# Planning Programs for Adult Learners

A Practical Guide
for Educators, Trainers,
and Staff Developers

Second Edition

## Rosemary S. Caffarella
Foreword by Malcolm S. Knowles

JOSSEY-BASS
A Wiley Imprint
www.josseybass.com

Published by Jossey-Bass
A Wiley Imprint
989 Market Street, San Francisco, CA 94103-1741   www.josseybass.com

Limit of Liability/Disclaimer of Warranty: While the publisher and author have used their best efforts in preparing this book, they make no representations or warranties with respect to the accuracy or completeness of the contents of this book and specifically disclaim any implied warranties of merchantability or fitness for a particular purpose. No warranty may be created or extended by sales representatives or written sales materials. The advice and strategies contained herein may not be suitable for your situation. You should consult with a professional where appropriate. Neither the publisher nor author shall be liable for any loss of profit or any other commercial damages, including but not limited to special, incidental, consequential, or other damages.

Readers should be aware that Internet Web sites offered as citations and/or sources for further information may have changed or disappeared between the time this was written and when it is read.

Jossey-Bass books and products are available through most bookstores. To contact Jossey-Bass directly call our Customer Care Department within the U.S. at 800-956-7739, outside the U.S. at 317-572-3986, or fax 317-572-4002.

Jossey-Bass also publishes its books in a variety of electronic formats. Some content that appears in print may not be available in electronic books.

**Library of Congress Cataloging-in-Publication Data**

Caffarella, Rosemary S. (Rosemary Shelly), 1946-
    Planning programs for adult learners: a practical guide for educators,
trainers, and staff developers / Rosemary S. Caffarella.—2nd ed.
        p. cm.
    Includes bibliographical references (p. ) and index.
    ISBN 0-7879-5225-7
    1. Adult education—United States–Administration. 2. Adult education—United
States—Planning I. Title.

LC5225.A34 C34 2001
374'.1973—dc21                                                    2001046201

The materials that appear in this book (except those for which reprint permission must be obtained from the primary sources) may be reproduced for educational/training activities. We do, however, require that the following statement appear on all reproductions:

*Planning Programs for Adult Learners: A Practical Guide for Educators, Trainers, and Staff Developers* by Rosemary S. Caffarella

Copyright © 2002 by John Wiley & Sons, Inc.

This free permission is limited to the reproduction of material for educational/training events. Systematic or large-scale reproduction or distribution (more than one hundred copies per year)—or inclusion of items in publications for sale—may be done only with prior written permission. Also, reproduction on computer disk or by any other electronic means requires prior written permission. Requests to the Author for permission should be addressed to the Permissions Department, John Wiley & Sons, Inc., 111 River Street, Hoboken, NJ 07030, 201–748–6011, fax 201–748–6008, or online at http://www.wiley.com/go/permissions.

Printed in the United States of America
SCEOND EDITION
PB Printing          10

The Jossey-Bass Higher and Adult Education Series

# Contents

# Figures, Exhibits, and Exercises

## Figures

## Exhibits

## Exercises

This book is lovingly dedicated to Ed Caffarella, my husband, and Christy Keeling, my daughter, who continue to provide love, laughter, challenges, and happiness in my life

A very special thanks to Lisa Matye Edwards for taking the "written text" for my figures, exhibits, and exercises and turning them into well-designed, highly readable, and useful materials

# Foreword

**WELCOME TO THE EXCITING** world of program planning for adults—exciting because this book makes it so.

In it, Rosemary Caffarella, one of the most effective scholar–practitioners of our era, explores the existing program planning models (which are mostly based on a linear, step-by-step process), extracts the best features of each, and incorporates these features into an essentially new model. This new model transforms program planning from a fundamentally mechanistic operation of following the steps to a creative operation of designing adventures in learning.

Because this new model involves cooperation between and among the planners, the organizational sponsors, and the participants in planning and implementing the program, Caffarella calls it an "interactive" model. I think of it also as a "dynamic" model, in contrast to a "static" or "routine" model.

You will find this book firmly grounded in clearly expressed concepts and principles derived from research-based theories of adult learning and loaded with practical suggestions for strategies and methods for applying these principles.

Whether you are new to the field or an old-timer, you will have one happy adventure.

*July 1994*                                                    Malcolm S. Knowles

# Preface

**PLANNING AND EVALUATING** education and training programs for adults is like trying to negotiate a maze. Sometimes we manage to get through the maze quickly and feel a real sense of satisfaction that we can do it with such ease. Other times we constantly run into dead ends and have to retrace our steps and find new paths, which can be frustrating yet challenging. So it is with program planning. Some programs run smoothly from beginning to end. Other programs have minor but fixable glitches, such as presenters being sick or equipment not being delivered to the right place. Still other programs seem to wander all over the place, with lots of revisions and changes along the way, and some even stall before they get off the ground. Often, when the norm is an evolving and ever-changing planning process, many of the alternative avenues that must be explored cannot be anticipated. Rather, new or reconfigured pathways will be added to the maze while you are still in it, with differing kinds of walls and openings along the way. For example, new staff members may have very different ways of planning programs than what has previously been accepted practice; program budgets may be cut with little or no warning; or senior management may ask for proof of learning transfer, while most of the available evaluation data focus on program delivery and content knowledge rather than application. Yet, when these seemingly unmanageable programs have successful endings, we feel a real sense of accomplishment and satisfaction with our work. I wrote this book to assist people who take on this challenge of "running the maze" of planning education and training programs for adults, whether the maze is simple, complex, and/or ever-changing.

Numerous models of planning education and training programs for adult learners exist, ranging from conceptual and data-based studies on program planning to how-to handbooks, guides, and workbooks. Some of these planning models are considered seminal works, such as R. W. Tyler's *Basic Principles of Curriculum and Instruction,* Cyril Houle's *The Design of Education* (1972, 1996), Malcolm Knowles's *The Modern Practice of Adult Education* (1980), and Ron Cervero's and Arthur Wilson's (1994) *Planning Responsibly for Adult Education: A Guide to Negotiating Power and Interests.* Other authors have provided very useful, but often brief and/or incomplete descriptions of the planning process. And most models of program planning for adults—especially those published more recently—have limited application to very specific contexts, such as training in the corporate sector, staff development in schools, or continuing education for the professions.

*Planning Programs for Adult Learners* is distinctive for two major reasons. First, the program planning model presented in this book both captures and reconfigures classical and current descriptions of the program planning process. The result is a comprehensive 12-component model, the Interactive Model of Program Planning, which draws on the best conceptual, empirical, and practice knowledge from across a variety of contexts—the corporate sector, continuing education for the professions, public schools, colleges and universities, health care, international development projects, government, community action programs, the military, religious institutions, and so on. In addition, the Interactive Model takes into account three key factors that make this model a viable resource for educational planners: the practicality and usefulness as a technical description of the planning process, the emphasis on people being the heart of the process, and the importance of context as a centering point for action.

Second, *Planning Programs for Adult Learners* provides both a concrete framework for program planning and a how-to guide and resource book for practitioners. This 12-component framework can be applied in many ways, as there is no best way of planning education and training programs. Program planners are asked, for example, to select which components of the model to use and when and how to apply these components based on professional judgment. Smart and effective planners make these decisions in collaboration with other key stakeholders. Planners also may start the process at varying points, focus on only one component at a time, or work on a number of components simultaneously, depending on their specific planning situation. In addition, they also may choose to give some tasks more emphasis than others and may need to revisit components or tasks more than once during the planning process. Therefore, program planning for adults, working within this framework, is an interactive and action-oriented process in which decisions and choices are made about learning opportunities for adults; thus, flexibility is a fundamental norm of the planning process.

The how-to part of *Planning Programs for Adult Learners* serves as a practical guide and provides hands-on resources for staff members who are constantly in the middle of planning one program or another. The many exhibits, figures, and lists presented throughout the text give the reader substantial information in a concise and easily usable format. Many of these could be used by planning staff as handouts related to specific tasks they must complete. In addition, there are application exercises at the end of most chapters to help readers apply the material addressed in the chapters to their own program planning situations.

This book is intended for both novice and experienced people who plan education and training programs for adults in a variety of settings. It is targeted primarily at people who either have or aspire to obtain full- or part-time positions as adult educators, trainers, staff developers, human resource developers, or performance improvement staff. These people already have (or will have) major responsibilities related to planning and evaluating education and training programs as all or part of their job. Their work settings are diverse. They may be, for example, in the corporate sector, public schools, non-profit organizations, colleges and universities, government, literacy programs, community action agencies, recreational programs, religiously affiliated groups, continuing education programs for the professions, and health care organizations. In addition, there are two other audiences for whom *Planning Programs for Adult Learners* can be helpful. The first is paid staff who plan education and training programs as only a small but important part of what they do, whether or not planning is a part of their official position descriptions. For example, many line staff, such as principals, division directors, and managers, are expected to provide education and training opportunities for their staff members; and in many cases, take leadership roles in and/or actually produce education and training activities. The second audience is the legion of volunteers who develop programs for adult learners—from committee and board members of social service agencies to community action groups. The commonality among all of the many audiences for this book is that they are all responsible in some way for planning and evaluating programs for adult learners, whether these learners are colleagues, other staff members, clients, customers, or the general community.

# Overview of the Contents

*Planning Programs for Adult Learners* is organized into two major parts, followed by a closing chapter that allows readers to revisit the Interactive Model of Program Planning. The first three chapters of the book lay the groundwork for the rest of the volume by introducing what program planning is all about—in other words, the Interactive Model that provides the framework for the remainder of the book. More specifically, Chapter One describes what education and training programs for adults look like, where these programs can be found, and who plans these programs. In addition, this chapter discusses the purposes and outcomes of education and training programs, and explores program planning models as one useful tool in the planning process. Chapter Two presents an overview of the Interactive Model of Program Planning for adults, the basic assumptions on which this model rests, the sources on which the model was built, the model as a guide to practice, and who currently uses the model. The 12-component model, discussed in detail in Chapters Four through Fifteen, is designed to assist people who develop, deliver, and evaluate programs for adults. The model helps program planners navigate the maze of people, ideas, organizational and wider environmental contexts, and administrative trivia (which is not trivial) that are part of the program planning process. Chapter Three addresses three important topics related to using the model in practice: identifying personal beliefs about program planning, developing upfront assumptions about each planning situation, determining what components and tasks of the Interactive Model to use in specific planning situations, and the use of technology in planning and delivering programs. The chapter closes with a challenge to program planners to be ethical in their practice.

The second part of the book makes the 12-component model come alive—the framework becomes a working guide for practice. Each component of the framework is explained, and practical tips and ideas related to concrete tasks within each of the components are given. The 12 components are reviewed as follows:

*Chapter Four.* Discerning the context

*Chapter Five.* Building a solid base of support

*Chapter Six.* Identifying program ideas

*Chapter Seven.* Sorting and prioritizing program ideas

*Chapter Eight.* Developing program objectives

*Chapter Nine.* Designing instructional plans

*Chapter Ten.* Devising transfer-of-learning plans

*Chapter Eleven.* Formulating evaluation plans

*Chapter Twelve.* Making recommendations and communicating results

*Chapter Thirteen.* Selecting formats, schedules, and staff needs

*Chapter Fourteen.* Preparing budgets and marketing plans

*Chapter Fifteen.* Coordinating facilities and on-site events

Application exercises are provided to assist readers in applying the material covered in each chapter to their own program planning situations.

The book closes with a chapter that offers an opportunity for readers to review and reflect on how they have or can use components and tasks centered in the Interactive Model of Program Planning. A brief discussion of the Interactive Model is presented, followed by a detailed checklist of the major tasks planners do within each component of the model, which provides a summary guide for practice. The chapter concludes with a short personal reflection from this author on the writing of the second edition of *Planning Programs for Adult Learners*.

# The Author

**ROSEMARY S. CAFFARELLA** is a professor in the Division of Educational Leadership and Policy Studies at the University of Northern Colorado. She earned her Ph.D. in adult and continuing education from Michigan University and also holds degrees in rehabilitation counseling and community development. Caffarella has held previous faculty and administrative appointments at Virginia Commonwealth University and the University of Maine. In addition, she has served as a visiting lecturer and scholar at a number of universities including the University of British Columbia, University of Calgary, University of Georgia, Pennsylvania State University, Texas A & M University, Universiti Putra (Malaysia), and University of Melbourne (Australia).

Caffarella's research and writing have focused on adult learning and development, program planning, and teaching and learning in higher and adult education. Her books include *Learning in Adulthood: A Comprehensive Guide (2nd ed.)* (1999, coauthored with Sharan Merriam), winner of the 2000 Cyril Houle Award for Literature in Adult Education; *An Update on Adult Development: New Ways of Thinking About the Life Course* (1999, coedited with Carolyn Clark); *Planning Programs for Adult Learners: A Practical Guide for Educators, Trainers, and Staff Developers* (1994); *Experiential Learning: A New Approach* (1994, coedited with Lewis Jackson); and *Program Development and Evaluation Resource Book for Trainers* (1988).

Caffarella has served as chair of the Commission of Professors of Adult Education, on the steering committee for the annual North American Adult Education Research Conference, and on the board of directors for the American Association for Adult and Continuing Education. In addition, she has served or is serving as a consulting editor for *The Canadian Journal for the Study of Adult Education, Adult Education Quarterly,* and *Adult*

*Learning.* She also has consulted and given many presentations for numerous organizations and groups, both in and outside of the United States, such as colleges and universities, health care organizations, public schools, state government, business and industry, and adult and continuing education programs.

Caffarella also enjoys her teaching and advising assignments, and has been awarded a number of teaching and research awards throughout her career. Outside of Caffarella's educational pursuits she takes pleasure in being with her family and friends, skiing, traveling, reading, and advocating for cancer survivors and research.

# Acknowledgments

**PLANNING PROGRAMS FOR ADULT LEARNERS** is a book for people who spend all or part of their time developing education and training programs for adults. The book was inspired by those practitioners, my students, and many others I have worked with from field settings and my university colleagues, who wanted a sound conceptual model—but one that is grounded in practice and has usable and practical guidelines and tools.

Many of those practitioners have provided invaluable assistance at various stages of the process. Gale Erlandson, Melissa Kirk, David Brightman, and Cathy Mallon worked well as a team to facilitate the book's publication. Student colleagues enrolled in my program planning courses during the summer of 2000 at the University of British Columbia, the fall of 2000 class of University of Northern Colorado (UNC), and Jean Fleming provided very helpful feedback on selected chapters of the manuscript, as did the outside reviewers when they read the first edition. A special thanks to Ron Cervero (who also did an earlier review of the book and the chapter on "Discerning the Context"), University of Georgia, and Ralph Brockett, University of Tennessee, for providing such useful feedback on my "next-to-last draft" of the book, when assistance was especially needed. Another very special thanks also to Lisa Matye Edwards, my graduate assistant at UNC, without whom I would have never made the manuscript deadlines. Her computer expertise in setting up the many charts and exhibits, her library skills, her assistance with copyediting, and her advice throughout the writing process was invaluable, as was her good humor and "we-can-do-this" attitude. My sincere appreciation to Lisa for the many late night, early morning, and middle of the day sessions. In addition, Betty Stewart, also a graduate student at UNC, gave very helpful assistance through her library work earlier in the writing process, while my UNC colleagues offered me continued support throughout the project. To all of you, I give a heartfelt thanks. Finally, I wish to say an extra special thanks to my husband, Ed Caffarella, who managed to survive yet another one of my major projects, and to Christy Keeling, my daughter, who always seemed to be around just when I needed a break. It is great to have a supportive and caring family like you! It goes to show how important for some of us the links are between the worlds of work and family. For me, they are inseparable.

*August 2001*                                                    Rosemary S. Caffarella
*Greeley, Colorado*

# Chapter 1

# Planning Programs for Adults: What's It All About?

**PLANNING PROGRAMS FOR ADULTS** is like swimming in the ocean. Some days the ocean is calm and welcomes people with open arms. It beckons people, even nonswimmers, to splash and play, jump the waves, float comfortably on their backs, and just enjoy the sun. On calm days like these, program planners, even those who are new at the business, feel like they are on top of the process—all is going smoothly and everyone just seems to agree on what to do, when, and how.

On other days, when the surf is somewhat rough and the waves higher, the ocean provides challenges for even the best of swimmers. On these days nonswimmers may just wade, while more experienced ocean adventurers eagerly dive through crashing waves and ride the surf. Experienced program planners on these rough days find their work especially exciting as they maneuver through the many tasks that just keep coming at them and negotiate with people with vastly different ideas and agendas. Conversely, novice planners may back away and just let the planning process take its course, unless more experienced planners willingly give them direction and support.

Then there are those stormy days when the ocean is dark and gray and the giant waves grab for anything they can find, toss it around with ease, and pull it every which way. Few people even want to be on the beach, let alone in the water. Both experienced and novice program planners on stormy days would prefer to sit tight away from the fray, and let whatever develops run its course. But staying on the fringes and not tackling the issues head on often means disastrous consequences for the planning process; the participants, planners, and other stakeholders; and the program itself. Thinking on one's feet and acting in the moment usually is what assists planners in getting through these turbulent and unpredictable times.

Playing and swimming in the ocean, even on the calmest days, also offers many surprises, some delightful and some downright frightening. On a chance day, dolphins might be seen leaping up and down close to shore, and for the very lucky swimmers the dolphins may come to swim with them. On the other hand, dangerous undertows and currents may suddenly grab swimmers and pull them away from where they want to be. So it is with planning programs for adults—some days planners find themselves with unexpected resources and support. Then, there are those days when nothing seems to go right no matter what they do, and staying afloat and on track seem hopeless. Instead program planners find themselves constantly being pulled in one direction or another, struggling to maintain a course toward their original destinations.

The purpose of this first chapter is to give people who plan programs for adults a glimpse of the waters in which they are playing and swimming—the what, who, where, why, and how of program planning for adults. To this end, described first are what education and training programs look like. Explored next are the many roles of people who plan programs, and the variety of settings where these programs are held. The purposes and primary outcomes of programs for adults are then examined. The chapter concludes with a discussion of how programs are planned, and it explores program planning models as one useful tool in the planning process.

## What Programs for Adults Look Like

Education and training programs for adults come in all shapes, sizes, and formats. They vary from information or skill sessions lasting only an hour or two to day-long workshops and conferences to highly intensive residential study at corporate training centers and universities. Organizations and groups who sponsor these programs may offer one or more of these kinds of program options. For example, a local book club meets once every other week for an hour and a half. They primarily use an open discussion format, with no set parameters. Members like this open-ended way of learning and have resisted efforts by some to make the meetings more formal with moderators and structured questions. They have also chosen not to engage as a group in any other educational activities, such as attending lectures or events hosted by the local bookstore. In contrast, most training programs in corporate settings offer a wide variety of education and training programs, such as courses, workshops, seminars, retreats, and activities like job shadowing and peer coaching. Although employees may choose to attend some of these programs, many are mandatory, such as orientation sessions for new employees and skill updates.

Programs for adults are also planned for individual learners, or designed for small or large groups of learners, including whole communities. Mechanisms like professional or individual growth plans are used to individualize programs for learners. For large- and small-group learning, participants often are expected to come to one location to attend, such as workshops and annual conferences hosted by many professional associations. With the advent of more sophisticated technology-based programs, learners also participate in group-learning experiences from their homes or offices through such means as teleconferencing and Web-based formats.

Finally, some programs are planned for a small, select group of people, such as senior managers from a given organization; others, such as classes and activities sponsored by community recreation programs or senior centers, are open to whoever signs up. Still others are planned for the general public, such as voter forums and summer concerts in the park.

## Planners of Education and Training Programs

Education and training programs for adults are planned and coordinated by people in numerous roles who have varied backgrounds and experiences. Chen-Seng, for example, a new trainer in the marketing department, has a business background and has been a successful marketing specialist for the past five years. Although he has attended many training programs and conferences, he has no formal background in training and development. Jana is a supervisor for a large staff in a state agency who, like Chen-Seng, also has no formal educational background in teaching or planning educational activities for adults. Yet she often finds herself coaching staff, helping staff prepare individual and team performance plans, and planning or facilitating staff training programs.

Dave, an elementary school principal, does have a bachelor's and master's degree in education, but little experience in planning programs for his adult staff. Yet Dave is expected to respond to a number of state and federal mandates that require his staff to take on new instructional practices. One of the ways he responds to these mandates is through planning and organizing, mostly by trial and error, inhouse and district-wide staff development programs. Malcolm, a local volunteer coordinator of a statewide group advocating social justice, also finds himself, like

Dave, planning numerous programs, such as community-wide forums and action-oriented events, by "just doing it." Although he and his volunteer staff are highly committed to their work, all of their planning expertise has come from earlier volunteer activities and a few training sessions hosted by the state organization. Unlike the people already described, Katrina, an assistant director of continuing education at a small private college, does have a graduate degree in adult and continuing education and five years of experience as a program specialist in that unit. Still, she finds that the program planning and delivery processes continue to change in many ways, driven mostly by technology and the changing nature of the clientele that her program serves.

While some staff, like Chen-Seng and Katrina, have clearly defined roles and responsibilities as program planners and carry official titles such as training specialist and assistant director of continuing education, most people who plan educational programs for adults do not (DuFour, 1991; Moller, 1999; Shipp, 1998; Winston and Creamer, 1998). For example, supervisors and line administrators, like Jana and Dave, are often expected to serve as staff developers and trainers through such mechanisms as coaching, the supervisory process, and even planning formal educational and training programs. Yet their job descriptions may or may not reflect these responsibilities and tasks, and some supervisors are not rewarded or even recognized for their efforts. In addition, many people also give countless hours as volunteer program planners for community groups, professional associations, and nonprofit organizations, like Malcolm and his volunteer staff.

This broad spectrum of responsibility for program planning is shown in Figure 1.1. Those who have primary roles as program planners spend the majority of their time developing, implementing, and evaluating programs, often with support from other people. In addition, they may take on other tasks, such as organizational development and facilitating change activities (Killion and Harrison, 1997; Rothwell and Cookson, 1997; Milano with Ullius, 1998; Lee and Owens, 2000). Program planning for others is one of multiple tasks for which they are accountable. Examples of roles that include numerous other responsibilities, in addition to planning programs, are managers of human resource development, deans of continuing education, and volunteer planners. Still others plan programs for adults as more of a tertiary activity, where although it is a minor, it is often an important part of their roles. This idea of the centrality of doing program planning as part of one's job, whether paid or as a volunteer, is further illustrated in the following three scenarios.

## FIGURE 1.1

# Centrality of Responsibility for Education Programs and Training

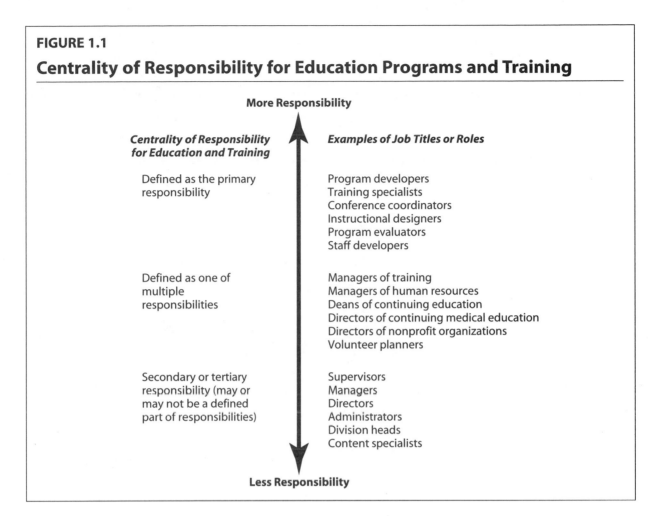

**More Responsibility**

| *Centrality of Responsibility for Education and Training* | *Examples of Job Titles or Roles* |
|---|---|
| Defined as the primary responsibility | Program developers<br>Training specialists<br>Conference coordinators<br>Instructional designers<br>Program evaluators<br>Staff developers |
| Defined as one of multiple responsibilities | Managers of training<br>Managers of human resources<br>Deans of continuing education<br>Directors of continuing medical education<br>Directors of nonprofit organizations<br>Volunteer planners |
| Secondary or tertiary responsibility (may or may not be a defined part of responsibilities) | Supervisors<br>Managers<br>Directors<br>Administrators<br>Division heads<br>Content specialists |

**Less Responsibility**

### *Program Planning As a Primary Responsibility*

Robert is employed as a training specialist for the Blackwell Corporation. His office is located at the corporate training center, and he reports to the associate vice president for human resource development. He is one of three training specialists employed at the corporate level. His major responsibility is to design training programs for both staff and customers of the company. These programs range from one-hour modules to three-week intensive seminars and Web-based programs. Though at times he may actually serve as the instructor for one of the programs, his major job is to develop and coordinate the various programs offered by the organization. In essence, Robert's major role is that of program developer. He functions as a program design specialist and is responsible for planning, coordinating, and evaluating training programs requested by the various divisions within the company, as well as for ensuring that transfer of learning happens. He rarely works alone. Instead, he works in tandem with content specialists, usually company personnel from the division that has requested the program and/or outside consultants, which calls on his group facilitation skills. In addition, he may work with the training center's production group on the development of the instructional materials to be used in the program (or, if the program is to be housed at the center itself with the center's conference coordinator). He also finds himself doing more internal consulting work, such as organizational development, and is a catalyst for change, in response to the problems he is asked to address.

### *Program Planning As One of Multiple Responsibilities*

Issabelle serves as the director of a nonprofit organization that has as part of its mission educational programming for the community. She reports to the board of directors and works a great deal with the board chair. Issabelle has a staff of five people: an assistant director, an educational specialist, two university interns, and one secretary. She also interacts with a large number of volunteers who serve on various committees and give their time to assist staff in their many tasks (for example, office duties, direct client services). In reviewing her calendar for the next day, Issabelle has made notations beside her commitments.

On that one day, Issabelle will concentrate on a number of different roles (meeting facilitator, problem solver, program planner, fund raiser, and instructor). If you were to examine her calendar on successive days, you would see that how much time she devotes to her tasks as a program planner changes, depending on what needs her attention (see Exhibit 1.1). For example, Issabelle may take charge of parts of the program planning process when she believes this is important or when her expertise is especially relevant (directing a fund-raising campaign targeted at specific educational programs or providing direct instruction). At other times, she will choose to be involved in a peripheral way, perhaps as an informal sounding board for program ideas, or by being present at major training sessions for volunteer groups. Therefore, although Issabelle is involved in program planning, it is only one of many primary roles that she assumes.

### *Program Planning As a Tertiary Responsibility*

John is the director of nursing of a medium-sized metropolitan hospital. He has a nursing staff of 300, including both full- and

**EXHIBIT 1.1**

# Issabelle's Calendar

| Times | | Appointments | Notes |
|---|---|---|---|
| AM | 8:00 | | |
| | 8:30 | | |
| | 9:00 | **Staff meeting** | *Note: Issues with volunteers, evaluation reports on two recent community programs, training for interns, review of new policy and procedures manual* |
| | 9:30 | | |
| | 10:00 | | *Note: Lay out the final plans for a statewide conference, revise the afternoon training session for interns based on comments made at staff meeting* |
| | 10:30 | **Joe** [the educational specialist] | |
| | 11:00 | | |
| | 11:30 | | |
| PM | 12:00 | **Lunch with Susan, Jim, and Marie** [chair of board and two members] | *Note: Discuss the upcoming statewide conference, issues with volunteers, next board meeting, and potential donors* |
| | 12:30 | | |
| | 1:00 | | |
| | 1:30 | | |
| | 2:00 | **Bill** [president of a local company that provides funds for agency operations and programs, and a state senator] | *Note: Discuss dinner with possible new donors, review his role as opening speaker of upcoming statewide conference* |
| | 2:30 | | |
| | 3:00 | **Conduct internship training with Joe (3–5 P.M.)** | *Note: Review last-minute program revisions* |
| | 3:30 | | |
| | 4:00 | | |
| | 4:30 | ↓ | |
| | 5:00 | | |
| | 5:30 | | |
| | 6:00 | **Dinner** with potential donors and two board members | *Note: Check with her administrative assistant that all informational packets are complete, review comments made by board members and Bill about the focus of the conversation at the dinner* |
| | 6:30 | | |
| | 7:00 | | |
| | 7:30 | | |
| | 8:00 | | |

part-time employees. He reports directly to the executive director of the hospital and serves on the executive council. He has learned that in two months a new charting system for patients will be installed in the hospital. His responsibility is to ensure that all his nursing staff will be able to use the new system in an effective and efficient manner. He has called a meeting of selected supervisory nurses to assist him in determining how he can get all the nurses trained to use this new system in such a short period of time. Meanwhile, he is having major problems in other areas, including the recruitment of new staff, the settlement of a two-year labor contract, and a high staff turnover rate.

John, in addition to responding to major mandates for training, is also involved in program planning and coordination for ongoing staff training, but he views this task as only a small part of his job. He knows he needs to complete these tasks, and although it is not in his official job description, the executive director has made it clear that he is accountable for training as part of his job functions. Yet planning and coordinating programs is a task to which he has assigned a fairly low priority. Most of what John has chosen to do in this area is to send staff to programs run by other departments in the hospital or by other organizations. He has invited a few university people to give "clinical updates," but he has delegated all the work on those activities to two of his supervisory nurses. He knows he has to lead this latest training effort himself, however, because the director of the medical staff and the executive director of the hospital have made it a priority item.

## Sponsors of Education and Training Programs

Many types of organizations sponsor education and training programs for adults (Craig, 1996; Sparks and Hirsh, 1997; Wilson and Hayes, 2000). As with the roles of staff, the centrality of these programs to these organizations varies by the mission and goals of the sponsors. For example, providing education and training programs for adults may be the primary mission, such as continuing education divisions or conference centers, or be one of many goals, with some groups placing more importance on the educational function than others (see Chapter Five).

Using a typology of organizations that offer education and training programs, proposed by Darkenwald and Merriam (1982), a sampling of organizational sponsors of education and training programs appears in Exhibit 1.2.

In addition to formal organizations, a number of more informal groups, such as hobby clubs, support groups, book clubs, and community action committees, also provide educational programs for their members.

**EXHIBIT 1.2**

## Sponsors of Education and Training Programs for Adults

| Sponsors | Independent Public and Private Adult Education Organizations | Educational Institutions | Quasi-educational Organizations | Non-educational Organizations |
|---|---|---|---|---|
| *Purposes* | *Primary purpose is to provide learning opportunities for adults (may be public or private).* | *One of the missions is providing educational programs for adults, but may be secondary to programs for youth, research, community service, and so on.* | *Consider education of their members and/or the general public to be an allied or corollary function of their primary mission.* | *Similar to quasi-educational organizations, their primary mission is not educational. The difference is they view education and training as a means to an end versus an allied or corollary mission.* |
| *Examples* | **Proprietary schools**<br>• Institutes for technology and other skill-based programs<br>• Freestanding distance learning programs<br>**Colleges and universities**<br>• Colleges designed for adult learners<br>• Distance learning enterprises<br>**Adult literacy programs**<br>• Literacy Volunteers of America<br>• Right to Read<br>**"Grassroots" community groups and organizations**<br>• Hispanic Coalition for Social Action<br>• Environmental education organizations<br>**International adult education groups**<br>• International Council of Adult Education<br>• The Indigenous Educator Network | **Public schools**<br>• Adult basic education<br>• Graduate equivalency diplomas (GEDs)<br>• Staff development programs<br>**Colleges and universities**<br>• Divisions and colleges of continuing education<br>• Cooperative extensions<br>• Faculty development<br>• Student leadership programs<br>**Community-based organizations**<br>• Community centers<br>• Recreation and outdoor centers | **Cultural organizations**<br>• Museums<br>• Libraries<br>• Arts councils<br>**Community organizations**<br>• Service clubs<br>• Civic organizations<br>**Religiously affiliated groups and organizations**<br>• Churches<br>• Synagogues<br>• Mosques<br>• YMCA<br>• Jewish community centers<br>**Public and private organizations**<br>• American Red Cross | **Business and industry**<br>• Training divisions<br>• Human resources development units<br>**Military**<br>• Recruit training<br>• Military colleges<br>• Leadership programs<br>**Government departments and agencies**<br>• Department of Transportation<br>• Bureau of Human Services<br>• Department of Corrections<br>**Unions**<br>• American Federation of Teachers<br>• AFL-CIO |

## Purposes of Education and Training Programs

Education and training programs for adults are conducted for five primary purposes and, as noted earlier, for a variety of audiences. These purposes are illustrated in the examples highlighted in Exhibit 1.3 (Craig, 1996; Daloz, Keen, Keen, and Parks, 1996; Merriam and Caffarella, 1999; Wilson and Hayes, 2000).

Education and training programs often serve more than one purpose. For example, workplace literacy programs are usually designed to assist

### EXHIBIT 1.3
### Examples of Program Purposes

| Program Purpose | Examples |
|---|---|
| To encourage continuous growth and development of individuals | • Continuing education course on Chinese art and culture of the nineteenth and twentieth centuries<br>• Session hosted by the local library: "Using the Library as a Lifelong Learning Resource"<br>• Workshop: "How to Use Your Home Computer to Tap into 101 Databases"<br>• Watching nature programs on public television |
| To assist people in responding to practical problems and issues of adult life | • Seminars on ways to cope with life transitions<br>• Combination information/support group for newly diagnosed cancer patients and their families<br>• Series of pre-retirement workshops offered for all interested employees<br>• Setting up Internet sites and chat groups related to areas such as divorce, parenting stepchildren, health issues, and changing jobs |
| To prepare people for current and future work opportunities | • New-worker orientation programs<br>• Formal apprenticeship and college and degree programs<br>• Workshop on applications of new software packages to daily work activities<br>• Teleconference on alternative job and career options |
| To assist organizations in achieving desired results and adapting to change | • Two-day seminar for all employees on responding positively to customers from diverse backgrounds<br>• Workshop offered by the Council of Economic Development: "Changing Demographics Through the Year 2020: Implications for the Workplace"<br>• A series of training sessions for volunteers on the changing role of volunteers and how they can adapt their current practice to those changes<br>• Web-based course for all supervisors and managers on working with difficult and hostile employees |
| To provide opportunities to examine community and societal issues, foster change for the common good, and promote a civil society | • Community Earth Day celebration consisting of numerous learning opportunities and events<br>• Nationwide teleconference on AIDS, focusing on health, economic, and social issues<br>• International UNESCO Conference focusing on adult literacy, role of women in society, globalization of the workforce, and social action movements<br>• Workshops for government personnel on concrete actions for promoting a civil society |

individuals to develop their language and computation skills while at the same time meeting organizational and societal needs for competent workers.

## Change as a Primary Outcome of Education and Training Programs

Implicit in each of these five purposes for conducting education and training programs is the expectation of change as an outcome or result (Rothwell and Kazanas, 1993; Welton, 1993; Rogers, 1995; Ewert and Grace, 2000; Tennant, 2000; Hall and Hord, 2001). Education and training programs foster three kinds of change: individual change related to acquisition of new knowledge, building of skills, and examination of personal values and beliefs; organizational change resulting in new or revised policies, procedures, and ways of working; and community and societal change that allows for differing segments of society (for example, members of lower socioeconomic classes, women, ethnic populations, the business sector) to respond to the world around them in alternative ways. Sample program outcomes in all three categories are outlined below:

### Sample Outcomes: Individual Change

- Individuals who attend the workshop on "How to Use Your Home Computer to Tap into 101 Databases" will be able to (1) describe at least five different databases they could use in their daily lives, and (2) demonstrate they know how to use at least two of the five databases they have identified.

- Sandy is taking an individual spiritual journey to discover what she really believes and how she wants to live her life. This journey was precipitated by the death of her husband and her entrance into middle age. The resources she is using are books, seminars, quiet retreats, and a spiritual guide. She also is committed to being in residence at a spiritual community for a three-month period. After the first six months of her journey she has already decided that she will change her place of residence and the kind of work she does.

### Sample Outcomes: Organizational Change

- Supervisors of staff who attend training sessions on the use of two new software packages will allow time on the job for program participants to practice using the software packages. Then, within a six-month time period, these same supervisors will implement new operational guidelines that require the use of these software packages for particular functions within the organization.

- Except for people who can demonstrate proficiency in Spanish, all new and current staff in the Division of Motor Vehicles who are responsible for providing information and services to the public will be required to enroll in an intensive Spanish language program. The end result of the program will be that staff will be able to effectively communicate verbally with customers in both English and Spanish. As part of this organization-wide training initiative, the personnel system will be modified to provide incentives for current staff members who are able to demonstrate or achieve language proficiency. In addition, one of the requirements for all new hires who work directly with customers will be a demonstrated language proficiency in both Spanish and English.

## Sample Outcomes: Community and Societal Change

- A cancer survivor organization will sponsor an action workshop on how to affect state and national policies related to cancer prevention, treatment, and education. One of the major goals of the workshop is to develop local networks of people who will lobby for legislative action in their districts.

- A group of medical personnel has agreed to undergo training for providing assistance in a third-world country. They will attend three regional workshops and one national meeting focused on a wide range of issues related to delivering medical services in a third-world country. In addition, they have agreed to partner with a medical specialist in their area who has given service overseas to learn and practice new techniques that have been shown to work in the countries they will be visiting. In return for this training they have agreed to serve at least three months in a third-world country and provide coaching for other medical personnel in their area who join the program.

Although change of some form is an assumption of most, if not all, education and training programs, the reality of these programs is that planning for change, that is, preparing concrete and workable transfer-of-learning plans, is often overlooked (see Chapter Ten). Also, contextual factors that affect the change process, such as organizational constraints and political and economic realities, are not routinely taken into account (see Chapter Four) (Cervero and Wilson, 1996; Cervero, Wilson, and Associates, 2001). Rather, people responsible for planning and implementing education and training programs have assumed that people attending these programs will be able to apply what they have learned, without planned assistance and support being an integral part of the programs they deliver. In addition, those who are responsible for ensuring that the desired changes actually take place rarely allocate enough time for these changes to be integrated into the daily lives of those affected, especially when these changes are major. As Hall and Hord (2001) so astutely observe: "Change is a process and not an event. In other words, change is not accomplished by having a one-time announcement by an executive leader [other people, or even oneself], a two-day workshop . . . , and/or the delivery of the [most modern equipment or other resources]. Instead change is a process through which people and organizations move as they gradually come to understand, and become skilled and competent in the use of new ways" (pp. 4, 5).

## How Education and Training Programs Are Planned

Some education and training programs are carefully planned, while others are literally thrown together. The following scenarios illustrate this point.

### *Throwing Together a Program*

George, the director of continuing education at a community college, has been asked to coordinate a half-day workshop for all part-time instructors on teaching adults. Somehow the date slips his mind, and a week before the workshop he realizes that he has no instructor. He calls the local university, hoping he can get one of the adult education professors to come for the morning. He is in luck, or so he thinks. Professor Bland gives a three-hour lecture on how to teach. Not only is the material old hat to most of the instructors, but the professor, well-versed in literacy education, uses examples primarily from that arena to illustrate his points. The workshop receives very low marks from all the participants.

### *Planning Thoughtfully*

Marie, a teacher on special assignment, has been asked to develop a half-day district-wide workshop on peer coaching skills as a staff development strategy. She calls together five teachers who are well-respected in their buildings to ask them what they think the teachers need to learn about this area. Based on the information she gleans from these teachers, and on some discreet observations of current practice in some of the schools in the district, she determines that a one-hour overview and demonstration of basic peer coaching skills is needed, followed by a two-hour practice session.

She asks three teachers from another school district, who are known for their ability in peer coaching, to assist in putting on the workshop. She also makes sure that a good lunch is served, at the district's expense, at the end of the morning. The workshop is well-received by all participants.

In addition, planning, delivering, and evaluating education and training programs for adult learners is both an organized and a haphazard endeavor. Like the ocean, on the surface, these processes may appear to be fairly logical and orderly, progressing from discerning the context to identifying ideas to program design and implementation to evaluation and transfer activities. Yet for those persons who actually develop and coordinate education and training programs, the progression seems to be more a mass of decisions, political maneuverings, details, and deadlines than precise and clear steps of what should be done, when, where, by whom, and how, as illustrated next by Jacquie.

### Despite Perfect Planning

Jacquie, a program coordinator for an international conference on experiential education, is frantically trying to get all of the program details in order. She is new to the business of conference coordination, yet thought she and her volunteer program committee had it all together. The conference theme, program objectives, site, and keynote speakers were all lined up well in advance. Also, all of the publicity and registration materials seemed well-designed, as well as the call for programs, and the program review process. In addition, Jacquie had received very good feedback on the training she conducted for the volunteer committees whose members had committed to complete specific program tasks, such as scheduling and on-site coordination. As the conference time draws closer though, there seems to be a million details still hanging out there—session presenters requesting time changes, hotel construction that seems to have appeared out of nowhere, problems with the equipment company, a change in the on-site conference manager, and so on. In addition, some of the members of Jacquie's volunteer committees, who had worked so well together, now seem at odds with both her and other committee members. The executive director is also not pleased with some of the arrangements, a sentiment that appears to stem from one committee member who is running for president of the association, and two board members. To top everything off, Jacquie has just learned that the worldwide

teleconference, which was a major draw for the conference, may
have to be canceled as the site coordinator now says the hotel has
neither the capabilities nor the facilities to host the event because
many more conferees than originally expected had registered.
Jacquie never thought this job would be so taxing—she just
assumed that once plans were set, all would be fine, except for a few
last-minute changes and tasks. In addition, although Jacquie is the
coordinator of this program, she also quickly became a learner and
even a teacher as part of making the program work.

Careful planning of education and training programs does not guarantee their success, nor does it mean that all tasks will run smoothly and people-related problems will not arise. Instead, as illustrated by Jacquie's experiences, a lot can and does go wrong, some of which is in her control, some of which is not. This lack of certainty in the planning process can be overwhelming, especially to novice planners, but also to more experienced ones. One avenue that helps many planners get through this maze of tasks, people issues, and political agendas is to have a guide or road map of the planning process to assist them in getting from start to finish. A program planning model is one way to provide this needed guide.

## Program Planning Models

Program planning models consist of ideas of one or more persons about how programs should be put together and what ingredients are necessary to ensure successful outcomes. These models come in all shapes and sizes. Program planning models may be simplistic in their orientation—with steps 1 through 5, for example—or very complex, using highly developed flowcharts or in-depth qualitative descriptions to depict a comprehensive array of issues and decision points (for example, Knowles, 1980; Nadler, 1982; Cervero and Wilson, 1996; Rothwell and Cookson, 1997; Sork, 2000).

Some models of program planning are linear. In these, the planner is expected to start at step one and follow each step in sequential order until the process is completed. This type of model may be helpful to newcomers; but it soon loses its appeal because it does not represent, as described in the previous section, the day-to-day working reality of most program planners. An alternative to the linear approach is to conceptualize program planning as a process that consists of a set of interacting and dynamic elements or components and decision points (Houle, 1972; Caffarella, 1985; Sork and Caffarella, 1989; Cervero and Wilson, 1994, 1996; Sork, 2000). This nonsequential model allows program planners to address a number of the components simultaneously, to rearrange the components to suit the demands of different planning situations, and/or to delete unneeded parts of the process. This type of model also allows planners to address the essence of the process working with people, which often involves negotiations between and among planning parties.

The Interactive Model of Program Planning, the model presented in this book, takes into account the dynamic and ever-changing nature of the planning process. In addition, the model acknowledges that people plan programs and that planning is not a neutral set of events. Rather, program planners often find themselves swimming their way through organizational, ethical, political, and social waves.

## Chapter Highlights

Variety and difference are key words that characterize the what, who, where, why, and how of planning education and training programs for adults. As such, these programs take on many forms, and the people who plan them, including paid staff and volunteers, have diverse backgrounds and experiences. Those for whom program planning is central to their work carry such titles as program planners, training specialists, staff developers, and instructional designers. Yet, often this role of program planner comes with work titles, such as manager and supervisor, where program planning is not considered a major or even secondary part of what they do. There are also a variety of organizations that sponsor programs for adults, and like the staff involved, the centrality of these programs to those organizations varies according to the mission and goals of the sponsoring groups.

Education and training programs for adults are conducted for five primary purposes: (1) to encourage ongoing growth and development of individuals; (2) to assist people in responding to practical problems and issues of adult life; (3) to prepare people for current and future work opportunities; (4) to assist organizations in achieving desired results and adapting to change; and (5) to provide opportunities to examine and foster community and societal change. Changes in individuals, organizations, and the wider community are the driving force and one of the underlying themes that link together all types of education and training programs for adults.

Some education and training programs are carefully planned, while others just seem to be thrown together. In addition, although on the surface program planning seems like a very rational and orderly endeavor, those involved know that it is often chaotic and unsystematic in nature. Therefore, in planning education and training programs for adults, it is helpful for program planners to have a model or guide to get them from the start to the finish. One such guide for action, the subject of this book, is the Interactive Model of Program Planning. This model is described in the next chapter.

# Application Exercises

This chapter's Application Exercises can help you understand your role as a program planner in your organizational setting and asks you to reflect on the variety of organizations you have been associated with as a participant or program planner. The final exercise can assist you in defining the purpose of your education and training programs.

---

## EXERCISE 1.1

### Understanding the Role of Program Planners in Organizational Settings

1. **List your present title and give a brief job description.**



2. **Is the role of program planner a *formal* part of your job description?**
   _____ Yes   _____ No
   If no, what roles if any, do you play as a program planner?




3. **Outline, on the following chart, the personnel in your organization (or a specific subunit of your organization) who are responsible for planning and conducting educational programs. Indicate whether this responsibility is a formal or informal part of their jobs. Then outline the tasks each person does as part of this work.**

   | Position, Name, and Program | Formal or Informal Responsibility | Tasks Related to Educational Programming |
   | --- | --- | --- |
   | _____ | _____ | _____ |
   | _____ | _____ | _____ |
   | _____ | _____ | _____ |
   | _____ | _____ | _____ |
   | _____ | _____ | _____ |
   | _____ | _____ | _____ |

4. **How might those who do program planning in your unit and/or organization be supportive of each other's efforts? List specific suggestions below.**

### EXERCISE 1.2

## Reflecting on Education and Training Programs
## You Have Participated In or Planned

1.   List all of the organizations you have been a participant in and/or the educational and training
     programs you have planned for the past two or three years.

| Organization | Roles |
|---|---|
|  |  |
|  |  |
|  |  |
|  |  |
|  |  |
|  |  |
|  |  |
|  |  |
|  |  |
|  |  |

## EXERCISE 1.3

# Defining the Purpose of Education and Training Programs

1.  **Within the framework outlined below, list examples of education and training programs you have participated in and/or planned within the last two to three years.**

    To encourage continuous growth and development of individuals

    To assist people in responding to practical problems and issues of adult life

    To prepare people for current and future work opportunities

    To assist in achieving desired results and adapting to change

    To provide opportunities to examine and foster change related to societal and global issues

2.  **Highlight the positive points of these experiences as either participant and/or planner and indicate what problems and/or disappointments you encountered.**

# Chapter 2

# The Interactive Model of Program Planning

**NUMEROUS MODELS OF** program planning for adult learners exist, as noted in Chapter One. A sample of classical and current models include those proposed by Tyler (1949); Houle (1972, 1996); Knowles (1980); Laird (1985); Cervero (1988); Cervero and Wilson (1994, 1996); Sork and Caffarella (1989); Rothwell and Cookson (1997); Sork (1997, 2000); and Milano with Ullius (1998). The commonalities between and among these models are the attention paid to: the needs and ideas of learners, organizations, and/or communities as central to the program planning process; the importance of context in the planning process; and identifiable components and practical tasks that are important to the planning process.

In building the Interactive Model of Program Planning for adults introduced in this chapter, many ideas were drawn from these previously proposed models of program planning (for example, Knowles, 1980; Houle, 1972, 1996; Sork and Caffarella, 1989; Cervero and Wilson, 1994, 1996; Sork, 1997, 2000). Therefore, the Interactive Model on the surface in terms of its key components and tasks appears similar to other models or ideas about program planning. This model differs, however, in four primary ways: by design, it is interactive and comprehensive; people and place are acknowledged as important in the planning process; differences among cultures are taken into account in the planning process; and practitioners find the model useful and therefore a practical tool. Discussed first in this chapter is the model itself and its components and key tasks. Explored next are the assumptions within which the Interactive Model is grounded and the sources and ideas on which the model is constructed. The chapter concludes with a discussion of who currently uses the Interactive Model.

## Description of the Interactive Model of Program Planning

The Interactive Model of Program Planning for adults is presented as a guide, not a blueprint for practice. The 12-component model, as shown in Figure 2.1, provides a map of the terrain of the planning process, but the map often changes in contour, content, and size.

What makes this model interactive is that first it has no real beginnings or endings. Rather, persons responsible for planning programs for adults are encouraged to use the relevant parts of the model in any order and combination based on the planning situation (see Chapter Three). Many experienced program planners, as noted in Chapter One, have found that planning programs is rarely, if ever, a linear, step-by-step process. Instead, program planners often work with a number of planning components and tasks at the same time and not necessarily in any standard order. For example, in planning a large national conference, the logistics of the meeting (such as place and date) often have to be handled before the theme or objectives of the conference are determined. In planning other programs, extensive needs assessments may be the starting point (see Chapter Six), while for others the

**FIGURE 2.1**

## Interactive Model of Program Planning

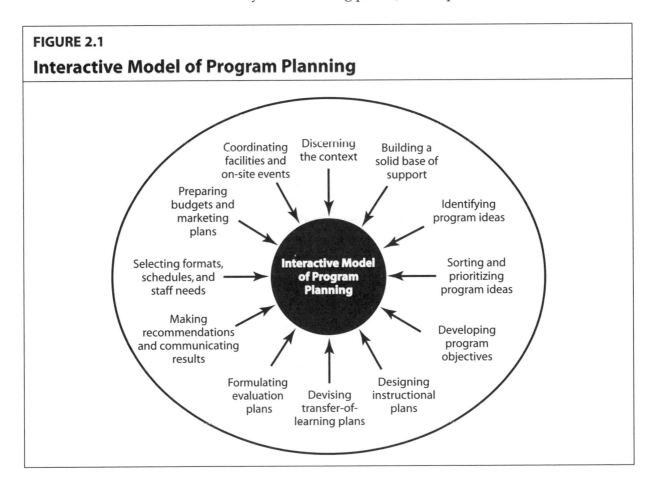

content (see Chapter Nine), transfer of learning (see Chapter Ten), and/or the context of the program (see Chapter Four) drive the planning process.

Second, experienced practitioners have found that the process of planning programs is essentially a people activity. As Wilson and Cervero (1996b) wisely observe: "In our view, real people plan real programs in complex organizations, which have traditions, political relationships, and needs and interests that profoundly influence the planning process" (p. 6). Therefore, program planning becomes a negotiated activity between and among educators, learners, organizations, and other stakeholders, all of whom bring their own beliefs and contexts with them to the planning table (Brookfield, 1986; Cervero and Wilson, 1994, 1996, 1998; Ottoson, 1995a). In this negotiations process, with its central issues of power and control, program planners use planning models that allow for adaptation of components and tasks.

Third, with education and training programs becoming global in nature, the interactive nature of this model allows planners to take into account the differences among cultures in the way these programs are planned and conducted (Rhinesmith, 1996; Funk and McBride, 2000; Merriam and Mohamad, 2001). For example, in working with planning groups from countries that are more centralized and autocratic in nature, planners may choose to use the model in a very linear fashion that better matches the nature of the "way things are done." These planners may also need to interpret the components somewhat differently and add or subtract some of the tasks that normally are associated with that component (see Exhibit 2.1 for an outline of these tasks).

Finally, practitioners find the Interactive Model of Program Planning a useful and practical tool. Program planners this author has worked with over the years have made three major observations about its use in practice. These planners have stated that it is one of only a few models that describe both what needs to be done and provides specific practical suggestions for how to tackle each component. Furthermore, these practitioners have found that the interactive nature of the model actually mirrors how they practice, and therefore confirmed for many of them that they actually do know what they are doing. In addition, these planners say that through using the model, they have expanded their thinking about what goes into the planning process. For example, many of them had never really thought about transfer of learning as being a part of their planning responsibilities, both in terms of designing and putting transfer plans into action. Adding this transfer component has, for many of them, given these practitioners a different way of perceiving their roles as planners. These planners are now providing a greater commitment of time and resources to assist learners in transferring what they have learned in their own settings.

**EXHIBIT 2.1**

# A Checklist for Planning Programs

*Discerning the Context*

— Be knowledgeable about the people, the organization, and the wider environmental contextual factors.
— Be well-informed about the issue of power dynamics in planning.
— Cultivate and/or enhance negotiation skills required to navigate situations in which power is a central issue.
— Ensure that beliefs and actions being displayed in one's practice are ethical.
— Know and be able to access sources of information about the context of planning situations.

*Building a Solid Base of Support*

— Ensure support from key constituent groups and other stakeholders.
— Cultivate continuous organizational support by establishing structural processes that work.
— Promote an organizational culture in which formal, job-embedded, and self-directed learning activities and continuous learning are valued.
— Obtain and maintain support from the wider community through formal and ad hoc groups and boards.
— Build and sustain collaborative partnerships with other organizations and groups.

*Identifying Program Ideas*

— Decide what sources to use in identifying ideas for education and training programs.
— Generate ideas through a variety of techniques.
— Be aware that highly structured needs assessments are not the only way to identify ideas for education and training programs.
— Ensure you can defend why a highly structured needs assessment is warranted, and choose and/or develop a model for conducting this assessment that is appropriate to the situation.
— Consider contextual issues that might affect how ideas for programs are generated.
— Be aware that in most planning situations program planners cannot use all of the program ideas that have been identified.

*Sorting and Prioritizing Program Ideas*

— Be knowledgeable about how priority ideas are defined, and what typical issues and problems are that call for interventions other than education and training programs.
— Analyze and sort the program ideas into two piles—those appropriate for educational activities and those that require alternative interventions.
— Select people who will do the actual prioritizing process.
— Be well-informed about two qualitative and quantitative approaches for prioritizing ideas.
— Use systematic methods for prioritizing program ideas.
— Be familiar with alternative interventions and how they are selected and implemented.

*Developing Program Objectives*

— Write program objectives that reflect what participants will learn, the resulting changes from that learning, and the operational aspects of the program.
— Ensure that both measurable and non-measurable program outcomes are included.
— Check to see whether the program objectives are written clearly so they can be understood by all parties involved.
— Use the program objectives as an internal consistency and "do-ability" checkpoint.
— Negotiate changes in program objectives among the parties involved with the planning process.

*Designing Instructional Plans*

— Develop clear and understandable learning objectives for each instructional session and ensure they match the proposed learning outcomes.
— Select and organize the content based on what participants "must learn."
— Choose instructional techniques that match the focus of the proposed learning outcomes, that the instructor is capable of using, and that take into account the backgrounds and experiences of the learners and the learning context.
   Select and/or develop instructional resources that enhance the learning effort.
— Choose an assessment component for each instructional segment.
— Use instructional assessment data in formative and summative ways for both instructional and program evaluation.
— Prepare clear and concise instructional plans.
— Make the instructional process work by ensuring instructors are competent and caring.

*(Continued)*

*Devising Transfer-of-Learning Plans*
— Be knowledgeable about the major factors that influence transfer of learning.
— Decide whether transfer-of-learning strategies should be employed before, during, and/or after a program.
— Determine the key players who should be a part of the transfer-of-learning process.
— Teach learners, supervisors, and other interested parties about transfer-of-learning strategies and techniques.
— Choose transfer strategies that are the most useful in assisting participants to apply what they have learned.
— Select and/or assist learners and others to opt for transfer-of-learning techniques that are the most useful to them in applying what they have learned.
— Negotiate and change the content, skills, and/or beliefs that are to be transferred.

*Formulating Evaluation Plans*
— Develop, as warranted, systematic program evaluation procedures.
— Use informal and unplanned evaluation opportunities to collect formative and summative evaluation data.
— Specify the evaluation approach or approaches to be used.
— Determine how evaluation data are to be collected.
— Think through how the data are to be analyzed.
— Describe how judgments are made about the program.

*Making Recommendations and Communicating Results*
— Examine program successes and failures, and formulate program recommendations.
— Tell the story well through carefully crafted program reports.
— Select the format for the report.
— Time the release of the report when the audience is most likely to review it.
— Follow up with appropriate individuals and groups.

*Selecting Formats, Schedules, and Staff Needs*
— Choose the most appropriate format or combination of formats for the learning activity.
— Take into account the desire to build a community of learners.
— Devise a program schedule.
— Identify staff requirements.
— Determine whether internal staff and/or external consultants are required.
— Make careful choices about instructors and/or learning facilitators.

*Preparing Budgets and Marketing Plans*
— Estimate the expenses for the program, including costs for the development, delivery, and evaluation of the program.
— Determine how the program is financed, and estimate the program income.
— Manage the program budget, and keep accurate budget records.
— Develop contingency budget plans for programs that are scaled back or cancelled.
— Be able to pay the bills for the program by managing the income side of the budget.
— Build and maintain program credibility, success, and market niches when marketing programs.
— Conduct a target audience analysis.
— Use already existing data or generate contextual information to help frame the marketing plan.
— Select and prepare promotional materials for the program.
— Prepare a targeted and lively promotional campaign.
— Ascertain and strengthen your promotional assets and capabilities.

*Coordinating Facilities and On-Site Events*
— Obtain suitable facilities, and arrange for instructional materials and equipment.
— Make sure facilities meet all Americans with Disabilities Act (ADA) requirements.
— Oversee all of the on-site program arrangements.
— Create a positive climate for learning from the moment the participants arrive.
— Provide systems for monitoring programs.
— Gather data for program evaluations.
— Give recognition to program participants, and thank both staff members and participants for being a part of the program.
— Tie up all loose ends after the program is finished.

In essence, the key to using the Interactive Model of Program Planning is *flexibility*. Therefore, the use of the model should be tailored to meet the demands of specific planning groups and situations (see Chapter Three).

## Tasks Within Each Component of the Model

Each program component of the model includes a set of tasks and decision points. As noted previously, not all of the components—and therefore not all of the tasks—are addressed in developing every program, and often need to be altered depending on the people and the context. For example, establishing and maintaining support systems for planning efforts are usually ongoing processes. However, once a solid base of support for an educational program is built, program planners may not have to address that task for each new program as long as this support remains relatively stable. The same could be said for the process of compiling a list of ideas, needs, and problems for possible educational programs. Some circumstances call for a well-conceived and well-executed needs analysis, while ideas for other programs may be more appropriately gathered through informal or less traditional means. In other situations the need for the program is a given, and therefore compiling program ideas probably is not even appropriate.

The tasks that make up each component, in a form of a checklist for planning, are presented in Exhibit 2.1. Each of the tasks is discussed more fully in Chapters Four through Fifteen. In using the checklist, planners may start with any one or more of the items that fit their planning situation (see Chapter Three).

## Assumptions on Which the Model Is Grounded

The Interactive Model of Program Planning rests on seven major assumptions. The assumptions are drawn primarily from the work of Brookfield (1986); Cervero and Wilson (1994, 1996); Houle (1972, 1996); Knowles (1980); Sork and Caffarella (1989); Wilson and Cervero (1996a, 1996b); Sork (1997, 2000); and Cervero, Wilson, and Associates (2001). Through these assumptions this author is conveying her personal belief systems about the planning process, and the foundational principles of the Interactive Model of Program Planning. In order to use the Interactive Model effectively and in an ethical manner, these assumptions have to be taken into account by program planners as they work their way through each planning process.

## Assumption 1: Focusing on Learning and Change

*Educational programs focus on what the participants actually learn and how this learning results in changes in participants, organizations, and/or societal issues and norms.* Program planners possess a clear understanding of why they are doing what they are doing. They are able to articulate what change will or could come about as a result of the education or training program. In addition, planners are aware that unintended changes might also occur, both good and bad. These changes may be work-related or focus on other practical issues and problems of adult life, on organizational adaptation, and/or on alterations in societal norms and practices. Some of these changes can be demonstrated almost immediately, such as learning a specific job skill; while other changes, such as abolishing discriminatory practices, may take years of continuous effort on the part of educators.

## Assumption 2: Recognizing the Nonsequential Nature of the Planning Process

*The development of educational programs is a complex interaction of institutional priorities, tasks, people, and events.* Developing education and training programs rarely is done in a logical fashion. Planners spend a great deal of time formulating and then reformulating the many facets of the process. In addition, the more organizations and persons added to the planning process, the less logical the process is. For example, when different people representing a number of organizations are responsible for different parts of a program, some people may make every planning deadline while others make none. The latter can be a program coordinator's nightmare, especially if the delinquent person's tasks are an essential element in getting the program off the ground. The key to keeping oneself sane as a program planner is to maintain flexibility throughout the process.

## Assumption 3: Discerning the Importance of Context and Negotiation

*Program planning is contextual in nature; that is, people plan programs within a social, economic, cultural, and political climate.* Planning then becomes "an integration of individual planners' actions and the organizational context within which they work" (Wilson and Cervero, 1996b, p. 8). As a result of the varying interests and needs of those involved in the planning process, the final program is often a negotiated product. Among those negotiating include people who are at the planning table and/or people who have influence with those who sit at the table. Planners therefore must take into account the power relationships among the parties involved, both those at and away from the planning table, and negotiate in responsible and ethical ways. This acknowledgment of power hopefully allows all parties who should be heard to become a part of the planning process. For example, "the boss" may want one kind of training program, while potential participants and trainers believe a different program is warranted. In addition, there may be another group that believes they have not been heard at all. It is up to program staff to negotiate between and among the participants—the group that believes it has not been heard, and the boss. Paying attention to concerns related to power and interests does not negate that planners need to be highly skilled in the tasks of program planning. Rather, greater responsibility is placed on people who plan programs to be technically competent, politically savvy, and ethically grounded.

## Assumption 4: Attending to Preplanning and Last-Minute Changes

*Program planning involves both systematic, preplanned tasks and "on-your-feet" (sometimes last-minute) decisions.* Persons responsible for planning programs can never know all the variables in the planning process. Even when the planning parameters and tasks are explicitly defined, they are often subject to change. For example, major presenters may cancel at the last minute, expected numbers of program participants may not show up, and weather conditions may prevent a specific event from taking place.

## Assumption 5: Honoring and Taking into Account Diversity and Cultural Differences

*People who plan programs for adults are sensitive to diversity and cultural differences in their many forms.* "Gender, race, ethnicity, and class remain the central concerns, but other forms of diversity—including sexual orientation, linguistic background, religious affiliation, ability or disability, and so on—represent differences" (Sork, 1997, p. 7) that must be taken into account in the planning process. Planners, for example, have to be aware of how people from different cultures communicate, take part in the educational process, regard instructors, and "relate to people from other cultures. . . . It is not enough to recognize and respect these differences; educational planners must be able to design workshops [and other program formats] that fully engage people in learning who might have very different cultural traditions and expectations" (Sork, 1997, p. 10–11).

### Assumption 6: Accepting That Program Planners Work in Different Ways

*Designing educational programs is anything but an exacting practice as there is no single method of planning education and training programs that ensures success.* Rather, program planners are very much like orchestra conductors. They are able to bring together diverse players and pieces in a harmonious and balanced effort. This task may not be easy: Some of the pieces may be much more difficult than anticipated, and some of the players may not be as adept at their parts as was hoped. Each orchestra conductor has his or her own way of making sure the orchestra is ready to play on opening night.

### Assumption 7: Understanding That Program Planners Are Learners

*Individuals, using one or more planning models as guides, can learn to be more effective program planners through practice.* Effective program planners are not born that way. Through trial and error, they become more skilled at balancing the various components and tasks of the process and negotiating among planning parties. It is important for planners to reflect upon and evaluate their planning efforts to see where they have been effective and where they can improve.

## Sources for the Model

The Interactive Model of Program Planning is derived from three major sources: classical and current descriptions of program planning, principles and practices of adult learning, and practical experience.

First, building on Tyler's (1949) and Walker's (1971, 1990) original descriptions of the curriculum development process, 14 sources that explore planning programs for adults provided the primary material for framing the model (Houle, 1972, 1996; Knowles, 1980; Caffarella, 1985, 1988, 1998/1999; Laird, 1985; Sork and Caffarella, 1989; Rothwell and Kazanas, 1993, 1998; Cervero and Wilson, 1994, 1996; Cervero and Wilson and Associates, 2001; Rothwell and Cookson, 1997; Sork, 1997, 2000; and Milano with Ullius, 1998). In addition, 14 other sources (Boyle, 1981; Nadler, 1982; Cervero, 1988; Munson, 1992; Richey, 1992; Tracey, 1992; Fleming, 1997; Driscoll, 1998; Mitchell, 1998; Birkenholz, 1999; Donaldson and Kozoll, 1999; Hartwig, 2000; Lee and Owens, 2000; and Wilson and Hayes, 2000) also provided some very useful information.

Second, as foundational material in building and using this model, it was important to consider how adults learn and change. Highlighted here are major principles and practices of adult learning that were used in developing the model.

▶ Adults have a rich background of knowledge and experience and learn best when this experience is acknowledged and new information builds on their past knowledge and experience.

▶ Adults are motivated to learn based on a combination of complex internal and external forces.

▶ All adults have preferred and different ways of processing information.

▶ Adults are not likely to willingly engage in learning unless the learning is meaningful to them.

▶ For the most part, adults are pragmatic in their learning; they want to apply their learning to present situations.

▶ Adults come to a learning situation with their own personal goals and objectives, which may or may not be the same as those that underlie the learning situation.

▶ Adults prefer to be actively involved in the learning process rather than passive recipients of knowledge.

▶ Adults learn in interdependent, connected, and collaborative ways as well as independent, self-reliant modes.

▶ Adults are more receptive to the learning process in situations that are both physically and psychologically comfortable.

▶ What, how, and where adults learn is affected by the many roles they play as adults (for example, worker, parent, partner, friend, spouse) and their own personal contexts as learners (for example, gender, race, ethnicity, social class, disabilities and abilities, and cultural background).

Current in-depth discussions about learning in adulthood are found in Merriam (1993); Tennant and Pogson (1995); Wlodkowski (1998); Clark and Caffarella (1999); Daloz (1999); Merriam and Caffarella (1999); Hayes, Flannery, and Associates (2000); Caffarella and Merriam (2000); and Silverman and Casazza (2000).

Consider these examples of how specific principles and practices of how adults learn and change are incorporated into selected components of the Interactive Model of Program Planning.

**Identifying Program Ideas**   Because adults are more willing to engage in learning activities when the content is meaningful to them, collecting ideas for programs from participants enrolled in current educational programs is a good way to generate ideas for future programs.

**Preparing for the Transfer of Learning**    To ensure that learners are able to apply their learning to their present situations, planners and instructors are familiar with the contexts in which the learning is applied. In addition, educational planners provide useful and timely transfer strategies and techniques prior to, during, and after the formal program to help facilitate this applications process.

 **Designing Instructional Plans**    Instructors design their learning objectives in such a way that participants, whenever possible, can incorporate their own learning agendas. The instructional content builds on the past knowledge and experiences of the participants and, where appropriate, is problem-oriented and practical. Teaching techniques permit active learner participation and provide opportunities to apply newly learned knowledge and skills. Learning activities encourage participants to assume responsibility for their own learning and allow for both independent and collaborative ways of knowing.

 **Coordinating Facilities and On-Site Events**    To ensure that the learning climate makes adults feel respected, accepted, and supported, instructors provide opportunities for the participants to set norms for the learning activities and are willing to modify the instructional objectives, content, and/or techniques based on learner needs and observations.

The third source used in developing the Interactive Model was practical experience—the author's own and that of other professionals in the field. The importance of this source is demonstrated by the work of Pennington and Green (1976); Brookfield (1986); Cervero and Wilson (1994, 1996); and Sork (1997). Pennington and Green were among the first to challenge the assumption that program planners always follow specific models of planning and include all the steps in those models. Although they found that planners could identify a clear set of tasks and decision points, they saw major discrepancies between what planners did and what popular models of program planning said they should do. For example, comprehensive needs assessments were rarely conducted as the basis for program development, and often those designing the actual instructional activities did not take into account the background, characteristics, and experiences of the particular group of learners who were to attend the program. Further, Brookfield (1986), Cervero and Wilson (1994), and Sork (1997) have observed as well that experienced program planners are often unable to recognize, in many program planning models, what they actually do. Planners also may not be aware of how they influence the planning process, and in return, how the planning process influences their decisions and their actions. In other words, program planning is an interactive and action-oriented process in which decisions and choices are made that do not necessarily follow what many of the planning models prescribe.

Among the major variables in how decisions are made in the program planning process is the experience that planners bring to the table. Therefore, in deciding on the components and tasks included in the Interactive Model and determining how this model is used, ideas and feedback were sought and received from novice and experienced practitioners. These sources included the author's graduate students, participants in workshops the author has conducted on program planning, and many practitioners (both paid and volunteer) in the field who are engaged in planning programs as part of their responsibilities. The ideas from these various constituents were incorporated in the many revisions of the Interactive Model that brought it to its present form.

## Who Finds the Interactive Model Useful?

Both novice and experienced planners find the Interactive Model of Program Planning useful. The Interactive Model assists novice planners to better use their planning resources of people, time, and money. For example, this model can help clarify the broad picture of what planning teams need to do to get a program up and running. Planning teams can save time by not having to figure out all the essential ingredients by themselves and not having to go back and do or redo parts they had forgotten and/or did not realize were important.

In addition, the daily work of novice program planners is made easier with the Interactive Model, because the model provides a list of specific tasks that they may need to address. Because the model helps novice planners choose and lay out needed tasks beforehand, they need not haphazardly limp along and then play catch-up at the last minute. Being on top of needed tasks is particularly feasible for those program elements that can realistically be preplanned, such as developing program objectives, preparing instructional and transfer of learning plans, and selecting satisfactory facilities.

For example, the first-time chair of a program committee for a city-wide conference on preventing violence, to be hosted cooperatively by the police department, area churches, and a community action group, prepares—using the Interactive Model—a checklist of tasks to be done. This checklist includes a column for writing deadline dates and the person or persons responsible for getting each task accomplished (as in Exhibit 2.2). The checklist then is used by those persons responsible for developing the conference as a practical guide for getting certain tasks done in a timely manner.

**EXHIBIT 2.2**

## Sample Program Checklist with Timetable

| Task to Be Accomplished | Person(s) Responsible | Timetable | |
|---|---|---|---|
| | | Immediate Deadline | Final Deadline |
| Identify theme and program objectives | Committee as a whole | Draft: Oct. 1 | Oct. 15 |
| Determine program format | Committee as a whole | | Oct. 15 |
| Prepare program budget | Susan | Draft: Oct. 1 | Oct. 15 |
| Identify possible presenters and session topics | John Roberto Joyce | | Oct. 15 |
| Line up major presenters | Joyce | | Nov. 15 |
| Finalize all sessions, topics, and presenters | Roberto John Kathy | | Nov. 15 |
| Prepare publicity | Joyce Roberto | Draft: Nov. 15 | Dec. 1 |
| Plan evaluation and transfer of learning | Joyce Roberto | Draft: Nov. 15 | Jan. 5 |
| Program delivery | | | Mar. 1, 2 |

When essential tasks are not done, holes are left in the planning process itself and in the final product of that process. For example, the checking of facilities and equipment for an upcoming program is of prime importance. Failure to complete this task can lead to disastrous results, as illustrated in the following scenario.

### *Unexpected Construction*

Jean had the responsibility for making all final arrangements for a continuing professional education conference. Although she had seen diagrams of the rooms to be used, she did not have the chance, nor did she really see the need, to visit the facilities herself. The hotel staff had assured her that the room space would be adequate and that they had an excellent sound system for the main banquet room. When Jean arrived on the morning of the conference, she discovered, to her horror, that not only was the sound system inadequate but a major remodeling project was under way in areas that the conference would be using.

Experienced planners often use the Interactive Model to revisit and expand their knowledge and skill base in planning programs for adults. They then adapt the materials so they can be applied to their own planning situations. For example, experienced planners may find that the ideas of discerning the context and working within the framework of power and negotiations (see Chapter Four) or preparing transfer of learning plans (see Chapter Ten) may be new. These concepts also may be ones they have to sell to both their organizations and staff members. They may choose to use selected tables or figures to illustrate what each of these planning components consist of to help their supervisors and other key players better understand the process.

Experienced planners also plan training sessions for those involved in the planning process that are unfamiliar with parts of or the entire program planning process. Putting everyone on the same page helps foster teamwork within the group responsible for planning a program and gives them a concrete guide for action. The model provides a means for clarifying roles and responsibilities for all involved, which can lead to a better spirit of team cooperation and less confusion over who is supposed to do what. The following scenarios, which include two possible descriptions of the same situation, illustrate this benefit. The scene is a mid-year planning meeting of a regional conference committee. The chair has asked each person to review his or her assignments for the upcoming conference to be hosted by the association in three months.

### Meeting Description One

Sue responds to the chair's request by asking if the chair can review again what each of the committee members is to do. She does not remember the specifics, nor does a colleague of hers who is not present and whom Sue has been asked to represent. (A second member is missing but unrepresented.) The chair fumbles through his notes of the last meeting trying to figure out just what was said. Meanwhile, two of the members fume—they have already completed their responsibilities and are ready to report on them.

### Meeting Description Two

Each person at the session describes what he or she has accomplished. The chair then gives a report for the two missing members. The group reviews the next set of tasks as described on the conference planning checklist they developed three months earlier. Due to some last-minute changes, some minor modifications need to be made to their workplan, but all agree they are right on target in their planning of the conference. They agree to meet via a conference call in one month to ensure that all the final arrangements are completed.

Whether program planners are novices or experts, five issues are critical to keep in mind when using the Interactive Model of Program Planning—personal beliefs about planning, setting planning parameters, determining which components and tasks of the model to use, technology, and ethical issues. Each of these issues is discussed in-depth in the following chapter.

## Chapter Highlights

The Interactive Model of Program Planning for adult learners consists of 12 components, with each component containing a series of tasks and decision points:

- Discerning the context for planning
- Building a solid base of support
- Identifying program ideas
- Sorting and prioritizing program ideas
- Developing program objectives
- Designing instructional plans
- Devising transfer-of-learning plans
- Formulating evaluation plans
- Making recommendations and communicating results
- Selecting formats, schedules, and staff
- Preparing budgets and marketing plans
- Coordinating facilities and on-site events

Program planners often work with a number of components and tasks at the same time and apply the model in different ways. In addition, they are required to continually negotiate and renegotiate both the processes and products of their work as they work within varying political and cultural environments. Therefore, the key to using the Interactive Model is remaining flexible in its application throughout the planning process.

The Interactive Model is grounded on seven major assumptions. Among those assumptions, the following three are the most critical for those using this model. First, education and training programs should focus on what the participants actually learn and how this learning results in changes in participants, organizations, and/or societal issues and norms. Second, planning education and training programs is usually a nonsequential process involving complex interactions among institutional priorities, tasks, people, and events; and third, discerning the importance of context and negotiation is important.

In constructing the Interactive Model, three major sources were used: classical and current descriptions of program planning, principles and practices of adult learning, and the day-to-day experiences of educators, trainers, staff developers, and others who plan programs. Although frameworks of earlier models and knowledge about learning in adulthood were helpful in building the model, without the voices of the practitioners the Interactive Model of Program Planning would be neither as rich nor as practical in its applicability.

Both novice and experienced planners find the Interactive Model helpful in their practice. Novice planners discover using the model makes their daily work easier as it provides a list of specific tasks that they may need to consider, depending on the planning situation. Experienced planners observe that the Interactive Model assists them in reviewing and expanding their own knowledge of program planning. In addition, the model assists them in framing education and training sessions for their own staff and other planning groups. Important considerations that should be taken into account when both novice and experienced planners use the Interactive Model of Program Planning are explored in the next chapter.

## Application Exercise

 The Application Exercise presented here can assist you in thinking more about the Interactive Model of Program Planning and the assumptions upon which this model is grounded.

## EXERCISE 2.1

### Examining the Components and Assumptions of the Interactive Model of Program Planning

1.  **Describe briefly a current or previous program planning process in which you are or were involved.**

2.  **What components and tasks of the Interactive Model of Program Planning are or were the most applicable to that planning situation and why? Are there components or tasks that also should be or should have been addressed to make that planning process more effective?**

    Components or tasks that are or were applicable:

    Components or tasks that should or should have been addressed:

3.  **Do some or all of the assumptions (see pages 26–28) that undergird the model fit your current or past planning situation? If so, which ones, and why? Are there additional assumptions you would add?**

    Stated assumptions that fit:

    Additional assumptions you would add:

# Chapter 3

# Using the Interactive Model of Program Planning

THE INTERACTIVE MODEL OF PROGRAM PLANNING is to be *used* rather than simply tucked in a file folder or left on a bookshelf. Both novice and experienced planners, as described in Chapter Two, find this model to be helpful in their practice. Before planners decide to try the Interactive Model, they should examine their own beliefs about planning programs for adults to determine whether the model fits with who they are and how they prefer to practice. If, for example, they are unwilling to negotiate with other parties in the planning process, the Interactive Model of Program Planning will not work for them. (Remember that one of the basic assumptions of the model is that education and training programs are a negotiated product among the people involved in the planning process.)

Once planners decide to use the Interactive Model, they review their current planning situation and set planning parameters under which they will be working (such as ongoing program commitments and resources). These parameters, which often result from a contextual scan (see Chapter Four), serve as reminders to planners of their current situation as they move simultaneously into new ventures. This movement forward may also result in modifications of the original parameters as programs evolve and change. As part of this movement forward, planning staff members have to make decisions about what components and tasks of the model are appropriate for them to use. In addition, with the advent of technological advances in both planning and delivering programs, planners face decisions of how to effectively integrate technology into their practice as they wind their way through the planning process. Finally, making decisions about how and what programs to plan requires more than just knowing which components and tasks to use, and using technology in a way that is productive for all parties. Rather, planners are often confronted with making decisions that have ethical consequences for the participants, the planners, and the program sponsors.

Each of these important topics, related to using the Interactive Model of Program Planning, is examined in this chapter. Addressed first is identifying personal beliefs about program planning, followed by a description of setting upfront planning parameters. Determining what components and tasks of the Interactive Model to use is discussed next. This discussion is followed by an exploration of using technology in program planning. The chapter concludes with a review of ethical issues that confront program planners and a framework for making decisions about those issues.

## Identifying Personal Beliefs Related to Program Planning

In applying the Interactive Model of Program Planning, planners construct personal platforms related to their practice as educators and trainers. More specifically, they identify and articulate their beliefs about the program planning process. By articulating these beliefs, program planners determine whether or not the Interactive Model fits what they value and how they work. (If it does not, perhaps they might be willing to reflect on their present practice and modify or change their beliefs so that the model could be a useful resource and enhance their practice.) For example, do they see the program planning process as sequential or a highly flexible and interactive process in terms of what planners do? Do they believe in the basic assumptions of the model, such as program planning being contextual in nature, and that people who plan programs must be sensitive to diversity and cultural issues? And do they believe that adults learn best when their experiences and prior knowledge are incorporated into learning activities, and when they have different ways of processing information?

Boyle (1981) and Apps (1991) provide useful categories to assist educators and trainers in articulating and examining their beliefs on program planning. These categories, as illustrated in Exhibit 3.1 with sample belief statements, incorporate ideas about what people believe about the purpose of educating adults, the program planning process, adults as learners, and the process of learning.

In constructing and revisiting these individual belief statements (see Exercise 3.1 in the Application Exercises, page 55), one useful instrument is Zinn's (1998) Philosophy of Adult Education Inventory. The purpose of this instrument is to help educators identify their personal beliefs about education as related to the categories described by Boyle and Apps. The inven-

---

**EXHIBIT 3.1**

# Sample Personal Belief Statements

---

### The Purpose of Educating Adults

- ❖ The purpose of education and training programs is to promote changes in the way workers behave so their job performance is enhanced.
- ❖ The purpose of education and training programs is to encourage the growth and development of individuals.
- ❖ The purpose of education and training programs is to assist adults to bring about change in societal norms and values.

### The Program Planning Process

- ❖ Program planners act as content experts and/or managers of the planning process, making sure that all necessary tasks are completed.
- ❖ Program planners serve as coordinators and facilitators in the planning process, enabling all parties (such as participants, supervisors, funding sources) to have active roles.
- ❖ Program planners facilitate negotiations among the various groups involved in the planning process. They also may simultaneously be content experts.

### Adults as Learners

- ❖ Adults have a rich background of knowledge and experience that should be incorporated into the learning process.
- ❖ Adults, for the most part, are pragmatic in their learning. They want to apply their learning to present situations.
- ❖ What, where, and how adults learn is affected by their own personal contexts (for example, gender, race, cultural background, ethnicity, social class, and disabilities and abilities).

### The Learning Process

- ❖ Participants learn best when new information or skills build on past knowledge and experience.
- ❖ Participants are more motivated to learn when a variety of instructional methods are used.
- ❖ Participants learn both in interdependent, connected, and collaborative ways as well as in independent and self-reliant modes.

---

tory is self-administered, self-scored, and self-interpreted, which makes it easy for planners to use in clarifying their personal beliefs about areas important to the program planning process.

In practice, rarely do persons involved with program planning fully articulate their personal beliefs about program planning, sometimes even to themselves; yet a system of beliefs guides their actions. Contrast, for example, two different people responsible for developing educational activities.

### More Is Better

Bob involves as many people as possible in designing the educational activities for which he is responsible. He has a very active education committee and uses a variety of ad hoc groups in the planning of new programs and other educational initiatives.

He strongly advises his instructors to use participatory methods in their program delivery and to gear their material to what is useful to the participants back on the job. He ensures that all participants receive prompt feedback on what they have learned, both during the sessions and when they apply the material to their specific work situations.

### The Lone Ranger

Cheri, on the other hand, prefers to plan educational activities by herself, although she occasionally hires outside consultants to assist. She finds working with committees and staff outside her unit very cumbersome. She does not like her instructors to waste any time in class, and she requests that they stick strictly to the topic at hand and make sure the participants know the content. Cheri requires pre- and post-tests for each session, but no follow-up training or evaluation are done once the program is completed. Cheri believes that follow-up activities are a waste of time and money. If the participants did not get the material the first time (she believes), they did not really want to learn it in the first place. Cheri also assumes that it is the participant's responsibility to apply the material, not hers.

Although most program planners do not take the time to spell out clearly and precisely their belief systems about program planning to either themselves or those with whom they work, there are consequences of not being cognizant of and acting on one's beliefs. Adult learners and program sponsors are usually quick at making judgments about planners who espouse one set of beliefs and then act in opposition to those beliefs. If, for example, potential program participants are asked for ideas for future programs, they want to see those ideas used; and if their ideas are not used, they want to know why. Likewise, if organizational sponsors expect that certain outcomes promised will be addressed, they do not like the planners of the event to respond to only some of their expectations. And when program planners say they are interested in fostering change in participants, organizational practices, and the like, administrators and participants expect them to take this charge seriously and not simply assume that the changes will happen through the good intentions of participants and/or sponsors. In essence, adult learners and sponsors of educational and training programs expect program planners to deliver what they say they will deliver. For program staff to do otherwise often results in angry—or even worse, indifferent—participants with the attitude that education and training programs are a waste of time and money.

# Setting Upfront Parameters

Setting explicit parameters about any planning situation is a very helpful starting point for applying the Interactive Model of Program Planning. These parameters are shaped initially within the confines of how the current reality of a specific situation is perceived. Through devising and keeping these parameters in mind throughout the planning process, planners can move forward with new activities without losing sight of their current situations. In addition, these planning parameters may also be modified through planners' recognition that they must change to allow program development to happen either through their actions as planners and/or changing circumstances. Although stating and using these planning parameters is generally a useful practice, it becomes especially critical when large programs, with their increased complexity and staffing, are being launched. Five major factors are considered in developing these planning parameters: current program commitments, organizational context, current and potential learners, planning personnel, and available resources. Each of these factors is discussed briefly below.

## Current Program Commitments

When deciding whether to initiate a new program it is important to have a clear understanding of both the new ideas for education and training programs and the present priorities and commitments of the organization. These commitments include all continuing programs and activities.

Interpreting new ideas in terms of present activities is handled in three ways. The first is to consider the present commitments as possible priorities, "along with other emerging and new concerns. Selecting this option means some present commitments eventually will be rated a lower priority" (Forest and Mulcahy, 1976, p. 17). A second approach is to recognize that prior or ongoing commitments take time, and therefore time must be set aside to meet them. Third, the past priorities and commitments can be ignored. This alternative will not be very popular, of course, because commitments are often made to get or keep the support of others. Whatever approach is used, all current programs and ongoing activities and commitments, as well as the emerging ideas, are considered when deciding whether to initiate a new program.

A sample parameter in the area of current program commitments reads as follows: *All present commitments, along with new ideas and concerns, will be considered as possible program priorities on an equal basis.*

## Organizational Context

Planning assumptions are also made in light of the sponsoring groups' or organizations' mission and goals. For example, does the organization expect that education or training programs will result in greater productivity (and thus cost savings)? Is it expected that the education or training unit will be a profit-making operation? Will innovative programs, along with those that have stood the test of time, be supported? Is the organization primarily interested in serving one major audience, or is a broader clientele accepted?

In addition, it is necessary to consider the politics of the organization and the wider community within which it is situated (Cervero and Wilson, 1994, 1996; Bolman and Deal, 1997; Cervero, Wilson, and Associates, 2001). How are decisions made, and who makes them? Are there power coalitions, both formal and informal, that program planners need to cultivate? How can staff wisely use the political structure to enhance their programs? "If planners are not politically astute, they surely will be ineffective" (Cervero and Wilson, 1991, p. 45).

A sample parameter in the area of organizational context reads as follows: *It is expected that training programs will result in increased productivity and effectiveness of employees. One measure of this productivity and effectiveness must be demonstrated through cost-benefit analysis.*

## Current and Potential Learners

It is crucial to take into account current and potential learners in thinking about initiating new programs. Considering the needs, interests, and characteristics of participants is important so that current clientele are not slighted, and planners should have at least basic knowledge about potential learners (see Chapters Six and Fourteen). For example, will programs need to be cut or reduced, and if so, will these changes adversely affect learners involved in those programs? Will the new program initiatives target or attract different clientele, and if so, are planners prepared to work with them? And, in cases where developing new markets is crucial, are these new markets an unrealistic vision of overly optimistic planners, or are there real people who will be attracted to the new ventures?

In addition, some current and potential participants may want to be involved in all or at least part of the planning process itself. Planners also may want the voices of learners included. Examples of ways to promote active learner participation is to request their assistance or leadership in getting a sense of the program context (see Chapter Four), designing instructional plans (see Chapter Nine), or providing marketing savvy (see Chapter Fourteen). Their involvement could encompass such activities as serving on advisory or ad hoc committees (see Chapter Five), being a part of chat room discussions, responding to program ideas via a listserv, and/or working in partnership with other learners and staff on specific tasks.

A sample parameter in the area of taking into account both current and potential learners reads as follows: *The new programs will address the interests and needs of both current and potential participants. Two of the goals of these new programs are to make programs affordable for all incomes levels, and expand their marketing campaign to reach a more diverse population. In addition, current or potential learners will be invited to participate in the planning process through a variety of ways.*

## Planning Personnel

Program planners rely on their own values, perceptions, and experiences in building program parameters. Therefore, it is important to know who the people are who will be involved in making these planning decisions. What are their educational backgrounds? What kinds of work and/or volunteer experience have they had? Are they oriented more toward service, organizational goals, the bottom line, social issues, and/or the growth and development of self and others? What are their perceptions of the value of education?

Although the views and leadership provided by program planners are important, they should not take precedence over the opinions and experiences of other people who are key stakeholders. Yet in the final analysis, the programs selected—whatever they are—become the personal agendas of the program planners, because it is they who are responsible for getting the program up and running.

A sample parameter in the area of planning personnel reads as follows: *The planning team for a regional-wide professional development program for literacy coaches will consist of three principals, three teachers on special assignment, the staff development specialist for that region, and an outside consultant. The outside consultant will be a content expert on current approaches to teaching literacy in the elementary- and middle-school settings. All members of the planning team have experience in using technology in the planning process.*

## Resource Availability

In determining program parameters, the type and amount of resources available for education and training programs must be clear. Resources include time, money, personnel, facilities, equipment, material, and supplies. Boyle has outlined three key questions that have to be answered about determining resources in setting program parameters: "Do we have the quality and quantity of resources necessary to affect change through a program? Are they the right kind of resources? Are we employing new personnel to coincide with changing program priorities?" (Boyle, 1981, p. 174).

A sample parameter in the area of resource availability reads as follows: *No new financial resources will be available to the Human Resource Division. The division may choose to reallocate present resources, however, including staff time and funds available for current programs.*

Program planners need to be aware, as noted earlier, that parameters can and do change as the planning process progresses. Therefore it pays to revisit the parameters from time to time. In addition, laying out these planning parameters assists planners in choosing whether they need to use all or just some of the components and tasks of the Interactive Model.

## Determining Which Components of the Model to Use and When

Although having planning parameters does help in determining which components of the Interactive Model program planners might use and which they might leave out, there is no exact method for completing this task. Selecting which components to use and when to apply them is based on professional judgment, and smart planners make these decisions in collaboration with other stakeholders. Even though there is no specific formula for applying the model, educational and training program planners have found four considerations, each of which are discussed in greater detail in this section, useful in making these judgments:

1. All of the components are commonly used in developing and revising comprehensive programs.

2. When choosing only selected components, the planning context and parameters of the program primarily affect which components and tasks are adopted.

3. There are essential components that need to be addressed at some point related to the program under consideration.

4. Unforeseen changes in planning circumstances often force planners to revisit some or all of the components of the Interactive Model.

### Using All of the Planning Components

Program planners developing and revising comprehensive programs for adults generally use all of the components of the model. Examples of such programs include:

▶ National and international professional and trade conferences

▶ Adult degree programs in colleges and universities

▶ Comprehensive community education or social action programs

▶ Regional job training and retraining programs

▶ District-wide or regional staff development programs for teachers or administrators

Even if program planners determine that they need to use all of the components of the model, they may apply the model in different ways, however, even for programs that are similar in nature. They may, for example, start the program planning process at any one of a variety of different points; focus on only one component at a time or work on a number of components simultaneously; choose to give some tasks more emphasis than others in the planning process; and/or revisit a component more than once during the planning process.

In planning a distance education degree program in higher education for adult learners, for example, the starting point may be for a college to first address the instructional design and staffing components of the Interactive Model. Does the college have the capacity for delivering such a program in terms of both the quality and effectiveness of the technology that is available? What is the current skill level of the staff in designing and providing instruction via distance learning? What support systems exist for both faculty and students in using technology as an instructional tool? If the responses to these questions were that the technology available is sufficient, but that faculty skill level and support are lacking, then the next steps in developing this program would be very different than for an institution in which all three questions can be answered in the affirmative.

For a college in which staff expertise and support are lacking, initiating a faculty development program for their staff on effective instruction via distance learning, and providing for technical support would be the first priorities. This same college then must go back and reassess both the instructional and staffing components of the model prior to moving forward with the planning of the distance learning degree. For a college in which the technology, staff skill, and support for distance education are adequate, planners could move forward with other components of the planning model, such as conducting a structured needs assessment of potential students and employers, discerning the context for planning, drafting program objectives, and developing transfer-of-learning plans. These tasks could be undertaken at the same time or in a certain order, depending on the planning parameters for new degree programs (for example, curriculum development guidelines for the college, and the state higher education coordinating body).

## Using Selected Components

Depending primarily on the planning context and the parameters that are set for a specific planning situation, often program planners use only selected parts of the Interactive Model. The planning context, for example, might demand that programs be developed in a very short amount of time. In this case, program planners must make quick decisions about which components and tasks are absolutely necessary to complete and which can be ignored or put on hold. In other cases, the program parameters, such as mandated content and formats, staff, and locations that are predetermined, help dictate what actions and tasks still need to be considered. Examples of such situations are listed in Exhibit 3.2.

Like program planners who use the whole model, planning staff who use only selected components may choose to address one component at a time or simultaneously work with two or more components depending on organizational expectations and other contextual factors.

## Essential Components

There are some components of the Interactive Model that are central to most planning processes; therefore, when choosing which components to use another question to ask is whether or not these components have been at least considered during the planning process. These critical components are: discerning the context, identifying program ideas,

---

**EXHIBIT 3.2**

## Examples of Parameters and Program Components

| Program Parameters | Components to Be Addressed |
|---|---|
| *Programs that are limited in scope and time and have set audiences, budgets, staff, and places to meet* | • Identifying program ideas<br>• Developing program objectives<br>• Designing instructional plans<br>• Preparing for learning transfer |
| *Already-developed programs being repeated in different locations with participants who have similar backgrounds and experiences* | • Coordinating facilities and on-site events<br>• Preparing for transfer of learning at the various locations<br>• Communicating program value |
| *Programs where attendance is mandatory and the goals and objectives, format, content, and evaluation are set* | • Determining program staff<br>• Coordinating on-site facilities and events<br>• Designing instructional plans<br>• Preparing for learning transfer |
| *Programs in which the delivery and content are being changed* | • Determining program format<br>• Designing instructional plans<br>• Preparing for learning transfer<br>• Formulating evaluation plans |

developing clear program objectives, designing instructional plans, devising transfer-of-learning plans, and formulating evaluation plans (Caffarella, 1998–1999).

To put these essential components in another light, it is not that the more administrative tasks, such as marketing and coordinating on-site events, are less important. Instead, what matters to learners and most sponsors is that the substance of the program is matched to the context in which the learning is to be applied, and that the program is instructionally sound. For example, glitzy marketing with content that is inadequate or irrelevant, or the use of the "latest and greatest technology," with little thought as to whether integrating this technology makes for good instructional practice, is neither a cogent nor ethical way for program planners to act.

## The Unforeseen in the Planning Process

Contextual or other outside forces, whether positive or negative, may dictate that planners revisit some or all of the components of the Interactive Model to get a program up and running or keep it functioning as they respond to these unexpected changes. A sampling of these program planning "interruptions" which either this author or her colleagues have experienced are highlighted.

A major new program initiative was announced on the assumption that start-up funds were available to get the new program up and running (after which it would be self-sufficient). Now, however, unanticipated budget cuts have eliminated that start-up funding. The question is whether alternative funds can be found or the program should be canceled.

• • •

A very popular program for volunteers of an organization has been oversubscribed. The instructors know that if all of the people who have registered in advance actually come, what they have planned in terms of format and teaching methods will not work. The organizers do not want to tell some of the participants not to come, because they are afraid they would lose some good volunteers. The questions are: (1) can they redesign the instructional part of the program and find additional instructors so a larger number of people are accommodated, or (2) should they offer the program a second time and give people the opportunity to choose one of the two times?

• • •

A fire has destroyed the headquarters hotel two days prior to the opening of a major national conference. The primary tasks to address are housing participants who were to stay at this hotel and finding enough meeting rooms for the program sessions.

• • •

A surprise snow and ice storm has kept all the major program presenters stranded at a hub airport all day. The airport was supposed to reopen, but now it has been shut down until the morning of the next day—and the program is scheduled to begin at 9:00 A.M. that morning. It is now 7:00 P.M., and there are no other transportation options available. Many of the program participants are either on their way or already at the program site, as they are all within drivable distance and it is only raining where they are. The major issue is what to do with the participants until the presenters arrive.

In summary, what is readily apparent in choosing which components to use and when, as stressed in Chapter Two, is the need for flexibility on the part of all involved in the program planning process.

## Increased Use of Technology in the Planning Process

Until recently, most programs for adults were planned either face-to-face, over the phone, and/or via U.S. Post Office "snail mail." With the advent of greater access to different mediums by planners, such as video conferencing and the use of the Internet, more programs or parts of programs are being planned, marketed, and delivered via technological means (Cahoon, 1998; Driscoll, 1998; Owston, 1998; Palloff and Pratt, 1999; Kruse and Keil, 2000). Using technology in the planning process is especially advantageous in planning national and international events, and in situations when face-to-face meetings are difficult to schedule.

In terms of incorporating technology into using the Interactive Model of Program Planning, the components of the model remain the same. What changes is that technology offers alternative ways for carrying through each component of the model, provides a different medium for the planning process itself, and may allow for shorter time frames for the planning process. Examples of alternative ways to complete tasks within sample components of the model include identifying program ideas through organization or division e-mail distribution lists, conducting program evaluations electronically, designing instructional units to include a combination of Web-based and on-site delivery modes, and using the websites of the various program sponsors as major marketing tools. More specific examples of how to use technology in addressing each of the components of the Interactive Model are given in Chapters Four through Fifteen.

Using technology also offers planners a different medium for completing all or parts of the actual planning process. Samples of these mediums include listservs, audio and video conferencing, chat rooms, and email. For example, this author has been involved in planning both national and international conferences using audio conferencing, listservs, and email.

In using technology for planning it is critical that all parties in the planning process have easy access to the needed hardware and software and either know how to use it effectively or have someone who can help them learn how to navigate the process. What planners cannot assume is that everyone is at the same level in terms of both knowing how and feeling comfortable with using technological means for planning. Care must be taken that people are not excluded from the planning process due to their lack of access and/or knowledge of how to use various forms of technological communication. In addition, planners take the risk of being misunderstood when only a one-way dialogue is used (for example, email and listservs). Synergy in the planning process also can be lost if "personal" commitment to the program is not taken into consideration for those who view electronic means as an impersonal medium. And finally, in using technological mediums for planning, those involved in the planning process should be deliberate in their choices of whether the entire process can or should be primarily technologically driven or whether face-to-face interaction is still critical in ensuring a fair and equitable process and quality product.

Through the use of technology planners may be able to cut down the time needed for planning as the communication among parties involved can be faster, depending on the medium chosen. For example, planning committees could share their ideas via a listserv or a chat room related to formats, facilities, staffing, transfer of learning, and marketing ideas. Depending on how this discussion is structured, they might choose to aim at consensus online and take action without a face-to-face meeting, or they may agree to at least get their ideas out prior to each meeting. These planners could also set norms that if no agreement is forthcoming, they would then meet, if possible, face to face for further discussions. Although time frames may be shorter, this lessened time period can also create frustration among planners. For example, a quick turnaround time among planners may be so demanding that little thought is actually given to the ideas presented. In short, others may set unrealistic expectations for how quickly programs can be put together.

## Making Ethical Decisions in Program Planning

One of the assumptions on which the Interactive Model of Program Planning is grounded is that using an ethical approach in making decisions about education and training programs for adults should be of concern to all parties involved in the process of planning such programs (see Chapter Four). "To overlook ethical concerns is a blatant disregard for the value of human beings" (Apps, 1991, p. 113). Perceiving ethical issues as unimportant diminishes what program planners do, but acting in an ethical manner is often easier said than done. Pressures abound as program planners try to meet deadlines, produce programs that will work, or (for some) simply stay in business. Examples of decisions reflecting ethical elements are illustrated below in relationship to selected components of the Interactive Model (Brockett, 1988; Apps, 1991; Wilson and Cervero, 1996b; Holt, 1998; Lawler, 2000; Sork, 1988, 2000; Aragon and Hatcher, 2001; Gordon and Sork, 2001):

### Discerning the Context

- Possessing accurate knowledge of the power and competing interests within a planning situation, but choosing out of self-interests not to act on that knowledge
- Using "insider" information about an institution to argue for programs that result more in personal gain rather than responding to issues and problems of the organization

### Building a Solid Basis for Support

- Asking people to serve on education or training advisory committees and then repeatedly ignoring their advice
- Publicly stating the beliefs of the education or training unit and then modeling those beliefs in program planning and delivery

### Developing Program Objectives

- Claiming that certain outcomes will happen as a result of the program when they are totally unrealistic
- Agreeing to unwritten program objectives that also enhance the stature of the educational unit, but at the same time ignoring either participant or organizational needs

### Coordinating Facilities and On-Site Events

- Setting participant fees so that diverse populations, including low-income families, can participate
- Offering programs at major ski resorts, with the only requirement that participants sign up and attend at least one session

### Designing Instructional Plans

- Employing big-name presenters who can draw a crowd, even though staff members know their presentations are usually of poor quality
- Requiring that instructors receive very good to excellent ratings from participants for them to continue to teach

▶ Stating in publicity materials that an organization is using the latest technology for program delivery, when they know they are not, as a ploy to get people to sign up for programs

**Formulating Evaluation Plans**

▶ Providing evaluation data on participants to supervisors of these learners without their prior knowledge or consent

▶ Challenging the criteria for program effectiveness when these criteria are unfair and biased

▶ Reporting only agreed-upon evaluation findings when unethical or harmful practices have been observed

Having a framework for responding ethically to the many decisions that are made in the course of planning programs for adults can be very helpful (Brockett, 1988; Starratt, 1991, 1994; Merriam and Caffarella, 1999). A sample framework is given in Figure 3.1.

As this figure shows, there are usually a multiple set of beliefs that are considered in making and acting on program decisions that have ethical elements. Obviously, the more comprehensive the scope of a program, the more difficult it becomes to respond in a way that all parties involved agree is ethical. For example, responding to ethical issues fostered by planning

**FIGURE 3.1**

## Sample Framework for Ethical Decisions in Program Planning

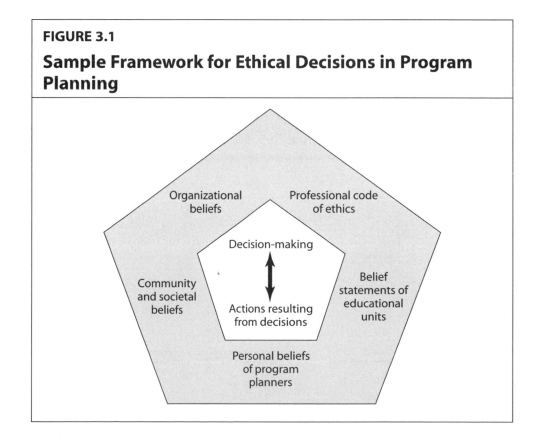

staff members who are not modeling belief statements of their department is easier to do than coping with ethical dilemmas resulting from major differences in beliefs among program planners, funding agencies, and powerful community or business groups. Chapter Four provides guidance on how to address these differences, especially when they are far apart or diametrically opposed.

In using this framework, program planners first start with themselves by examining their own beliefs about program planning. Affirming their own beliefs may be the only part of the equation over which planners are able to exercise any control. (The process of identifying one's beliefs is discussed earlier in this chapter.) The next step is to make public the belief statements of the education or training unit or the organization as a whole as they relate to educational programming. In order for this public sharing to be meaningful, these belief statements must be definitive and clear (see Chapter Five). Examples of groups who should be cognizant of these statements include program participants, colleagues, the leadership of the organization, and/or the general public. Sample belief statements for education and training units and organizations are:

### Educational Unit Belief Statements

- Human growth and development are lifelong pursuits.

- Organizational and individual development are both important elements of the educational programs sponsored by this division.

- Being caring and ethical is fundamental to the practice of planning educational programs.

### Organizational Belief Statements

- Change is a continuing phenomenon within this organization.

- Validated knowledge and active inquiry form the basis of professional practice in this organization.

- Quality individual and teamwork are highly valued by this organization.

The third task is to identify any codes of ethics or statements of beliefs of professional groups or other groups and organizations that are part of the planning process. These belief statements and ethical codes should be brought into the decision-making practices throughout the planning process. One practical source for thinking through how to use belief statements to promote ethical action is *Ethics and Integrity in HRD* (Aragon and Hatcher, 2001).

The last operational step, and definitely the most difficult (in some cases, nearly impossible), is to identify the beliefs and values of the community and wider society in which program planners work. Although locating documents that explicitly outline community or societal beliefs can be a very difficult task, especially when there are competing and constantly changing belief systems, there are some planning situations in which they are vital. Examples of such situations include planning educational programs on major social concerns (for example, school reform or family planning) or for large numbers of people (for example, all state or federal employees, participants in national and international forums). Being able to find this information is especially critical when program planners find themselves in unfamiliar territory, in touchy situations, or in environments where subterfuge is the norm.

## Chapter Highlights

In applying the Interactive Model of Program Planning, planners have to know what they stand for—their personal beliefs about the purposes of education, the program planning process, adults as learners, and the process of learning. Does the model, and the assumptions upon which it is grounded, fit with their implicit or explicit beliefs as portrayed in their actions as program planners? If their actions are different, are they because of the circumstances of the planning situation or because their beliefs and actions as planners are truly incompatible with the model? Knowing one's beliefs is one of the cornerstones of ethical practice.

In using the Interactive Model in specific planning situations, planners benefit by delineating parameters of that situation. Explicitly stated parameters about the organizational context; the backgrounds and experiences of planning personnel and current and potential learners; how current program commitments fit in with new programs; and available resources are all helpful guideposts throughout the planning process. These parameters can and will change, but having people on the same wavelength at the start of the process provides a solid foundation for open communication among the planning parties.

Depending on the planning situation, program planners may choose to use all or only selected components of the model. Although choosing which components to use and when is a professional judgment call, educational planners find four considerations useful in making these decisions.

◆ All of the components are commonly used in developing and revising comprehensive programs.

◆ When choosing only selected components, the planning context and parameters of the program primarily affect which components and tasks are adopted.

◆ There are essential components that need to be addressed at some point related to the program under consideration.

◆ Unforeseen changes in planning circumstances often force planners to revisit some or all of the components of the Interactive Model.

Whether all or only parts of the model are used, the key word in applying the model is *flexibility*. Experienced planners know that even the best programs rarely come together without a lot of juggling of ideas, strategies, resources, and people.

With the ever-increasing use of technology, educators and trainers have to take into account both how technology can enhance the way programs are planned and delivered. What technology provides is alternative ways to accomplish the components and task of the Interactive Model and alternative mediums for carrying out the planning process itself. Although there are drawbacks to using technology in the planning process, there are also many advantages.

Regardless of whether program planners use one, many, or all of the components of the Interactive Model, a critical operating principle is that an ethical approach is fundamental to making planning decisions. Program planners often face ethical dilemmas as they move through the planning process—from questionable reasons for conducting programs to poor teaching and learning practices. In handling problems and issues of an ethical nature, it is helpful for program planners to have a framework for making these kinds of decisions, which are often complex and have no right or wrong responses (except in the eyes of the beholder).

The remainder of this book outlines in detail each of the components and corresponding tasks of the Interactive Model of Program Planning, starting with discerning the context for planning. The major purpose of these chapters is to provide "hands on" practical tools for program planners.

## Application Exercises

The three Application Exercises presented here can help you adapt the Interactive Model of Program Planning to your own planning efforts. The first exercise helps you identify your personal beliefs related to program planning, and the second assists you in clarifying preliminary assumptions about specific planning situations. The third exercise assists you in determining which components of the Interactive Model of Program Planning are appropriate for your situation and whether using technology could assist you in the planning process.

## Identifying Personal Beliefs Related to Program Planning

1. First identify your own beliefs in the four areas listed on the chart. Then, using the chart, outline specific actions related to what you do as a program planner that illustrate your belief statements and actions that appear to contradict those statements.

| Beliefs | Personal Belief Statements | Your Actions that . . . | |
|---|---|---|---|
| | | Illustrate Your Beliefs | Appear to Contradict Your Beliefs |
| About the purpose of educational programs for adults | | | |
| About the program planning process | | | |
| About adults as learners | | | |
| About the process of learning | | | |

2. Ask others with whom you plan programs to identify their beliefs. Where are your beliefs similar and where they are different? Have these similarities and differences enhanced the planning process; and if so, how? Have the differences created difficulties in program planning?

## EXERCISE 3.2

## Developing Upfront Assumptions

1. Briefly outline a situation in which you have or have had the responsibility for developing program planning assumptions.

2. For the following four factors, list the assumptions you made before you initiated your program planning process. Be as specific as you can.

   Current program commitments:

   Organizational context:

   Planning personnel:

   Available resources:

## EXERCISE 3.3

### Determining Which Components of the Interactive Model to Use and How Technology Could Assist in the Planning Process

1. Describe briefly an educational program you are or have been involved with as part of the planning effort.

2. Indicate with a check mark those components of the Interactive Model of Program Planning that you believe need to be or were addressed. Place a second check by those that are receiving or did receive special emphasis for this program (and briefly note why). Using Figure 2.1 (page 21) and Exhibit 2.1 (pages 23–24) will assist you in completing this exercise.

| Components to Address | Components to Emphasize | Interactive Model Components |
|:---:|:---:|---|
| ❏ | ❏ | Discerning the context for planning |
| ❏ | ❏ | Building a solid basis for support |
| ❏ | ❏ | Identifying program ideas |
| ❏ | ❏ | Sorting and prioritizing program ideas |
| ❏ | ❏ | Developing program objectives |
| ❏ | ❏ | Designing instructional plans |
| ❏ | ❏ | Transfer-of-learning plans |
| ❏ | ❏ | Formulating evaluation plans |
| ❏ | ❏ | Making recommendations and communicating results |
| ❏ | ❏ | Selecting formats, schedules, and staff needs |
| ❏ | ❏ | Preparing budgets and marketing plans |
| ❏ | ❏ | Coordinating facilities and on-site events |

3. Has using technology assisted you in the planning process for the program you have described above? If so, outline which specific tools (for example, planning video conferencing, email, chat rooms) were useful and for which components of the process.

_____

_____

_____

_____

# Chapter 4
# Discerning the Context

**PEOPLE WHO DEVELOP EDUCATION** and training programs for adults do not work in a vacuum, as seen in the following scenarios.

### *A Program Failure*

Peter, who is employed by a large human resource development (HRD) consulting firm, is responsible for presenting a "canned" program for supervisory personnel that his firm has marketed for a number of years. Peter has always updated the basic materials he presents and usually makes some minor changes in content to fit the needs of the clients. He, as well as the president of the company, is perplexed that this program, which has always been well-received, failed miserably in two recent major contracts. Peter is feeling frustrated and angry about the whole thing, as the participants' feedback from both organizations was that they did not like what he said, nor did they appreciate how he presented the materials. Peter did know that one of the companies had just gone international, and that the participants in the second company just seemed "different" than those he had worked with in the same organization three years ago. Yet to Peter, these differences were not as important as his concept of basic supervisory practice and that the materials are relevant no matter what the participants' backgrounds or the setting.

### *New Directions*

Jamie also works for an established HRD consulting firm, but the partners in the firm made some very deliberate decisions in the last five years to respond to the changing nature of the workforce.

These changes are reflected in their mission and beliefs statement and in the competencies of the staff they hire. Examples of their belief statements are:

- Diversity in thought, action, background, and experience are viewed as strengths.

- Collaborative planning and assisting clients to negotiate among planning partners are operating norms.

- Ethical practice is foundational to how staff members work internally and with clients.

- The external environment is an important consideration to take into account in working with clients.

Planning education and training programs within these belief systems has paid off well. Their profits have increased in the past three years, as has their market share. The firm, for example, has expanded their work with multinational corporations, and this expansion has opened new markets with a sizable number of organizations where staff members speak many languages, although English is the "official language" of the business.

Program planners can no longer ignore the context in which they practice, as demonstrated by these two scenarios. Organizations are constantly changing. Political and economic climates are ever-fluctuating, and sometimes even volatile. And there is a growing diversity among people who plan and attend education and training programs. Rather, discerning the context, which is both a skill and an art, is a major component that planners address as they design educational programs. Described first in this chapter are the many facets of the planning context that are explored by planning personnel. This description is followed by a discussion of three key issues program planners consider when using this contextual knowledge. Reviewed in the final section are ways planners obtain information about the contexts in which they work.

## Facets of the Planning Context

Context is defined as the human, organizational, and environmental factors that affect decisions planners make about programs (Cervero and Wilson, 1994, 1996, 1998; Newman, 1995; Houle, 1996; Rothwell and Cookson, 1997; Guy, 1999b; Sork, 2000). These factors are not unconnected in how they affect the planning process, and often merge into major issues that educational planners address as they navigate through their planning tasks.

## The People

People plan programs, whether this planning is face to face through technological means or a combination of the two. As such, "planners are constantly confronted with issues that involve people" (Wilson and Cervero, 1996b, p. 5), such as who should be invited to the planning table, which persons should do what tasks and when, whose email or telephone calls should be responded to first, and who really holds the power over which programs actually get constructed. Therefore, planners must have finely tuned social and communication skills; and the ability, in most planning situations, to constantly negotiate among all involved parties (Forester, 1989; Cervero and Wilson, 1994, 1998; Ottoson, 1995a; Wilson and Cervero, 1996a, 1996b).

Different planning situations call for different groups of people to be involved. Some programs, such as an Attention Deficit Disorder (ADD) adult support group, only require learners and facilitators, whereas others, like workplace learning programs, include a number of key stakeholders—learners, program planners, work supervisors, instructors, and senior-level management. Still other programs, such as welfare-to-work programs or community development projects, also involve governmental bodies and the general public. The more stakeholders, the more complex the interactions among the various groups are. Add to this complexity issues of diversity among and within groups of people, as program planners work in increasingly culturally diverse settings and a global marketplace.

The following scenario illustrates these complex issues and how different players might react to the same planning situation. This scenario illuminates how important it is to consider who the people are and where they are coming from in a planning situation.

### *Revisiting a Program Failure*

Peter, the HRD consultant introduced earlier in scenario one, knows there are some things he thought about, but would have never said and/or did not want to be bothered to do. He wonders what the others involved in the planning process were thinking and either would not or chose not to share.

### Organization One: The Organization Goes International

▶ *Peter, the consultant serving in the roles of lead program planner and instructor.* This job is a breeze. I have worked with this company for a number of years and they have always responded well to my materials and presentations. I know I should check out this "international thing," but I just don't have the time with all of the pressures I am under.

▶ *Senior level management.* This consulting firm has a good track record with our organization so we know their staff will do their homework about the major changes we have made in our structure and staffing patterns, especially in relation to supervisory responsibilities over the last year.

▶ *Human resource development director who is serving as the liaison for the company with the consulting firm.* I know I should have more meetings with Peter and his assistant as they finalize the plans for the program, but further sessions from my perspective would be unproductive. Peter has done very little listening to how our organization has changed since we bought out two major Asian corporations. I even tried bringing in some staff who have recently moved to international assignments, but he kept stressing that "supervision is supervision" no matter where you are working. Peter also made all of us aware of how well he knew our president, how often he had worked with us, and the successful track record his firm had with the various training programs they have conducted for us. Actually I felt somewhat intimidated by him, as I am new to the organization. I also did not want to "ruffle any feathers" over this one program.

▶ *Program participants.* Some participants were really looking forward to the program, hoping to learn new ways of supervising employees within the company's new structure, especially employees whose first language was not English. Other participants really resented the fact they had to take three days out of their overbooked schedules, especially after they had reviewed the program description describing the content and the format.

### Organization Two: The Participants Were Just Different

▶ *Peter, the consultant serving as both lead program planner and instructor.* Peter knew this organization well and had worked with them over a long span of time, although he himself had not planned nor delivered a training program for them in at least three years. Peter always enjoyed working with this group and knew quite a few of the senior supervisory personnel, most of whom he had trained. He spent his time planning the program primarily with one of the current supervisors, an old buddy of his, and Juan, a new training manager, who was just promoted to that position from within the company. Peter believed he had a solid product.

▶ *The in-house planning team.* Bill, one of the senior supervisors, is delighted to have a chance to work with Peter again. He really likes their long lunches, and a chance to play a round or two of golf as part of the "planning process." Juan, on the other hand, has never met Peter and is highly skeptical of the written material he reviewed prior to their first planning meeting. Juan thought he had gotten his point across in their initial planning meeting about how the training program should be changed to address the needs of supervisors who are now managing a very different workforce than they did three or four years ago—more non-English speakers, a high percentage of first-generation immigrants, and more women. Juan also attempted in this initial meeting to describe the supervisors who would be attending this training session (for example, that the majority were women, many were bilingual, and a large number were new to the company). He also made the point that this group would be very different than the one he worked with three years ago. Peter's response was that he would work into the program the changes Juan suggested, and that he felt comfortable with any audience because of his subject matter expertise. A second planning meeting was postponed, and the last planning meeting was held on the golf course with Bill and two other senior supervisors, as Juan was ill. These supervisors all liked and approved his final plan, and Juan did not have a chance to closely review it as the training sessions were scheduled for the next week.

▶ *Program participants.* Many of the participants, especially those who just recently joined the company, are required to take this three-day training workshop on supervisory practices. Some of these personnel really wanted to participate, while others did not want to attend as they already had acquired the content and skills through previous training and supervisory experience, albeit with another organization. There were a few supervisors who were very vocal, at least with each other, that they should have been involved in the planning process and resented the fact that "the good old boys" were asked again and they were not.

As can been seen through the thoughts of the different people involved in these two planning processes, what these people were thinking about the planning process, the content of the program, and their role in the planning was often very diverse. Although Peter might have been a good planner and instructor, his people skills and especially his ability to facilitate communication among the planners are not evident in his actions. One thing that Peter's actions did was to allow him to keep control of the planning process and the final product. This control led to program failures, whereas if he had been willing and had had the skills to facilitate an open dialogue and negotiate the end product, he may have experienced very different outcomes—useful and successful programs.

## The Organization

Inherent contextual factors that are imbedded within organizations are broadly categorized under three headings: structural, political, and cultural (Forester, 1989; Mills, Cervero, Langone, and Wilson, 1995; Bolman and Deal, 1997; Rothwell and Cookson, 1997; Daley and Mott, 2000). *Structural factors* include the mission, goals, and objectives of organization; administrative hierarchy; standard operating policies and procedures (for example, how staff are selected, supervised, and trained); the system of formal organizational authority; information systems; organizational decision-making patterns; financial and other resources; and physical facilities. *Political factors* comprise coalition building; bargaining and jockeying for position; power relations among individuals and groups; and the politics of funding and providing other resources. *Cultural factors* incorporate the history and traditions of the organization; organizational beliefs and values; and organizational rituals, stories, symbols, and heroes. Representations of specific contextual factors from each category are given here:

### Structural Factors
#### Standard Operating Procedures

▶ Staff members at all levels are given the opportunity to attend the equivalent of three days of educational programs per year at the organization's expense.

▶ Before participating in an educational program, a person must receive permission from a specified person (such as work supervisor or executive director).

#### Organizational Decision-Making

▶ Decisions about educational programs within the organization are made primarily through a formal, hierarchical chain of command.

▶ Decisions about educational programs are made in a collaborative and democratic manner, with each staff member having an equal voice.

### Political Factors
#### Coalition Building

▶ Planning staff and clients from community-based and governmental agencies meet monthly to strategize how to best meet the educational needs of new immigrant populations coming into their community.

▶ Coalitions of special interest groups internal to a large multicampus university have a long history of jockeying for power over sparse resources for educational programs.

### Power Relations Among Individuals and Groups

▶ A networking system, which includes key program sponsors, sympathetic legislators, and public figures (such as the governor's wife, and the husband of the president of the local community college), has a good track record for increasing public funding for literacy programs.

▶ A small but powerful group of people, none of whom hold formal positions of authority, manage to continually thwart efforts by other staff members to change the program planning practices of the organization.

## Cultural Factors
### History and Traditions of the Organization

▶ Offering educational programs for adults has a long history at this institution, with an emphasis on quality and service to the participants.

▶ This organization has a strong tradition of viewing education for job advancement as the responsibility of the individual worker.

### Organizational Symbols

▶ The organizational logo includes the words "learning for life," visualized in the symbol of a continuous circle.

▶ Persons who complete the Senior Management Institute are given pewter mugs engraved with the organization's symbol; they are expected to display these mugs in their offices.

Returning to the scenario at the beginning of the chapter and Jamie's situation, it is clear that all three major categories of organizational factors were addressed when the partners reframed how they would practice. For example, they reworked their mission statement and their business plan; they took into account the reality of political power in planning by making negotiations an active part of their planning process; they revisited and committed to a different set of values and beliefs that drive what and how they practice; and they hired staff who wanted to work within their belief system.

When taking into consideration contextual factors related to organizations, programs planners are cognizant of those factors internal to their own organizations, such as portrayed in the previous example. In addition, they are aware of these same factors operating within the external groups with whom they plan and sometimes compete. Of particular concern to educators and trainers are the structural, political, and cultural aspects of:

▶ Organizations and groups (for example, professional associations, regulatory bodies, governmental and quasigovernmental agencies, private non-profit entities, and grassroots community groups) that have major influence and/or control, including regulatory and/or funding responsibilities, over the programs being planned.

▶ "Official" planning partners for a specific program event (for example, a consortium of colleges and universities in cooperation with local businesses).

▶ Sponsoring organizations, whether or not they have a role in the planning process.

▶ Other providers of similar education and training programs.

## The Wider Environment

The more general economic, political, and social climate within which planners work is increasingly becoming more important, especially as program planners work across numerous types of borders, from geographic to cultural to ideological (Forester, 1989; Sork and Caffarella, 1989; Newman, 1995; Rothwell and Cookson, 1997; Sparks, 1998; Cervero and Wilson, 1999; Longworth, 1999; Sork, 2000). This importance is seen in how specific program topics such as diversity in the workplace, AIDS education, how children are educated, and the changing nature of work have become more and more politicized. These topics are all seen as major economic and social issues that must be addressed not only by organizations but also by society in general.

For example, the current welfare-to-work program in the United States is primarily politically driven, with the mandate to provide training to move welfare recipients off public assistance. Whether or not this program has served the "public good" is questionable, but many voices have attested to the economic viability of the program and how it has made those who have successfully completed the program more socially responsible; for example, participants no longer on the welfare rolls.

The increasing role of nongovernmental organizations within UNESCO provides another good example of how social, economic, and political pressures are important ingredients in how programs are planned, by whom, what content they focus on, and who the recipients are. A sampling of critical programs resulting from recent UNESCO meetings includes programs for women from many countries and a continuing agenda of economic development through literacy and work-related programs.

In considering these more encompassing environmental factors, program planners filter the work they do through a variety of specific interest groups to the larger community to the societal sphere in which they practice. Sample questions include:

▶ What are the economic conditions planners work within and who benefits from these conditions?

▶ How does the competitive marketplace influence what and how educational planners work?

▶ What political agenda am I representing and perhaps even championing?

▶ Is what planners are doing for the "common good," or does it serve the needs of a limited few?

The people, organizational, and wider environmental factors of the context give rise to some common issues and concerns spanning all three arenas.

## Common Issues When Using Contextual Knowledge

Using contextual knowledge as a program planner is neither an easy nor "sure fire" answer to ensure program success. Using this knowledge is complex and challenging, even to the most experienced planners. The knowledge planners have about the context, especially when all three types are considered (such as knowledge about people, organizations, and the wider environment), is often contradictory and sometimes even paradoxical. For example, when governments at all levels are mandating school reform, devising an educational program for the public about these reforms can be a nightmare. Whose stance do planners take when the views of different stakeholders are in conflict, stakeholders who more often than not include national or local governments, teachers, unions, court systems, the general public? Should planners attempt to present all sides, or might that be impossible in the current political climate in which they practice? What about the fallout for the organizations for which these planners work? Will the program help or hinder the reputations of these organizations?

Running through these questions and concerns are three primary issues that planners using contextual knowledge of any kind consider: issues of power, their willingness to negotiate, and ethical considerations (Forester, 1989; Cervero and Wilson, 1994, 1996, 1998, 1999; Mitchell, 1998; and Cervero, Wilson, and Associates, 2001). As Wilson and Cervero (1996a) observe: "Planners must learn to negotiate power and interests responsibly, because their actions (that is, their planning tasks) validate whose interests matter. . . . Planners must know who they are responsible to (that is, whose interests matter, both politically and ethically)" (pp. 98–99). Each of these major issues—power, negotiating, and ethics—are now explored in greater depth.

## Power Is Central

In responding to contextual clues, power is a central issue to address in the planning process. "If planners ignore those in power, they assure their own powerlessness. Alternatively, if planners understand how relations of power shape the planning process, they can improve the quality of their analyses" (Forester, 1989, p. 27), and have the opportunity to empower both themselves and those with whom they work. These dual aspects of power are illustrated in the following scenario.

### Shandra—Caught in the Middle

Shandra, who serves as chair of the planning committee and is the director of professional development for the major sponsoring organization, is perplexed about how she should respond in the next planning meeting. Although she knows that the program as currently proposed will probably end in disaster for all involved— the planners, the instructors, the participants, and the sponsoring organizations—she is not quite sure how to get her point across that the content level is inappropriate to meet the outcomes that have been proposed for the program. Shandra knows she has some power over decisions being made, but she is also keenly aware that Joyce, the vice president for human resources of the main sponsoring group, has given a mandate of sorts, albeit not directly, about what she thinks the major content for the program should be. Shandra knows that most participants will be insulted at the level of content the vice president wants. The instructors will be frustrated at best and angry at worst, because they will have little say about what should be presented. Some of the other sponsors will be appalled at how little the participants will actually learn that is new and applicable to their work situations.

The other members of the planning team include an instructional design specialist from Shandra's organization, a content expert who is a faculty member at a local university, Joyce's assistant, the vice president (Joyce), and two people who represent two of the other sponsoring organizations, one of which is the major funding agency. The dynamics of previous planning meetings, which Shandra chairs, are that the instructional designer has primarily been concerned that the latest technology be incorporated into the teaching process. The faculty member has never attended. The assistant to the vice president says little, but when he speaks, everyone listens. The other two representatives know little about the content being proposed, even the person representing the major funding agency. The program itself is possibly the first in a series of programs, providing that this first one is a success; the potential for major funding for future programs is a definite possibility.

Shandra is a subject-matter expert and has primarily served as a facilitator for the earlier meetings and contributed little in substance. She feels she is caught between a rock and a hard place as she is cognizant of the strong political connections that Joyce has throughout the state, the vice president's willingness to wield her power with these connections, and Joyce's intolerance for being slighted, either publicly or privately. Shandra also knows that the vice president's assistant speaks softly, but likes his own position of control and power in any planning situation. In addition, Shandra is a final candidate for a new position over which Joyce has the final say on who will be hired. To help support her own power base, Shandra has built a strong coalition within the group as a result of having met a number of times with the representatives from both the funding agency and the other sponsoring group. As a result of these meetings, these two people, one a male of Hispanic origin and the other a Black female, have great respect for her judgment.

It is clear who the power players are in this case—Joyce (the vice president for human resources), her assistant, and Shandra. The power of Joyce and her assistant are a combination of positional and political clout, while Shandra's power comes primarily from her knowledge base and ability to build coalitions with important individuals and groups. The people who are the direct actors in this power drama are the assistant and Shandra, with the supporting cast being Joyce and the two agency representatives. Shandra can choose to use her power to act as a catalyst to empower others—first, the members of the planning committee and then if she is successful, the participants, the instructors, and the sponsoring organizations, including her own organization. But Shandra runs a risk by promoting this way of working, as the assistant to the vice president may interpret her actions as a challenge to his authority as representative of the vice president and report this message back to her. Shandra may be able to minimize this risk by directly communicating her concerns with Joyce prior to the next meeting or by asking the funding agency representative to do so. On the other hand, the assistant to the vice president may also attempt his own power play, but unless Joyce is unequivocally on his side, his chances of remaining a key player in this power arena are nil.

### How Power Influences the Planning Process

There are a number of ways that power is used to influence what happens in the planning process. The most common are: shaping "felt" needs, setting program agendas, determining populations to be served, making decisions, allocating types and amounts of resources, and choosing who benefits from the program (Forester, 1989; Mills, Cervero, Langone, and Wilson, 1995; Archie-Booker, Cervero, and Langone, 1999; Cervero, Wilson, and Associates, 2001). Specific examples of positive and negative influences on these elements of the planning process are given in Exhibit 4.1.

Using information as a source of power is often how people involved with the planning process, whether directly or indirectly, make their influences known. How, to, and by whom this information is communicated, examined, and debated is critical. The actual language planners use is an important variable in this communications process (Rees, Cervero, Moshi, and Wilson, 1997). Planners must carefully choose their words to get their

**EXHIBIT 4.1**

## How Power Influences the Program Planning Process

| Elements of Program Planning Process | Sample of Positive Influence | Sample of Negative Influence |
| --- | --- | --- |
| **Shaping needs** | Ensure that all voices that need to be heard are included. | Apply pressure on planning teams in order to have them accept your version of what is needed, based on what you have to offer as a consultant and your connections to senior management. |
| **Setting agendas** | Consult with a number of divergent sources, and bring the alternative ideas to the planning table. | Use a political agenda as a basis for an agenda setting that is popular, although not in the best interests of those being served. |
| **Determining populations** | Find funding sources so opportunities can be given to any community member to attend no matter what their income level. | Choose the populations to be served totally on their ability to pay large program fees. |
| **Making decisions** | Set norms with the planning group for decision making that ensure a democratic process is used. | Suppress any differences of opinion and conflicts that arise among planning members. |
| **Allocating resources** | Provide for adequate staffing with excellent content and instructional skills. | Mandate that technology-based programming be used although the technical support is inadequate. |

message across so it can be heard in a world of competing interests. This information-sharing process is made even more complex by the advent of technology where "instant communication" via fax and email is often the expectation, whether or not that information is even complete or useful to the planning situation. In addition, Forester (1989) also observes that "misinformation of several distinct types—some inevitable, some avoidable, some systematic, and some ad hoc—can be anticipated and counteracted by astute planners" (p. 28). Therefore, as stressed earlier, it is critical for program planners to have excellent communication and people skills. One communication skill in particular that is essential for program planners when addressing issues of power is being willing and able to negotiate between and among the various stakeholders involved in the planning process. This skill, which is both an art and a science, is discussed later in this section.

### A Practical Way to Measure Planners' Power and Influence

Yang (1999) has developed a valid and reliable instrument to assess what kinds of tactics educators and trainers use when confronted with issues of power in a planning situation. This instrument, the *Power and Influence Tactics Scale* (POINTS), measures seven different behavioral patterns associated with negotiating organizational political processes. These seven power and influence tactics are shown in Figure 4.1.

The POINTS instrument is used by planners "to reflect on their planning practice and to identify effective planning strategies" (Yang, 1999, p. 1). What is crucial in interpreting these data is that what tactics planners employ are situation specific. Two variables, which are also measured by the instrument, are key to which tactics planners use—the amount of conflict among the various stakeholders in the planning process, and the power base of the planner in relation to the planning situation. For example: If there are no serious *conflicts of interests* and you (as the planner) hold no less *power base* than the target person (or groups), the effective tactics are *reasoning* and *consulting*. However if your *power base* is limited by the situation, you might want to use tactics of *appealing and networking*. . . . When the *conflicts of interest* are significant and your *power base* is limited, such tactics as *pressuring, counteracting,* and *reasoning* are more plausible (Yang, 1999, p. 7). In other words, "an effective planner should be a tactical agent who understands the planning situation well and is able to use a variety of power and influence tactics according to the situation" (Yang, Cervero, Valentine, and Benson, 1998, p. 242). Hendricks (2001), although she views the POINTS instrument as reliable and useful, cautions that this "instrument should be refined with the purpose of increasing the reliability of the influencing subscales" (p. 233), which are related to the choice and nature of the most appropriate tactics to be used.

**FIGURE 4.1**

# Power and Influence Tactics

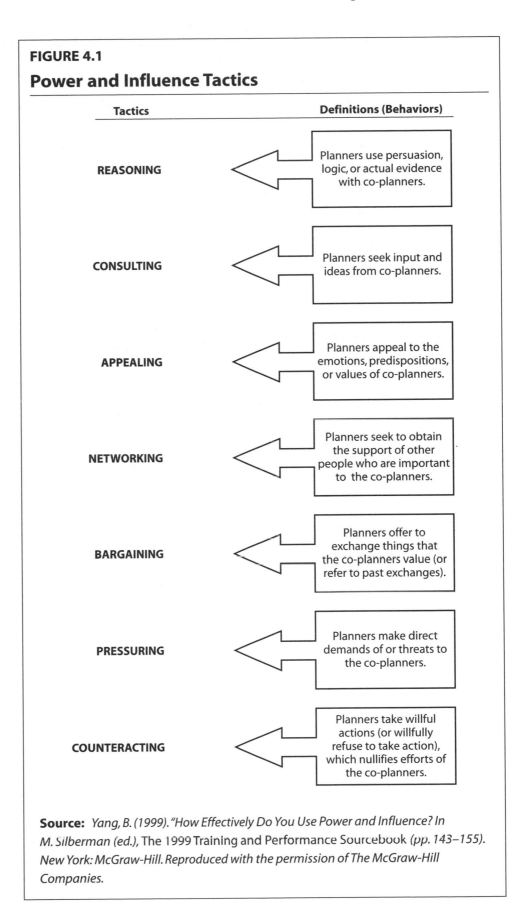

| Tactics | Definitions (Behaviors) |
|---|---|
| **REASONING** | Planners use persuasion, logic, or actual evidence with co-planners. |
| **CONSULTING** | Planners seek input and ideas from co-planners. |
| **APPEALING** | Planners appeal to the emotions, predispositions, or values of co-planners. |
| **NETWORKING** | Planners seek to obtain the support of other people who are important to the co-planners. |
| **BARGAINING** | Planners offer to exchange things that the co-planners value (or refer to past exchanges). |
| **PRESSURING** | Planners make direct demands of or threats to the co-planners. |
| **COUNTERACTING** | Planners take willful actions (or willfully refuse to take action), which nullifies efforts of the co-planners. |

**Source:**  *Yang, B. (1999). "How Effectively Do You Use Power and Influence? In M. Silberman (ed.),* The 1999 Training and Performance Sourcebook *(pp. 143–155). New York: McGraw-Hill. Reproduced with the permission of The McGraw-Hill Companies.*

### Closing Observations on Power as Central to Planning

Cervero and Wilson (1999) and Cervero, Wilson, and Associates (2001) argue that people who plan programs for adults are always operating in "socially organized relations of power [which] define both the possibilities for action as well as the meaning of the learning for all stakeholders" (1999, p. 34). The primary role of educators and trainers then is twofold: to use these power relations to provide top quality and accessible programs, and to challenge the status quo in terms of "the distribution of knowledge and power in society" (1999, p. 27). Therefore, in developing programs planners continually ask: Are the best products being prepared? Who benefits from taking this program? Who has been overlooked or excluded? Sork (1996) cautions program planners not to invent power relations in situations where perhaps they do not exist. Rather, planners need to take each planning situation as it comes, and use their analytical, experiential, and intuitive knowledge in determining their plans of action.

## Willingness and the Ability to Negotiate Is Essential

When planners acknowledge that discerning contextual factors is a crucial part of the planning process, then being willing and able to negotiate is an accepted and essential task. Negotiation requires that planners have finely tuned people skills, listen to multiple voices, are good analytical thinkers, and are willing to take unpopular stands. More specifically, program planners are able to communicate effectively through a variety of means, have excellent group process skills, understand what taking risks really means, and have the ability to operate effectively within relationships of power.

Negotiating begins early in the program planning process through determining who is invited to the "planning table" (Cervero and Wilson, 1998; Wilson and Cervero, 1996c). Looking back to Shandra's situation, it was probably no accident that the vice president's assistant was included on the planning committee. His membership on the committee allowed the vice president a voice at the table without actually being present. Having a representative of the funding agency was also probably strategically planned. Representatives of other groups who possibly should have been at the table were program participants and their supervisors. Shandra may have decided purposely not to include them, as she foresaw their input could have created a conflict level that would have been detrimental to the planning process; or, less likely, she did not believe their voices were important.

Negotiations usually continue throughout the planning process and address various components and tasks of that process depending on the specific planning situation. Selected components from the Interactive Model of Program Planning that are most dependent upon the negotiation process are highlighted in Exhibit 4.2.

---

**EXHIBIT 4.2**

## Sampling of Negotiated Tasks and Items

| Components of Interactive Program Planning Model | Sample Negotiated Tasks |
|---|---|
| *Building a solid base of support* | • Who becomes a part of the support base and why?<br>• Will a specific group that holds political clout be excluded from the support base if this group's agenda is to change the fundamental mission of the sponsoring organization? |
| *Sorting and prioritizing program needs and ideas* | • Who decides which organizations and/or people will prioritize what programs should be offered?<br>• Who will have control over choosing which criteria are used in the prioritizing process? |
| *Preparing transfer-of-learning plans* | • Can the information that is applied from a workplace learning program be negotiated and, if so, who decides when and how?<br>• Will there be recognition for learning transfer, and if so, what forms will it take? |
| *Formulating evaluation plans* | • Who has control over what will be evaluated and the criteria for success?<br>• Will the evaluation data be shared, and if so, with whom (for example, learners, work supervisors, general public)? |
| *Preparing budgets and marketing plans* | • When multiple organizations are sponsoring a program, who will have primary control over the budget?<br>• What will the primary purpose be for marketing (for example, to give useful information about the program, to provide a "slick" brochure that will make the sponsoring organizations look good)? |

---

Cervero and Wilson (1998) and Umble, Cervero, and Langone (2001) alert planners that they are usually operating simultaneously on two levels when they are acting as negotiators in the planning process: substantive negotiations and metanegotiations. Substantive negotiations, that is, "negotiating about the important features of educational programs" (Cervero and Wilson, 1998, p. 20), are also illustrated in Exhibit 4.2. Most program planners are aware that they are acting at this level and often even gladly take on this challenge. On the other hand, many planners are not cognizant they are also operating at the metanegotiations level; that is, negotiations "about the social and political relationships of those who are included and excluded" (Cervero and Wilson, 1998, p. 20) while at the planning table. The task of the planner at the metanegotiations level is quite different, as is seen in the next scenario. Rather than bargaining about specific aspects of the program being planned, program planners may find themselves negotiating between and among angry stakeholders, all of whom want a place at the planning table.

### *Fireworks over the Fourth of July Celebration*

Stacey, the director of the city's recreation department, has been trying for months to get the Fourth of July Committee and the Hispanic Coalition to meet and discuss their mutual interests for a festive Independence Day celebration. The Hispanic Coalition wants more programs that would appeal to the large Hispanic population, while members of the Fourth of July Committee like the program just the way it is. Members of the Fourth of July Committee, consisting primarily of established families in the community, are adamant that it is their job to plan the day's activities, and if members of the Coalition want a voice, they should try to get on the committee next year. As this impasse continues, ugly rumors begin to spread about both groups, the local paper does a series of stories on the increasingly unsettled situation, and letters to the editor about the standoff are quite common. There is even pressure from the mayor's office and city council members to get these two groups to talk. Yet, even with all of this pressure, Stacey is still unable to persuade either group to offer a compromise they both could accept.

As illustrated by this scenario, Stacey is negotiating simultaneously at both the substantive negotiations level (about what activities should be included in the Fourth of July celebration) and at the metanegotiations level (the social and political context that influences the interactions and relationships between the two groups). Metanegotiations are difficult and often highly risky for program planners. These risks and difficulties are especially apparent in organizations and communities where there are deep social and political fissures existing between and among groups.

Planning at the intersection of these two kinds of negotiations also brings with it ethical dilemmas and contradictions. For example, in doing a credible job in serving one population, do planners need to exclude other groups who also have the same need? Do planners serve the "greater good" by delivering programs they know are not a major priority yet make a huge profit, so they can then use those profits to sponsor programs they believe are really needed but for which funding is not available? Do planners "call an organization" on its shoddy practices in a desperately needed program, like workplace literacy, and run the risk of losing the program entirely? Cervero and Wilson (1998) assert that resolving these types of situations "[is] the fundamental political problem of our work as . . . educators [and trainers]" (p. 20). These authors also stress that more detailed and practical descriptions of how educational planners carry out this important work are needed.

## Ethical Practice Is Foundational

As stressed in Chapter Three, one of the values on which the Interactive Model of Program Planning rests is that using an ethical approach in making decisions about educational programs for adults should be of concern to all parties involved in the planning process. Being ethical in one's practice becomes even more complicated when contextual factors are brought into the picture (Cervero and Wilson, 1994; Wilson and Cervero, 1996b, 1996c; Sork, 2000). Planners most easily reflect on their own beliefs related to the "rights" and "wrongs" of practice. In collaborative units, they can probably also construct belief statements that guide their practice (for example, being caring and ethical is fundamental to our practice of program planning). Staying true to one's own values and beliefs and those of the unit becomes much more problematic when these beliefs clash with those of the organization for which they work, other stakeholders involved in the planning process, and/or with the ethical stance of the wider community.

These differences in ethical practices are especially difficult when the espoused values of the parties involved are contrary to how they act behind closed doors. For example, a university's mission and goals statement says explicitly that the university is committed to educating adult students. Yet, at the same time, the same university is closing the Office of Adult Students, increasing tuition and fees for off-campus and technology-based courses, charging more for on-campus child care, and bowing to the pressure of the state legislature to have undergraduates complete their degrees within a four-year period, almost an impossibility for adults who are working and/or have parenting responsibilities. A number of questions then arise: Where are the on-campus voices that support adult students? Are these advocates, such as the dean of continuing education and staff, faculty who support adult students, and the students themselves, included in the decision-making processes that impact these programs? If some or all of these groups are included, are they allowed to champion their cause? If they do not speak, are there reasons they do not or cannot voice their concerns? Are they intimidated by the powers that be or ambushed by armloads of data on cost-saving measures? Or are these voices silenced by excluding them from the decision-making process entirely? Do administrators, faculty, and students learn of the decisions after the fact, either through the campus grapevine or perhaps in the local press in an editorial praising the university president for cost-containment strategies and response to state mandates?

Operating ethically in a climate in which ethical practices are not the norm is difficult at best and downright impossible at its worst. Program planners make choices about if and how they want to work in a context where thinking in ethical ways is not even a part of the process for developing and closing programs. If planners choose to stay in this environment, there are ways they may infuse small steps to move the organization or group into different ways of thinking.

▶ Establishing advisory boards with members outside of the organization who have links with key power players and openly advocate for program areas that staff members believe are critical

▶ Making oneself available to be a member or chair of ongoing and ad hoc committees where decisions are made that affect the direction of one's program or other programs to which the organization is committed

▶ Attending open forums and meetings with key decision makers to keep one's knowledge base about the context current

▶ Forming coalitions with like-minded people, both internal and external to the organization, so that the messages come from a group, rather than a lone voice

▶ Mentoring future program leaders to be ethical in their practice

There are times when planners choose to leave an organization or group as there is no meeting of the minds on ethical issues, or the sponsoring organization and/or other parties involved have stepped "over the line" in terms of the planners' values and beliefs. For example, Ramone has decided to leave his position as the director of the African-American Cultural Center, as the center is not receiving the promised financial support from the local city council, which is composed primarily of White and Hispanic middle-class men and women. The city council has continually cut the funding to the center over the past three years, despite the fact that full funding was promised for the center's operations for at least five years. The reason given by council members for the funding cuts is that center staff members should be generating even more of their own funding than they currently are.

Ramone's decision to leave has been very difficult as he is very committed to the center and its programs, and he believes the center has provided a positive place for gatherings and learning opportunities for people of all ages and colors. Ramone also thinks, as do his staff and those who use the center, that he has been an effective director. In addition, he is also a well-respected leader in the Black community. Ramone is fraught with all kinds of feelings and thoughts, from anger at the city council to self-doubt about the way he has handled the funding situation. Now that Ramone's decision to leave is final, he needs to decide how he will make his exit—in silence, telling a chosen few about why he decided to leave, or by making a public announcement.

When a public announcement is the chosen path, this statement must be crafted with both head and heart. Good questions to ask in deciding when and what to say are: What is the worst thing that can happen if I make public my reasons for leaving? Who might be helped by my statement, and who might be hurt? When and where will my announcement have the most impact? Returning to Ramone's situation, he made a public statement, as he believed it was both an ethical and practical obligation for him to do so. From the ethical side, he wanted the general community to be aware of how city council members had reneged on their funding commitment, especially as the center has been successful in all of their programming endeavors. On the practical side, he hoped that his public announcement would generate support for restored funding from the city, as well as additional support from private foundations and individuals. Ramone truly wants the center to both survive and thrive, and he believes his resignation and a public statement of his leaving are the only ways this outcome might happen.

## Obtaining Information About the Planning Context

Where is information about the planning context found? Five basic sources are accessible to program planners: written documents, people, group meeting and gatherings, professional and trade associations, and technology-based sources. Examples of each information source follow:

▶ *Written documents.* Annual reports; organizational descriptive materials; policies and procedures manuals; newspapers; magazine and journal articles; government documents; books; newsletters

▶ *People.* Colleagues; supervisors; key managers; program participants; program planners from other organizations; professional networks; community and business leaders; elected or appointed government officials; economists; political and social scientists; professional educators; community activists

▶ *Group meetings and gatherings.* Boards and committees; work teams; ad hoc groups; community meetings; planning meetings; open forums; local gathering places (like grange halls, community centers, coffee rooms, school athletic events, hallways, union halls); governmental hearings and sessions; social gatherings; formal lectures and seminars on economic, social, and political conditions

► *Professional and trade associations.* International, national, regional, and local conferences and meetings; committee and ad hoc groups within these associations; formal and informal networking groups; chats with key formal and informal leaders

► *Technology-based sources.* Websites; public chat rooms; bulletin boards; email; listservs; online forums and threaded discussions; video and video conferences; Web-based conferences

In addition, planners have access to other informal sources of information. For example, they may be invited to eat in the executive dining room, to attend meetings with senior management personnel, go to a ball game or play golf with a group of people "in the know," or shop and have dinner with colleagues.

The level and depth of the information that people need to have about the context for planning varies, depending on the role of the planner, the planner's background and experience in this context, the education and training programs being planned, and the nature of the organization and the wider environment in which the planner works. Consider two very different scenarios in relation to how much information is required.

### From Insider to Trainer

Rodney has just been appointed as a training specialist for computer operations in the commercial division of the Jones Bank. A new operating system is to be brought online within the next six months. Rodney is responsible both for developing the user manuals and for conducting the actual training of employees. He has been promoted through the ranks to his present position and has a clear understanding of how the unit presently functions. In addition, his supervisor has briefed him on the proposed changes and their importance to both the commercial division and the general operation of the bank. The supervisor has also explained to Rodney the evolving nature of commercial banking, especially how their bank is changing. Rodney has obtained for review a copy of the last two annual reports and some in-house reports on the commercial division to better understand his particular situation.

### From Outsider to Insider

Marie has just assumed the position of corporate vice president for human resource development and training for the Jones Bank. Though familiar with the banking industry, she was hired from the outside. Marie did her homework prior to her interview, however. She has a very clear "outsider's understanding" of the overall mission and expected future direction of the bank, based on written materials, her interviews, informal talks with colleagues, and Web-based sources. Now she needs to convert that data to an insider's perspective. Marie decides on six basic strategies to achieve those ends: (1) review all available in-house documents related to the present and future operations of the organization; (2) interview members of the senior management team, key middle managers of each major division of the bank, and her own staff; (3) manage by "walking around"; (4) attend all strategic planning meetings at both the corporate and division levels; (5) make herself visible in key business, professional, and community organizations; and (6) scan material related to how her organization and the banking industry in general are viewed in political, economic, and social terms, both in her local community and in the wider markets that her bank serves. Marie hopes through her efforts to gain an in-depth understanding of her new organization and how her unit fits into the practices of that organization.

Both Rodney and Marie have to gain a basic understanding of the context in which they are planning and/or managing education and training programs. But, the types and levels of information that are essential for them to effectively function are quite different.

## Chapter Highlights

Discerning the context, which is both a major skill and an art, is a critical component that planners continually explore as they design education and training programs for adults. Three facets of the planning context are key: interacting with people, the organizational component, and the wider environmental conditions. People plan programs, and as such program planners are constantly bombarded with issues related to the people with whom they work. Therefore, planners must have finely tuned social and communication skills, and the ability to negotiate among all involved parties—other individuals, groups, organizations, and/or the wider community. Major factors that are rooted within organizations are broadly categorized under three headings: structural, political, and cultural. When taking into account these contextual organizational factors, planners are cognizant of those internal to their own organization, as well as those of external groups with whom they plan and/or compete in the programming arena. In the context of the wider environment the factors that planners take into account include the general economic, political, and social climates. This "macro-picture" of planning has increasingly become more important as people cross numerous borders in their work as educational planners, from geographic, to cultural, to ideological.

In discerning the context for planning it is important to address the following tasks:

◆ Become knowledgeable about the people, organizational, and wider environmental contextual factors that affect decisions made throughout the planning process.

◆ Be well-informed about the issue of power that is present in most planning situations and the influences that power relationships have in the planning process.

◆ Cultivate and/or enhance negotiation skills required to navigate situations in which power is a central issue. Negotiation requires that planners have finely tuned people skills, are able to listen to multiple voices, are good analytical thinkers, are willing to communicate effectively through a variety of means, have excellent group-facilitation skills, understand what taking risks really means, and have the ability to operate effectively within relationships of power.

◆ Ensure that beliefs and actions convey ethical practices. Being reflective in one's practice and stating personal, unit, and organizational beliefs related to planning programs for adults (see Chapter Two) are essential elements of being consistently ethical in practice.

◆ Know and be able to access sources of information about the context of the planning situation (for example, written documents, technology-based sources, professional and trade associations, group meetings and gatherings, and interactions with individuals).

Gathering, reflecting on, and using contextual knowledge as a program planner is challenging, even to the most experienced planners, as this knowledge is often contradictory and sometimes even paradoxical.

The importance of having sound knowledge about the contexts in which planners work will become apparent in subsequent discussions of the other components and corresponding tasks included in the Interactive Model of Program planning (see Chapters Five through Fifteen). Without having credible contextual knowledge, it is difficult, if not impossible, to complete the other parts of the planning process.

## Application Exercises

The two Application Exercises presented here help you analyze and reflect on the contextual component of program planning. The first exercise is designed to assist you in analyzing the facets of the planning context in which you work. In the second exercise, you have an opportunity to reflect on your own actions as an educational planner when you take into account the context in which you are planning.

## EXERCISE 4.1

## Analyzing the Context for Planning

1. Describe briefly an organizational setting—either your present one or one in which you worked previously—where part of your role is or was to plan education or training programs for adults.

2. Identify, within the framework outlined below, key contextual factors that have or could influence the program planning process in the organization that you described above.

   *People Issues*

   *Organization Elements*

   Structural

   Political

   Cultural

3. Identify critical aspects of the wider economic, political and social environment in which the organization is situated that has or could affect how programs are planned within the organization you described above.

4. Using the chart provided here, list sources you could use to investigate further the contextual environment in which you have or do work. Using the items listed, be as specific as you can in highlighting what types of sources you would seek out.

| Written Documents | People | Group Meetings and Other Gatherings | Trade and Professional Associations | Technology-Based Sources |
|---|---|---|---|---|
| _____ | _____ | _____ | _____ | _____ |
| _____ | _____ | _____ | _____ | _____ |
| _____ | _____ | _____ | _____ | _____ |
| _____ | _____ | _____ | _____ | _____ |
| _____ | _____ | _____ | _____ | _____ |

5. Review this material with a colleague and add additional ideas as needed.

### EXERCISE 4.2

## Acting in Context: Reflecting on Your Beliefs and Actions as a Program Planner

Understanding that using contextual knowledge in planning programs is complex and challenging, this exercise gives you an opportunity to reflect on your beliefs and actions as a program planner when using this type of knowledge.

1. **How do you react when confronted with power issues when planning education and training programs? What might you change about your current beliefs and actions when acting within power relations as a planner?**

2. **What negotiation skills do you possess that you use well in planning education and training programs? What skills and beliefs about negotiating might you want to revise or add to your repertoire and belief system?**

3. **What ethical beliefs do you have about planning programs for adults? When these ethical beliefs are challenged, how do you respond? How do you feel? Are there ethical beliefs that you would like to change or add to your practice as a program planner?**

4. a. **Has there been a situation where you have chosen to resign from a position and/or a planning group because you refused to compromise your own values and beliefs? If so, describe why and how you left. Would you leave the situation differently if you had the chance to do it over, and if so, how?**

   b. **If you have not left a planning situation even though you experienced clashes of values and beliefs between yourself and the other planning parties, why not? How did you act and feel in that situation? What would it take to make you resign from a position or planning committee? How might you leave that situation?**

# Chapter 5
# Building a Solid Base of Support

Pam, the new associate vice president for nursing services, sees a real difference between her previous organization and the one in which she is now employed. Rather than staff fighting every new directive imposed upon them, staff members are willing to try out new ways of working as long as the focus is on quality patient care and that the care is not compromised. What is really unique to this facility is that these changes in practice are not always top down, but often are initiated by frontline nursing personnel. There also appears to be a spirit of collaboration, and for some, even adventure as staff members seek to find more effective and caring ways to work with patients and families. In addition, there seems to be an openness in communication among units, rather than continual in-fighting. Although resources are tight, as they are in many health care organizations, the Executive Council, of which Pam is a member, is quite vocal about the importance of continued learning and encourages both attendance at formal workshops and conferences and job-embedded learning. Changes in practice that result in optimal patient care and cost containment, two major goals of the organization, are rewarded in numerous ways from hallway acknowledgments by supervisors and upper-level management to increased pay and benefits, including additional monies for education and training pursuits. Pam senses there is a firm basis of support for learning and growth for both individuals and the organization as a whole.

Establishing a firm base of support for planning and conducting education and training programs is critical for program planners to embrace. This support takes the form of both commitment and action. *Commitment* is viewed as a recurrent promise, which usually comes in the form of written and/or verbal statements. For example, the chief executive officer of Pam's organizations emphasizes in his annual "state-of-the-union" address that continuing learning is foundational to the mission of the organization. *Action* involves having people at all levels of an organization respond to that commitment in the form of budgetary and other resource allocations and actual involvement in the education and training function. In Pam's situation, she sees actions present in the variety of education and training activities embedded as a part of the job and the availability of formal programs, both internal and external, for all staff and/or volunteers. In addition, there are resources allocated to these activities, transfer-of-learning activities are the norm, and one of the major goals of supervisory personnel is to promote both individual and organizational learning. In advocating for education and training programs, as in discerning the planning context, program planners must pay attention to how to garner people and organizational support, including assistance from the wider environment in which their organizations reside.

Addressed first in this chapter are strategies for ensuring people support. Among the groups discussed are learners, supervisors, and middle- and top-level managers. Discussed next is building organizational support, which includes taking into account the centrality of the education and training function and promoting an organizational culture that supports continuous learning and development. The chapter concludes with a discussion of the importance of obtaining and maintaining the support of the wider community within which the organization resides. More specifically, two strategies are discussed, the use of advisory committees and collaborative partnerships.

## Ensuring People Support

In building people support for education and training programs, one or more of the following types of people should be included in the planning process:

► Potential and current learners

► In work situations, supervisors of potential participants

► Mid- and senior-level management of the sponsoring organization(s), sometimes including members of the board

► Other stakeholders who have a vested interest in either the planning process or the results of the education or training program (such as grassroots community groups, funding agencies)

As seen in Chapter Four (context), and also discussed in Chapters Ten (learning transfer) and Nine (instructional plans), this concept of the importance of the people factor in program planning is crucial.

In many organizations, there are certain key people who continually are tapped for support, especially when planning education and training programs is part of a centralized unit or the major mission of the organization. For example, in securing people support for an adult education program housed within a public school system, it is important to gain support from the superintendent, the principal of the building in which the program is housed, the participants, and the various organizations and community groups that the program impacts (such as specific businesses and industries or other literacy programs).

Although there will, in all likelihood, be a fairly set group of people who support education and training programming for an organization, the supporters may need to change for different programs, depending on the context in which the program will be held, goals and objectives of new programs, needs and backgrounds of potential audiences, and organizational sponsors. For example, if a public school adult education program was asked to extend its operations to deliver, in cooperation with the local community college and literacy volunteers, a new program for adults to learn English as a second language, an expanded network of people support would be needed. This network might include the president and other key opinion leaders at the college, the leaders and volunteers of the local literacy organization, and the leaders of groups that have regular contact with the potential learners for this program (such as local churches, the migrant worker association, local businesses).

There are numerous ways to gain support from key people for planning education and training programs. Outlined here are ideas for obtaining support from learners, immediate supervisors in work situations, and mid- and senior-level managers and administrators. Some of the ideas presented could also be used to respond to needs of potential participants and sponsors (see Chapter Six), be used as transfer strategies and techniques (see Chapter Ten), assist in choosing instructional techniques and formats (see Chapters Nine and Thirteen), and provide sources of data for evaluating instructional activities and programs (see Chapters Ten and Eleven).

## Support from Learners

Support from learners is best produced by providing meaningful and useful programs (Munson, 1992). Most former participants will spread the word if a program is well-presented and useful to them. And if they perceive an education or training program as poor or ineffective, they will probably be even more vocal about it. Therefore, attendance at future programs, especially for those programs where participation is voluntary, is definitely influenced by former participants. But even in programs where participation is mandatory, former participants can and do affect the support of those who must attend. For example, if the word is passed around in a work situation that a particular program is a waste of time, participants are more apt not to pay attention, to bring other tasks to do during the sessions, or to come late and leave early. This kind of behavior is especially prevalent when the immediate supervisors of the participants also believe that the program and the time away from the job are not worth it.

A second strategy for building learner support is to actively involve current and potential learners in planning and conducting the program.

### Before the Program, Planners Can . . .

▶ Ask learners what they want to learn, how they see themselves as learners, and what formats and instructional techniques they prefer.

▶ Invite selected learners to assist in planning the program, with part of their input being how they can apply what is being learned into their work roles or other life situations.

▶ Ask learners who have been involved in previous programs to help recruit new participants.

### During the Program, Planners Can . . .

▶ Invite learners to serve as instructors and/or resource persons.

▶ At specified intervals ask participants to provide feedback on how the sessions are going and make changes, as appropriate, based on their suggestions.

▶ Pair experienced practitioners with novices, asking them to serve as assistants in the learning process.

▶ Ask participants to reflect on what they have learned and develop specific application plans.

▶ If specific transfer strategies and techniques have been chosen, review with participants how they can integrate these into their applications plan.

▶ If there is no specific transfer-of-learning plan, provide an overview and discussion of the various transfer strategies and techniques, and assist participants in choosing ones that are useful and appropriate to their situations and ways of learning.

**After the Program, Planners Can . . .**

▶ Follow up with participants either on-site or through electronic means to help them reflect on whether the learning-transfer strategies and techniques they are using actually are assisting them in applying what they learned. Assist those who are not finding these strategies and techniques useful to choose alternative ones. Also probe whether the transfer process may be blocked by other factors (for example, lack of supervisory support, motivation, and/or resources).

▶ Encourage learners to serve as peer coaches or mentors to each other in applying what they have learned.

▶ Ask selected participants to assist in collecting and reviewing evaluation data.

▶ Act as advocates for learners if they need to negotiate program outcomes as they are applying what they have learned into their own settings.

## Support from the Immediate Supervisors of Participants

In programs for work settings, whether for paid or volunteer staff, support from the immediate supervisors of participants and potential participants is crucial at all points in the educational cycle, from assessing needs to learning transfer and evaluation. To illustrate, consider the following scenario.

### The Influence of Supervisors

The enrollment for Corporation X's training seminar on working with difficult employees is always good. But on the day of the training session, there are always high percentages of both no-shows and attendees who wander in and out of the session. Despite this, participants consistently rate the program very highly, especially in usefulness for on-the-job activities. In investigating this problem, program staff discover that for a period of six months, the no-shows and leave-early participants have all come from four of the 10 departments involved in the program. They also notice that the supervisors in two of these four departments have complained loudly and often about the enormous amount of time that their people spend on training activities.

As can be seen in this scenario, supervisors exert considerable influence over staff attending education and training programs. Supervisors also play a very important part in whether whatever has been learned in these programs can actually be applied on the job. If supervisors understand and support the objectives of the education and training efforts, it is easier for staff to change their practice (and for supervisors to positively reinforce that change).

As with participant support, support for education and training activities from immediate supervisors of paid and volunteer staff is best gained by providing worthwhile programs and involving the supervisors at various times in the programming cycle. The opportunities for supervisory involvement are many.

### Before the Program, Planners Can . . .

▶ Invite supervisors to assist in assessing the learning needs of staff, including asking staff what they perceive their needs are for doing their jobs more effectively and efficiently.

▶ Have supervisors assist in scheduling education and training activities and select staff for these activities.

▶ Invite supervisors to work with participants to help them prepare for the upcoming session, with a focus on how the material can be applied. This activity could involve hosting a training session for supervisors on alternative transfer strategies and techniques.

▶ Ask supervisors to assist in collecting baseline evaluation data.

### During the Program, Planners Can . . .

▶ Invite supervisors to attend parts of the program that would be helpful to them in assisting participants to apply what is being learned.

▶ Request that supervisors avoid calling participants out of sessions to handle work-related problems.

▶ Encourage supervisors to serve as instructors or resource persons for specific programs.

▶ Ask supervisors to provide informal feedback on how the program is being received by staff.

### After the Program, Planners Can . . .

▶ Ask supervisors to provide feedback to the planning staff and instructors on whether programs are addressing adequately the needs that were identified and whether what has been learned can actually be applied in practice.

▶ Serve as a mentor to supervisors as they assist their staff in applying what they have learned.

▶ Urge supervisors to provide opportunities and resources for learning transfer and facilitate how what has been learned can realistically apply to their work (for example, time for participants to share their learning with colleagues, and encouraging learners to serve as peer coaches to each other in applying what they have learned).

▶ Coach supervisors in choosing alternative strategies and techniques for learning transfer if the current ones are not effective. Also probe with them other possible barriers to the transfer process.

▶ Ask supervisors to assist in collecting data for evaluation and follow-up.

Although the support of supervisors is crucial to all aspects of the educational process, it is especially important that planners seek the active involvement of supervisors before and after the programs. Supervisors might need assistance from program planners, as noted in the previous examples, in order to help their staff members apply what they have learned in the actual work situation. Guiding staff through this applications phase can be a time-consuming activity for supervisors, but can be very beneficial to all parties involved and the organization as a whole.

## Differing Levels of Support of Immediate Supervisors

Supervisors often provide differing levels of support throughout the educational process from lip service to full support. When these differing support levels are primarily negative (for example, from viewing education and training programs as a waste of time to sincerely doubting that what is being learned will be helpful back on the job), learners can find themselves being caught between wanting to implement what they have learned, yet being either overtly or covertly blocked at every step by their supervisors.

Although this blocking behavior by supervisors often causes frustration and even anger, there are ways learners can work with, or if necessary around, supervisory staff. A sampling of these ways is outlined in Exhibit 5.1.

A word of caution: When, how, and by whom these strategies are undertaken depends a great deal on how the work group interacts (for example, is the group collaborative or is in-fighting more the norm?) and the relationship supervisors have with their staff (for example, open and receptive to staff ideas versus a top-down approach).

A final way for staff to respond to supervisors who block the application of their learning is to ask for or build upon the support already given by mid- and senior-level managers. Finding ways to ask and use this support, especially for those with little job security, is difficult at best and at worst may result in being fired. Yet, there are times when some staff members are willing to take that risk, usually when these staff know the changes being fostered will result in better products and services, working conditions, and/or personal well-being.

**EXHIBIT 5.1**

# Ways Staff Can Work with or "Around" Supervisory Personnel

| Reactions from Supervisors | Strategies Used by Staff |
| --- | --- |
| **Openly hostile** | ❖ Have leaders among the staff seek to understand why the supervisor is expressing these feelings. (For example, is there a legitimate reason for not wanting this change in practice? Are there ways the proposed changes could be altered to better fit with how work is currently done in the unit?)<br>❖ If no resolution can be found, does this supervisor have a consistent pattern of not wanting to change the way things are done? If so, this person's behavior becomes a personnel issue to be addressed by his immediate supervisor. |
| **No overt responses** | ❖ Choose staff who interact well with the supervisor and have them explore with the supervisor why she has responded neither positively nor negatively to how the practices of the staff could change as a result of the educational program. Is it that the supervisor has no knowledge about what the training was about and how it might impact the unit? Is the supervisor just overloaded and can't find time in an already heavy workload to assist staff even if she wanted to do so? Does the supervisor know how she can be helpful to staff?<br>❖ Depending on the supervisor's response, staff could provide information about the learning transfer expectations and then propose ways that the supervisor could assist staff in changing their practice that are reasonable and doable. |
| **Covert blocking** | ❖ Have selected staff try to detect a pattern of this supervisor's covert blocking. Is it focused on all or parts of the change? On certain staff members? In addition, these staff members could use their informal networks to get a sense of why the supervisor is against the proposed changes, yet will not speak openly about her opposition.<br>❖ If patterns can be detected, key leaders among the staff can strategize how they could respond to the covert actions of the supervisor to enable them to continue applying what they have learned. Their informal data might allow them to modify the change to respond to some of the supervisor's reservations. |
| **Openly questioning the value of the learning applications** | ❖ Have key leaders meet with the supervisor to learn the reasoning behind the questioning of the proposed changes in practice.<br>❖ If the supervisor agrees with some of the changes, but not others and has sound reasons, ask if the supervisor would be willing to negotiate, perhaps with members of staff, what the outcomes of the transfer process should be. |

## Support from Mid- and Senior-Level Managers

It is important to garner support from both middle- and senior-level managers. Although the assumption of having support from top management is often viewed as a given, less attention has been paid to middle managers.

As Wiggenhorn (1996) has astutely observed: "Middle managers . . . often have to mediate between what is and what should be, making them primary players in creating and managing change. This in no way is intended to dilute the power and influence of top management's commitment to change programs. But it is often middle managers who have the task of forging connections between reality and the vision"(p. 30–31).

Support for educational programs from both middle- and senior-level managers is reflected in individuals' style and practice as leaders and managers, their budgetary commitment to these programs, and their public support of the educational function in organizational publications and key organizational meetings. Their support can be gained in a number of ways, a sampling of which is listed here (Munson, 1992).

**Planners can . . .**

▶ First and foremost, do good work! Set specific goals and objectives for the education and training activities and then meet them. Provide documentation, in an easily understood form, of the successful results and benefits of the program.

▶ Demonstrate they know the business of the organization. Whatever the business of the organization is, from computer technology to educating children, know well what the mission, goals, products, and services of the organization are.

▶ Request that senior management issue formal policy and procedural statements concerning the education and training activities of the organization.

▶ Ask selected visible and respected mid- and senior-level managers to be actively involved in the design and evaluation of highly visible programs. For example, a manager could serve as a consultant to a planning group designing a program in an area of his or her competence; or a group of managers could serve in an ad hoc capacity to preview proposed education and training programs that have organization-wide impact.

Munson (1992) warns that it is easy to get discouraged trying to gain the support of key organizational leaders, an effort that can take a considerable investment of time, yet offer few initial concrete results. However, time may be one of the keys in gaining managerial support. Because education and training programs for adults are not the primary focus of many organizations, it will, in most cases, take longer for senior executives to take note of such activities and to give them more than nominal support. Therefore, it is important to develop a consistent track record of successful programs and communicate that record in effective ways (see Chapter Twelve).

## Building Organizational Support

In building organizational support two major facets are considered. The first facet is structural in nature and focuses on how the education and training function is positioned within the organization. Is education and training the central "job" or "product" of the organization or are these activities a secondary or even a random occurrence? The culture of the organization is the second major aspect. Does the organization view continued learning as a basic tenet of that organization's way of doing business? Is learning just an unplanned byproduct of what goes on in the life of the organization? Or, is the importance of learning and development just given "lip service"?

### Centrality of Education to the Organization

Establishing the type of structural support that program planners need depends primarily on how central the education and training function is to the organization. Therefore, planners need to carefully and realistically evaluate their position and function within their own organizations. The ways in which education and training programs are incorporated into organizations vary widely, but most organizations fall into three general categories.

1. Organizations that sponsor education and training programs for adults as their primary mission (such as consulting firms that provide only education and training services, and schools for adult students only)

2. Organizations that have as a major function of their operations a centralized division or unit charged with managing education and training programs (such as colleges of continuing education in universities, staff development units in public schools, and human resource divisions in business and industry)

3. Organizations that provide education and training programs as one of their services but do not have separate units charged with managing or coordinating functions (for example, organizations offering programs in which nurses teach patients in primary-care settings, principals plan staff-development programs, and managers are mentors and coaches to selected staff)

A sampling of specific ways to build structural organizational support—organizational mission and goals, standard operating procedures, and organizational authority—within each of the three organizational frameworks are explored next.

### Organizations Whose Primary Mission Is Educating and Training Adults

If you are part of an organization dedicated to the education of adults, you can build organizational support as follows:

- *Mission and goals.* The mission and goals statement clearly defines the main focus of the organization as developing and providing education and training programs for adults. The language of the mission statement is understandable to all organizational personnel, current and potential program participants, key external organizations, and other stakeholders.

- *Standard operating policies and procedures.* All staff members respond to requests by learners in a timely and helpful manner; and all management systems related to the program (systems for registration and for obtaining instructional materials, for example) are designed for the convenience of the participants and instructional staff. Staff members are continuous learners, who take advantage of professional development programs, opportunities for job-embedded learning, and learning of a more informal or self-directed nature. Managers and supervisors support the learning efforts of staff by actively being a part of the transfer activities and through continued recognition of all forms of learning.

- *Organizational authority.* The president of the organization has the decision-making authority related to all education and training programs. She is a member of the governing board, and all executive-level staff members serve as either ex-officio members or staff to the board.

### Organizations with a Centralized Education or Training Division

If you are part of an organization that has a centralized division or unit, you can build organizational support as follows:

- *Mission and goals of the organization.* The mission and goals statement refers to the importance of continued individual and organizational learning as a function of the organization. In addition, the education or training division has its own mission and goals statement and clearly communicates this statement to all appropriate parties, internal and external to the organization.

- *Standard operating policies and procedures.* The operating procedures of the division (and any changes in these procedures) are clearly communicated to all other divisions of the organization. In turn, each division in the organization keeps the staff of the central education or training unit informed of its education and training needs on a quarterly basis. Expectations of staff members and managers related to continuous learning by all staff are the same as in those outlined for organizations whose primary mission is the education of adults.

- *Organizational authority.* The directors of the education or training division have the authority to direct and manage all educational activities within their own division. They are part of the organization's executive council and serve on committees and teams that set the central focus and ways of operating for the organization (for example, strategic planning committees, visioning teams). In addition, each division has its own advisory council composed of representatives from all departments that receive services and, as appropriate, external constituents important to the operation of the program.

### Organizations That Provide Education and Training Programs Noncentrally

If you are part of an organization that supports and offers education and training programs, although it has no specific educational division, you can build structural organizational support as follows:

- *Mission and goals of the organization.* The organizational mission and goals statement refers to the importance of continued individual and organizational learning as an important function of the organization.

- *Standard operating policies and procedures.* Participants who complete a certain number of education and training programs are recognized by their supervisors and given either bonuses or pay increases. All staff members are allowed an equivalent of at least three days per year of paid leave to take part in education and training programs and activities. Managers support staff in their efforts to apply what they have learned from formal programs, as well as recognize and encourage job-embedded and more informal self-directed learning activities.

- *Organizational authority.* The directors of each operating division have given the authority for planning education and training opportunities for staff as part of their official job description. In addition, there is an organization-wide advisory council on education and training programs composed of staff from all levels and units of the organization and staffed by the human resource department or its equivalent.

### Supportive Organizational Cultures

Promoting an organizational culture or climate that supports continuous learning and educational programming as part of the organization's basic beliefs and actions is often a difficult and frustrating task. This task is especially challenging when a climate that fosters learning and development has not existed before or exists in name only. For example, even in divisions or organizations whose major focus is educating adults, such as continuing education units in universities and proprietary schools, the major outcome expected may be revenue generation. If this revenue generation means shortchanging students and staff and creating a less-than-favorable environment for learning, so be it; generating a 20- or 30-percent profit margin is the major goal of any programs offered.

Despite the difficulties and frustrations, there are ways to build favorable organizational climates for learning and for planning education and training programs (Apps, 1988; Hiemstra, 1991; Watkins and Marsick, 1993; Dixon, 1997; DiBella and Nevis, 1998; Donaldson and Kozoll, 1999). Most of these strategies have been reviewed earlier in this chapter, in the discussions of building people support and taking into account the centrality of mission related to education, because developing these kinds of support is often critical to ensuring a positive culture or climate for learning. In all support efforts, a strong commitment in words and action from mid- and top-level leaders and managers is most often stressed, including active endorsement of policies and procedures that support quality education and training activities (Munson, 1992; Wiggenhorn, 1996).

Apps (1988) and Schein (1999) suggest a process of transformational action through which organizations can become more supportive of programs for adults. The center of this transformational process focuses on questioning the basic assumptions and values about how the organization perceives programs for adults. The process includes five phases:

1. Developing awareness—recognizing that something is fundamentally wrong with the planning and delivery of education and training programs

2. Exploring alternatives—searching for new beliefs and ideas from other institutions and acknowledging that changes are needed in how, when, where, and by whom education and training programs are developed

3. Making a transition—leaving the old system of values, beliefs, and approaches behind (or dramatically changing them) and adopting a different set of beliefs and ways of operating related to planning programs

4. Achieving integration—putting the pieces from the transition back together

5. Taking action—putting the new ways of planning and conducting education and training programs into actual practice. This type of process

demands the backing of senior-level personnel and the involvement of all key players in the program planning process (such as staff, learners, other stakeholders)

In organizations whose primary purpose is to deliver education and training programs for adults or where program delivery is decentralized, one result of the previously described transformational process could be a revision of both the mission of the organization and the policies and procedures related to the education and training programs. In organizations where a centralized division for managing education and training programs exists, in addition to changes in the overall mission and policies, that division itself can also revise its mission or, if none exists, draft one. Mission or policy statements for education and training units clearly and precisely outline the "why, what, who, where, and how" of those units (Munson, 1992; Rothwell and Kazanas, 1993).

- ▶ *Why?* Outlines the basic values and beliefs of the division and the end results to be accomplished, in terms of overall purpose and goals

- ▶ *What?* Describes the broad functional areas for which the education and training divisions are responsible (such as management development, technical training, organizational development, volunteer training, community education)

- ▶ *Who?* Identifies the current and potential audiences with whom staff in the education and training divisions work

- ▶ *Where?* Defines the parameters within which the education and training units function (that is, the whole organization; specific departments, divisions, or sites within the organization)

- ▶ *How?* Describes the major delivery modes used in education and training programs (such as classroom instruction, on-the-job training, computer-based instruction, self-directed learning options, off-site programs and conferences, community action projects)

A sample mission statement of a centralized division is shown in Exhibit 5.2.

A new or revised mission or policy statement should be approved by senior management prior to its circulation among organizational personnel. Once it is approved, care should be taken that all appropriate individuals (for example, division directors, supervisory personnel, union representatives, external stakeholders) receive a copy. This distribution ensures that key players have at least some basic information about the overall scope and responsibilities of the education and training unit.

**EXHIBIT 5.2**

# Sample Mission Statement

*Purpose*

The purpose of the Department of Human Resource Development is threefold: (1) to prepare people to enter the workplace, improve their present job performance, or advance and/or change their chosen occupation; (2) to assist the overall organization to adapt to changing markets, products, and ways of operating; and (3) to assist people in the organization to respond and cope with both work and personal problems and issues they encounter.

*Values and Beliefs*

The staff of this department believe that the purpose of education and training programs is to encourage the growth and development of the organization and individuals within the organization. They view continuous learning, diverse forms of inquiry, and collegiality as fundamental values of the organization. The staff believes that all adults and organizations can and want to learn and continue to grow and change. The role of the staff is to serve as both process and content experts in the program planning process.

*Functions*

The staff of this department are responsible for five primary functions:

1. To coordinate all existing educational activities within the organization
2. To develop and manage all educational activities for support staff and supervisory and management personnel
3. To serve as consultants to senior management on issues related to organizational change and development
4. To provide education and training programs that address both the work and personal development needs of individual employees
5. To design education and training programs for clients and suppliers of the organization related primarily to new product development

*Audience and Parameters of Programs*

The primary audience includes all levels of people working throughout the organization. This audience includes central office staff and personnel located within all divisions and locations of the organization. The staff of this department works primarily with the training and human performance staff personnel located within each unit of the organization and with management and supervisory personnel. Only the senior staff serve as consultants to executive-level managers. Secondary audiences are suppliers and clients of the organization.

*Primary Ways Education and Training Programs Are Delivered*

Education and training programs are delivered through inhouse programs (such as seminars, workshops, computer-based instruction, job-embedded learning) and off-site programs (such as conferences and institutes). Both formally designed educational programs and self-directed learning activities are considered legitimate ways for participants to learn.

# Obtaining and Maintaining Support of the Wider Community

As discussed in Chapter Four, the wider community and forces within that community (such as the economic, political, and social climate) are critical considerations in planning programs for adults. Therefore, thinking through strategies for obtaining support from the wider community is essential in the planning process. Depending on the nature of the program, this wider community spans from more localized groups (such as cities and regions) to a more national and international focus. Specifically, two strategies are discussed: the use of advisory groups and legally constituted boards, and learning partnerships.

## Support Via Groups and Legally Constituted Boards

Using different group configurations and legally constituted boards is one way to build support from the wider community for education and training programs. The most common type of group is an *advisory board* or *committee*. These boards and committees are given a variety of formal titles, such as steering committees, advisory boards, coordinating committees, and planning boards (Rothwell and Cookson, 1997; Birkenholz, 1999). Although these boards and committees are advisory and therefore not empowered to make decisions that must be followed, members can nonetheless influence staff and affect the direction and form of the education and training function in organizations.

These groups and boards may be permanent, or be put together on an ad hoc basis. For example, a vocationally orientated program for low-income adults, funded through federal and state dollars and currently housed in a local community college, may ask for representatives from a number of different groups to serve on a program advisory council (for example, the business sector, community activist groups, funding agencies, and learners). This advisory council's function stems from offering advice and counsel for planning specific programs to wider environmental scanning and intervention activities. These council members could provide, for example, assistance in understanding general economic conditions and trends, recommending new markets where employees are needed, providing information on funding options, using their political clout to ensure funding continues, and designing programs that fit the diverse populations being served. If this program were to become a legally constituted organization unto itself, then the choice could be to move from an advisory council to a legally constituted board. In addition, under either structure, ad hoc teams might be useful in addressing specific program issues, such as possible loss of funding, retention of program participants, or opportunities for growth that require immediate action.

## Principles and Operating Norms

Whatever the format selected, the choice to form advisory groups or legally constituted boards for education and training programs for adults should be grounded in three major principles (Birkenholz, 1999; Donaldson and Kozoll, 1999):

1. The input from groups or boards are really wanted, with the assumption that members' ideas and observations are both heard and used.

2. The working philosophy of these bodies is that democratic ways of planning are fostered.

3. These groups and boards are collaborative in nature, and where necessary instructing committee members in group facilitation and collaborative ways of decision making are a part of the groups' agendas.

In addition, the purpose, function, and authority of groups or boards should be understood by all involved, including group members, staff, and top-level leadership.

Guidelines for achieving these principles and ways of operating and therefore fostering successful groups and boards include the following (Knowles, 1980; Birkenholz, 1999):

▶ Members clearly understand what they are supposed to do and what the parameters are for making decisions and taking action.

▶ Members have a working knowledge of the program.

▶ Leadership is provided by experienced members who are skilled in facilitating meeting and use collaborative ways of working.

▶ Members have real tasks to do and they are responsible for decisions that are still in the "idea stage"; they should not be asked merely to rubber-stamp decisions already made by others.

▶ Meetings are well-planned, which includes timely notification, a detailed agenda, and other support materials sent well in advance of the meeting so members can review the material prior to the meeting.

▶ Operating norms and procedures for meetings are clear and either applied consistently or, if they are not working, modified (for example, meeting times and duration, starting and ending on time, respectful ways of interacting).

▶ Individual and group tasks accepted by members are clear, specific, and definitive, and a tracking system is used to ensure that all assignments are carried out in a timely and effective manner.

▶ Members are kept informed about how their decisions and actions have been incorporated into the work of the sponsoring unit or organization.

Groups and committees, whether they are permanent or ad hoc, should not outlive their usefulness. When members believe they are wasting their time—or even worse, know that they are nothing more than names on a piece of paper—it is time to refocus or disband the group or board. This notion of refocusing includes both advisory and legally constituted entities.

## Member Tasks

It is essential, as noted earlier, that members of advisory groups and legally constituted boards have real tasks to do. Knowles (1980), Birkenholz (1999), and Cervero and Wilson (1999) have outlined sample tasks appropriate for such groups and boards:

▶ Assist with environmental scans, including the economic, social, and political climate in which the organization is situated.

▶ Ensure voices of all constituents that need to be heard are encouraged to be a part of the conversation related to planning programs.

▶ Participants use the power base they have, for example, economic or political, for the "common good" of all stakeholders.

▶ Provide whatever assistance is needed to build partnerships with other organizations in order that programs can be both effectively designed and successfully delivered.

▶ Identify problems and issues for which education and training programs might offer solutions.

▶ Assist in gathering ideas for programs and defining program objectives.

▶ React to initial drafts of program design and content.

▶ Communicate past achievements and efforts for key individuals and groups, such as senior management, current and potential learners, and community groups.

▶ Ensure that program ideas, especially ones that are potentially controversial, are considered by staff.

▶ Help locate and secure resources (for example, funding, equipment, people, and space).

▶ Give advice regarding program logistics (for example, availability of child care, where programs should be held).

▶ Assist in program review and evaluations.

Having a clear picture of the members' tasks helps in selecting the best members of these groups and boards.

### Selecting Members

Selecting members for the groups and boards requires careful deliberation. Three major factors to consider are:

1. Diversity (for example, age, gender, race, class, ethnic background)

2. Competence and experience (for example, leadership skills, political and economic clout, knowledge of the industry and the subject matter, excellent people skills)

3. Geographic location, especially for regional, national, and international programs

One way to ensure that these specific factors are taken into account when choosing members is to use the two-way grid portrayed in Exhibit 5.3.

In addition to these three major factors, program planners address other criteria as well. Birkenholz (1999), for example, emphasizes that care must be taken to select individuals who "are respected among their peers; reflect the diversity of the target audience . . . ; are sincere, dedicated, conscientious, credible, [and] principled; speak their own mind, but can compromise . . . ; and are available [and] willing to meet and serve" (p. 60).

### Support Through Partnerships

Partnerships for planning programs for adults, according to Donaldson and Kozoll (1999) and Highum and Lund (2000), come in all shapes and sizes. More specifically, Donaldson and Kozoll (1999) assert, although there are many forms of partnerships, the most highly developed and complex are those which are grounded in collaboration. Collaborative partnerships are characterized by being "organizations [unto] themselves [although often of a short duration], . . . employ unconventional kinds of governance, and rely more on informal mechanisms" (p. 3). In addition, the leadership functions differ for planners who operate in partnerships versus those who work from one organizational base. These planners span boundaries of culture, space, and ways of operating as they move between and among the organizational partners. Other forms of partnership arrangements include

**EXHIBIT 5.3**

# Two-Way Grid for Selecting Group and Board Members

| Criteria | Existing Committee and Current Committee Members | | | | | | Potential Committee Members | | | |
|---|---|---|---|---|---|---|---|---|---|---|
| | 1 | 2 | 3 | 4 | 5 | 6 | a | b | c | d |
| *Age* | | | | | | | | | | |
| Under 30 years of age | X | | | X | | | | | | |
| From 30 to 55 years of age | | X | X | | | | | | | |
| Over 55 years of age | | | | | X | X | | | | |
| *Gender* | | | | | | | | | | |
| Men | X | | | | X | X | | | | |
| Women | | X | X | X | | | | | | |
| *Ethnicity* | | | | | | | | | | |
| Caucasian | | | X | | X | X | | | | |
| African-American | X | | | | | | | | | |
| Hispanic/Latino(a) | | | | | | | | | | |
| Native American | | | | | | | | | | |
| Asian/Pacific Islander | | X | | X | | | | | | |
| Other | | | | | | | | | | |
| *Social class* | | | | | | | | | | |
| Upper middle | X | | | X | X | | | | | |
| Middle | | X | | | | X | | | | |
| Lower | | | X | | | | | | | |
| *Competence and experience* | | | | | | | | | | |
| Leadership skills | | X | X | | | | | | | |
| Political and economic clout | | | | | X | | | | | |
| Industry and subject-matter knowledge | | | | X | | X | | | | |
| Excellent people skills | X | | | | | | | | | |
| *Geographic location of members* | | | | | | | | | | |
| Local area | | | | X | X | X | | | | |
| State and region | X | | | | | | | | | |
| National | | X | | | | | | | | |
| International | | | | X | | | | | | |

**Source:** *Adapted from Houle, C.,* Governing Boards: Their Nature and Nurture, *1989. p. 40. Reprinted by permission of Jossey-Bass, Inc.*

cooperation (that is, providing assistance on an ad hoc basis to each other), and coordination, where institutions take into account consistently what types of programs for adults are being offered by similar groups, and find their own market niches rather than being in direct competition.

### Relationships Among Partners

In addition to how partnerships are defined, the relationship between or among partners may be informal or formal, voluntary or involuntary, and result in a variety of interactions, as described in the next scenario.

### *Voluntary Joint Planning*

Five organizations join forces to acquire the needed technologies to foster Web-based learning programs for professional and support staff of nonprofit agencies. Some of these programs are offered jointly, combining the expertise of two or more of the institutions, while other programs are institution specific. The common bond among these institutions is the use of the same hard- and software systems, in addition to sharing one instructional support unit. Although the decision was voluntary on the part of the institutions, the major motivator was the funding sources required that partnerships be established as part of the funding guidelines. Due to the nature of the funding, a formal agreement had to be developed and agreed upon by all five organizations. Some of the factors supporting this venture were the close physical proximity of the institutions in the partnership, an established positive track record of collaboration among three of the five institutions, and shared values, including being learner-centered and quality-focused. A few negatives also appeared as the initial grants were being negotiated, the most apparent being when one of the institutional planners attempted a power play to gain control over both the planning and implementation phases of this venture (see Chapter Four related to contextual elements of the planning process). Unfortunately for her, but fortunately for the organizational partners, she was asked by the director of her organization to step out of the project, and she eventually left that institution.

### *Mandated Joint Planning*

In contrast to the partnership just described, another set of partners was mandated to join forces through legislative action in the delivery of initial teacher-preparation and professional development for teachers. The legislation was very specific—school districts, colleges and universities, and private sector representatives must work together in order for any funding to be awarded. As these partnerships were formed across one particular state, major differences among the various partnership groups emerged. For example, the private sector contingent in some regions was adamant about how poorly managed these monies had been in the past, and therefore insisted that these partnerships frame the budgeting practices and accountability systems from a business model orientation. Although some districts were very much in agreement with this way of operating, there were others that were opposed and, in some cases, even openly hostile to the idea. In addition, there were disagreements about how the program should be delivered, with some believing that most, if not all of the program should be job-embedded, while others favored a combination of classroom and experienced-based learning. Some of the regional partnerships were able to resolve their differences through collaborative interactions: open communication, continual negotiations, and compromise. Other partnerships appeared to resolve their differences in terms of the actual grant proposal, but internal jockeying for control continued throughout the life of the project; and still others never made it through the proposal stage. In the case of some of the latter two groups, the internal bickering, and sometimes open and hostile conflict, resulted in deep-seated distrust among and between planning partners, which in some regions will probably be felt for years to come.

## Building, Maintaining, and Dissolving Partnerships

As described in the previous scenarios, building and maintaining partnerships among organizations can be characterized as admirable to openly hostile. A number of authors describe fundamental principles or ways of operating to ensure that the partnerships are truly collaborative in nature (Cervero and Wilson, 1994; Saltiel, 1998; Sgroi and Saltiel, 1998; Donaldson and Kozoll, 1999; McCullum, 2000; Sparks, 2000). More specifically, there are nine critical operating principles for building and maintaining partnerships:

1. Sharing dreams, values, and ideas "that lead to a vision and goals for the collaborative effort" (Donaldson and Kozoll, 1999, p. 10)

2. Generating a "compelling stretching purpose that motivates and directs the work of all parties" (Sparks, 2000, p. 3)

3. Cultivating and nurturing trusting relationships among organizations and persons within those organizations

4. Developing an open and honest communication system in which all parties believe they are being heard

5. Recognizing, and where necessary, challenging power relationships among organizations and individuals within those organizations

6. Ensuring that democratic decision making is the norm and ethical issues are brought to the planning table

7. Fostering a sense that working together is an equitable and reciprocal process, in that all parties believe the benefits they receive equal what each has contributed (for example, time, staff resources, funding, space)

8. Valuing differences among the partners, and using this diversity to foster stronger partnerships while still focusing on core issues and interests

9. Enabling effective leadership at all levels of the partnership effort, including acknowledging the importance of both formal and informal leaders

Putting these principles into practice is not an easy task; more often than not, it is messy and can feel like an endless process as partnerships evolve. Put in more positive terms, one of the challenges members of successful partnerships gladly embrace is the education of members related to these critical principles, and continuous feedback to each of the partners on their interactions and actions. Sample strategies of meeting this challenge are described in Exhibit 5.4.

An excellent source of questions to assist planning partners in assessing the strengths and intensity of their work has been developed by Donaldson and Kozoll (1999, pp. 128–131). These questions focus on program complexity and scope, leadership and vision, tensions, strategies, and fragile relationships.

In addition to thinking about building and sustaining partnerships, participants in partnership arrangements also need to acknowledge that there is a time for many of these groups to end (Donaldson and Kozoll, 1999). This disbanding of partnerships may be on friendly terms—for example, the goals of the partnerships have been successfully met and therefore their task is done. These endings may also be due to continued inaction or even hostile relationships between or among partners. Whatever the reason, members need to address these endings, whether they are positive or negative (Bridges, 1991). For those partnerships that have had

**EXHIBIT 5.4**

# Strategies for Building and Sustaining Partnerships

| Building Partnerships | Sustaining Partnerships |
| --- | --- |
| ➡ Invite possible partners to a "brainstorming" session where dreams and ideas for programs are shared using a nominal group process. | ➡ Set up mechanisms to monitor the interactions of the partner groups to ensure the operating norms established by the partners, both in formal meetings and other interactions, are being adhered to in a reasonable way. For example, appoint a person with excellent group facilitation skills to observe key meetings and assist members in adhering to the norms that have been set, assist in revising those norms, design self-monitoring systems for individuals and informal and formal task groups. |
| ➡ Secure the support of key leaders from each organization and, where appropriate, the wider community as the partnership begins to form through meetings of these key leaders with people who are representative of the various groups who can both tell and sell their story. | |
| ➡ Set norms or ways of operating as one of the first major tasks of "formalizing" the partnership, taking into account cultivating healthy and trusting relationships, developing open and honest communication systems, ensuring democratic decision making and ethical practice, and valuing differences. | ➡ Continue to provide education and training opportunities (for example, regular meetings or separate programs) to provide assistance to members in terms of both the content and process elements of the partnership (for example, facilitating groups, addressing ethical issues, confronting power relationships that impede the group's work). |
| ➡ Develop a shared vision and purpose, with the assistance of a trained facilitator, through both face-to-face meetings and electronic means (for example, listservs or threaded discussions). | ➡ Design ways that partnership members can negotiate positive changes in the goals, objectives, activities, and outcomes of the partnership. |
| ➡ Determine areas where knowledge and skills are needed by partnership members related to the key operating principles. Devote a specific time at each meeting to educating members about the identified topics (for example, recognizing power relationships that both enable and impede the work of the partners, building effective and open communication systems). | ➡ Continue to build and nurture relationships among groups and individuals through action teams, celebrations of partnership accomplishments, electronic interactions, educational opportunities, and dealing with fragile relationships. |
| | ➡ Recognize that sustaining partnership activities is a continuing and often time-intensive process, and that partner members still need energy to fulfill responsibilities at their own organizations or groups. Create "resting" or "downtimes" for the partners to reflect on what they have done thus far, and recover from the "costs of energy and time committed to [the partnership] so that capacity is renewed for future efforts" (Donaldson and Kozoll, 1999, p. 108). |

great working relationships there may be feelings of sadness and even loss, as well as celebrations of accomplishments, all of which needs to be acknowledged. Where little activity is the major issue, someone just has to take the initiative to end the relationships, which is fairly easy for informal partnerships, but more complex for groups that have legal ties. If open conflict and purposeful noncooperation are the problems, steps have to be taken to dissolve the partnership as amicably as possible, which can be a difficult undertaking. However, it is important to take on this task, as the aftermath of open hostility can last for long periods, resulting in continuing squabbles and lack of cooperation between and among these groups. What is really disheartening is when these partnerships are a major ingredient in any change process, but either refuse to work with each other or sabotage each others' best efforts. Examples of these destructive types of endings include planning such events as parades that honor one ethnic or cultural group, but are opposed by other groups; professional development programs on procedures that are mandated by law or administrative fiats, but are diametrically opposed by program participants; and community action activities that are for the "common good" of the whole community, but are attacked by a few powerful interest groups with political clout.

## Chapter Highlights

In building a solid base of support for program planning, planners concentrate on five major tasks:

- Ensure support from key constituent groups including current and potential learners, all levels of organizational personnel, and other stakeholders through such mechanisms as active participation in planning and conducting education and training activities, transfer-of-learning strategies, and formal and ad hoc group and board work.

- Cultivate continuous organizational support through establishing appropriate structural mechanisms (for example, mission and goals statements, standard operating procedures and policies, what formal authority the unit has over programs), the choice of which depends primarily on the centrality of the education or training function.

- Promote an organizational culture in which formal, job-embedded, and self-directed learning activities and continuous learning are valued.

- Obtain and maintain support from the wider community through formal and ad hoc groups and boards, with key underlying assumptions that ideas and observations from members are heard and used, democratic planning is fostered, and collaborative interaction is the operative norm.

◆ Build and sustain collaborative partnerships with other organizations and groups that provide different vehicles for program planning and delivery that are in the best interests of all involved parties.

These tasks, if viewed as an ongoing and integral part of the planning process, often are revisited in a more formal way only at the start of major new program initiatives, when people take on new positions or additional planning responsibilities, and/or on a scheduled periodic basis. As in discerning the context for planning, establishing a solid basis of support for education and training programs is vital in carrying through the other components and corresponding tasks of the Integrated Model of Program Planning (Chapters Six through Fifteen).

## Application Exercises

The three Application Exercises presented here help you establish a solid base of support for program planning. The first exercise is designed to assist you in ensuring people support, the second in building organizational structural support, and the third addresses obtaining and maintaining support from the wider community.

## EXERCISE 5.1

## Ensuring People Support for Education and Training Programs

1. Complete the chart with ideas for how you could involve learners, supervisors, and mid- and upper-level managers in an organization's education and training activities. Be as specific as possible in naming the persons and/or types of personnel you would like to include or have included.

|  | Before the Program | During the Program | After the Program |
|---|---|---|---|
| **What Learners or Participants Can Do** |  |  |  |
| **What Supervisors Can Do** |  |  |  |
| **What Mid- and Upper- Level Managers Can Do** |  |  |  |

2. Review your ideas with a colleague and/or your planning committee and revise as needed.

## EXERCISE 5.2

## Building Structural Support for Education and Training Programs

1. Describe briefly your current organizational setting or one that has as all or part of its function planning education and training programs for adults.




2. Indicate whether planning these programs is:

    1. The primary mission of the organization

    2. One of the functions of the organization, with a centralized unit to manage that function

    3. One of the functions of the organization, but with no centralized unit to manage that function

3. Identify, within the organizational framework you have indicated above, how you would build structural support for planning education and training programs within that organization.

| Structural Factors | Specific Examples of Ways to Build Support |
|---|---|
| **Mission Statements** | |
| **Policies and Standard Operating Procedures** | |
| **System of Formal Organizational Authority** | |
| **Organizational Decision-Making** | |
| **Financial Resources** | |
| **Physical Facilities** | |

---

## EXERCISE 5.3

### Obtaining and Maintaining Support from the Wider Community

1. Choose and briefly describe an education or training program that you are currently planning or have planned in the past two years in which the wider community has or has had involvement in some way.

2. Identify what ways you currently or did involve people and groups outside of your immediate organization.

3. If you are using or did use an advisory board or other types of groups, do or did members of these groups help or impede the planning process? List each group and explain briefly actions or attitudes that either helped or impeded the group's or board's function.

| Group | Helpful Actions or Attitudes | Unhelpful or Impeding Actions and Attitudes |
|---|---|---|

4. If you currently or did use partnership arrangements, describe briefly: the partners; roles each partner plays or played; parameters for how the partnership is or was set up (for example, formal or informal, long- or short-term, mandated or voluntary); operating principles (for example, cultivate and nurture trusting relationships, recognize and work within power relationships, value differences among the partners); and ways you built and do or did sustain that partnership.

Partners

Role of Partners

Parameters of the Partnership

Operating Principles

Ways You Built and Are Sustaining or Did Sustain the Partnership

---

# Chapter 6

# Identifying Program Ideas

John, director of computer training, is not quite sure why the training activities he has been coordinating are, as his boss terms it, "not overly successful." He has hired what he believes are top-flight instructors and includes a free lunch as part of each program event. However, the enrollments are low, and a small but noticeable number of participants leave at the morning coffee break. Participant evaluations (at least for those programs John remembers to have participants evaluate) praise the presenters and the food, but are critical about the lack of usefulness and immediate transferability of the information presented. John cannot understand this reaction, because the programs are exactly like those run by one of his close friends, a training specialist at a similar organization, and his friend's sessions have received rave reviews. Perhaps, John thinks, he should reevaluate how he decides what the content of the programs should be, but he is unsure how to go about doing this. He has just assumed, based on his previous experience as an expert computer operator and programmer, that what is successfully working in one organization should work in another, providing one gets the operating systems (in this case, the training programs) properly installed and up and running.

Identifying relevant ideas and needs—the program content—is one of the major tasks of people involved with planning education and training programs (Witkin and Alschuld, 1995; Houle, 1996; Gupta, 1999). Although some educational programs may be "borrowed" from other organizations, as John has done in the scenario, this borrowing is not the only or necessarily the best way to generate ideas for education and training programs. For example, program ideas may come from such diverse sources as personal observations and hunches to highly structured needs assessments.

In most program planning models, this component of identifying ideas is called a needs assessment, needs analysis, or more recently, a performance analysis, which is usually conceived as a highly structured process, sometimes rather lengthy, with a series of steps. "Although (a formally structured) needs assessment can be a powerful tool to justify and focus the planning effort" (Sork, 1990, p. 78), conducting this form of needs assessment, as noted previously, is only one of many ways ideas are generated for education and training programs. In actual practice, a highly structured needs assessment may not be necessary or even useful in identifying program ideas, either in terms of time or money spent (Sork, 1990, 2000; Rossett, 1996). For example, when an educational program is mandated as part of federal or state regulations, identifying ideas for programs that address this mandate, through a formally structured mechanism, to see whether either the organization or the staff desires such a program is a waste of time. Likewise, if an organization installs a new computer system or other new equipment, whether staff members like it or not, they must become knowledgeable about this system in order to keep their jobs.

This chapter addresses first what planners are looking for in this phase of the planning process. This discussion is followed by a description of the most often used sources from which program ideas and needs are derived and the multiple techniques for identifying these ideas and needs. These techniques are appropriate for all forms of generating program ideas, from informal to highly structured. Examined next are reasons why program planners choose to conduct highly structured needs assessments, and one model for doing this process is discussed. An exploration of contextual issues in identifying program ideas and needs is discussed next. The chapter concludes with a brief overview of what to do with these ideas and needs once they are identified, a topic covered in more detail in Chapter Seven.

## Knowing What You Want to Accomplish

A number of concepts or descriptors have been used to define what program planners are looking for in generating ideas for education and training programs—educational needs, performance problems, new opportunities, changing conditions, areas for improvement, data-driven practice, societal issues, customer demands, resource availability, and images of ideal practice (Kaufman, Rojas, and Mayer, 1993; Gupta, 1999; Rossett, 1998; Dick, Carey, and Carey, 2001). No matter what term is used, program planners are seeking to respond to what they and the people, organizations, and/or communities they work with perceive as important topics, skills, and belief or value systems adults should examine and/or know more about.

The term *educational need* is by far the most common descriptor in the literature and rhetoric of practice as the focal point for identifying ideas for education and training programs. An educational need is most often defined as a discrepancy or gap between what presently is and what should be (Rothwell and Cookson, 1997; Kaufman, Rojas, and Mayer, 1993; Kaufman and Stone, 1983; Milano with Ullius, 1998; Birkenholz, 1999; Leigh, Watkins, Platt, and Kaufman, 2000; Dick, Carey, and Carey, 2001). This "what should be" is described in a number of ways—as desired results, future states or conditions, changes in performance, or expected outcomes. The discrepancy or gap can appear in many forms. For example, an unemployed individual may enroll in a class on job-seeking skills because he wants to get another job yet cannot seem to find one. An organization might offer "outplacement" seminars for employees being laid off in hopes that the seminars can help these employees learn to sell themselves elsewhere. Or a community or adult education program believes a job-skills training program should be developed to address the high rate of unemployment in the community. In each case, an individual, an organization, or the community recognizes a gap in knowledge and skills.

Although defining educational needs as gaps is often used and can be helpful in identifying ideas for education and training programs, it can also be limiting. This limitation stems primarily from the negative connotation inherent in seeing "need" as a discrepancy or gap—the perception that because there is a need, something is missing or *wrong* with a person, an organization, or society and has to be *fixed*. For example, the implementation of efficiency management programs (which are mandated by senior management) is sometimes interpreted by staff members and customers as an administrative statement that services and/or products are less than acceptable. Only with this new training will staff members perform in ways that are truly oriented to efficient products and service. If staff members believe they are already performing at high efficiency levels, they may resent both the implication that their operations are not up to standard and the intrusion on the successful way they are currently doing business. Likewise, previously satisfied clients may be frustrated that staff members are not as available as they were before (because they always seem to be in training sessions) and that procedures they liked and trusted are changing. Clients may also fear that their costs will escalate because of this new way of doing business.

Responding to needs as a way to justify program planning also implies that developing education and training programs is primarily a *reactive* versus a *proactive* process; the trainer or educator may be viewed as the person asked to put out organizational or community fires rather than one who proactively initiates innovative changes. For example, colleges and universities and community organizations often sponsor educational programs on gay and lesbian rights as a response to students' and community members' fears rather than proactively using the educational process to assist in changing people's negative stereotypes about differences in sexual orientation.

In addition, developing programs on identified educational needs of learners, organizations, or communities may have little to do with programs being successful (Sork and Caffarella, 1989; Sork, 2000). For example, opportunities for good programs might just present themselves. Perhaps a well-known content expert is in town—one who is recognized as an excellent, on-target presenter with cutting-edge material—and all you have to pay is a speaker's fee. An organization has new facilities (such as a new conference center) that the board expects to be used. Program ideas just "feel right," based on a hunch, a chance conversation with friends or colleagues, or recent experiences.

To further complicate the planning process, individual, organization, and/or community ideas for what is needed are not always in sync. This lack of agreement comes from many sources, such as practical arguments for and against proposed changes, strong disparities in beliefs and values, as well as ethnic and cultural differences.

Organizational ideas and needs, for example, which often drive education and training programs, are frequently at odds with what individuals in the organizations believe they need or perhaps want to know more about. Top-level administrators of a family services division, for example, may decide that a more efficient client reporting system for children in foster care is desirable in order to meet recent funding cuts. There are many among the staff members who believe this new system does not allow for critical information to be recorded, which in turn will get in the way of them providing helpful services to children and families. There are also staff members who see this budget cutting as racially motivated, as most of the department's clientele are people of color. These staff members are very vocal in not wanting any part of the training or the proposed changes. In addition, some staff members who are not opposed to this change do not see any need for formal training because the form is so simple to complete.

External groups are also strong voices in opposing specific programs being planned or currently offered by organizations and community groups. This opposition frequently comes in the form of specific changes or programs they request, or in some cases demand, and through community or legislative action. For example, antiabortion groups may demand that Planned Parenthood programs not be allowed to continue educational activities that contain information on abortion. Instead they want staff to counsel young women only on certain options, such as adoption and raising the child themselves. On the other hand, other external groups believe providing information on all alternatives, including abortion, is critical. As demonstrated by this example, there is often an added dynamic to these messages sent by external groups, which are often contradictory and even diametrically opposed. Therefore, either overt or covert conflict often results, which can then create difficult questions and issues for planners. For example, can program planners realistically respond in a way that will satisfy all of the conflicting parties? If not, which group or groups should be listened to, and why? How do staff members respond to those groups whose ideas were rejected?

## Sources of Ideas for Education and Training Programs

Ideas for education and training programs surface in a number of ways, as described in the previous section—from identified needs to specific problems and opportunities. These ideas are gathered through informal to highly structured processes and stem from four primary sources: people, responsibilities and tasks of adult life, organizations, and communities and society in general. Examples of specific sources, drawn primarily from the work of Knowles (1980); Tracey (1992); Kaufman, Rojas, and Mayer (1993); and Pearce (1998) are given in Exhibit 6.1.

Often the first sign that education and training programs are warranted surfaces as a specific idea, need, problem, or opportunity from one of these four primary sources:

### People

▶ Adult literacy teachers comment to their supervisor that they are not receiving telephone messages in a timely fashion, and this communication problem is affecting relationships with their students.

▶ Program participants are very vocal about how difficult it is to register for programs and how unhelpful staff members are when answering questions.

### Responsibilities and Tasks of Adult Life

▶ Balancing work and family is problematic for a number of women and men, especially those who are committed to both their families and time-consuming careers.

▶ Coping effectively with life events (such as the illness of a parent, job changes, returning to school, parenting teenagers, retirement) is a major challenge for many adults.

---

**EXHIBIT 6.1**

## Sources of Ideas for Education and Training Programs

| Sources | Specific Examples |
|---|---|
| **People** | • Former, current, and/or potential participants<br>• Educators, staff developers, and trainers in other organizations<br>• Employers<br>• Colleagues<br>• Friends and family<br>• Content experts<br>• Consultants |
| **Responsibilities and tasks of adult life** | • Being a spouse or partner<br>• Being a parent<br>• Being a volunteer<br>• Being a friend<br>• Jobs and careers<br>• Living in a community<br>• Personal development<br>• Leisure activities<br>• Health and fitness<br>• Spiritual life |
| **Organizations** | • Changes in the mission of the organization<br>• Changes in policies, procedures, and/or structure<br>• New products or services<br>• Identified problems (for example, absenteeism, low employee morale)<br>• Government regulations<br>• Legislative mandates<br>• Recommendations from professional associations |
| **Communities and society** | • Identified problems at community, state, and national levels<br>• International issues and problems<br>• Changes in the political, economic, and/or social climates<br>• Social issues (for example, gay and lesbian rights, health care, workplace violence)<br>• Technological innovations |

### Organizations

▶ On an organization-wide basis, supervisors are having trouble outlining for their subordinates a new set of policies and procedures concerning benefits, overtime work, and sick leave.

▶ Community organizations that depend on volunteers are having a difficult time recruiting and maintaining volunteer staff for their programs.

**Communities and Society**

▶ Violence in schools and the community is a major issue.

▶ Issues related to diversity (for example, race, ethnicity, gender, sexual preference, social class) continue to surface on national and international levels.

At this point, the job of educator and trainer is to define the ideas in more depth. This process of problem clarification and analysis, which can be done in a number of ways, often occurs during the gathering, analyzing, and prioritizing of program ideas (also see Chapter Seven).

# Generating New Program Ideas

Ideas for education and training activities are identified in a number of ways, as discussed earlier in this chapter, and as illustrated by the following scenarios:

### New Ideas from a Conference

Matt, a staff member in the College of Continuing Education, attended a teleconference called "Gender Issues and Leadership Development." Because he believed the ideas presented would be very helpful to the administrative staff of his unit, he reviewed the materials he had received (including two suggested videos he had not previously seen). He then tried out the idea over lunch with three key staff members, including the associate dean for continuing education, and they were enthusiastic about the proposed program.

### Problems with Efficiency

Joyce, a training specialist for a large paper company, has been informed that the level of productivity on two pieces of newly installed equipment has been steadily declining, even though there was an initial production rise a month after the machines were fully operational. After closely examining the analysis of efficiency indexes (data on downtime, repairs, and waste, for example), she decides, in consultation with two of her line supervisors, to do a formal job analysis to get a better handle on the problem. Joyce forms an ad hoc task force to assist her.

### Needs Assessment

The director of legal education for a national organization has been asked to conduct a nationwide comprehensive needs assessment related to planning a program on sexual harassment in the court system. She convenes a committee of five people to assist her in planning and conducting this effort. The committee is charged with outlining the specific purposes for this assessment, what data collection and analysis methods will be used, and how and to whom the results will be reported and used.

### *Social Action*

Consortiums of groups opposed to the International Monetary Fund (IMF) are working together to stage protests at different meeting sites. They are committed to making these demonstrations a worldwide social activist movement. Numerous educational programs for protesters are being planned as part of these activities. Program ideas have come from a variety of sources, including experienced social activists, observations from earlier rallies, conversations with demonstrators, responses to questions asked on their websites, and leaders of the movement.

These four scenarios illustrate the broad range of ways to collect ideas for programs, from observations based on personal experiences to more highly structured comprehensive needs assessments. Key techniques used by program planners to get a sense of what potential program participants might want or have to know are described in the next section.

## Key Techniques

Ten of the most widely used techniques for generating ideas and needs for education and training programs are given in Exhibit 6.2. A description of each technique is provided, along with basic operational guidelines.

Many of these same techniques are also used to collect data for instructional and program evaluations (see Chapters Nine and Twelve). In addition, the actual data collected about program ideas and needs can be, where appropriate, all or parts of the database for discerning the context (see Chapter Four), both program and instructional evaluation (see Chapters Nine and Twelve), and formulating learning-transfer plans (see Chapter Nine).

In addition to the techniques described in Exhibit 6.2, there are numerous other methods for eliciting program ideas. Some of these other methods, such as social network and trend analysis, are quite technical in nature and are primarily used by the corporate sector and selected government agencies (Witkin and Altschuld, 1995; Scott, 2000). Other techniques, such as reviewing prepackaged education and training programs and bringing back ideas from various conferences and trade shows, are employed by a variety of organizations. Especially helpful resources that include more in-depth descriptions of techniques for generating program ideas and needs

**EXHIBIT 6.2**

# Techniques for Generating Ideas for Education and Training Programs

| Technique | Description | Operational Guidelines |
|---|---|---|
| **Paper and computer-based questionnaires and surveys** | Gathering opinions, attitudes, preferences, and perceptions by means of print or electronic questionnaires (such as climate and attitude surveys, questionnaire on current practices). | Should pretest and revise the questions and format unless the questionnaire's reliability and validity are reported at acceptable levels and appropriate for the population being tested. Can use a variety of question formats (open-ended, ranking, checklists, and forced choice, for example), and can be administered through the mail, given to individuals or groups to complete, or delivered by electronic means (for example, an attachment to an email, Web documents). |
| **Observations** | Watching people doing actual or simulated tasks and activities. Individuals and/or groups of people are observed. | Can use observations that are open-ended or structured (with specific variables to investigate). Examples of specific types of observations include time–motion studies, task listings, behavioral frequency counts, the recording of critical activities or events, and unstructured observations. |
| **Interviews** | Conversing with people individually or in groups, in person, by phone, and online. | Can use interviews that are open-ended, non-directed, or formally structured (with specific questions to ask). Should pretest and review interview questions unless they have been successfully used before with a similar population. Interview respondents can be chosen randomly, consist of a convenience sample, and/or be key informants (people who are highly respected and knowledgeable about the areas being addressed). |
| **Group sessions and community forums** | Identifying and analyzing ideas, problems, and issues. Start with an idea, problem, or issue known to be of concern to those in the group. | Use one or more group facilitating techniques such as brainstorming, nominal group techniques, focus groups, consensus ranking, large and small group (or a combination of the two) facilitated discussions. Ensure there are competent group facilitators to lead the process and group members who are both knowledgeable and willing to participate. |
| **Job and task analysis** | Collecting, tabulating, grouping, analyzing, interpreting, and reporting on the duties, tasks, and activities that make up a job. Tasks may be cognitive and/or skill-based. | Be sure the analysis is of a current job and performance. Provide for data collection from all knowledgeable parties (for example, job incumbents, supervisors, managers, human resource personnel, volunteers, and/or clients and customers). Use a variety of techniques to collect data, such as questionnaires, task checklists, individual and group interviews, observations, a jury of experts, work records, and analysis of relevant technical publications. |

| Technique | Description | Operational Guidelines |
|---|---|---|
| **Tests** | Using paper-and-pencil or computer-based tests to measure a person's knowledge, skill, problem-finding and -solving capabilities, and/or attitudes/values. | Know what the test measures (knowledge, skills, problem finding and solving, attitudes, and values) and use it as a diagnostic tool for only those areas. Choose a specific test carefully. Be sure that what the test measures is relevant and important to the particular situation. (For example, do not use a test for knowledge if you are really interested in a hands-on skill.) Make sure the test is both reliable and valid. |
| **Information from printed and computer-generated materials** | A variety of forms of these materials exists: strategic planning reports, websites, policies and procedures manuals, performance evaluations, minutes of meetings, employee records, job efficiency indexes, monthly and annual reports, research and evaluation studies, curriculum reviews, statements of professional standards and competencies, books, professional and trade journals, legislation, and contents of file drawers. | Maintain up-to-date, active computer and/or print files that pertain to your current and future educational activities. Materials on past programs may be useful, but these materials should be culled on a regular cycle. |
| **Performance and product reviews** | Review of specific skills, procedures, and/or tangible items that potential participants are currently doing or have produced. | Choose carefully what to review to ensure the performace and/or product is relevant to what needs to be analyzed. Determine what tool will be used in the review process (for example, checklists, expert judgment, rating scales). |
| **Social indicators** | Variables representing important characteristics of a group or social situation that are kept over a number of years by government, education, and social service organizations. These data, usually quantitative in nature, describe such areas as level of education, economic status, and demographic information. | Choose carefully the sources to ensure the data are up-to-date and accurate. Determine whether these data are pertinent to the target audience or local situation. |
| **Conversations with colleagues, friends, family, and acquaintances** | Talking informally with people about ideas for educational programs. These conversations take place over coffee, at lunch, in the hallways, in meetings, at professional conferences, and so on. | Record ideas in print and/or computer-based files for current and future reference. Use a variety of ways to check out these ideas (for example, check them once a month, make a "tickler" file). |

are contained in materials by Zemke and Kramlinger (1982); Tracey (1992); Witkin and Altschuld (1995); Rossett (1987, 1998); Lee and Owens (2000); and Piskurich (2000).

No one technique for generating ideas and needs for programs is better than another. Each technique has its own strengths and weaknesses, depending on the context and the data required. How, then, do program planners determine which technique or combination of techniques is best for their situation? The following six criteria, extracted primarily from the work of Newstrom and Lilyquist (1979) and Witkin and Altschuld (1995), are helpful to those selecting techniques:

- Consider characteristics of the target group(s) for the potential program(s).

- Determine how much involvement is reasonable in collecting data from potential respondents.

- Estimate time, cost, and other constraints.

- Ascertain type and depth of data required.

- Consider ability of planning staff members to use the technique(s).

- Use, where appropriate, a combination of techniques that yield different kinds of data.

Observations, for example, normally require a low level of involvement by those being observed, while interviews and group sessions require a higher level of involvement. Costs and time requirements for well-designed questionnaires and job analyses are usually high; in contrast, costs and time requirements for conversations with colleagues and friends, and for reviewing print and computer-based materials are generally low or moderate.

One additional factor to consider in selecting techniques for generating ideas and needs is the nature of the paid or volunteer work. Some techniques are better suited for particular kinds of job categories than others, as shown in Exhibit 6.3.

This evaluation of the appropriateness of various techniques for particular job types is not ironclad, but generally reflects the experience of practitioners.

The techniques just described in this section for generating program ideas and needs, as noted earlier in the chapter, are appropriate for all forms of identifying program ideas, ranging from highly structured to informal ways. Explored next are reasons why program planners choose to conduct highly structured needs assessments; included is one model for carrying out this process.

**EXHIBIT 6.3**

**Appropriateness of Techniques for Selected Job Classifications**

| Techniques | Job Classifications | | | |
|---|---|---|---|---|
| | Manual | Technical | Clerical | Professional |
| Observations | ✓ | ✓ | ✓ | |
| Written surveys and questionnaires | | | | ✓ |
| Group sessions | | | ✓ | ✓ |
| Job and task analysis | ✓ | ✓ | ✓ | |
| Tests | | | ✓ | ✓ |
| Print and computer-based materials | | ✓ | ✓ | |
| Conversations | ✓ | ✓ | ✓ | ✓ |
| Performance and product reviews | ✓ | ✓ | ✓ | ✓ |

# Conducting a Highly Structured Needs Assessment

A highly structured needs assessment is defined as a systematic way, usually involving a rather lengthy process and based on formal needs assessment models or analyses for identifying education and training problems, needs, issues, and the like. The focus of the assessment is not to find solutions for specific problems but to clarify and define the problems. Conducting a highly structured needs assessment, as noted earlier, is one of many ways that ideas and needs are identified for education and training programs. Although programmers often do not use them, nor are they a necessity, the myth still prevails that conducting this form of needs assessment is one of the major components of the program planning process. As Pearce (1998) has observed: "Much to the dismay of authors extolling the many virtues of [highly structured] needs assessment, programmers are not exhibiting poor professional judgment if they choose not to use them. Many highly successful programs have no needs assessment component" (p. 267), let alone ones that are highly structured in nature.

Because conducting a highly structured needs assessment is not the way many planners identify ideas and issues, how do planners decide when using this way of generating program ideas is appropriate? Although there is no single definitive method to determine whether a highly structured needs assessment is warranted, there are some general guidelines that planners consider when making this decision:

▶ When little is known about an idea, issue, or problem and more depth analysis is justified, because planners and other stakeholders deem the idea worthwhile and important.

▶ When more in-depth knowledge is required about the characteristics of the target audience and their perceptions about the idea, issue, or problem (for example, who is really interested in this idea? Who would be interested in planning an education or training program based on this idea? What does this idea mean to them?).

▶ When the expected results of responding to the idea, problem, or issue require major in-depth changes in people, organizations, or communities.

In addition, Pearce (1998), has provided a useful four-stage process for thinking about whether this form of needs assessment is warranted. The process begins with voicing program ideas, and then moves to doing an initial assessment. Planners' reasons for planning the program are then considered, followed by asking whether a more in-depth structured needs assessment is necessary. Pearce provides as part of this fourth stage focused questions that planners can ask themselves as they complete this stage.

In addition, there are three specific programming situations that stand out as ones that usually necessitate and in some cases even mandate a highly structured needs assessment. First, many funding agencies, both governmental and private, require that a highly structured needs assessment be completed as part of the justification for why a grant should be funded. Second, planners may choose to use a highly structured needs assessment in tandem with a marketing thrust to provide needed visibility for a new, and often risky, program prior to it formally being planned. Finally, conducting a highly structured needs assessment may be a way planners can contend with power issues that arise (see Chapter Four). For example, through using this process planners can empower those who are disenfranchised by asking them to be members of a needs assessment planning committee, and by making sure they are a part of the respondent group. Giving these groups a legitimate vehicle for expressing their opinions and needs can be a useful way to ensure their insights have a chance of being heard.

In thinking through how to plan and conduct a highly structured needs assessment, it is important to remember that there is no single accepted process. Rather, a number of models or descriptions of procedures have been developed (Tracey, 1992; Caffarella, 1994; Witkin and Altschuld, 1995; Kemp, Morrison, and Ross, 1996; Kaufman, Rojas, and Mayer, 1993; Pearce, 1998; Gupta, 1999). A composite description of how to design a highly structured needs assessment, consisting of 11 elements, is outlined in Exhibit 6.4. For each element, specific examples of how to carry out each step for an organization-wide needs assessment are presented.

Although a highly structured needs assessment may occur in logical order or in a step-by-step fashion, often, as with the Interactive Model of Program Planning, the various elements overlap, need to be revisited, or

**EXHIBIT 6.4**

# Elements of a Formally Structured Needs Assessment

| Elements | Examples |
|---|---|

*Decide to conduct needs assessment*

➤ Make a conscious decision to complete a needs assessment with a commitment to planning.

 ◆ The Division of Continuing Medical Education, as part of the requirements for three major grant proposals, conducts a systematic statewide needs assessment of physicians in a variety of settings.

*Identify staff and develop management plan*

➤ Identify individuals to be involved in planning and overseeing the needs assessment, and develop a management plan.

 ◆ A steering committee of six people is appointed, composed of three members of the Continuing Medical Education (CME) staff, a medical school faculty member, the assistant dean of the medical school, and an outside consultant. One of the CME staff is appointed as the project manager.

*Determine context, purpose, and objectives*

➤ Develop context, purpose, and specific objectives for the needs assessment (to ensure that it answers the questions one really wants to know).

 ◆ The political and economic climate of the state, current trends in health care, and changes in the delivery of medicine constitute important contextual factors. The purpose for the needs assessment is to fulfill grant requirements for the proposals CME staff are preparing. With this context and purpose in mind the steering committee focuses the needs assessment on the following questions: (1) What are the major issues, problems, and opportunities that physicians face in their practice? and (2) In three years, how might these identified areas change, based on future forecasts and trends?

*Determine logistics*

➤ Lay out the target dates, time lines, budget, and staff.

 ◆ The steering committee determines that it has to complete the needs assessment in six months. Two members of the CME staff and an outside consultant are named as staff for the project, and $20,000 is allocated for expenses.

*Choose respondents*

➤ Choose the specific individuals and/or groups to be the respondents for the needs assessment.

 ◆ Two different sample groups are chosen through two sampling procedures: (1) a stratified random sample of all physicians who are employed full-time, with this sample weighted for rural respondents; and (2) a nomination process of key opinion leaders within the physician community.

*Select techniques*

➤ Determine data collection techniques.

 ◆ The techniques chosen for data collection include a written survey, focus groups with the key opinion leaders, and a review of printed and computer-based materials and documents.

*(Continued)*

**EXHIBIT 6.4**

# Elements of a Formally Structured Needs Assessment (*Continued*)

| Elements | Examples |
| --- | --- |

### Collect data

➢ Ensure data are collected in an appropriate and timely manner.

◆ The survey is developed in consultation with the steering committee, with the outside consultant taking the lead, and administered by staff members from the CME. These same staff members, plus four other trained facilitators, conduct the focus groups with the nominated opinion leaders. Steering committee members review selected print and computer-based materials.

### Analyze data

➢ Breakdown collected information to determine: (a) the basic findings in terms of quantitative (numerical) and qualitative descriptions, (b) points of agreement and disagreement, and (c) agreed-upon findings and conclusions concerning identified needs and ideas.

◆ An analysis of the data that includes an in-depth description of each identified major problem, issue, and opportunity is completed by staff members from the Division of Continuing Medical Education, in consultation with the consultant. The steering committee then reviews and critiques this analysis. Changes are made based on group consensus, in consultation with the outside consultant.

### Sort and prioritize needs

➢ Sort and prioritize each of the identified needs and indicate (a) which needs should be responded to first, second, and so on, and (b) needs for which alternative interventions are more appropriate (for example, changes in the reward system, installation of needed equipment, changes in organizational structure).

◆ The steering committee puts aside those "need descriptions" that in their judgment call for other interventions. Using a priority rating instrument followed by group discussions, they arrive at a consensus of what needs should receive priority rankings for each of the three grant proposals (see Chapter Seven).

### Communicate results

➢ Distribute the results of the needs assessment to appropriate individuals and groups within and external to the organization.

◆ A full report of the needs assessment process, findings, and conclusions is submitted to the Division of Continuing Education and the dean of the medical school. This report includes how the data are being used in writing the three grants. After the report has been approved by the dean and dean's council, the director of the Division of Continuing Medical Education, and the CME advisory council, an executive summary of the report, in the form of an informational brochure, is given to all of the key opinion leaders who took part in the study. In addition, a journalistic report on the results of the needs assessment is placed in each of the major newsletters of the different state-level physician associations.

have already been addressed through other planning activities. For example, planners may already have made a conscious decision to conduct a formally structured needs assessment as part of an initial overall planning session and may also have appointed an ad hoc task force at that time. In addition, even as data are being collected, the process may have to be revised, as the initial findings may not be realistic due to contextual factors or budgetary concerns.

One of the most important outcomes of a highly structured needs assessment may be a commitment by those involved in the process to ensure that the ideas from the needs assessment are actually used in the program planning process. According to Bradley, Kallick, and Regan (1991), "This [statement] may seem self-evident, but we would be wealthy if we had one dollar for every [highly structured] needs-assessment process that was undertaken and the data not used. Don't raise false hopes in those who contribute to [this form of] needs assessment" (p. 168). Ensuring this use of the data for planning means making sure at the outset that those who have the authority to implement the findings of such assessments are willing to listen to the voices of those who respond, and that they will actually implement programs based on these findings. One helpful way to let respondents know that they have been heard is to inform them (through newsletters, mail, meetings, follow-up cards, and so on) how the results have been translated into upcoming programs and why some of the ideas have not yet been or will not be implemented.

Whether identifying ideas and needs for education and training programs is a highly structured, less structured, or informal process, program planners are not immune from the context in which they operate. Rather, contextual factors may end up driving the process.

## Contextual Issues in Identifying Program Ideas

Often people, organizational, and wider environmental factors (see Chapter Four) are interwoven with the process of identifying ideas and needs for programs, whatever form that process takes. The initial phase of an idea generating process to set new program directions for a community-based Hispanic cultural center is described in the following scenario to illustrate how these contextual variables can come into play.

### A Community Cultural Center

Manuel, the new director of the cultural center, and a group of volunteers were charged by the Board of Directors to collect ideas for new education and community action programs. The main purpose of completing this process was to assist the board in setting new directions for the center. He and his team of volunteers collected ideas from various sources, including groups who meet regularly at the center, Hispanic community leaders, and agencies in the community who primarily serve Hispanic families. From these sources a wide variety of suggestions, impressions, and opinions were gathered. Manuel's next steps in the process involved bringing these ideas back to the Board of Directors for their reactions, and gauging the wider communities' reactions to the ideas presented.

The Executive Committee of the board and many of the Hispanic community leaders that he interviewed impressed the importance of this second step upon him. These individuals conveyed to him that the center itself has often come under attack by the wider community for raising unpopular issues, such as school drop-out rates of Hispanic children and the underemployment of a large percentage of the Hispanic population. These attacks had often been instrumental in blocking any programs the center wanted to initiate. As Manuel was not a "local" and had only been on the job for three months, this past history was new information and a bit disconcerting to him, especially with his personal commitment to social action and change.

There was quite a bit of heated discussion by the board, as they were currently split on the direction the center should take. Although Manuel was aware of this split, he was under the impression he was hired because a majority of the board was committed to more community action programs, which was his forte and passion. In fact, more than half of the board was highly vocal at the board meeting against many of the ideas that were community action-oriented, and they appeared unwilling to entertain these ideas further. One person in particular, who continually spoke loud and clear about moving away from a community action focus, seemed to be using her position on the board to advance her own political career in the community.

In addition, a number of community leaders, neighborhood groups, and a local reporter were also in attendance at the board meeting. The resulting newspaper article, talk among local leaders, and neighborhood gossip created additional obstacles to moving the process of collecting ideas for education and community action projects forward. A number of letters to the editor also appeared in support or rejection of this possible change in direction of the center.

As demonstrated in this scenario, this idea generating process definitely has to be changed in order for it to go forward and result in any positive change for the center. In order for this change to happen, Manuel and key board members and leaders in the Hispanic community have to carefully analyze the major contextual factors currently influencing the process. A sampling of these factors include Manuel's lack of experience in this community and his own values and commitment to community action programs; who the key stakeholders are in this process; how to construct a workable decision-making process; who to build coalitions with around ideas judged to be worthwhile; and who has the political clout to make this process work for both the Hispanic and wider community. As noted in Chapter Four, using contextual knowledge is neither an easy nor "surefire" answer to ensuring the success of using these ideas to set new directions for the center. Rather, using this knowledge calls for a willingness by Manuel and others to address issues of power, to negotiate differences, and to confront ethical issues that have already and will continue to emerge.

## What to Do with Identified Program Ideas

There are no magic formulas, even when the idea origination process goes smoothly, for deciding which program ideas are the best, however they are generated. This lack of a formula is because often there are too many good ideas that "must" be addressed and/or problems that "must" be solved. Ideas for programs may contradict each other, be unclear, or be unrealistic in terms of time, staff expertise, and cost. So even with enormous amounts of data and/or long lists of good ideas, program planners must figure out ways to make decisions about what ideas and needs are important, affordable, necessary, and the like. This prioritizing process is normally an element in most highly structured models of needs assessments (see Exhibit 6.4), but also may need to be a part of less structured or informal processes. Developing an education or training program also may not be the best or even a viable way to respond to the ideas and problems that have been identified.

Therefore, program planners at this point have to translate the ideas that have been identified into clear statements of priorities for programs and set aside those for which an education or training program, in their judgment, is not warranted (see Chapter Seven). Planners often seek assistance with these decisions, both through official channels (such as program committees, advisory boards, and opinion leaders) and through more informal ways (such as running ideas past colleagues and learners and paying attention to the local press).

## Chapter Highlights

Identifying relevant ideas for education and training programs range from informal hallway conversations to comprehensive, highly structured needs assessments. These ideas take the form of educational needs, performance problems, new opportunities, client demands, images of ideal practice, and so on. Program ideas surface from a number of sources—people, responsibilities and tasks of adult life, organizations, and communities and society in general—and are generated in numerous ways. It is important to address the following tasks in identifying program ideas:

◆ Decide what sources to use in identifying ideas for education and training programs (for example, current or potential program participants, employers, organizational and community leaders, personal issues, government regulations and legislative mandates, community and societal problems).

◆ Generate ideas through a variety of techniques. Example of the most often used techniques include questionnaires, interviews, observations, group sessions, job analyses, review of print and computer-based materials, social indicators, and conversations with colleagues. Remain open to gathering program ideas using a wide variety of techniques that may not have been predetermined or even considered.

◆ Be aware that highly structured needs assessments are not the only way to identify ideas for education and training programs. In reality, this way of generating program ideas is not often used. Rather, less formal and informal ways are more often employed than highly structured processes.

◆ Ensure you can defend why a highly structured needs assessment is warranted, and choose and/or develop a model for conducting this assessment that is appropriate to your situation.

◆ Consider contextual issues that might affect how ideas for programs are generated.

◆ Understand that in most planning situations program planners cannot use all of the program ideas that have been identified, and therefore planners usually have to sort and prioritize these ideas.

This sorting and prioritizing of program ideas is described in the following chapter. In addition, the notion that education and training programs is not the only way to respond to these ideas is explored.

## Application Exercises

This chapter's Applications Exercises are designed to help you identify appropriate sources of ideas for education and training programs and select the best technique or techniques by which to solicit program ideas from those sources.

---

### EXERCISE 6.1

### Identifying Sources of Ideas for Education and Training Programs

1.  **Describe briefly an education or training program that you are currently planning or have recently planned.**

2.  **Outline what sources of ideas you are using or did use for the program you described above. Be as specific as possible in naming those sources (for example, names of individuals and groups; specific life problems and opportunities; political, economic, and/or social climate), and indicate where the sources are or can be located.**

    **People:**

    **Organizations:**

    **Responsibilities and tasks of adult life:**

    **Communities and society:**

3.  **Based on the material you outlined in response to the previous question, make a list of those sources you are using or did use first, second, and third. Are there any you did not or would not choose to use at this time?**

    **Sources you did use/are using first:**

    **Sources you did use/are using second:**

    **Sources you did use/are using third:**

    **Sources you did use/are not choosing to use at this time, and why not:**

---

## EXERCISE 6.2

### Generating Ideas for Education and Training Programs

1. Briefly describe an organization or group you currently work or have worked with, in either a paid or volunteer capacity:

2. Suggest different techniques this group or organization could or did use to generate ideas for specific education or training program and indicate why these might be or were useful:

3. Might there be or were there any contextual factors (people, organizational, or environmental factors) that might or did influence why certain techniques might be or were chosen?

4. Of those techniques you listed in response to the previous question, which ones do you prefer to use, and why?

# Chapter 7

# Sorting and Prioritizing Program Ideas

Christy has just been appointed the statewide director of staff development for the Cooperative Extension Service. She has been with Cooperative Extension for 12 years, eight of those years as a county agent and four as an extension specialist. Because the position has been vacant for six months, there is already a pile of requests for staff development activities sitting on her desk. In addition, her predecessor had conducted a statewide needs assessment, but none of the recommendations have yet been implemented. Christy decides she should get some programs up and running fast.

In reviewing all the program requests and the needs assessment data, she comes to two major conclusions: there are too many good program ideas to start up all at once, and some of the items appear to be problems that cannot be addressed by an educational program (for example, the problem of staff being repeatedly asked to take on too many assignments). After consultation with her staff, Christy puts aside those items for which an educational intervention is clearly not appropriate. She plans to talk with the assistant director about what alternative ways she should recommend to tackle those issues. Next, she decides to plan, with a quickly constructed ad hoc committee, a series of workshops on volunteer leadership development. She knows that this topic of improving volunteer leadership addresses one of the major goals of the statewide strategic plan, was cited as a major problem in the needs assessment report, and is viewed by county boards as a critical issue. In addition, Christy decides to respond to three of the many requests she has on her desk that seem amenable to an educational intervention. It just so happens that these three requests are from colleagues whom she knows she can count on to get people to the programs, and the programs deal with issues that the Extension Service needs to demonstrate to the county and federal government officials that they are doing something about.

As is seen in this scenario, identifying ideas for education and training programs is usually not enough. People involved with program planning also have to sort through these ideas to determine which of them make sense in terms of planning an education or training program, and which call for alternative interventions. Then, from the pool of ideas considered appropriate for educational activities, they decide which ideas should have priority in the planning process. These two tasks, sorting ideas into categories and prioritizing needs and ideas, are often not considered by program planners, at least not in any systematic way. Rather, some planners just assume they are supposed to do everything, while others may prioritize ideas and needs, but in a haphazard manner with little thought to interventions other than education and training programs. There have been some planners, primarily human resource development and performance improvement staff involved in workplace learning, who have moved from a training paradigm to focusing on performance problems and multiple solutions to those problems, with training and education programs being only one of many solutions (Fuller and Farrington, 1999).

Discussed first in this chapter are what constitutes priority ideas, and typical issues and problems that require solutions other than education and training programs. Described next are the processes of analyzing and sorting ideas, which include a description of three major factors used in making decisions about whether the ideas are appropriate for education and training programs or alternative interventions. Who is involved in the actual priority setting process, as well as two primary ways for determining program priorities, are then explored. The chapter concludes with an overview of the most often used alternative interventions and how these are selected and applied.

## Priority Ideas and Alternative Interventions

Planning education and training programs is not the only or necessarily the best way to respond to various ideas, needs, problems, and opportunities that have been identified. Therefore, program planners have to make decisions about whether education and training programs or alternative interventions are a more useful response (Laird, 1985; Rothwell and Kazanas, 1998; Witkin and Altschuld, 1995; Fuller and Farrington, 1999; Piskurich, 2000). In order to make decisions about whether educational programs or alternative interventions provide a more appropriate solution, planners have to be knowledgeable about what constitutes priority ideas and typical issues and problems that could require alternative interventions.

## Defining Priority Ideas

What constitutes priority ideas in the context of program planning? Priority ideas are often thought of as ones that are among the most important and/or the most feasible to address. Depending on the specific planning situation, however, other factors are considered, such as the number of people affected and availability of resources. As Sork (1982) states, "What is being done in determining priorities is to assign preferential ratings to [ideas and] needs which are in competition for available resources so that judgments can be made about how those resources will be allocated" (p. 1).

Which program ideas become priorities is also tied to the context within which the decisions are being made (see Chapter Four). For example, do those responsible for planning programs have the power to make decisions about priorities, or must all such decisions be cleared with someone higher up? Are planners expected to use a collaborative style of making decisions; and if so, is collaboration a genuine operational norm or one that senior staff just "parrot," with the real expectation being quick results or an ever-increasing number of program participants? Can the planners make decisions within the confines of their own organizations, or must they form decision-making networks with outside groups, like funding, regulatory agencies, or other outside agencies? Do the current economic, political, and/or social situations block or enhance ideas that may be viewed as priorities? Again, flexibility is the key, because the context for planning programs can change overnight. For example, major budget cuts or public infighting between and among the leadership of an organization could drastically change how decisions are made about future programs.

## Typical Issues and Problems

There are a number of issues and problems that require solutions, other than planning or conducting education or training programs, that often surface in identifying ideas and needs for programs. Some of these include:

- Lack of knowledge of the change process
- Low learner motivation
- Poor quality physical facilities
- Inadequate communications systems
- Lack of support for transfer-of-learning activities
- Reward and compensation systems that do not match expected changes in practice
- Organizational norms and expectations that are in conflict with the proposed ideas
- Political and other outside environmental pressures

A sample of these issues and problems are illustrated in the following scenarios.

### One Too Many Education and Training Programs

Staff members are literally moaning and groaning about yet another training program, the outcomes which will demand still more changes in their practices. They have been hit with too many expectations for altering their practice over the past two years, with little time to really understand the proposed changes, let alone actually use them. Although they are not directly talking with their supervisors, the hall and coffee break conversations make it clear that they are ready to rebel—they just will not even try to use any of the proposed ideas until the pace slows down.

There are two major underlying issues that relate to a problem of this nature: lack of knowledge of the change process by either program planners or other stakeholders, and lack of motivation by participants to change their practice as they feel overwhelmed by unrealistic expectations. Unless the major underlying problems are adequately addressed, there is little chance that this training program will foster long-term changes in practice.

### I Can't Hear and I'm Just Plain Uncomfortable

A group of senior citizens have been complaining for months that the installation of a new heat and air conditioning system has been troublesome because they cannot hear when volunteers come to the center to conduct learning activities. These activities range from discussion groups on local political issues to learning email so they can communicate with their grandchildren. They also are too cold or too hot much of the time because the new system has been difficult to regulate. This group has finally collectively said "no more," and they have refused to attend any more programs, no matter how much they want to learn about the topic being discussed, until these problems are solved.

The problem in this scenario is that although the ideas related to program content are addressed well, another need of the learners is not—poor physical facilities that interfere with their learning. Conducting education and training programs requires an environment that takes into account the physical needs of the participants. Older adults, as illustrated here, often require acoustical adjustments in learning environments, especially when changes are made in which extra background noise is added. In addition, many are also sensitive to the heat and cold, and if they are placed in uncomfortable physical facilities for too long, they will not return no matter how interested they are in the programs provided.

### I Just Can't Remember

Joan and Paul, two faculty members who participated in a faculty development program on how to develop PowerPoint presentations, were sharing with each other their frustrations on trying to remember all of the helpful hints the instructor gave on how to put together a good presentation. They remember her talking about font size, how to import graphics, and how to change the background colors; but they do not have a clue how to go about doing these things. They are in a time crunch to get a presentation ready for a national meeting and have decided they will have to go back to their old presentation style once again, which they really do not want to do.

The issue in this scenario is that even though the original educational program fit Joan and Paul's needs, little thought was given to the transferability of this material into practice. It is not atypical that adults have difficulty remembering the details of new skills they are trying to acquire, especially when they are not using these skills on an everyday basis. This lack of learning transfer is also a problem that surfaces when ideas and needs are being generated for future programs.

What these three scenarios all have in common is that formal education and training programs, even ones that have already been completed, will not solve the problems and issues presented. Program planners have to look at alternative interventions and often need to rely, as discussed later in this chapter, on the assistance of others to find useful resolutions to these problems so they can move forward with any further educational programming.

## Analyzing and Sorting Program Ideas

Sorting and deciding whether to respond to ideas for education and training programs through education and training activities or alternative interventions may or may not be an easy task. Sometimes these decisions are clear-cut: the idea fits well in either the educational programming pile or the alternative interventions pile. Other ideas are not as easy to sort. For example, some ideas may not lend themselves to clearly defined ways of responding. For others, a combination of strategies, including education and training programs, may be the best way to go. In sorting through ideas, it is wise to err on the side of keeping ideas that are not easy to categorize in the educational pile.

As with other planning tasks, asking for assistance with this sorting process is usually a good strategy, especially when large numbers of ideas have been generated from diverse sources. This assistance, for example, could come from the same individuals or groups who are involved in actually determining which ideas for education and training programs should be given priority, or a combination of some of these individuals and/or groups with some new people. People who are important players in these processes include learners, colleagues, education and training committee members, external parties, and/or other stakeholders. Personnel who have experience in human resource management or human performance improvement are often especially helpful in this sorting process.

Three major factors, alone or in combination, are used to make judgments about whether an education or training program should be developed or an alternative intervention chosen: people, organizational and environmental factors (see Chapter Four), and cost (see Chapter Fourteen). The major question program planners ask in examining each of these factors is whether an education or training program can really address the problems, new opportunities, changing conditions, societal issues, and/or images of ideal practice that are presented. The *people factor* centers on the knowledge and skills of individuals and groups (Laird, 1985; Rossett, 1998). Is the content being proposed something people do not know or already know or can do, but either choose not to demonstrate or are blocked from demonstrating by other people? For example, an office assistant may be knowledgeable about how to respond in a positive manner to phone inquiries, but fails to use that knowledge because she does not want to be bothered, especially when calls interrupt other tasks she considers to be more important. Another office assistant may want to respond in a helpful way to those who call for information, but has been told repeatedly by his supervisor that she believes he is spending far too much of his time on the phone, answering what she considers to be unimportant questions. The problem in these cases is not that the office assistants need more information or skill development; they need another intervention so that they and/or their supervisors can change their actions and responses. Examining the people factor is often the most puzzling, and yet critical factor.

The *organizational* and *environmental factors* focus on conditions external to the person (Witkin and Altschuld, 1995; Rothwell and Kazanas, 1998). Are the issues identified readily amendable through education and training programs, or do other interventions constitute a more realistic response? Examples of types of environmental or situational conditions that may need to be altered in lieu of offering an educational program include communication systems, personnel practices, physical environments, organizational norms and expectations, and the nature of the task or job itself. For example, an educational program on how to live with a continually stressful work situation might be much less effective in assisting staff to cope than making changes in the work environment itself (for example, ensuring adequate physical facilities and equipment and/or altering the unwritten work ethic from 60 or 70 hours a week to 40 or 50 hours). Other examples and further discussion of these organizational and environmental factors were discussed in the previous section.

The third factor for consideration is the *cost factor*, which includes time, money, and staff. Are the costs of a proposed education or training program more than the benefits it provides? If the costs are higher, unless there are other compelling reasons to conduct education and training programs, it is time to consider other alternatives to get at the same issue or idea (Kaufman, Rojas, and Mayer, 1993; Witkin and Altschuld, 1995). One way to assess these issues is through a cost-benefit analysis, which is discussed more fully in Chapter Fourteen.

Once the ideas have been analyzed and sorted, the next step for planners is to prioritize those ideas appropriate for education and training programs. Rarely can personnel responsible for planning these programs design activities for *all* of the ideas identified. Therefore, program planners must have a system for choosing those who determine which ideas take priority in the planning of actual activities and events, and they must be able to use alternative systematic processes for determining these priorities.

## Selecting People for the Prioritizing Process

People who are involved in the actual priority-setting process, as noted in the previous section, may be the same individuals and/or groups who did the analyzing and sorting, or a combination of some of these people with additional individuals and/or groups. Yet, still at this stage, some planners often ignore the importance of having others be a part of this decision-making process. Rather, they tend to think that the most urgent issues and ideas will be obvious to everyone involved (and thus will be handled first). Even worse, some program planners simply accept the fact that part of the program planning business is being "overwhelmed," and they use that as an excuse for not being responsive to why ideas and needs have or have not been translated into education and training activities.

Depending on the planning context, any combination of the following people may be involved in setting program priorities:

▶ Past, current, and potential participants

▶ Content experts

▶ Paid or volunteer staff members

▶ Supervisors of potential participants

▶ Key management and administrative personnel

▶ Other colleagues from different divisions of the organization

▶ Education committee and board members

▶ Representatives of funding and/or regulatory bodies

▶ Community leaders

▶ Consultants

▶ Legislative leaders

▶ Other stakeholders or interested parties (for example, social agencies and recreational organizations)

Those responsible for planning programs may consult with these people on an individual basis and/or involve them in group discussions. Group meetings may be of an informal nature, or they may be formally organized committees (such as formally constituted education or training committees), as shown in the following scenario.

### Collecting and Prioritizing Ideas for Training

John, the director of management development, is planning a program for entry-level managers. He first talks informally with selected key managers in the organization. The focus of their conversations centers on an executive summary of a report that outlines the ideas identified for the entry-level management program. These ideas were generated through a structured needs assessment. From these interactions he makes notes on the ideas these key managers believe to be the most important to consider in developing new programs. He then asks a group of entry-level managers and their supervisors to form an ad hoc committee to review this report and also prioritize these ideas and problems. John's next step is to have the training committee (two members who were part of the original needs assessment process), using the priorities generated by both key management personnel and the ad hoc committee, make the final recommendations on what specific programs will be offered for entry-level managers.

In selecting ideas for program development, planners should bear in mind that the more systematic the process, the greater likelihood that the resulting education and training activities will reflect the most important and feasible ideas. Examples of systematic processes for determining program priorities are given in the next section.

## Systematic Processes for Determining Priorities

There are two primary systematic approaches for prioritizing ideas for education and training programs: quantitative and qualitative. Quantitative methods are based on numerical measures and usually involve some sort of rating charts. Qualitative strategies are more descriptive in nature, with choices being made primarily through open-ended group and/or one-on-one meetings. Planners can choose to use both of these approaches in a priority setting process or just one, depending on the nature of the ideas and needs identified, the time frame allotted to the process, and/or the preferences of the decision-making group. Each approach to priority setting is described later in this section. Whatever approach is used, a key element of the priority setting process is to select or develop criteria.

### Selecting and Developing Criteria

Criteria provide the basis on which priorities are judged, and also serve as the justification for the eventual choices. Kaufman, Rojas, and Mayer (1993); Witkin and Altschuld (1995); Mitchell (1998); and Sork (1998) have offered a variety of criteria for making priority judgments. These criteria generally fall under two major categories: those dealing with importance and those dealing with feasibility (Sork and Fielding, 1987; Sork, 1998). An overall judgment about an idea or need can be made only by its relative importance or feasibility, or on both importance and feasibility. Under each major category, examples of criteria that fit that category are given in Exhibit 7.1.

These sample criteria are only a partial set of guidelines on which decisions about priorities are made. Not all of the criteria under each category may be useful, and other criteria not outlined might be more appropriate, depending on the planning context. As Sork (1998) has observed: "No single set of criteria is suitable for all adult education settings. . . . It is likely that most priority decisions are based on a few criteria considered important by decision makers" (p. 281).

### Quantitative Approach

An example of two quantitative approaches, one based on equally weighted ratings and a second on unequally rated weights, is described (Sork, 1982, 1998). These two processes can help planners, in a timely and organized manner, determine priorities among identified ideas and needs for programs. These priority rating charts, using numerical data, are especially helpful when priorities are determined by a number of individuals or groups. The charts can be completed individually and then the ratings compiled, or a group as a whole may complete them. The size and complexity of the chart depends on how many criteria have been chosen and whether

**EXHIBIT 7.1**

# Two Major Categories of Criteria with Examples and Descriptions

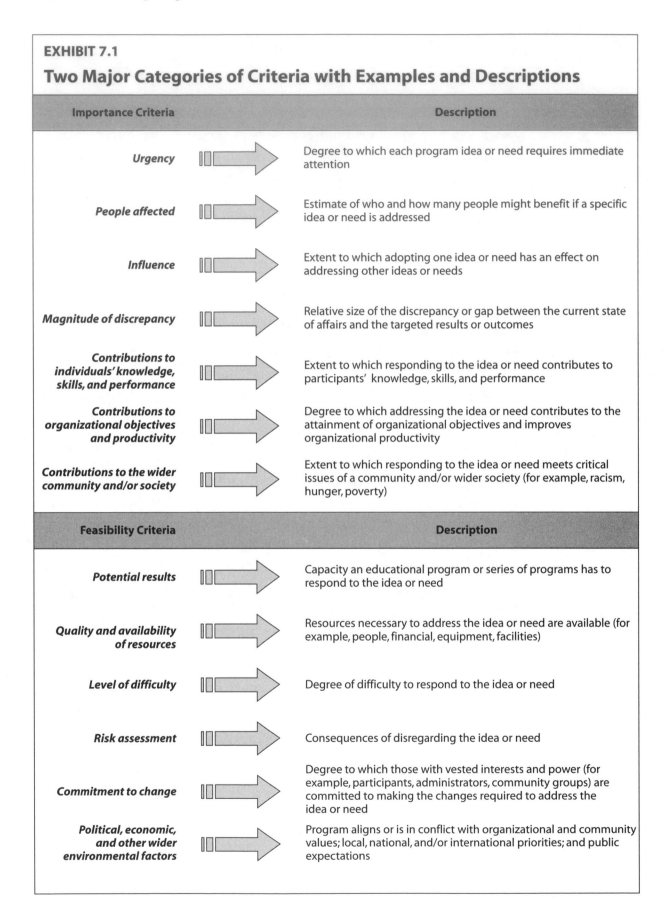

| Importance Criteria | Description |
|---|---|
| *Urgency* | Degree to which each program idea or need requires immediate attention |
| *People affected* | Estimate of who and how many people might benefit if a specific idea or need is addressed |
| *Influence* | Extent to which adopting one idea or need has an effect on addressing other ideas or needs |
| *Magnitude of discrepancy* | Relative size of the discrepancy or gap between the current state of affairs and the targeted results or outcomes |
| *Contributions to individuals' knowledge, skills, and performance* | Extent to which responding to the idea or need contributes to participants' knowledge, skills, and performance |
| *Contributions to organizational objectives and productivity* | Degree to which addressing the idea or need contributes to the attainment of organizational objectives and improves organizational productivity |
| *Contributions to the wider community and/or society* | Extent to which responding to the idea or need meets critical issues of a community and/or wider society (for example, racism, hunger, poverty) |

| Feasibility Criteria | Description |
|---|---|
| *Potential results* | Capacity an educational program or series of programs has to respond to the idea or need |
| *Quality and availability of resources* | Resources necessary to address the idea or need are available (for example, people, financial, equipment, facilities) |
| *Level of difficulty* | Degree of difficulty to respond to the idea or need |
| *Risk assessment* | Consequences of disregarding the idea or need |
| *Commitment to change* | Degree to which those with vested interests and power (for example, participants, administrators, community groups) are committed to making the changes required to address the idea or need |
| *Political, economic, and other wider environmental factors* | Program aligns or is in conflict with organizational and community values; local, national, and/or international priorities; and public expectations |

the criteria are rated equally or whether some criteria should have greater impact on the decision than others.

When applying criteria that are weighted equally, people are asked to give a ranking on each idea using a range of 10 (highest) to 1 (lowest). The rankings are then totaled, and the idea receiving the highest number is considered the top priority. An example of this system, related to ideas for a train-the-trainer program, is given in Exhibit 7.2. The top priority in this example is "the ability to incorporate transfer of learning strategies," followed closely by "facilitation skills."

When the decision makers believe that some of the criteria should have more impact on the decision than others, weighting factors are assigned to each criterion. To carry out this task, assign the criteria weights, starting with criteria that should carry the most weight. Those criteria that carry the most weight are assigned the highest numbers, while those that carry the least are given the lowest. These numbers, on a scale of ten to one, are

---

**EXHIBIT 7.2**

## Sample Priority Rating Chart with Equally Weighted Criteria

| Items to Be Prioritized | Criteria | | | | | Total Score | Final Ranking* |
|---|---|---|---|---|---|---|---|
| | People Affected | Magnitude of Discrepancy | Potential Results | Resources | Commitment to Change | | |
| Knowledge of adults as learners | 6 | 5 | 8 | 7 | 7 | 33 | 4 (tie) |
| Instructional design skills | 6 | 6 | 6 | 8 | 7 | 33 | 4 (tie) |
| Facilitation skills | 8 | 8 | 9 | 9 | 7 | 41 | 2 |
| Ability to incorporate transfer of learning strategies | 10 | 9 | 8 | 7 | 8 | 42 | 1 |
| Ability to use a variety of instructional techniques | 7 | 6 | 7 | 8 | 7 | 35 | 3 |

*The final rankings are based on 1 being the highest priority and 4 being the lowest.*
*Adapted from Sork, T. J., 1998, p. 287.*

decided by those who are responsible for coordinating the prioritizing process.

An example of assigning a weight for each criterion is as follows:

*Importance Criteria*

> *People Affected: Weight = 3*
> *Magnitude of Discrepancy: Weight = 7*

*Feasibility Criteria*

> *Potential: Weight = 9*
> *Resources: Weight = 8*
> *Commitment of Change: Weight = 5*

When program planners use a priority system in which the criteria are not equally weighted, the process is more complex than when each criteria is equally weighted. A suggested way for completing this system, adapted from Sork (1982, 1998), is outlined:

1. For each criterion, assign an individual weight ranging from 10 (representing the highest priority) to 1 (representing the lowest priority).

2. Then for each item, assign a rank ranging from 10 (representing the highest priority) to 1 (representing the lowest priority).

3. Multiply the rankings by the weight for each item.

4. Add the weighted ranks for each idea (across the columns) and record the sum in the "Sum of Weighted Ranks" column.

5. Divide the sum of ranks by the number of criteria used in this rating process and record the result in the "Mean Weighted Rank" column.

6. Assign a final rank to each idea based on the "Mean Weighted Rank." The item that receives the highest score becomes the top priority (number one), with each descending numerical score representing the high to low continuum of ideas identified.

An example of a completed chart using the weighted system is pictured in Exhibit 7.3.

As a result of the weighted system, the top priority is "Facilitation Skills," with "Ability to Incorporate Transfer of Learning Skills" as a close second. These weighted results reversed the top two choices of the equally weighted chart that was pictured earlier in Exhibit 7.2 (page 143). The next three priority items remained the same. This result is not unusual as different priorities are often adopted when an unweighted versus a weighted priority ranking system is used, even when the criteria and items on that list are the same.

**EXHIBIT 7.3**

## Sample Priority Rating Chart with Criteria Weighted Differently

| Items to Be Prioritized | Criteria | | | | | Sum of Weighted Ranks | Mean of Weighted Ranks | Final Ranking* |
|---|---|---|---|---|---|---|---|---|
| | People Affected | Magnitude of Discrepancy | Potential Results | Resources | Commitment to Change | | | |
| Weights for Each Criteria | *Weight = 3* | *Weight = 7* | *Weight = 9* | *Weight = 8* | *Weight = 5* | | | |
| | Rank/ Weighted Rank | Rank/ Weighted Rank | Rank/ Weighted Rank | Rank/ Weighted Rank | Rank/ Weighted Rank | | | |
| Knowledge of adults as learners | 6 / 18 | 5 / 35 | 8 / 72 | 7 / 56 | 7 / 35 | 216 | 43 | 4 (tie) |
| Instructional design skills | 6 / 18 | 6 / 42 | 6 / 54 | 8 / 64 | 7 / 35 | 213 | 43 | 4 (tie) |
| Facilitation skills | 8 / 24 | 8 / 56 | 9 / 81 | 9 / 72 | 7 / 35 | 268 | 54 | 1 |
| Ability to Incorporate transfer-of-learning strategies | 10 / 30 | 9 /56 | 8 / 72 | 7 / 56 | 8 / 40 | 254 | 51 | 2 |
| Ability to use a variety of instructional techniques | 7 / 21 | 6 / 42 | 7 / 63 | 8 / 64 | 7 / 35 | 225 | 45 | 3 |

*\* Final rankings are based on 1 as the top priority and 4 as the lowest.*
*Adapted from Sork, T. J., 1998, p. 287.*

## Qualitative Approach

Qualitative approaches to setting priorities are also used, as noted earlier, either in concert with a quantitative approach or by themselves. The central element of these types of approaches is that the priority-setting process is completed through in-depth group discussions and/or a series of one-on-one interactions. The criteria used in these deliberations are usually more fluid and open to the interpretation of the parties included in the dialogues, as demonstrated in the following scenario, than those that are quantitatively based.

### *Priority Setting Through Group Discussions*

Michael and his priority-setting group, in working through a set of highly controversial ideas and needs for a community action program, decide that giving numerical rankings to these ideas could cause more consternation among those who had suggested the ideas and the community at large if the numbers became public. In addition, the ideas all have merit in one way or another, and this group wants to give each idea its due through in-depth conversations among the members. The group members first discuss how they want to go about this prioritizing process. They decide that two or three group meetings are warranted, and that during these meetings the group will work in both small and whole group sessions.

To start this process they analyze each idea or need separately in small groups, with each group discussing an equal number of the ideas and needs presented. The small groups then report their analysis back to the whole group, which is followed by a discussion to clarify what is being presented. Members usually add other observations, which they believe are important to hear, after this clarification discussion. Once this analysis process has been completed, the whole group then brainstorms and discusses criteria that might work in choosing among the ideas and needs presented. Again, small groups review a set of ideas and needs, different than the ones they discussed earlier, based on the initial set of criteria (for example, people affected; influence; resources; risk assessment; and political, economic, and other wider community factors). Each group also revises or makes additions to these criteria as part of these small-group discussions. The small groups then report back to the whole group, and this process of small- and large-group interaction continues until clear criteria are agreed upon, as well as which ideas and needs have the greatest priority at this time.

Groups doing a qualitative prioritizing process may also want to include rating charts to assist them in their deliberations, but how items are rated is different than when using a quantitative approach. Rather than assigning numbers, word descriptors are used. These word descriptors are general in nature and usually open to a wide variety of interpretation by those completing the ratings. The completed rating charts serve as a starting point for discussions between and among members of priority setting groups.

Kaufman, Rojas, and Mayer (1993) have suggested one set of descriptors to use in qualitative rating systems:

- This need is very critical.
- This need is moderately critical.

- This need is *not* critical (therefore, ignore it).
- This is not a need. (p. 97)

  Another set of qualitative criteria for categorizing ideas and needs is:

- High/High (address in 30 days)
- High (address in three to six months)
- Medium (address in six months to a year)
- Low (address in one to two years)
- Not a need or idea (do not consider)

An example of a qualitative rating chart, again focused on the train-the-trainer program, is given in Exhibit 7.4. The results of this rating, as described previously, can then be discussed for points of agreement and disagreement, with the goal of consensus among members about what constitutes the priority ideas and needs.

---

**EXHIBIT 7.4**

## Sample Priority Rating Chart Using High/High, High, Medium, Low

| Items to Be Prioritized | Criteria | | | | | Total Score | Final Ranking* |
|---|---|---|---|---|---|---|---|
| | **People Affected** | **Magnitude of Discrepancy** | **Potential Results** | **Resources** | **Commitment to Change** | | |
| **Knowledge of adults as learners** | Medium | Medium | High | Medium | Medium | Medium | 3 |
| **Instructional design skills** | Medium | Medium | Medium | High | Medium | Medium | 3 |
| **Facilitation skills** | High | High | High/High | High | Medium | High | 2 |
| **Ability to incorporate transfer-of-learning strategies** | High/High | High/High | High | High/High | High | High/High | 1 |
| **Ability to use a variety of instructional techniques** | Medium | Medium | Medium | High | Medium | Medium | 3 |

*\* Final rankings are based on a 1 as high/high to 4 as low.*
*Adapted from Sork, T. J., 1998, p. 287.*

If just this example rating chart was used without discussion, the apparent priority ideas are "ability to incorporate transfer-of-learning strategies" and "facilitation skills." Yet, after deliberations between and among group members, there is a good chance that some of the original ratings will be altered, and therefore the program priorities will change.

# Alternative Interventions

After completing the prioritizing process for education and training programs it is important to return to that "other pile of ideas"—ideas and needs inappropriate for education and training programs. In examining this other pile, planners have to view alternative interventions as viable options to ideas originally suggested for educational programs. Examples of alternative interventions are shown in Exhibit 7.5. For some program planners, taking on the responsibility for addressing this second pile may require a new way of thinking, especially for people who work with organizations and groups in which developing formal education and training programs has always been the norm for responding to ideas and needs generated for education and training programs.

How the alternative intervention pile is handled depends on the role and function of the planning staff. Some planning personnel are responsible for determining alternative interventions and ensuring that they are used. These people usually have specialized training in such areas as organizational development, human resource development, and/or performance improvement. More often, however, program planners pass these ideas along to other units or groups, which then decide what should be done. This sharing of responsibility means, as stressed in Chapter Five, that people who plan education and training programs must have good people networks, know their organizations and communities, and have access to sources outside of their immediate situation. In addition, they require some basic knowledge of alternative interventions and how they are selected and used. This knowledge is helpful because they are often asked to define more specifically the ideas, needs, or problems, and what might be done about them.

## Frequently Used Interventions

A description of some of the most-often used alternative interventions to education and training programs is outlined in Exhibit 7.5 (Rossett, 1996; Rothwell and Kazanas, 1998; Langdon, Whiteside, and McKenna, 1999; Piskurich, 2000).

In considering what alternative interventions might be the most useful, planners often find it helpful to focus on who or toward what the intervention

**EXHIBIT 7.5**

# Alternative Interventions

| Intervention | Description | Examples |
| --- | --- | --- |
| *Job aids* | Information given in a variety of print or computer-based forms to provide learners quick references when a "need to know" arises | • Checklists<br>• Worksheets<br>• Fold-out cards<br>• Flowcharts<br>• Audio- or videotapes<br>• Memory joggers<br>• Booklets<br>• Index cards with notes |
| *Organizational development* | A systematically planned change effort for the purpose of developing and implementing action strategies for organizational improvements | • Team building<br>• Total quality management<br>• Third-party facilitation<br>• Organizational redesign<br>• Redesign of communication systems<br>• Changes in decision-making processes<br>• Building learning organizations<br>• Strategic and business planning |
| *Electronic support systems* | Electronic systems that provide assistance and coaching for computer-based tasks, work-related issues, and other life tasks | • Help desks<br>• Online assistance (ability to ask and receive responses online)<br>• One-on-one tutoring or coaching<br>• Expert systems<br>• Websites<br>• Chat rooms |
| *Changes in organizational environment, facilities, and/or tools* | Alterations in the conditions where the job or task is performed and/or the tools used to do the job or task | • Effective heating and cooling units<br>• Good air quality<br>• Renovated facilities<br>• New equipment<br>• Physical and cognitive ergonomics |
| *Redefining the job or task* | Changes in the content, activities, and/or responsibilities of a job or task | • Job enrichment<br>• Job enlargement<br>• Job rotation<br>• Performance standards altered |
| *Action research* | Research in which the major goal is improving practice | • Testing of new techniques or methods<br>• Examination of alternative strategies<br>• Exploration of specific tasks and activities<br>• Investigation of learner characteristics<br>• Analysis of the context of practice |
| *Feedback systems* | A process for providing written or oral critiques and/or commentaries to individuals and/or groups about specific tasks or activities being performed or completed | • Individual meetings<br>• Written materials<br>• 360° feedback<br>• Team meetings<br>• Quality circles<br>• Results from customer or client surveys |
| *Personnel practices* | Changes in the way people are recruited, screened, hired, trained, evaluated, and rewarded | • Recruitment and selection practices<br>• Staff education and training<br>• Performance standards<br>• Appraisal and evaluation systems<br>• Job transfer or terminations<br>• Flexible work hours<br>• Assessment centers |

is directed: individuals and/or groups, jobs or tasks, whole (or parts of) organizations, and/or communities. Examples of alternative interventions for each of these categories are in Exhibit 7.6.

The most frequently used alternatives to education and training programs are individually oriented or job- or task-specific. Job aids and electronic system support, for example, are standard items for many organizations and community groups. Examples of such aids are flowcharts on how to start or turn off a piece of equipment or lists of key contact people with their phone numbers and email addresses. There is also a widespread use of organizational processes and techniques, such as development activities or the building of learning organizations. For example, when organizations are presented with internal communications problems, they may look to redesign the communications system, rather than sponsor training programs for staff on how to communication more effectively.

---

**EXHIBIT 7.6**

# Examples of Alternative Interventions by Group

| Individual or Group Alternatives | Job- or Task-Specific Alternatives | Organizational Alternatives | Community-Based Alternatives |
|---|---|---|---|
| • Create job aids (for example, checklists, charts, manuals, reference aids).<br><br>• Provide electronic support systems (for example, online assistance, coaches or tutors, chat rooms).<br><br>• Encourage regular feedback sessions.<br><br>• Transfer or terminate the individual.<br><br>• Host team meetings.<br><br>• Change the reward system (for example, allow for individual choice of schedule, provide educational opportunities at no cost to the individual). | • Redefine the job.<br><br>• Encourage job rotation.<br><br>• Install new equipment.<br><br>• Change the environment in which the job is performed (for example, lighting, cooling, air quality).<br><br>• Change the performance standards.<br><br>• Communicate the performance standards differently.<br><br>• Eliminate the job. | • Improve the personnel system on an organization-wide basis.<br><br>• Conduct an action research project on the climate of the organization.<br><br>• Use an organizational development process to build trust levels among units in the organization.<br><br>• Change the organizational structure and/or patterns (such as who reports to whom within the organization). | • Provide electronic support systems (online assistance, in-person coaching and tutoring, Web pages).<br><br>• Encourage regular feedback sessions through individual and team meetings.<br><br>• Conduct an action research project on new action learning strategies.<br><br>• Redesign the communication and decision-making systems. |

## Selecting and Implementing Alternative Interventions

Although, as noted earlier, many program planners do not have the responsibility for selecting and implementing alternative interventions, it is helpful for them to know who is responsible for these tasks, comprehend how these processes work, and understand what role, if any, they do or should play. Having this knowledge can help planners have more success with the initial sorting process, have a better sense of who they need to talk with about possible alternative interventions, and give useful observations to those who have the responsibility for implementing these different responses.

As Langdon (1999) observes: "Intervention selection is no easy matter" (p. 24). A thorough discussion and analysis of the problem or issue is required, resulting in the identification of what specific changes are needed, and which intervention or interventions could best foster these changes. In this analysis phase, representatives of those most affected by the problem or issue are involved in the decision-making process, as are those who are most likely to implement the intervention (for example, supervisors, directors, content experts). Deciding on what interventions to use can become highly politically charged, depending on the nature of the issue or need. For example, if what is required is basic changes in the personnel system, these interventions may not be welcome by those who are responsible for developing policy and operating procedures for this system. Or, if what is called for is a change in response to a highly sensitive community issue, such as racism, those who have benefited from the current status quo may try to block any interventions, no matter how well conceived.

Implementing alternative interventions, similar to education and training programs, requires a well-developed "master plan" (Langdon, Whiteside, and McKenna, 1999). The more comprehensive and politically charged the problem and intervention strategies, the more important it becomes to ensure that effective communication systems are in place and that support bases are cultivated and nurtured. In order to do these two tasks, it is critical that the persons or groups responsible have a clear sense of the context of the target population in which they are working (see Chapters Four and Fourteen). These alternative interventions may be implemented one at a time or simultaneously. "Building credit with one intervention can earn you the right to plan and develop others" (Langdon, Whiteside, and McKenna, 1999, p. 31). One can also use this initial intervention to collect additional data for future interventions, including education and training programs.

## Chapter Highlights

Planning an education or training program may not be the only response, or even an appropriate response to some of the ideas and needs generated for programs; other interventions may be of more use in solving some of the problems and issues that surface. In addition, even for those ideas where conducting an education or training program makes sense, there are often more ideas than program planning staff can handle. Therefore, planning staff members have to decide which idea or ideas should be acted upon first, second, and so on. In this sorting, analyzing, and prioritizing process, it is important to address the following tasks:

◆ Be knowledgeable about how priority ideas are defined and typical issues and problems that call for inventions other than education and training programs.

◆ Analyze and sort the program ideas into two piles—those appropriate for educational activities and those that require alternative interventions.

◆ Select people who will do the actual prioritizing process. These may or may not be the same individuals who analyzed and sorted the original program ideas.

◆ Be well-informed about quantitative and qualitative approaches for prioritizing ideas for education and training programs.

◆ Use a systematic method for prioritizing program ideas. The critical ingredient in this process is the establishment of clear criteria for making decisions about each of the ideas.

◆ Be familiar with alternative interventions and how they are selected and implemented. Work on creating and nurturing networks of people who will listen and act when these alternative interventions are required.

Once the program ideas have been sorted and prioritized, program planners can realistically move to developing program objectives for a given program or set of programs. Developing program objectives that are clear and understandable is the subject of the next chapter.

## Application Exercises

The Application Exercises presented here can help you gain a clear understanding of how to use one method for determining which program ideas to develop and alternative interventions. The first exercise helps you set program priorities using a quantitative process, and the second assists you in assessing when alternatives to education and training programs are appropriate and what alternative interventions you might select for a specific situation of your choice.

## EXERCISE 7.1

## Setting Program Priorities

Using the instructions given here and in Exhibit 7.3 (page 145) as a model, complete the following priority rating chart.

1. List five ideas or needs identified by your organization as appropriate for education and training activities.
2. Select appropriate criteria to judge these ideas and needs.
3. For each criterion, assign an individual weight ranging from 10 (representing the highest priority) to 1 (representing the lowest priority).
4. Then for each item, assign a ranking ranging from 10 (representing the highest priority) to 1 (representing the lowest priority).
5. Multiply the rankings for each item by the weight that has been chosen for that item.
6. Add the weighted ranks for each idea (across the columns) and record the sum in the "Sum of Weighted Ranks" column.
7. Divide the sum of ranks by the number of criteria (in this exercise that number is 5) used in this rating process and record the result in the "Mean Weighted Rank" column.
8. Assign a final rank to each idea based on the "Mean Weighted Rank." The item that receives the highest score becomes the top priority, with each descending numerical score representing the high-to-low continuum of ideas identified.

| Items to Be Prioritized | Criteria | | | | | Sum of Weighted Ranks | Mean of Weighted Ranks | Final Ranking |
|---|---|---|---|---|---|---|---|---|
| **Weights for Each Criteria** | **Weight =** <br> **Rank/Wt. Rank** | **Weight =** <br> **Rank/Wt. Rank** | **Weight =** <br> **Rank/Wt. Rank** | **Weight =** <br> **Rank/Wt. Rank** | **Weight =** <br> **Rank/Wt. Rank** | | | |
| | | | | | | | | |
| | | | | | | | | |
| | | | | | | | | |
| | | | | | | | | |
| | | | | | | | | |

*Adapted from Sork, 1998, p. 287.*

## EXERCISE 7.2

## Using Interventions Other Than Educational Programming

1. Give a description of an idea or problem in an organization where you are currently working or have worked for which you believe developing an education or training program might not be appropriate.

2. List people who could or did assist you in deciding whether alternative interventions would be more appropriate than an educational program.

3. Identify one or more possible alternative interventions (other than or in addition to an education or training program) that could or did address the idea or problem you have described.

4. Outline at least two reasons why you believe this different intervention or interventions could be or was the best choice in this situation.

   1.

   2.

# Chapter 8

# Developing Program Objectives

Carolyn, the director of education for the Department of Human Services, is now ready to plan her first program on the department's new policies, services, and procedures related to child abuse cases. This subject is one of the top three areas for training that have been mandated by the state. Therefore, she knows that all staff who work with child abuse cases must attend. But where does she start? Carolyn knows she must address basic items, such as developing program objectives, finding instructors, estimating costs, locating facilities and equipment, and figuring out evaluation strategies, but which task should she do first? Carolyn decides some assistance from Pam, a colleague who is an experienced educator, would be helpful. In talking over her dilemma with Pam, she discovers that there is no single order to the various tasks. Rather, each program planning situation she faces, and her own daily schedule, will influence which task or tasks she might do first. Pam stresses to Carolyn that three major elements should be addressed at this point in the planning process, however:

1. Where you want to go (program objectives, instructional plans, transfer of learning)
2. How you will determine if you have gotten there (program evaluation, communicating program value)
3. How you want to get there (formats, staffing, budgeting, marketing, and logistical details)

Logically, the first task seems to be to determine program objectives, based on the identified priority ideas; but in practice, as stressed in Chapters Two and Three, how programs are actually planned usually defies logic (at least it seems so to the external observer). What is important is that each of these elements is addressed in such a way that the final product has internal consistency and is doable. For example, does the program fit within the parameters of the overall mission and goals of the sponsoring organization(s) or group(s)? Is there a clear match between and among the program objectives, how these objectives will be evaluated, and how the learning activities are designed? Does the "instructional" portion of the program actually reflect the program objectives focused on participant learning? Are the transfer-of-learning plans workable and consistent with the evaluation component, especially with any plans for follow-up evaluation? Do the program formats and schedules fit with the instructional and transfer plans? Is what has been said in marketing brochures reflective of the program objectives, and the instructional and learning-transfer plans? Does the budget allotment meet the requirements to implement the plan in all areas, from staffing to facilities to transfer-of-learning activities?

Each of the major elements of program planning highlighted above is discussed in Chapters Nine through Fourteen. The focus of this chapter is on developing program objectives. Discussed first is how program objectives are defined. This discussion is followed by a review of how program objectives are constructed and how planners judge the clarity of these objectives. Explored in the final section of the chapter are ways program objectives are used to determine whether a program is internally consistent and/or doable.

## Defining Program Objectives

Thinking through program objectives is one of the most difficult tasks people who plan programs do. The difficulty stems from two sources. First, at the heart of formulating program objectives are defining program *outcomes;* and these are often elusive, especially at the beginning of the process. For example, those working in literacy programs know that one of the major objectives of these programs is that adults who lack literacy skills will be able to read and write. But what does being able to read and write mean? Does it mean reading at a specified grade level, having the reading and writing skills necessary to be a productive worker or member of society, or both of these outcomes and more? Second, in the actual writing of program objectives, the parameters are not always clear. The terms *program objectives* and *program goals,* for example, are sometimes used interchangeably in practice: what one organization terms a *program goal,* another may call a *program objective.* There is a useful distinction between the two terms, however.

*Program objectives* provide clear statements of the anticipated results to be achieved through education and training programs. In addition, they serve as the foundation for instructional plans (see Chapter Nine), concrete guidelines for developing transfer-of-learning plans (see Chapter Ten), and benchmarks against which programs are evaluated (see Chapter Eleven). In contrast, *program goals* usually refer to broad statements of purpose or intent for education and training programs. They answer the questions: "Why are we doing this?" (Milano with Ullius, 1998), and " Why is the program worth doing?" (Rothwell and Cookson, 1997). For programs sponsored by organizations whose primary function is the education and training of adults (such as community-based literacy programs sponsored by community colleges), the major program goals are usually a part of the organizational mission statement (see Chapter Five). This statement is also true for organizations that have centralized units charged with the education and training function; but in these organizations, the goals are usually a part of the unit's mission statement.

Sample program goals include:

- *Community-Based Literacy Program.* The central goal of this program is to ensure that all adults in this community are able to read and write at a level sufficient to carry through their life roles as adults (for example, as workers, parents, contributing members of the community). In addition, services are provided to enable these same adults to complete their Graduate Equivalency Diploma (GED) and have the entry-level communication skills to enter a community college.

- *Reach for Recovery Program.* Women who have had breast cancer surgery have special physical, social, emotional, and cosmetic needs. These needs are why Research for Recovery was created. With the help of a volunteer who has had breast cancer herself, women learn to adjust and return to normal activities (American Cancer Society, n.d.).

- *Human Resource Development Department.* The goals of the Human Resource Development Department are: (1) to provide new hires with entry-level training and initiation into the corporation; (2) to improve the job performance of current staff; (3) to advance and/or enable employees to change their work roles and functions; and (4) to assist the overall organization to adapt to changing markets, products, and ways of operating. The end result of the activities of this department will be well-educated employees who can work effectively, within an ethic of care, in an organizational environment of constant change.

Program objectives focus primarily on what participants are expected to learn as a result of attending a specific education or training program. This learning results in changes in individual participants, groups of learners, organizational practices and procedures, and/or communities or segments of society. Program objectives that focus on change in individual participants are often translated into learning objectives (see Chapter Nine). These learning objectives in turn assist planners in developing or revising program objectives. In addition, program objectives outline how program staff will improve the quality and quantity of program resources and other basic operational aspects of the program. This second kind of program objective is also termed an *operational objective* (Knowles, 1980). It is important to include, as appropriate, program objectives that focus on the learning outcomes as well as outcomes related to improving the program operations. See Exhibit 8.1 for examples of program objectives focused on participant learning and on program operations.

People who plan programs often overlook those program objectives that are directed at improving the quality of the program operations. Yet, if

---

**EXHIBIT 8.1**

## Examples of Program Objectives by Type

| Program Objectives Focused on Participant Learning | Program Objectives Focused on Program Operations |
|---|---|
| • *Individual change.* To provide an educational support group for adults with Attention Deficit Disorder (ADD) with three primary outcomes: (1) knowledge gain about their condition, (2) opportunities to express their feelings about living with ADD, and (3) times for sharing what they are doing to help themselves deal with adult life roles and how they can help each other. | • *Adequate physical facilities.* To provide adequate physical facilities for the educational program, including refurbishing three seminar rooms and adding a space designed for individualized instruction. |
| • *Organizational change.* To provide a training program on two new software packages for all staff who will be required to use them on the job within a six-month period. Two outcomes are expected as a result of this program: (1) staff will be able to demonstrate that they know how to use each new package, and (2) managers, in cooperation with the technology support staff, will develop operational guidelines that clearly define how these two packages are to be integrated into existing work systems. | • *Equipment.* To locate and equip five computer labs so that computer-based learning can become a more integral component of the program.<br><br>• *Revenues.* To increase program revenues by 10 percent, through higher participant fees, with the money used for innovative programming. |
| • *Community change.* To provide a two-day workshop for leaders from all segments of the community (for example, police, government agencies, businesses, schools, social service agencies) on how to curb violence in their community. The major outcome expected is that an interorganizational team will be formed, which will then provide the leadership for future decisions and actions related to controlling and preventing violent acts of all kinds. | • *Training program.* To establish a volunteer training program for volunteers who could assist program staff in planning and carrying out programs for low-income families. |

developing these kinds of objectives is included as a regular part of the process of constructing program objectives, the overall quality and efficiency of programming will, in many cases, improve. In addition, although operational program objectives are probably more applicable to programs housed in formal education and training organizations or units, these types of objectives are also useful to persons who conduct educational activities as part of their other job responsibilities. For example, a director of a community action agency responsible for the in-service training of her staff may observe that she does not have adequate audiovisual equipment. Therefore, she defines as one of her program objectives to locate and secure by April 1 the following equipment: a laptop computer and computer projector, a videotape player and monitor, and a hanging screen.

## Constructing Program Objectives

There are differences of opinion among program planners whether program objectives should be stated in behavioral terms, and therefore are measurable, or whether these objectives can also encompass outcomes that cannot be expressed in "seeable" performance (Brookfield, 1986; Mehrens and Lehmann, 1991; Milano with Ullius, 1998; Sork and Caffarella, 1989). Some program planners take the position that education and training programs have some outcomes that are measurable and some that are not. Likewise, outcomes can be either intended or unanticipated, because it is almost impossible to know beforehand all the benefits a program could produce. Therefore, in constructing program objectives, it is important to state both measurable and nonmeasurable objectives and to be flexible in renegotiating and reshaping those objectives so that unanticipated but important achievements and outcomes of the program are highlighted. This notion of measurable and nonmeasurable and intended and unanticipated results is illustrated in Exhibit 8.2 with examples of specific program objectives.

Program planners should not develop program objectives in a vacuum. It is relatively easy to sit in one's office, carefully crafting program objectives, but there is always the risk of producing impractical and/or irrelevant projected outcomes. Instead, other people, such as program participants, work supervisors, and external stakeholders, should be asked to help in developing or at least reviewing these objectives. This involvement can be handled in a number of ways. For example, education and training staff could request that key supervisors of potential participants help draft and/or review program objectives for their people. They could also ask a sample of potential participants to help with this same process. Questions and comments from both these groups could be solicited on the relevance

**EXHIBIT 8.2**

## Examples of Unintended and Intended Measurable and Nonmeasurable Program Objectives

| | | Intended Achievements (stated before the program is carried out) | Unanticipated Achievements (stated during the program or after it has been carried out) |
|---|---|---|---|
| Program objectives focused on participant outcomes | *Measurable achievements* | To provide an educational program on time management for all new entry-level principals on ways to construct their day to save at least one hour of time per week. These time savings must be verified by the assistant superintendent for instruction. | About 50 percent of the office assistants for the new entry-level principals told them that it took them less time now to manage their calendars and monitor their telephone calls. |
| | *Nonmeasurable achievements* | To assist new trainers to feel they have more control over their daily work lives. | A number of the trainers remarked on the program evaluation that they felt more confident in their ability to carry out their jobs. |
| Program objectives focused on operational outcomes | *Measurable achievements* | To purchase a new computer to be used by participants in the instructional process through generating more income than what the program costs. | As more revenue was generated than expected, the agency staff members were able to purchase four new computers, all to be used for instructional purposes. |
| | *Nonmeasurable achievements* | Through training programs for volunteers, funded with revenue-producing programs, these volunteers would feel they were an important part of the staff. | A number of the volunteers remarked that this training program inspired them to recruit other volunteers to work with the organization. |

and usefulness of the objectives and on their understandability (especially concerning actual practical application and usefulness). In addition, if a formal education or training committee exists, this committee may serve as a review board and give advice and counsel in the initial writing and/or the redrafting of the objectives (see Chapter Five).

Program objectives, whether they are learning or operational, "should be stated clearly enough to indicate to all rational minds exactly what is intended" (Houle, 1996, p. 193). Houle goes on to describe a number of properties that characterize clearly articulated program objectives; three of them are highlighted.

- *Program objectives are essentially rational and thus impose a logical pattern on the educational program.* This rationality does not mean that the objectives do or even could describe all the possible outcomes of education and training programs over a specified period of time. For example, for large programs, usually program objectives that are learner and operational in scope are not comprehensive enough to speak to all aspects of the program. Nor do these objectives address the usually accepted but often unstated motives, aspirations, and objectives of those persons who plan and/or participate in education and training activities.

- *Good program objectives are practical and concrete.* As practical guides for action, program objectives neither describe things as they ideally should be nor focus on esoteric problems that have no basis in reality. "The ultimate test of an objective is not validity but achievability" (Houle, 1996, p. 183).

- *Good program objectives are discriminative.* By stating one course of action, another is ruled out. For example, if resources for the next calendar year are targeted at new personnel, other staff members for the most part are excluded from education and training activities. Whether this course of action is appropriate depends on a number of factors. For example, was an education or training program for new staff viewed as a priority need? Does senior management support this decision? Do the supervisors of the new staff believe the programs being planned meet the needs of their people?

More specifically, people who plan programs ask themselves the following questions to help them judge the clarity of the program objectives they have developed for both those that focus on participant learning and program operations, as applicable (Boyle, 1981; Sork and Caffarella, 1989; Milano with Ullius, 1998):

1. Is there a clear relationship between the objective and the ideas, problems, and needs that have been identified as priority areas?

2. Do the objectives reflect the prior knowledge, experiences, and abilities of potential participants?

3. Does the objective focus on a crucial part of the program?

4. Is the objective practical and doable?

5. Is the objective attainable in the time frame proposed?

6. Does the objective clearly communicate the proposed outcomes or accomplishments?

7. Is the objective meaningful, and will all interested parties understand it?

8. Is the objective supposed to be measurable; and if so, is it?

Program objectives often are negotiated and reworked at some point (or points) in the life of a program. Practically speaking, these changes in the program objectives mean program planners are willing to eliminate, revise, and/or add program objectives as the situation warrants (see Chapter Four). This updating of program objectives ought to be done in a thoughtful way. Staff should not modify or eliminate certain objectives just because they do not want to do them or because those objectives cannot be met as proposed; rather, staff have to reflect carefully when revising or adding to initially agreed upon program objectives.

## Using Objectives as Checkpoints

Clearly stated program objectives, both learning and operational, provide one of the major checks for ensuring that a program has internal consistency and is doable. As noted earlier, use of program objectives as checkpoints does not mean these objectives are necessarily constructed prior to working on or completing planning tasks. However, once these objectives have been developed, other aspects of the plan (for example, the transfer-of-learning activities, budget, marketing, and staffing) or the planning process itself can be revisited to see if what is being proposed really addresses the expected outcomes and can be done. The following scenarios illustrate this point.

### Ensuring Objectives Are Realistic

In planning a continuing education program for practicing physicians on a new online insurance management system, the planning team at its third meeting reviews a draft of the program objectives. One of the major expected outcomes is that participants will be able to integrate this new system as part of their practice within the next six months. Three of the planning team members caution the team that the potential participants are probably at many different stages in integrating this type of technology system into their current practices and question whether this objective is realistic. Based on these observations, team members then decide to reexamine the activities planned for the program itself to determine whether they can develop a transfer-of-learning plan that addresses this issue.

### Ensuring Objectives Are Feasible

In reviewing a draft of a revised training program for new teachers, Cassie, the director of the statewide literacy program, notices that what has been proposed is probably not feasible, given some recently projected funding cuts in the training budget. She decides to ask the ad hoc committee that put the plan together to continue to meet and revise the plan in light of these projected budget shortfalls. In discussing with the committee chair how she might go about this task, Cassie suggests that the committee might start with reviewing the program objectives. For example, which of the objectives are more critical than others? Could some of the objectives be achieved in a different way, one that would require less cost? Might some of the objectives be scaled back in terms of the projected outcomes? Can operational objectives be developed, focusing on replacing this lost funding? The chair agrees that using these questions is a good starting point for revising the whole plan.

Using the program objectives as an internal consistency check is especially helpful in matching instructional, transfer-of-learning, and evaluation plans to what people want to see happen (see Chapters Nine, Ten, and Eleven). For some programs, the connections between and among the program objectives, the transfer activities, and the evaluation process are readily apparent—the strategies and techniques for instruction, learning transfer, and evaluation may overlap or be one and the same. For example, selected supervisors might be asked to be part of the instructional team and require that participants, as part of the instructional process, develop learning applications or transfer plans. All supervisors could use the formal supervisory process as a strategy to ensure that participants use what they have learned on the job. In turn, the evaluation plan may include interviewing supervisors about the usefulness of the program as well as reviewing performance appraisal data. Therefore, checking to see that these components of the plan line up with one another and get at proposed outcomes may be relatively easy. In other programs, seeing that these elements match may be more difficult. This matching process is especially so, for example, when the sponsoring organizations or groups are not responsible for monitoring and/or evaluating the transfer-of-learning activities and outcomes.

## Chapter Highlights

Program objectives provide clear statements of the proposed outcomes or anticipated results of a specific program. Although primarily centered on what participants learn, program objectives may also address the operational aspects of a program. Participants' learning may result in individual, organizational, community, and/or societal changes. In constructing program objectives, program planners should be cognizant of the following tasks:

◆ Write program objectives that reflect what participants will learn, the resulting changes from that learning, and the operational aspects of the program. The program objectives related to participant learning are often then translated into learning objectives (see Chapter Nine).

◆ Ensure that both measurable and nonmeasurable program outcomes, as appropriate, are included.

◆ Check to see whether the program objectives are written clearly enough so they can be understood by all parties involved (for example, participants, sponsoring organizations).

◆ Use the program objectives as an internal consistency and "do-ability" checkpoint (to determine, for example, whether the instructional, transfer-of-learning, and evaluation plans match the objectives).

◆ Negotiate changes in program objectives, as appropriate, among the parties involved with the planning process.

The program objectives, in either draft or final form, often serve as the point of departure for preparing instructional, transfer-of-learning, and evaluation plans, which are addressed respectively in the next three chapters.

## Application Exercise

This Application Exercise is designed to help you develop and evaluate program objectives within your own organization.

| EXERCISE 8.1 | | | |
|---|---|---|---|
| **Developing and Evaluating Program Objectives** | | | |

1.  Develop two or three clearly written program objectives for a program area of your choice. As appropriate, include both objectives focused on participant learning and objectives focused on program operations. List each of these objectives on the chart provided.

| **Initial Program Objectives** | | | |
|---|---|---|---|
| Is there a clear relationship between the objective and the problems, ideas, or needs identified? | | | |
| Does the objective focus on a crucial part of the program? | | | |
| Is the objective practical and doable? | | | |
| Is the objective obtainable In the time frame you have proposed? | | | |
| Does the objective clearly communicate the proposed outcomes or accomplishments? | | | |
| Is the objective meaningful and can it be understood by all interested parties? | | | |
| Is the objective supposed to be measurable, and if so, is it? | | | |
| Do the objectives reflect the prior knowledge, experiences, and abilities of the potential participants? | | | |
| **Revised Program Objectives** | | | |

2.  Ask one or two of your colleagues to help you critique those program objectives using the questions noted on the chart. Using the feedback, rewrite those objectives that need revising in the space provided. (Please note that you may need or want to do this critiquing and revising process a number of times with the same and/or different colleagues.)

# Chapter 9
# Designing Instructional Plans

Alicia Two-Trees, director of community programs for the Paugusset Reservation, is in the process of developing an environmental awareness day for residents of the reservation and the surrounding communities. The reservation has not sponsored a program of this nature before, but a number of the reservation members have expressed their excitement about providing the leadership and sharing their expertise on environmental issues. With the assistance of an ad hoc planning committee, Alicia has chosen the basic format for the program, and established a draft of the program objectives. She and the committee spent the last meeting identifying possible learning activities and people who could facilitate these activities. She and one of her committee members have contacted those who were recommended to serve as instructors and facilitators and have received positive responses from all of them. Alicia has asked these people to come to a meeting to put together instructional plans for the activities for which they are responsible. About half of these volunteer instructors have either formal or informal teaching experience, some with children and a few with adults. The other half, to her knowledge, have never taught or facilitated a learning activity before. Alicia ponders the best way to assist these volunteers in preparing specific instructional plans for their sessions, which range from formal presentations to hands-on workshops to interactive exhibits. She decides that the easiest way is to have a work session where each person will prepare a draft of her or his actual instructional plan. Alicia also decides to ask those in the group who have a reputation for being good instructors to assist her in this work session as well as develop their own plans. She will provide resources for this meeting on how to develop learning objectives, select specific content, and choose instructional techniques. Alicia will then ask the volunteer instructors to return for a second session where they will actually practice what they have designed, and revise their plans as needed.

Preparing instructional plans involves designing the interaction between learners and instructors and/or learners and resource materials for each education and training activity. Those who are delivering the instruction often are involved in developing these instructional plans. These individuals receive assistance in putting the plan together, but the responsibility for the final product is theirs. There are times, though, when designing instructional plans is a team effort, especially when the education and training activities are very complex and comprehensive and/or if software packages are used in the actual design phase (Piskurich, 2000; Alessi and Trollip, 2001). The composition of these design teams varies, depending on the purpose, format, and content of the education and training activity. Four types of staff can be members of these teams, especially on major programs: instructional designers, subject-matter experts, instructors, and persons representing the overall planning team or education and training unit (Kemp, Morrison, and Ross, 1996; Smith and Ragan, 1999). For example, the design team for a combination of a one-day intensive workshop and Web-based instruction for trainers who want to incorporate Web-based instruction into their teaching is composed of an instructional designer, an expert on Web-based instruction, and the directors of human resource development from the sponsoring organizations. The staff responsible for designing instruction may be paid or volunteer, and internal or external to an organization.

This chapter addresses the various components of instructional plans, how they are put together, and helpful hints for instructors as they put their plans into operation. Described first are the learning objectives and how they are constructed and then suggestions are offered for selecting and organizing the content to be taught. Selecting instructional techniques and resources and preparing the instructional assessment are reviewed next. The chapter concludes with providing an example of an instructional plan and an exploration of ways instructors make the instructional plans work for them and their learners.

## Developing Learning Objectives

Learning objectives, along with the terms performance objectives or learning targets, describe what participants will learn as a result of attending an education or training session (Mager, 1984; Diamond, 1998; Smith and

Ragan, 1999; Dick, Carey, and Carey, 2001; McMillan, 2001). These learning objectives are set in the context of the program objectives that focus on participant learning, so there is continuity between the two sets of objectives. The major difference between learning and program objectives is that learning objectives center on individual participants and sessions within a larger program, while program objectives are focused on the education or training program as a whole. Illustrations of program objectives, which are drawn from Chapter Eight, and how they are translated into learning objectives are shown in Exhibit 9.1.

---

**EXHIBIT 9.1**

## Translating Program Objectives into Learning Objectives

| Program Objectives | Learning Objectives |
|---|---|
| To provide an educational support group for adults with Attention Deficit Disorder (ADD) with three primary outcomes: <br><br> 1. Up-to-date knowledge about their condition <br> 2. Opportunities to express their feelings about living with ADD <br> 3. Time for sharing what they are doing to help themselves deal with adult life and how they can assist each other | The participants will: <br><br> 1. Identify new sources of accurate information about ADD (for example, from books, websites, people) <br> 2. Discuss with experts current knowledge about ADD and how to use this knowledge in their everyday lives <br> 3. Express and explore their feelings with group members about living with ADD <br> 4. Share strategies of how they deal with ADD as part of their life as adults <br> 5. Provide assistance to group members who ask for help in addressing specific life issues |
| To provide a training program on two new software programs for all staff that will be required to use them on the job within a six-month period. Two outcomes are expected as a result of this program: <br><br> 1. Staff will be able to demonstrate they know how to use each new package <br> 2. Managers, in cooperation with the technology support staff, will develop operational guidelines that clearly define how these two packages are to be integrated into existing work systems | The participants will: <br><br> 1. Demonstrate that they are able to use two new software packages <br> 2. Understand and use the new guidelines for integrating these new software packages into their existing work systems <br> 3. Apply effectively what they have learned about integrating these new software packages to their everyday practice in their own departments and units |

Learning objectives are selected carefully, because they set the tone and direction for what participants are expected to do and learn during the instructional activity. Therefore, in preparing learning objectives, the developer must have in mind a clear picture of the proposed learning outcomes for the instructional unit.

There are five major categories of learning outcomes: acquiring new knowledge; enhancing cognitive skills; developing psychomotor skills; strengthening problem-solving and -finding capabilities; and changing attitudes, beliefs, values, and/or feelings (Bloom, 1956; Kemp, Morrison, and Ross, 1996; Smith and Ragan, 1999). Following are examples of learning objectives illustrating each category of learning outcomes for participants who enroll in an intensive ropes course (Rohnke, 1990; Johnson, 1999).

▶ *Acquisition of knowledge.* Participants will be able to describe what a ropes course is and identify the basic principles of team building.

▶ *Enhancement of cognitive skills.* Participants will analyze each of the team-building exercises and translate what they have learned into one or two proposed changes in their professional practice and/or personal lives.

▶ *Development of psychomotor skills.* Participants will demonstrate they can do at least two of the physically challenging exercises included in the ropes course.

▶ *Strengthening of problem-solving and -finding capabilities.* Participants will explain how the various activities they have undergone have augmented or reinforced their problem-finding or -solving abilities, and how they will apply this learning to a specific work and/or life situation.

▶ *Changes in attitudes, values, beliefs, and or feelings.* Participants will share their feelings about experiencing the ropes course and discuss how taking part in course activities has affected them either personally or professionally.

Learning objectives are useful for four major reasons (Smith and Ragan, 1999). They provide a focus and consistency for the design of instruction; guidelines for choosing course content and instructional methods; a basis for evaluating what participants have learned; and directions for learners to help them organize their own learning.

As with program objectives, learning objectives should be "stated clearly enough to indicate to all rational minds exactly what is intended" (Houle, 1996, p. 193). Tracey (1992) has outlined five general rules for communicating objectives clearly and correctly: avoid unfamiliar words; do not confuse or misuse words; be concise; seek simplicity; and review what has been proposed to make sure the objectives say what you want them to say.

The focus of each learning objective, as noted earlier, is on the program participants. Therefore, these objectives should be stated in terms of what learners will be able to know, do, or feel (refer to the previous example of outcomes for ropes course participants). Objectives should consist of an opening statement ("The participant will . . ."), an action verb, and a content reference (which describes the subject being taught). Five additional sample learning objectives are given in Exhibit 9.2.

In developing learning objectives, people sometimes have difficulty coming up with a variety of action words that fit each category of learning outcomes. To assist in this task, a sampling of such words is given in Exhibit 9.3 (Tracey, 1992; Kemp, Morrison, and Ross, 1996; Rothwell and Cookson, 1997; Vella, 2000).

Although the three essential elements of all learning objectives are a statement of *who* (the learner), *how* (the action verb), and *what* (the content), other authors have suggested additional components that may be useful in clarifying further what learners are able to know or do. More specifically, Mager (1984); Smith and Ragan (1999); Dick, Carey, and Carey (2001); and McMillian (2001) have described two more elements of learning objectives: conditions under which the learning is to be demonstrated and the

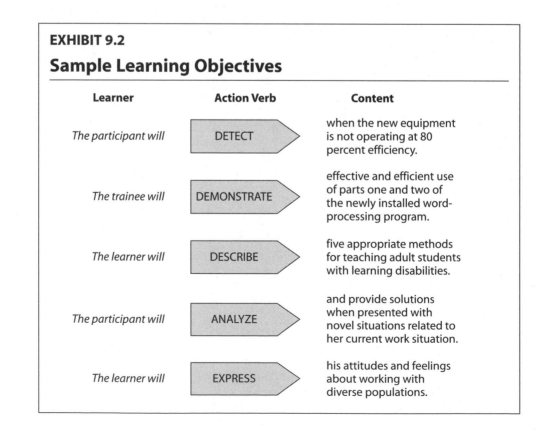

**EXHIBIT 9.2**

# Sample Learning Objectives

| Learner | Action Verb | Content |
|---|---|---|
| *The participant will* | DETECT | when the new equipment is not operating at 80 percent efficiency. |
| *The trainee will* | DEMONSTRATE | effective and efficient use of parts one and two of the newly installed word-processing program. |
| *The learner will* | DESCRIBE | five appropriate methods for teaching adult students with learning disabilities. |
| *The participant will* | ANALYZE | and provide solutions when presented with novel situations related to her current work situation. |
| *The learner will* | EXPRESS | his attitudes and feelings about working with diverse populations. |

**EXHIBIT 9.3**

## Examples of Action Words for Learning Objectives

| Acquiring Knowledge | Enhancing Cognitive Skills | Developing Psychomotor Skills | Strengthening Problem-Finding and -Solving Capabilities | Changing Attitudes, Values, Beliefs, and/or Feelings |
|---|---|---|---|---|
| To identify | To reflect | To demonstrate | To propose | To challenge |
| To list | To compare | To assemble | To practice | To defend |
| To define | To contrast | To adjust | To enhance | To judge |
| To describe | To catalogue | To install | To recognize | To question |
| To state | To classify | To apply | To clarify | To accept |
| To name | To examine | To operate | To determine | To share |
| To prepare | To evaluate | To detect | To decompose | To adopt |
| To recall | To forecast | To locate | To consider | To advocate |
| To express | To formulate | To isolate | To deconstruct | To bargain |
| To categorize | To investigate | To arrange | To fetter out | To cooperate |
| To chart | To modify | To build | To discover | To endorse |
| To rank | To organize | To conduct | To uncover | To justify |
| To distinguish | To plan | To manipulate | To select | To persuade |
| To explain | To research | To fix | To analyze | To resolve |
| To outline | To study | To lay out | To evaluate | To select |
| To inform | To translate | To perform | To search | To dispute |
| To label | To differentiate | To sort | To practice | To approve |
| To specify | To analyze | To construct | To construct | To choose |
| To tell | To compute | To draw | To simulate | To feel |
| To memorize | To devise | To employ | To employ | To care |
| To reproduce | To review | To design | To examine | To express |
| To recognize | To synthesize | To set up | To change | To reflect |
| To recite | To relate | To practice | To diagnose | To protest |
| | To group | To exhibit | To prioritize | To sort |
| | To estimate | To diagram | | To control |
| | To edit | | | To value |

standards or criteria for acceptable performance. Sample wording describing the given conditions are:

- Given a problem of the following type . . .
- Given a list of . . .
- When provided with a specific set of tools . . .
- Without the use of any reference materials . . .
- By checking a flowchart next to the property equipment . . .
- When a client is angry or upset . . .

Sample wording describing the criteria for acceptable performance are:

- . . . with 98 percent accuracy.

- . . . getting 16 out of 20 correct.

- . . . in a 20-minute time period.

- . . . by brief responses (fewer than five sentences).

- . . . with no mistakes.

- . . . with all irate clients.

The latter two elements are appropriate only for learning objectives that are measurable through quantitative means. There are certain kinds of learning outcomes, as stressed in Chapters Eight and Eleven, that do not lend themselves to precise behavioral or performance criteria (Knowles, 1980; Caffarella, 1992; Apps, 1996). Using specific behavior or performance criteria is especially not applicable in most situations when creativity, confidence, sensitivity, feelings, attitudes, and values are the focus of the learning activity. For example, changes in deep-seated values and attitudes about race, gender, and cultural differences are learning outcomes that are extremely difficult, if not impossible, to express in any meaningful way in behavioral terms. However the learning objectives are written, it is key that they have meaning for both the participants and the instructors, are understandable, and provide a clear direction for the education or training activity.

## Selecting and Organizing Content

Selecting the content—that is, choosing what will be learned during a learning activity—is a challenge because instructors can rarely include all the material they would like to teach. These limitations stem from the amount of time, types of delivery systems, backgrounds and experiences of the participants, materials available, and staff capabilities (Alessi and Trollip, 2001).

The starting point for selecting content is the learning objectives. Milano with Ullius (1998) recommends "playing" with the proposed content until key topics and points are arrived at for each learning objective. What may happen as designers categorize and rethink what might be covered is that some of the learning objectives may need to be revised or even dropped. Some designers, to arrive at what they believe to be important and essential to learn, construct visual maps to assist them in this process, while others prefer either just talking it through or using a combination of methods.

Smith and Delahaye (1987) provide a framework for moving towards the final content:

- *What participants must know.* Content that is essential to the objectives.

- *What participants should know.* Content that supplements the essential material and should be included if time allows.

- *What participants could know.* Content that is interesting and relevant but not essential for clear understanding.

As Tracey (1992) cautions, care must be taken to avoid leaving out important points and ideas, overemphasizing topics that do not merit extensive attention, and repeating the material presented.

The organization (or sequence) in which the content is delivered is also important. There is no one way to organize content. For example, should the content flow from general to specific or vice versa? Should it emanate from abstract to concrete or concrete to abstract? The ordering of the content depends on the participants' knowledge and experience, the nature of the content itself, the required level of achievement, and teaching and learning styles of those involved (Houle, 1996; Farquharson, 1995). The guidelines in Exhibit 9.4 are ways to think about what sequence might work best (Tracey, 1992; Farquharson, 1995; Kemp, Morrison, and Ross, 1996).

There are three common pitfalls that designers stumble into when organizing instruction: they plan too much material for the time allowed; they

---

**EXHIBIT 9.4**

## Guidelines for Organizing Content

- ❖ Start by acknowledging and reviewing what participants know about the content.

- ❖ Give participants a framework to use in organizing what they are to learn ("an advanced organizer") and understand how this learning could be transferred into their own settings.

- ❖ Introduce key concepts, ideas, and terms early and revisit them throughout the instructional unit.

- ❖ Explore materials familiar to the participants and then proceed to the less familiar.

- ❖ Ensure prerequisite knowledge and skills are taught prior to moving to content that builds on these materials.

- ❖ Proceed from the most important to the least important.

- ❖ Teach the less difficult to the more difficult.

- ❖ Do not overload any activity with ideas and/or skills that are difficult to learn.

- ❖ Provide for instructional activities that allow for learning transfer throughout the instructional segment.

want instructors to impart more than learners are motivated to absorb; and they discount the context in which the learning is to be applied (Farquharson, 1995; Milano with Ullius, 1998). Those designing instruction need to constantly remind themselves that planning instruction, like program planning, is an iterative process—objectives, organization contexts, and evaluation mechanisms will change both during the planning and implementation phases.

## Selecting Instructional Techniques

How does an instructor decide which instructional technique might best fit a specific situation?

### Training for the Christmas Rush

Roberta, a department manager and training specialist for a large retail outlet, has set up a two-hour training session for all part-time sales personnel who have been hired to handle the Christmas rush. She knows she will have both experienced salespeople and people who have never sold before—about 25 in all. Roberta has outlined what she believes to be a good set of learning objectives in areas such as customer relations, selling techniques, and general store operations. She is now trying to decide just how she should cover that broad array of content in a short period of time. Roberta has delineated two possible alternatives. The first is to use a combination of lecturing and small- and large-group discussions. She would ask the more experienced people to serve as resource people and leaders in the small groups. Her second idea is to use role playing, followed by small- and large-group discussions. She would then fill in with lecture material as needed. Roberta decides to review her ideas with three of her experienced sales staff. She believes that an offer of a paid lunch would entice them to help her out.

Underlying Roberta's quandary about instructional techniques is the fact that there is no one best way of assisting people to learn. Rather, there are ten major factors instructors take into consideration when choosing instructional techniques (Tracey, 1992; Milano with Ullius, 1998; Smith and Ragan, 1999; Vella, 2000; Dick, Carey, and Carey, 2001). (See Exhibit 9.5.)

Of these ten factors, the first four—the focus of the learning objectives, the capability of the instructor to use the chosen technique, the experiences and backgrounds of the learners, and the learning context—are key. These four factors are discussed in the following sections.

**EXHIBIT 9.5**

# Ten Major Factors for Consideration Regarding Instructional Techniques

| FACTOR 1 | *Learning objectives* | • Is the focus of the objectives acquiring new knowledge, enhancing cognitive skills, developing psychomotor skills, strengthening problem-solving and -finding capabilities, or changing attitudes, values, and/or feelings? |
|---|---|---|
| FACTOR 2 | *Instructors* | • Are instructors capable of using the techniques, and do they feel comfortable doing so? |
| FACTOR 3 | *Learners* | • How many learners are involved?<br>• What are the characteristics of these learners? (See Chapter Fourteen.)<br>• What are their cultural backgrounds?<br>• What expectations do the learners have in terms of the techniques to be used?<br>• Are the participants capable of learning through these techniques? |
| FACTOR 4 | *Context* | • How does where the learning takes place influence the usefulness and appropriateness of the instructional techniques?<br>• Can the learning context enhance the use of the techniques chosen? |
| FACTOR 5 | *Transfer-of-learning* | • Do the techniques promote the transfer-of-learning process?<br>• What techniques have the greatest potential for simulating the context in which the learning will be applied? |
| FACTOR 6 | *Content* | • Is the content abstract or concrete?<br>• What is the level of complexity and comprehensiveness of the material? |
| FACTOR 7 | *Technique characteristics* | • What can realistically be done with the techniques?<br>• How difficult are the techniques to use?<br>• What kind of time is needed to use the techniques effectively? |
| FACTOR 8 | *Variety* | • Are there plans to use a variety of techniques that take into account the various backgrounds and experiences of the learners and the different ways they process information? |
| FACTOR 9 | *Logistical constraints* | • Are the costs, if any, associated with the techniques chosen realistic?<br>• Are the space, equipment, and/or materials necessary to use the techniques readily available? |
| FACTOR 10 | *Time* | • Are techniques being used that fit into the time frame allotted (for example, is there too little or too much time available)? |

### Learning Objectives

To address the first factor, the focus of the learning objectives, a variety of instructional techniques appropriate for each category of learning outcomes—acquiring knowledge, enhancing cognitive skills, developing psychomotor skills, strengthening problem-solving and -finding capabilities, and changing attitudes, values, and/or feelings—are listed and described in Exhibit 9.6. More in-depth descriptions of these and other

---

**EXHIBIT 9.6**

## Examples of Techniques by Learning Outcomes

### Acquiring Knowledge

*Lecture*
A one-way organized, formal talk is given by a resource person for the purpose of presenting a series of events, facts, concepts, or principles.

*Panel*
A group of three to six people present their views on a particular topic or problem.

*Face-to-Face Group Discussion*
A group of five to 20 people have a relatively unstructured exchange of ideas about a specific problem or issue.

*Buzz Group*
A large group is divided into small "huddle" groups for the purpose of discussing the subject matter at hand.

*Symposium*
People qualified to speak on different phases of a subject or problem offer presentations.

*Computer-Based Tutorial*
Participants are presented information and guided through the content via computer-based programs. The most common way of stimulating interaction with the learner is through questions that require learner response.

*Computer-Based Drills*
These drills provide a way for learners to determine what knowledge they have gained through practice exercises. The drill cycle begins by selecting an item which is then displayed. The learner responds to the item, the program judges the response, and the learner receives feedback about the response. Drills are often a part of computer-based tutorials.

*Web-Based Searching*
Participants search the Internet for information related to specific topics using search engines such as Yahoo (www.yahoo.com) or AltaVista (www.altavista.com).

*Email and Listservs*
Information and questions can be shared between and among instructors and learners via email or listservs. While email allows more for one-on-one interaction, a listserv provides communication among all participants and instructors.

*Asynchronous Online Forums*
Computer online forums allow learners and instructors to post messages, share ideas, ask questions, and read about topics of interests. Sample types of forums include threaded discussions, news groups, notes files, bulletin boards, and e-forums.

*Hypermedia*
These computer-based instructional products connect various forms of media (for example, text, audio, graphics, and animation) and allow participants to acquire knowledge at their own pace, sequence, and depth.

*Real-time (Synchronous) Internet Relay Chats*
Internet relay chats allow for moderated discussions, private conversations, and question and answer times between and among participants, instructors, and outside invited experts, all of whom are online at a specific chat time.

*Audio and Video Conferencing*
This two-way communication system allows learners to interact in real-time with each other and outside resource people, with the expressed purpose of gaining specific knowledge. These types of conversations can be done via telephone, satellite, or through Web-based means.

| Enhancing Cognitive Skills | Developing Psychomotor Skills |
|---|---|

*Case Study*

A small group analyzes and solves an event, incident, or situation presented orally, in written form, or through computer-based means.

*Debate*

Two people or two groups present conflicting views, which helps to clarify the arguments between them.

*In-basket Exercise*

In a form of simulation that focuses on the "paper symptoms" of a job, participants respond to materials people might have in their in-baskets in a work situation.

*Critical Incident*

Participants are asked to describe an important incident related to a specific aspect of their lives. This incident is then used as a basis for analysis.

*Drawing*

Learners are asked to draw a concept or an idea as individuals or in groups. They then discuss with the whole group why they drew what they did.

*Observation*

After an individual or group systematically observes and records an event using a specific focus (for example, leadership style, group interactions, instructor behavior), the data are analyzed and discussed (either one-on-one or in a group format).

*Quiet Meeting*

Participants who know each other well sit quietly and reflect on a topic or question, sharing from time to time an idea on the area presented. No reaction is given to these comments, although others are free to share their ideas also. The power of this technique is in the silence, not the talking or listening.

*Game*

An individual or group performs an activity characterized by structured competition that provides the opportunity to practice specific thinking skills and actions (such as decision-making). Games are done both live and through computer-based means.

*OnLine Forums and Real-Time Internet Relay Chats*

Online forums and chat rooms can be designed in such a way that participants are raising and discussing critical questions, debating ideas, and challenging each other's ways of thinking.

*Computer-Based Simulations*

This is a Web-based tool that reproduces a real-life situation, with the focus on analyzing and making decisions related to that situation.

---

*Demonstration with Return Demonstration*

A resource person performs a specified operation or task, showing others how to do it. The participants then practice the same action.

*Live or Computer-Based Simulation*

Participants practice skills in a learning environment that simulates the real setting in which those skills are required.

*Trial and Error*

Participants are encouraged to figure out individually or in groups a way to do a hands-on task effectively. The tasks may be simulated or set in "real-life" settings.

*Skill Practice Exercise*

Participants repeat the performance of a skill with or without the aid of an instructor.

*Behavior Modeling*

A model or ideal enactment of a desired behavior is presented via an instructor, videotape, or film, and is usually followed by a practice session on the behavior.

*Electronic Performance Support Systems (EPSS)*

EPSS computer programs provide support at the time a specific action is needed. "An EPSS may be a hypermedia database, a question-and-answer online help system, or a more complete tutorial" (Alessi and Trollip, 2001, p. 306).

*Game*

An individual or group performs an activity characterized by structured competition that provides the opportunity to practice specific psychomotor skills (such as hitting a ball). These are usually done live.

*Simulation*

In this learning environment a real experience is simulated, with the focus on learning or enhancing psychomotor skill (for example, an indoor rock climbing wall).

*(Continued)*

| Strengthening Problem-Solving and -Finding Capabilities | Changing Attitudes, Beliefs, Values and/or Feelings |
|---|---|
| **Suggestion Circles**<br>In circles of no more than 12 people, participants are asked to provide high-quality, concisely stated solutions to a specific problem posed by one of the members within a time frame of no more than 5 to 10 minutes.<br><br>**Problem-Based Learning**<br>The content for the instruction is centered on fundamental or critical problems of practice. Participants focus on solving the presented problems with the end product being enhanced problem-solving skills, content knowledge related to the problems presented, and improved thinking skills. Problem-based learning can be carried out face to face, through computer-mediated formats, or a combination of both.<br><br>**Socratic Dialogue**<br>Through interaction with an expert, whose role it is to provide examples and guiding questions, learners are challenged to solve problems through clear reasoning and thinking.<br><br>**Simulations**<br>Participants are asked to solve problems in activities that closely mimic real-life situations. The feedback given as they move through the simulation is life-like and immediate, especially in computer-based simulations.<br><br>**Reflective Practice**<br>This practice involves thoughtful reflection on one's actions, focusing on alternative ways one would approach a similar problem or incident, which can be done individually, as part of a small group discussion, or some combination of the two.<br><br>**Web-Based Applications Sharing**<br>Learners work collaboratively on solving real-life or simulated problems using software applications like spreadsheets and whiteboards.<br><br>**Microworlds**<br>Participants, through the use of computer programs, "manipulate objects to accomplish what they want" (Alessi and Trollip, 2001, p. 308). These microworlds are sophisticated forms of computer simulations that provide "good opportunities for learners to create their own views of the universe defined by the microworld" (Alessi and Trollip, 2001, p. 308) included in the parameters of the situation.<br><br>**Audio and Video Conferencing**<br>Using either an audio or video two-way communication system, participants can collaboratively solve problems that are posed by either the instructors or themselves. Experts could also be brought into these real-time discussions. | **Role Playing**<br>The spontaneous dramatization of a situation or problem is followed by a group discussion.<br><br>**Simulation**<br>A simulation, which could be computer-based, emulates a real learning environment, with the focus on attitudes, beliefs, and feelings related to the situation presented.<br><br>**Group Discussion**<br>A group of five to 12 people have a relatively unstructured exchange of ideas focused on the attitudes, beliefs, and values they hold about a specific issue or problem.<br><br>**Storytelling**<br>Participants "tell their stories" about an experience that all or most group members have in common and/or an experience that opens vistas unknown to the rest of the group.<br><br>**Metaphor Analysis**<br>Participants construct metaphors—concrete images—that describe, in a parallel yet different way, a phenomenon being discussed.<br><br>**Exercise, Structured Experience**<br>People participate in planned exercises or experiences, usually using some instrument or guide, with a focus towards learning about and discussing their feelings, beliefs, values, and attitudes.<br><br>**Reflective Practice**<br>This practice involves thoughtfully reflecting on one's actions, including the assumptions and feelings associated with those actions, which can be done individually or as a part of a small group discussion.<br><br>**Listening Circle**<br>The main focus of this activity is to listen closely to what each participant is saying about a question or topic that is raised and to suspend his or her own thinking about the topic at the same time. A person speaks only when they have the symbol (where possible, from indigenous peoples) to talk, which is passed around the circle while the other learners listen intently to what is being said. The keys to this process are to ask all participants to guard against thinking about how they want to respond, and to make connections to what others are saying, and above all, to just listen.<br><br>**Listening to Music**<br>This practice uses music as a stimulus for participants to write down feelings and memories related to what is being taught or discussed.<br><br>**Online Forums and Chat Rooms**<br>Online forums and chat rooms are designed to allow a discussion related to feelings, attitudes, beliefs, and values learners hold related to the topic or area being shared or studied. In having computer-based conversations of this nature, instructors need to build first a sense of trust and caring among the participants. |

instructional techniques can be found in Mezirow and Associates (1990); Apps (1996); Silberman (1996); Driscoll (1998); Galbraith (1998); Smith and Ragan (1999); Burge (2000); Collison, Elbaum, Haavind, and Tinker (2000); Kruse and Keil (2000); Taylor, Marienau, and Fiddler (2000); and Alessi and Trollip (2001).

Although this categorization of techniques offers a good representation of how each instructional technique fits with a type of learning outcome, in actual use the categories of techniques are not that clear-cut. One technique may be appropriate for two or three categories of learning outcomes. For example, as discussed above, many of the Web-based techniques can be used across most of the categories, while different forms of group discussion could be used to impart knowledge, teach cognitive skills, enhance problem-solving abilities, or examine beliefs, values, attitudes, and feelings.

## Capability of the Instructor

The second key factor in choosing instructional techniques, as stated earlier, is the capability of the instructor. Does the instructor have the knowledge, skill, and confidence to handle a particular technique? Does he or she feel comfortable using it? If not, the instructor's discomfort may be distracting. For example, an instructor who employs a new technique that does not seem to work the way she thought it would may continually apologize to learners. Or even worse, the instructor may embarrass or even blame the participants for being unable to use the technique well, when in actuality it is the instructor's problem. There are ways that instructors who choose to employ new or unfamiliar techniques can try out these techniques. For example, instructors could request that participants join them in experimenting with these new techniques and ask for feedback on whether they worked, and if they did, how effective were they. This feedback could come in the form of written responses to open-ended questions or through group discussions where both the instructor and the participants could discuss what transpired in terms of the "positives" and "areas for improvement."

Capable instructors of adults also are aware and use well the principle of active learner participation in choosing techniques (Knowles, 1980; Silberman, 1996; Vella, 2000). "Given the choice between two techniques, choose the one involving the learners in the most active participation" (Knowles, 1980, p. 240). A sampling of techniques with high, medium, and low participant involvement are provided in Figure 9.1. In addition, competent instructors also acknowledge differences among learners, which is the third key element in choosing instructional techniques.

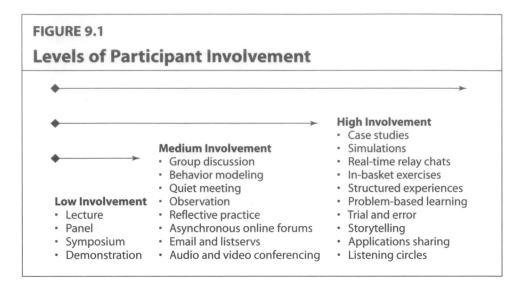

**FIGURE 9.1**

**Levels of Participant Involvement**

**High Involvement**
- Case studies
- Simulations
- Real-time relay chats
- In-basket exercises
- Structured experiences
- Problem-based learning
- Trial and error
- Storytelling
- Applications sharing
- Listening circles

**Medium Involvement**
- Group discussion
- Behavior modeling
- Quiet meeting
- Observation
- Reflective practice
- Asynchronous online forums
- Email and listservs
- Audio and video conferencing

**Low Involvement**
- Lecture
- Panel
- Symposium
- Demonstration

## Learner Characteristics

In instructing adults, thoughtful teachers have always been challenged by the differences learners bring with them to learning activities and what these differences mean for choosing instructional techniques. Traditionally, these instructors, for example, have recognized that adults bring rich but often divergent experiences to learning activities, are immersed in various life roles, have preferred ways of learning, and want practical solutions to problems and issues (Knowles, 1980; Merriam and Caffarella, 1999; Dick, Carey, and Carey, 2001). With the changing demographics in the United States and other western countries, the advent of "global classrooms," and the recognition that factors such as race, gender, class, and culture do affect the learning process, responding to differences among learners has become even more complex and challenging. Hayes (1994); Hayes and Colin (1994); Blankespoor (1997); Guy (1999a, 1999b); Merriam and Caffarella (1999); Wlodkowski (1998); and Hayes, Flannery, and Associates (2000) advise instructors to first acknowledge their own biases, both the obvious and the hidden, as a starting point for addressing issues of diversity when teaching adults. For example, it is obvious when this author first walks into any teaching situation that she is a White, middle-aged female. By her dress, learners also may easily judge that she is at least middle class and, through her language, that she is well-educated and a primary English speaker. When her reputation as a scholar is known, she also carries into the learning situation an air of authority and power, which for some learners is daunting and intimidating. The less obvious factors (although readily apparent for some in the room) are her beliefs regarding people of color, gender, class, cultural background, sexual orientation, learning abilities and disabilities, and language use.

Hayes (1994) and Guy (1999a) also challenge instructors of adults to go beyond just acknowledging their own biases in teaching. Their view is that instructors must be willing to change their views about learners, the way they teach, and even what content they choose to include. This task of making teaching situations more inclusive is not easy, either for instructors or participants. As Wlodkowski (1998) has astutely observed:

> *When we are teaching, exclusion is usually an indirect act, an omission of opportunity or of someone's voice. We're usually not mean-spirited, but, more likely unaware that a perspective is missing, that a biased myth has been perpetuated, or that we aren't covering topics of concern to certain adults. In fact, most adult learners, usually those who have been socialized to accommodate our method of instruction, may like our course or training. Things seem pretty pleasant. Why go looking for trouble? (p. 89).*

Instructors who take into account the many differences among learners adopt three key norms for practice:

1. The multiplicity of ways people learn and respond to learning situation is a given.

2. Instructors have the responsibility for designing instruction so these differences are acknowledged and used to enhance the what, when, where, and how of learning situations.

3. Instructors and learners together work to form learning communities that encompass an awareness and feeling of connection among adults and respect for all involved in the instructional process (see Chapter Thirteen).

Helpful resources that provide examples of learning techniques that acknowledge differences, and ways to create inclusive learning environments for adults, include: Hayes and Colin (1994); Tisdell (1995); Wlodkowski and Ginsberg (1995); Roth (1997); Brookfield and Preskill (1999); Guy (1999b); Pratt, Kelly, and Wong (1999); Wlodkowski (1998); and Hayes, Flannery, and Associates (2000).

## Learning Context

The learning context, the final key factor that influences the choice of learning techniques, is the setting where the learning takes place (Smith and Ragan, 1999; Vella, 2000). Adults learn in a variety of settings, from formal class and training rooms, to their homes and workplaces, to the great outdoors (see Chapter One). Some learning situations are more conducive to using certain techniques than others. For example, solving problems of practice in the settings where participants actually work calls for using "real-life" case studies, in-basket exercises, observations, and problem-based learning. Other places, such as multiple learning sites in a number of countries, are better suited for computer-based instruction and audio and video conferencing, providing the technology is available.

In turn, some learning contexts can enhance the use of techniques that are used, while other settings can inhibit the use of those same techniques. For example, teaching in a residential setting on an island in Alaska lends itself to using a number of learning techniques, like reflective practice, Socratic dialogue, storytelling, and listening circles, all of which take time and work especially well when participants have a chance to build a learning community (see Chapter Thirteen). In contrast, using these same techniques in a busy workplace is often frowned upon, as the expectations are that participants will be in and out of training fast and will be able to immediately apply whatever they are learning to their specific job tasks.

## Selecting Instructional Resources

In addition to choosing appropriate instructional techniques, it is important that staff members who design instruction also know how to select and use appropriately a variety of instructional resources, as illustrated by the following scenario.

### *If One Is Good, Twenty Must Be Great!*

Carol, a new part-time instructor in the continuing education division, attends a workshop on selecting and using different instructional resources in the classroom. She really gets turned on to the use of these materials and decides to incorporate them into her classes as often as she can. Carol's colleagues can always tell who the instructor is for a particular class by the amount of equipment, handouts, and other resources in the room. She has noticed that learners seem distracted at times, but she writes this off to the hour of the day and the numerous pressures her students face. To Carol's surprise, she finds through her mid-term evaluations that students are complaining bitterly about the overuse of handouts. The resources don't seem to fit with their own experiences, especially the "canned programs" that Carol uses. Students report that instead of helping, the resources actually are hindering their learning, and they feel "off-track" or disconnected to the class content and process. Carol sincerely thought the materials and ways of presenting made her class much more interesting and lively, but she knows now that she needs to cut back and reassess her use of materials. She decides to ask a small group of the students to assist her in determining what resources and equipment use is best suited for the class and most helpful in enhancing student learning.

In choosing which resources to use there are numerous guidelines that are helpful to instructors (Tracey, 1992; Kemp, Morrison, and Ross, 1996; Mitchell, 1998; Sugrue and Clark, 2000; Dick, Carey, and Carey, 2001). Among those guidelines, the following are the most salient:

▶ Select materials that fit the experiences, interests, and abilities of the learners, and are useful to them in applying what they have learned in their own situations.

▶ Choose resources that effectively take advantage of the context in which the learning is taking place.

▶ Choose materials that explain and illustrate well what is being taught (for example, knowledge versus problem-solving capabilities).

▶ Select resources that focus attention on the essence of the topic.

▶ Adopt materials that "can take you where you cannot otherwise go" (Mitchell, 1998, p. 213); for example, an inside look at the brain, practices which cannot be brought to the learning situation, sounds of a work environment.

▶ Use a variety of resources.

▶ Avoid the overuse of materials and other aids.

▶ Select resources that are available now or can be designed in the needed time frame and can be delivered effectively in the environment where the learning activity is to be held.

Carol violated at least two, if not more, of these basic guidelines—avoiding the overuse of materials and choosing resources that did not fit the learners' experiences and interests.

## Types of Resources Available

A wide variety of instructional resources and aids can be used. A categorized listing of the most popular resources is depicted in Exhibit 9.7 (Kemp, Morrison, and Ross, 1996; Driscoll, 1998; Mitchell, 1998; Smith and Ragan, 1999). Again, competent instructors carefully select resources and aids to enhance the learning efforts of the participants.

**EXHIBIT 9.7**

## Sample Instructional Resources and Aids by Category

| Category | Resources and Aids | |
|---|---|---|
| **Real Things** | • People<br>• Objects and devices<br>• Models, mock-ups, or simulators<br>• Outdoor environment<br>• Job aids | |
| **Printed Materials** | • Handouts<br>• Notebooks<br>• Manuals<br>• Pamphlets<br>• Articles | • Books<br>• Forms for guided note-taking<br>• Worksheets<br>• Reference lists<br>• Workbooks |
| **Visual Aids** | • Transparencies<br>• Graphs<br>• Storyboards<br>• Charts<br>• Posters<br>• Slides | • Chalk and white boards<br>• Photographs<br>• Flip charts<br>• Maps<br>• Diagrams<br>• Pictures |
| **Audio and Video Materials** | • Videotapes<br>• Digital videodiscs<br>• Audiotapes and CD recordings<br>• Television | |
| **Computer-Based Resources** | • PowerPoint presentations<br>• Computer-generated images<br>• World Wide Web<br>• LCD panel<br>• Listservs<br>• Asynchronous threaded discussions and forums | |
| **Interactive Technologies** | • Interactive CD-ROMs<br>• Web-based tools (for example, chat rooms, synchronous threaded discussions)<br>• Video and audio conferencing | |

## Buying or Making Instructional Resources

Before developing or contracting for instructional resources, program planners explore what materials and people resources already exist in-house. Are suitable materials and aids available that could be used as is or with some modification? If not, is organizational staff available and able to develop the needed materials, or would it be more cost-effective to buy materials from an external vendor (Diamond, 1998; Mitchell, 1998; Kruse and Keil, 2000)?

If the decision is to make the materials in-house, this is done in a number of ways (Milano with Ullius, 1998; Mitchell, 1998; Dick, Carey, and Carey, 2001). For simple materials, such as handouts and content outlines, the instructor or the coordinator of the program usually develops the materials. The same is now true for such aids as transparencies, notebooks, charts, diagrams, and manuals for staff who have access to computer graphics and word-processing programs.

When preparing more elaborate materials, such as videotapes or the components of computer-based instruction, a more complex process is used, usually involving a team effort (Kemp, Morrison, and Ross, 1996; Smith and Ragan, 1999; Alessi and Trollip, 2001). A typical team is composed of a program or instructional designer, a content expert, and a technology specialist. The team's role is to plan and oversee the production of the needed materials. Individual members of the team, depending on their expertise, may also do the actual production activities. It is important to validate complex materials with actual participants prior to using them on a large-scale basis (Tracey, 1992; Smith and Ragan, 1999). The validation process is done with individuals or with groups, depending on the nature of the materials developed and how they are used.

Nadler (1982) and Kruse and Keil (2000) recommend that program planners who decide to contract for all or part of the instructional resources for an educational program consider five questions that address possible restrictions on the use of those materials:

1. Who owns the content? For technology-based programs, who owns the source code?

2. What are the copyright restrictions on the use of the material?

3. Is there a cost for subsequent use of the same resources?

4. Can the purchaser reproduce some or all of the materials, or must these materials be continually bought from the vendor?

5. What will program updates cost and can you do them in-house or must the outside vendor be involved?

Resources purchased from outside vendors do not always meet all the requirements of a particular program. Therefore, modifications may have to be made to the materials themselves or to the instructional activities. For example, the sequencing of content of a particular program may need to be changed to match more closely the sequence of the purchased materials. In most cases permission must be sought from the outside vendor to make these changes, unless this right has been negotiated in the initial contract.

Whether the decision is made to use or prepare in-house materials or obtain resources from an outside source, Tracey (1992) notes that "the major criterion of selection is simply this: Will it advance learning; is it needed? A training aid must actually aid learning and not be mere 'eye wash' " (p. 292).

## Preparing for Instructional Assessment

Instructional assessment or evaluation is done for five major reasons (Brookfield, 1992; Diamond, 1998; Wiggins, 1998; McMillian, 2001):

- To assess participants' background, experiences, and readiness for learning when they enter an activity or program
- To improve the instructional process and materials
- To ascertain whether the instructional event has actually produced the desired results
- To assist participants to be more effective learners
- To provide data for the overall program evaluation (see Chapter Eleven)

Some of these assessment instruments that address these five purposes are now constructed and administered online as well as through more traditional ways (Alessi and Trollip, 2001; Dick, Carey, and Carey, 2001). Each of these purposes for doing instructional assessment is discussed in the following sections.

### Assessment at Entry

Assessment done either prior to or at the start of a learning activity allows the instructors to know what the participants know and can do and/or how they feel about the content to be presented. This entry-level assessment activity may also be done as part of identifying program ideas (see Chapter Six) and/or as a part of preparing marketing plans (see Chapter Fourteen). Evaluation methods at this stage range from asking participants to complete simple questionnaires (on who they are, what background knowledge and experiences they have related to the content, and the like) to administering comprehensive tests on prerequisite knowledge or skills (Angelo and Cross, 1993; McMillan, 2001). These data can also be used, as discussed later in this section, as baseline information for assessing the results of the instructional activity and the program as a whole (see Chapter Eleven).

### Assessment of the Instructional Process and Resources

Using instructional assessment to improve the instructional process and resources is done prior to offering the instructional event (alpha and beta testing), during the instructional event (formative evaluation), and afterwards (summative evaluation) (Brookfield, 1990; Angelo and Cross, 1993; Smith and Ragan, 1999; Alessi and Trollip, 2001; Dick, Carey, and Carey, 2001). This type of assessment is usually completed by the instructors themselves and/or by the participants.

Instructors can benefit greatly by checking and reflecting on the instructional process and the content before, during, and after the session is over. For example, one way for instructors to formalize this reflection is to keep a teaching journal or log in which they jot down and reflect on what was done well, what could have been done better, and what could be done differently. Team-teaching with a colleague also encourages instructors to reflect on instructional activities, as long as both instructors agree that debriefing sessions will be a regular part of their team-teaching process (Buckley, 2000).

Participant assessment of the resources and process are also very useful. This form of assessment is especially useful when the session is still in progress, but only if instructors are willing to make changes based on the feedback given to them. Again, this assessment is done in a variety of ways, from questionnaires to small-group feedback sessions to large-group discussions. Sample questions to guide participant reactions are in Exhibit 9.8.

With instructional segments that will be used on a large scale with a variety of groups, a more comprehensive process of formative evaluation is used to evaluate the instructional materials and process. Usually this alpha and beta testing is done with small test groups before the materials are used

---

**EXHIBIT 9.8**

## Sample Questions to Guide Participant Assessment of Resources and Process

1. Were the handouts and other materials understandable and useful to you?

2. Which instructional techniques were the most helpful to you in the learning process? Which were the least helpful?

3. What was especially good about the session, and what could have been improved?

4. Were the facilities comfortable and appropriate for the learning activities?

5. Was the instructional climate welcoming, or did it inhibit your learning? Please give specific examples of factors that enhanced and/or blocked your willingness and/or ability to learn.

6. Was the participation level appropriate and helpful to you as a learner?

7. Were there any points and/or specific skills covered that you do not understand or do not know how to do? What do you believe would help you in gaining a better grasp of the content?

8. Did the instructor respect differing viewpoints?

9. Did the instructor and other learners acknowledge learner differences and capitalize for these differences?

10. Did the instructor invite and encourage participation from the group and individuals?

11. Were the instructional resources (for example, PowerPoint presentations, videotapes, charts, and Web-based materials) helpful, or did they distract from the learning?

on a regular basis. For a more complete description of this type of formative evaluation for instructional units, see Smith and Ragan (1999).

### Assessment of the Results

The starting point for assessing the results or outcomes of the instructional unit is the learning objectives. The assessment techniques chosen need to match the focus of those objectives—acquiring knowledge, enhancing cognitive skills, developing psychomotor skills, strengthening problem-solving and -finding capabilities, and/or changing attitudes, beliefs, values, and/or feelings. Some of the most widely used techniques for assessing what has been learned are in Exhibit 9.9 (Angelo and Cross, 1993; Wiggins, 1998; Guskey, 2000; McMillan, 2001).

Although categorizing assessment techniques is helpful, program planners should note that depending on how a technique is designed, it (like instructional techniques) may fit into more than one category of learning outcomes. For example, tests and reflective journals, depending on how they are constructed, are used to assess knowledge, cognitive skills, problem-solving and -finding capabilities, and changes in attitudes, beliefs, values, and/or feelings, or all of the above. In addition, another assessment tool—the portfolio—has become more popular in recent years in the educational community. Depending on how it is constructed, it can address all of the different types of learning outcomes (Jackson and Caffarella, 1994; Wiggins, 1998; Dietz, 1999; McMillan, 2001). Portfolios provide direct evidence of learning through a collection of carefully selected materials (for example, written papers, memos, artistic materials, audio and videotapes, computer-based materials, published articles, honors and awards, work-related products). Accompanying this evidence are descriptive and reflective entries that allow the instructor and/or fellow participants to gain a clear understanding of what each artifact represents. Portfolios are powerful tools for both individual and group learning.

Smith and Delahaye (1987); Angelo and Cross (1993); Wiggins (1998); and McMillan (2001) have outlined key ideas to consider when choosing and managing instructional assessments. In choosing assessment tools, instructors should ask themselves:

▶ Are the assessment techniques of high quality? That is, "are they technically sound and provide results that demonstrate and improve" participant learning (McMillan, 2001, p. 52)?

▶ Are the assessment techniques appropriate for the targeted learning results (for example, acquiring knowledge, changing attitudes, beliefs, values, and/or feelings)?

**EXHIBIT 9.9**

# Assessment Techniques by Learning Outcomes Category

## Acquiring Knowledge

- *Closed-Answer Tests.* Participants answer a set of standardized or instructor-developed test items. The test may consist of multiple-choice, true/false, matching, and/or sentence-completion items.
- *Essays.* Participants respond in writing to one or more questions or problem situations. They may be asked to compare, discuss, analyze, criticize, evaluate, apply, or the like.
- *Oral Tests.* Learners react to a set of oral questions either individually or in groups.
- *Oral Presentations.* Participants give a formal presentation to a selected group on a specific topic area.
- *Self-Report Evaluation Forms.* Learners respond to structured or open-ended questions or matrixes and describe what they have learned.

## Enhancing Cognitive Skills

- *Case Studies.* Participants analyze and give alternative solutions to an event, incident, or situation that is problematic. This process may be done in written or oral form and can be either a group or individual exercise.
- *Concept Maps.* Learners make diagrams and drawings that represent the mental connections between and among major concepts and ideas.
- *Interviews.* Participants conduct individual and/or group interviews. The focus of the exercise is to demonstrate the ability to analyze, criticize, or evaluate a specific problem or situation.
- *Analytic Memos.* Learners write a memo responding to a real-life problem or issue that demonstrates their analytical abilities (for example, work-related issues, community problems).

## Developing Psychomotor Skills

- *Performance Reviews and Tests.* Participants perform a skill, operation, or practical application. Specified equipment and/or materials are often used. A clear statement of the required standards is used, and all parties have to understand those standards prior to initiating the testing procedure.
- *On-the-Job Observations.* Participants, under the eye of the evaluator, carry out a set of performance behaviors on the job. Again, clear standards for performance are set.
- *Product Reviews.* Learners develop a product for examination by the instructor and/or an outside expert or panel of experts (for example, a model, a videotape).

## Strengthening Problem-Finding and -Solving Capabilities

- *Documented Problem Solutions.* Participants document specifically how they have solved a problem in their own or a simulated context.
- *Audio- and Videotaped Protocols.* Learners are audio- or videotaped while engaged in a problem-finding or -solving situation.
- *Reflective Journals.* Participants are required to keep written reflective entries on how they solved specific problems and/or the processes they used in problem identification.
- *Computer-Based Simulations.* Learners solve problems through computer simulations that allow them a range of responses to the various problem-based situations they encounter.
- *Observations.* Learners are observed by instructors of other interested parties to ascertain whether useful and appropriate new ways are being used to strengthen their problem-finding and -solving capabilities.

## Changing Attitudes, Beliefs, Values, and/or Feelings

- *Role Playing.* Learners role play a situation, focusing on attitudes, beliefs, values, and feelings.
- *Closed-Ended Tests.* Participants answer questions that focus on specific attitudes, beliefs, values, or feelings. Although these tests are difficult to construct, they can provide a very useful measure, provided they are both reliable and valid.
- *Reflective Journals.* Learners record in their journals two types of entries: one that describes an event or situation, and a second that focuses on their feelings and attitudes about that event.
- *Free Form Writing.* Participants are asked to respond to a stem sentence or just write about a specific topic, responding primarily to how they feel about a topic, situation, or proposition.

▶ Is the assessment tool practical and efficient to use?

▶ Is the assessment tool fair and can it account for individual differences?

▶ Does the assessment technique appeal to your professional judgment and intuition about its usefulness?

▶ Will the assessment technique be seen as credible and user-friendly to the learners?

▶ Is the assessment going to turn into a "self-inflicted chore or burden" (Angelo and Cross, 1993, p. 31) for both you and the participants?

▶ Have you planned enough time to use the assessment in an effective manner?

▶ Have you tried this assessment out on yourself?

In managing the assessment process, instructors first need to understand that many adults are very anxious about any type of assessment related to what they have learned. Educators and trainers have to respond to this anxiety with both concern and respect for the participants' feelings. Second, clear and complete instructions about how the assessment will be conducted must be provided. Specify the date, time, and place of the assessment; the format and length; and what the assessment requires participants to do. Third, a comfortable environment should be provided. Fourth, all resources (such as computer stations, test booklets, and equipment) to complete the assessment process should be readily available and in working order.

## Assessment to Assist Learning

The next reason to do instructional assessments is to assist learning (Brookfield, 1990, 1992; Wiggins, 1998). As Brookfield (1992) notes:

> *To be helpful an evaluation should be educative. . . . (1) It should help the recipient become more adept and critically reflective in regard to the specific learning activity involved, (2) it should assist learners to develop insight into their own habitual learning process and rhythms so that they can make some judgments about when these should be given free rein and when they should be held in check, and (3) it should assist adults to develop self-concepts of themselves as learners as a way of nurturing their self-confidence and encouraging their belief that areas of skill, knowledge, action, and insight that they had formerly considered as being closed to them are actually accessible. [p. 22]*

Brookfield (1992); Dirkx and Prenger (1997); and Wiggins (1998) go on to describe nine indicators that help instructors judge whether their assessment processes are useful and significant to learners engaging in the learning process. See Exhibit 9.10 for the indicators and a description of each indicator. Of the nine indicators in Exhibit 9.10, the indicators of affirmation and focusing on changes that can be made are the most challenging and helpful to both instructors and participants.

### Assessment to Provide Data for the Overall Program Evaluation

The final rationale for doing instructional assessments is to provide data for the overall program evaluation (see Chapters Eleven and Twelve). Yes, there are differences in the focus of instructional and program assessment; that is, a "program evaluation focuses on larger organization questions and social contexts of the program (macro level), [while] evaluation of learning focuses on what and how learners learn and how educators help or hinder the process of learning (micro level)" (Deshler, 1998, p. 305–306). Despite these different foci, data from learning or instructional assessments are valuable sources of information to use in making judgments about the program as a whole. These data are useful, as shown in Exhibit 9.11, in both formative and summative processes of program evaluation (Rothwell and Cookson, 1997; Dick, Carey, and Carey, 2001).

Instructional assessment data are not used as often as they ought to be in program evaluations, although there is an obvious link between whether

---

**EXHIBIT 9.10**

## Nine Indicators of Useful Assessment

1. **Clear.** Describing clearly, precisely, and in language understandable to the learners the criteria that will be used to judge their learning.

2. **Specific.** Outlining precisely the criteria for what is expected of learners (for example, in terms of in-class participation, written assignments, other products) and specific actions they can take to enhance their learning efforts.

3. **Timely.** Giving feedback as soon as possible after the activity has been completed.

4. **Ongoing and frequent.** Providing feedback on an ongoing and regular basis throughout the instructional process.

5. **Accessible.** Providing opportunities to learners for additional discussions about their evaluation.

6. **Affirming.** Acknowledging participants' efforts and achievements, no matter how large or small.

7. **Changeable.** Giving clear suggestions for future changes and actions.

8. **Justifiable.** Making sure that learners understand how the evaluation will help them in their learning efforts.

9. **Stated with Care and Concern.** Giving feedback in such a way that learners know you care about their learning and wish to provide helpful and nonpunitive assistance.

the instructional activities provided the intended results and the overall value and worth of the total program. For example, at professional conferences, participants are usually asked at the end of each session to provide an assessment of that session. Common questions include: Were the session objectives clear and did the presenter successfully address each objective? Were the instructional techniques and materials helpful? Did the session contribute to your knowledge and/or skill level? What happens to these data after they are collected is often mysterious. Sometimes these data go

**EXHIBIT 9.11**

## Examples of Using Instructional Assessment Data in Program Evaluation

| Aspect of Instruction | Formative Evaluation | Summative Evaluation |
|---|---|---|
| **Selecting and organizing content** | → Check whether content and the organization of this content are appropriate in helping participants determine whether any changes need to be made in either the content itself or the organization of that content. | → Document strengths and weaknesses in selection and organization of instructional content to decide whether to continue, revise, and/or delete some or all of the content and how it was organized. |
| **Choosing instructional techniques** | → Ensure the instructional techniques match the outcomes of the learning objectives, are being used well by instructors, and take into account the backgrounds and experiences of the participants and the learning context to decide whether revisions are appropriate. | → Provide evidence the instructional techniques were suitable for the content being taught, instructional staff were capable of using them, learners found the techniques appropriate, and the learning context was taken into account in selecting the techniques. Decisions are then made to determine whether these instructional techniques should be used again for programs of this nature. |
| **Preparing instructional assessments** | → Make certain the instructional assessments are appropriate for evaluating the focus of the learning outcomes, are being used in both a formative and summative way, and provide useful feedback to learners in a caring way to determine whether any of these processes should be revised or dropped. | → Substantiate that overall the instructional assessments actually centered on the focus of the learning outcomes, were used in both formative and summative ways, and provided useful and caring feedback to learners on what and how they were learning. These data are used to conclude whether these instructional assessments should be the same, or if parts or all of these assessments should be revised, and/ or not used again in programs of this nature. |

directly to the presenters and are definitely not used in evaluating the overall conference. Other times, planning teams use these data primarily to decide whether a person should present at future conferences, but this reason is often not shared beyond the planning team. In other cases, the conference evaluators integrate these data into their program evaluation reports, but even when this action is taken, it is not always clear how this integration has been done. But most often, conferees and presenters are not sure what has happened to the data collected at each individual session. One way to make sure these data are used is to build into the program evaluation plan how instructional assessment data are being collected and utilized in terms of assessing the overall program.

## Sample Instructional Plan

Clearly and concisely developed instructional plans provide roadmaps that help instructors get where they want to go and remind them of their intended route (Milano with Ullius, 1998; Mitchell, 1998; Van Kavelaar, 1998). Three major advantages of preparing these plans are that they assist instructors to stay within the timeframe for various parts of the educational activity; know whether they have wandered too far off the topic (and how they can regain their focus); and complete the learning activity in the allotted time.

There is no set form for an instructional plan as long as these major components of the activity are outlined:

- Course or session title
- Date and time frame
- Learning objectives
- Session activities
- Instructional techniques
- Assessment plan
- Estimated time for each major part of the learning activity or activities
- Instructor and learner materials
- Room arrangements
- Equipment and other resources

A sample instructional plan is given in Exhibit 9.12.

The instructional plan should be used as a guide for how the instructor and the participants spend their time in the session, not as a document that dictates precisely what each person must do and when. There must be room for flexibility and change in both the content and the learning process, depending on the learners and what happens in the learning situation.

**EXHIBIT 9.12**

# Sample Instructional Plan

**Title:** A Program Planning Model—Checklist for Planning Successful Programs

**Date and Time:** Wednesday 9:30 A.M. to Noon

| Learning Objectives | | | | |
|---|---|---|---|---|
| *The participants will be able to . . .* | **Content Heading** | **Key Points to Emphasize** | **Instructional Techniques** | **Estimated Time** |
| Describe a 12-component program planning model. | Present program planning model. | Point out that the model is a set of interacting and dynamic elements and that most program planners work concurrently on a number of the components. Describe the 11 components of the model. The key word in using the model is *flexibility*. | Lecture Question-and-answer period | 30 minutes |
| Analyze a case study using the model presented. | Analyze the case study. | In groups of five people, have participants analyze a case study. Appoint a discussion leader and a recorder who will report back to the whole group the results of each small group's work. | Small-group discussion Report from small groups Large-group discussion | 45 minutes |
| Critique the model in terms of its usefulness for on-the-job applications. | Critique the model. | Discuss the strengths and weaknesses of the model. How could the model be revised? | Buzz groups Large-group discussion | 30 minutes |
| List two ways they can use one component of the model in their daily work activities. | Apply the model. | Point out how the model can be applied to what participants do in their jobs. | Dyads Round-robin listing of ideas in the larger group | 30 minutes |

**Assessment plan:** Pre-test and post-test on the program model. Review of case study analysis.

**Instructional resources and equipment needed:**

| **For Instructor** | **For Participants** |
|---|---|
| PowerPoint presentation | Handout on program planning model |
| LCD Panel | Case study |
| Critique form | Reference list on program planning |
| Notes for instructor about process or content | |

**Room Arrangement Needed:** Chairs arranged around tables, table up front for the instructor

## Making the Instructional Plan Work

Whether they are leaders of individual sessions or keynote speakers, how instructors put their instructional plans into action can either foster or block a positive climate for learning. Instructors enhance learning by sharing their content mastery, being helpful facilitators, using instructional techniques and assessment strategies appropriately and well, and establishing good rapport with the participants (Brookfield, 1990; Apps, 1996). All these actions assume that instructors have knowledge about the participants and are well-prepared for the instructional event.

Motivating participants upfront is a very important part of making the instructional plan work (Wlodkowski, 1998). One major way to capture participants' interest is to get them personally involved with the material. Starting with a question-and-answer period or breaking the group into dyads or small work teams can set the stage for learner engagement with the content. In very large groups, presenters can use human-interest stories or prepare participants by highlighting two or three new and exciting ideas at the outset. However participation and interest are fostered, the method should be well thought-out and applicable to the program content. There is nothing worse than starting a session in an unorganized and vague manner.

A second way to motivate the group is by encouraging instructors to be enthusiastic and energetic. Instructors who are open to questions and comments, use humor, and interact with the crowd spark the interest of even the most reluctant participants. In assisting the participants to learn content, instructors have to present the material in an organized manner. A number of different instructional techniques, as described earlier in this chapter, can be used, with the emphasis placed on active learner participation whenever possible and appropriate. Some helpful hints for instructors as they move through the instructional plan are listed in Exhibit 9.13.

Useful resources that describe more fully what instructors can do to ensure a positive learning experience include: Brookfield (1990), Brookfield and Preskill (1999); Vella, (1994, 2000); Tisdell (1995); Apps (1996); Roth (1997); Silberman (1996); Guy (1999); and Wlodkowski (1998). Whenever possible, instructors should assist participants in examining how the new knowledge, skills, problem-solving and -finding capabilities, beliefs, and/or feelings they have learned can be applicable to their lives (see Chapter Ten). Four key transfer-of-learning or applications strategies are: (1) use active learning techniques that enhance transfer (for example, critical reflection, developing action or learning plans); (2) incorporate having learners try out their new skills in either their own or similar settings; (3) provide learners opportunities to develop specific applications plans; and

---

**EXHIBIT 9.13**

## Helpful Hints for Instructors

- Remove or lessen anxieties of the participants.
- Create safe and inclusive learning environments.
- Spell out clearly and up front the expectations for participants.
- Set or develop group norms. (Let participants know, for example, that active participation is encouraged, divergent opinions are welcomed, and a question-and-answer period is a part of the presentation.)
- Talk about the commonalities among all parties involved (for example, the instructor, the participants, invited resource people).
- Let learners know the role of the instructor is to help them learn.
- Acknowledge and celebrate learner diversity as a strength of the learning process.
- Use nondiscriminatory language that all participants can readily understand, and treat participants in an unbiased way.
- Develop professional and caring relationships between and among learners and instructors.
- Give participants advanced "organizers" (such as five key points) to help them follow the ideas presented.
- Use the resources and expertise of the participants.
- Use an outline or notes rather than reading a formally prepared paper or script.
- Use active learning techniques that allow time for reflection.
- Restate important ideas.
- Be generous with examples.
- Listen carefully to all ideas presented by the participants and respond appropriately.
- Keep a good pace, and be aware of time.
- Provide feedback and positive reinforcement to participants throughout the session.
- Recognize that emotions play an important part in the learning process.
- Be flexible with the presentation, instructional plans, and techniques (for example, build on the unexpected).
- Be caring and openly committed to the participants' learning.
- Use humor and laughter.
- Have fun.
- Be ethical in instructional practice.

---

(4) ensure assistance is given for learning transfer (for example, coaching, refresher courses, mentoring) (see Chapter Ten).

When participants develop individual action or learning plans, in most cases a draft should be prepared during the program (Caffarella, 1993; O'Donnell and Caffarella, 1998). In helping participants complete these plans, instructors encourage participants to indicate specific individuals who could provide assistance and/or support, especially when they are committed to making major personal, work, or community changes. (This assistance and/or support can be given by a variety of people, such as fellow participants, work colleagues and supervisors, family and friends, and professional educators.) A sample form for an individual action plan is provided in this chapter's Application Exercises.

## Chapter Highlights

Instructional plans provide the framework for the interactions between and among learners and instructors and/or learners and resource materials for each education and training activity. These plans spell out the anticipated end product, the content, the instructional techniques, and the assessment strategies that make up the instructional process. In designing instructional plans, instructors, program planners, and/or instructional designers complete the following tasks:

◆ Develop clear and understandable learning objectives for each instructional session and ensure they match the proposed learning outcomes (acquiring new knowledge, enhancing cognitive and psychomotor skills, problem-solving and -finding capabilities, and changing attitudes, beliefs, values, and/or feelings).

◆ Select and organize the content on what participants "must learn," which is based on the learning objectives. Content that supplements the essential material should be included only if time allows. Be cognizant that there is no best way to select and sequence the content.

◆ Choose instructional techniques that match the focus of the proposed learning outcomes, that the instructor is capable of using, and that take into account the backgrounds and experiences of the learners and the learning context (for example, lectures, case studies, Web-based instruction, storytelling, games, or metaphor analysis).

◆ Select and/or develop instructional resources that enhance the learning effort (for example, "real things," printed materials, visual aids, audio and video materials, computer-based resources, or interactive technologies).

◆ Choose an assessment component for each instructional segment that improves participants' learning and ascertains whether the instructional event actually produced the desired result.

◆ Use instructional assessment data in formative and summative ways for both the instructional aspects of the program as well as the program as a whole.

◆ Prepare clear and concise instructional plans as roadmaps that can assist instructors to stay focused as they move through the instructional process.

◆ Make the instructional process work by ensuring instructors know their content, are competent learning facilitators, care about learners, use instructional and assessment techniques appropriately and skillfully, and are well-prepared for each instructional event.

The information provided through the program objectives (see Chapter Eight) and the instructional plans often inform the design of learning-transfer activities and program evaluations and, in turn, the learning-transfer and evaluation plans inform the development of program objectives and instructional plans. Devising transfer-of-learning plans and formulating program evaluations are discussed, respectively, in the next two chapters.

## Application Exercises

 The Application Exercises in this chapter help you to develop learning objectives, select instructional techniques, develop an instructional assessment process, complete an instructional plan, and prepare for the application of learning.

---

### EXERCISE 9.1

### Developing Learning Objectives

1. Describe briefly an educational program for which you will act as the instructor or be part of an instructional team.

2. Develop a set of learning objectives for your part of the program using the following format. Complete each part for each objective, as appropriate.

| The Learner . . . | Action Verb | . . . Content | Conditions Under Which the Learning is to Be Demonstrated?* | Criteria for Acceptable Performance* |
|---|---|---|---|---|
| _____ | _____ | _____ | _____ | _____ |
| _____ | _____ | _____ | _____ | _____ |
| _____ | _____ | _____ | _____ | _____ |
| _____ | _____ | _____ | _____ | _____ |
| _____ | _____ | _____ | _____ | _____ |

*These two elements of the learning objective are not applicable for learning objectives that cannot be stated in behavioral or performance terms.*

## EXERCISE 9.2

## Selecting Instructional Techniques

1.  For the same session you described in Exercise 9.1, develop two alternative ways the material could be taught. Keep in mind the focus of the learning outcomes, your expertise, the backgrounds and experiences of the learners, and the context for learning.

Alternative 1:

Alternative 2:

## EXERCISE 9.3

## Developing an Instructional Assessment Process

1. **For the same session you described in Exercises 9.1 and 9.2, describe the major reason or reasons for completing an instructional assessment.**

2. **Select and describe one or more techniques you will use to evaluate this instructional session.**

   Technique:

   Description:

   Technique:

   Description:

3. **Describe how you will ensure that the assessment process exhibits the following qualities:**

   Clarity:

   Specificity:

   Timeliness:

   Ongoing and Frequent:

   Accessibility:

   Affirmation:

   Be About Something That Can Be Changed:

   Justifiability:

   Stated with Care and Concern:

## EXERCISE 9.4

## Completing an Instructional Plan

**Using the material from Exercises 9.1, 9.2, and 9.3, develop an instructional plan (refer to Exhibit 9.12 as a guide) for a session for which you serve as the instructor.**

*Title:*

*Date and Time:*

| Learning Objectives The participants will be able to . . . | Content Heading | Key Points to Emphasize | Instructional Techniques | Estimated Time |
|---|---|---|---|---|
|  |  |  |  |  |
|  |  |  |  |  |
|  |  |  |  |  |
|  |  |  |  |  |

*Assessment plan:*

*Instructional resources and equipment needed:*

**For Instructor**                          **For Participants**

*Room Arrangement Needed:*

## EXERCISE 9.5

## Preparing for the Application of Learning

1.  **Briefly describe an educational program you recently attended.**

2.  **Complete an individual plan, as outlined in the following chart, specifying how you will apply what you learned.**

### Individual Action Plan

| | |
|---|---|
| List knowledge; skills; problem-solving and -finding capabilities; and/or attitudes, values, feelings learned. | |
| Specify when, where, and how you want to apply what you have learned. | |
| Name people who could offer assistance, support. | |
| List other resources that might be helpful (such as books, training programs). Specify how you will know you are successfully using the new knowledge; skills; problem-finding or -solving capabilities; and/or values and attitudes. | |
| Specify a time frame. | |

3.  **Review this plan with at least one other person and make changes as appropriate.**

# Chapter 10

# Devising Transfer-of-Learning Plans

**ONE OF THE BASIC TENETS OF PEOPLE** who attend, plan, and sponsor education and training programs is that what has been learned is something participants can use after the program is completed. Yet in the planning of most programs, until fairly recently, it has been assumed that this transfer of learning would somehow just happen. Neither program planners nor instructors paid much attention to intentionally how program participants could integrate what they had learned back into their personal, work, and/or public lives. Rather, it was primarily left up to learners to apply, as they thought appropriate and needed, what they had learned.

In some cases, as illustrated in this scenario, leaving the application piece in the learners' hands makes sense:

### Recreational Mountain Biking

Dave has just completed a workshop sponsored by a local community recreation association on mountain biking. He has always enjoyed the out-of-doors and thought this would be a sport that might be fun and relaxing. One thing that he had not counted on is how expensive the sport is. Dave had hoped he could start riding on a regular basis right away but has decided, except for one short trip (for which he will rent a bike), that he will need a few months to save up so that he can buy the kind of bike he really would like. He also wants to entice one or two of his friends to join him in this venture, because there is greater safety in numbers, especially for the longer rides into the backcountry.

In other cases, as shown in the next scenario, program participants do need assistance in applying what they have learned:

### I Am Back at Work—Now What?

Susan, the dean of continuing education, took an intensive three-week summer course on leadership development four months ago. She is still very excited about what she learned in the program and about her plan (developed at the suggestion of the program facilitators) for putting into practice some of the key ideas. But reality set in on her first day back on campus as she faced a mountain of mail, phone messages, and meetings. Although the plan stayed in her "to do" file for the remainder of the summer and into the fall semester, she never got to it. And she *still* has no time. In addition, she now has a gut feeling that the new vice president for academic affairs would probably block one of the major changes she wants to initiate, even though she knows her staff members are supportive. As she reflects informally with a colleague about the summer experience, she comments that a more explicit transfer-of-learning component to the course—including specific support from the institute staff—would have been very helpful.

Discussed first in this chapter is what transfer of learning is all about, and what learning-transfer plans are based upon. This discussion is followed by an exploration of why transfer of learning is an important component of the program planning process. Examined next are the key factors that influence the transfer-of-learning process. The next sections present a framework for planning transfer of learning and highlight a number of strategies and techniques that are used prior to, during, and after education and training programs to assist participants in applying what they have learned. The final section explores the challenge that program planners face in the applications process.

## What Is the Transfer of Learning?

Transfer of learning is the effective application by program participants of what they learned as a result of attending an education or training program (Kemerer, 1991; Killion and Kaylor, 1991; Broad and Newstrom, 1992; Ottoson, 1995a, 1997a; Taylor, 2000). It is often referred to as the "so what" or "now what" phase of the learning process. "So what does this all mean, and how can what was learned be applicable to my situation?" Transfer of learning (also termed transfer-of-training or applications process) is not a new component of the planning process (Nadler, 1982; Fox, 1984; Baldwin and Ford, 1988). Rather, it is an element of the process that is receiving increased attention as both participants and sponsors of education and training programs demand more concrete and useful results. Not all educational programs for adults need to have a plan for this part of the process, however. In fact, for some programs—a public lecture series or a weekend retreat for spiritual renewal, for example—a plan for how the transfer of learning should happen may be totally out of place. But for many programs, it is essential that a plan be developed for helping participants apply what they have learned.

Transfer of learning has most often been thought of in behavioral terms—that is, what is to be transferred can be clearly specified in terms of observable changes in knowledge, skills, and attitudes (Broad and Newstrom, 1992; Yelon, 1992). Therefore, the assumption has been that as long as everyone knows ahead of time what is to be transferred and how this learning transfer will be accomplished, that transfer will happen without any additional interventions. Although this assumption is true in some situations, learning transfer is often more complex and multifaceted than just simply being clear about what learning needs to be applied and having a plan to do that (Ottoson, 1995a; Yelon and Ford, 1999; Holton III, 2000; Yelon and Sheppard, 1999; Baldwin, Ford, and Naquin, 2000; Broad, 2000). As Ottoson (1995a) has so aptly observed: "Application is a complex, multidimensional process that takes more than just a good idea. It takes knowledge, skill, endurance, and artistry. Application requires multiple kinds of knowledge, including knowledge of the *thing* (emphasis in the original), the context, the practical, and the skill to put it all together" (p. 24 ).

Viewing the transfer process from this venue requires that program planners and others involved in the transfer process have the "skills of translation, negotiation, adaptation, and decision-making" (Ottoson, 1995a, p. 26), as illustrated in the following scenario.

### The Multifaceted Dimensions of Learning Transfer

A regional school association funds a program for assisting teachers to implement new content standards in literacy for grades one through five. The design of the program includes three one-day workshops for selected teachers from each district in the region over a period of nine months. In addition, literacy coaches have been assigned to work with those teachers after each of the workshops. The expectation is that as a result of these workshops specific instructional practices will be adopted, including more use of technology in the instructional process. After the first workshop, through informal observations and feedback from the coaches and some of the teachers, it was found that at least two of the instructional practices teachers were expected to use did not work with the children in their classes. In fact, if anything, these practices created more confusion related to basic skills. In addition, there was resistance from a small percentage of the schools involved, primarily from the principals, at having the literacy coaches involved in the project at all. Although it was not said directly, these principals appeared not to like the idea of "outsiders" coming into their schools. In addition, a number of the schools were having problems adopting the technology-based instructional tools either because of the lack of teachers' skills, and/or the availability of useable hard- and software.

In order for the transfer of learning to be a success in this case, the lack of usefulness of some of the instructional strategies had to be acknowledged, as well as the contextual factors of leadership, equipment, and teacher experience and skills. One action that Bill, who was the program planner in the previous scenario, took immediately to alleviate some of the problems was to drop from the transfer plan those instructional practices that were just not working. Bill then followed up by visiting those schools where the literacy coaches were not welcomed. He found a number of different scenarios in terms of why the assistance of these coaches was viewed as negative, and for each case he negotiated with the principals and teachers as to what transfer strategies would be more appropriate in their settings. In addition, Bill made connections with the technology unit of the state department to receive some assistance with both procuring the needed equipment and training for those teachers who lacked the technological skills.

As demonstrated in the last scenario, assisting people to make changes is the heart of what transfer of learning is all about—changes in themselves, other people, practices, organizations, and/or society (Loucks-Horsley, 1989; Rogers, 1995; Ottoson, 1995a, 1997a; Holton III, 2000; Hall and Hord, 2001). Some of these changes may be easy and even fun, like learning how to be a better gardener or skier. Other changes may be difficult and painful, such as learning to cope with a major illness or how to lay off large numbers of staff members due to funding cuts or national emergencies.

Although many education and training programs focus on individuals' learning, often some of what has been learned cannot be applied, as noted in the previous case, unless changes are also made in the context in which the changes are expected (Ottoson, 1995a, 1997a; Xiao, 1996; Holton III, Bates, Seyler, and Carvalho, 1997; Bennett, Lehman, and Forst, 1999; Latimer, 1999; Taylor, 2000). These contextual factors, such as transfer climate, cultural differences, and structural issues, are especially important when what is learned is to be applied primarily in a work or other organizational setting, in a different cultural milieu, and/or depends on others having to agree to or also make those changes (see Chapter Four). For example, a frontline customer representative may want to use some alternative strategies of working with customer complaints as a result of attending a series of professional development seminars, but encounters a stumbling block in his departmental supervisor who voices strong opposition. This departmental supervisor claims that the new procedures will take too much time and thus will be less efficient. A more global example would be assuming that workers are highly self-directed in their transfer activities in a cultural context "where they are more accustomed to being told what to do and letting someone else take both the credit and the responsibility" (Latimer, 1999, p. 4). These contextual factors are one of the bases, among others, upon which transfer-of-learning plans are grounded.

## What Learning-Transfer Plans Are Based Upon

Transfer-of-learning plans are based upon and linked primarily to five components of the Interactive Model of Program Planning: the context (people, organization, and wider community), as noted previously, program ideas and needs, program objectives, instructional plans, and program evaluation as illustrated by the following scenario.

### Linking Learning-Transfer Plans to Other Planning Components

Sheila is chairing a committee that is planning an outdoor adventure experience for recovering alcoholics. Sheila knows her population well as she has worked in drug and alcohol programs for a number of years, and she is a recovering alcoholic herself. She is a bit worried as the potential participants are all from urban areas, and only a few of them have any experience with hiking in the mountains, rafting, or wilderness camping. Also, she is wondering, with other committee members, about how to "sell" the relevancy of this kind of program to her audience, for whom these kinds of physical activities are foreign and who think trees only grow in parks. In addition, although she has funding for this program, a number of the other stakeholders in the planning process, including her own organization and the local Alcoholics Anonymous groups, have serious doubts about whether a program of this nature can have any positive impact on the people who will attend. She and her committee know the program must have clear outcomes, in terms of what it can offer to recovering alcoholics that fits the participants needs. She also is aware that she must respond to the many questions she has received from sponsors and other stakeholders.

In addition to working with her local program committee, Sheila has contracted with a private outdoor adventure group, using grant funds, to plan and lead the actual activities for the program. Sheila and two of her committee members have met twice with this group and have asked them to draw up program and learning objectives and specific activity plans that fit with what she and her committee hope the outcomes of the program will be. Sheila and her committee members also discussed with this outdoor adventure group how the participants could apply what they learn from this experience in helping them stay on the road to recovery, especially as the learning context and activities will both be novel to these participants. In addition, as this program is government-funded, Sheila will need to demonstrate that both the outdoor adventure experience itself and the transfer strategies and techniques they use to apply what has been learned from this experience actually produce the desired outcomes.

Sheila's next step is to have the whole program committee meet with the outdoor adventure group and hammer out the various complexities of the program plan:

- Do the instructional and transfer plans meet the stated program and learning objectives?

- How will they demonstrate to Sheila's organization, the funding agency, and other stakeholders that they really met the program outcomes with these plans?

- How will the learning context and the participants' backgrounds, experiences, and needs affect what are selected as instructional techniques?

- How will the transfer-of-learning strategies and techniques fit into the whole picture, as these are key to the learning outcomes being met?

Sheila knows this part of the planning process will be challenging because as one part of the plan changes, so will others.

Although this scenario describes well the linkages among devising transfer plans and the five components mentioned earlier in this section, the bases for preparing transfer-of-learning plans are not always connected to all or even the majority of these components. Rather, in some planning endeavors the transfer process is connected only to instructional plans, and more specifically as one means of meeting the learning objectives. As is seen from Sheila's planning endeavors, the transfer-of-learning strategies and techniques often hold the key to whether or not program outcomes can be achieved. Therefore, planning for learning transfer is a critical part of the planning process.

## The Importance of Planning for Learning Transfer

There are a number of reasons why planning for the transfer of learning is so important. First, as noted previously, both sponsoring organizations and participants are asking for outcomes that are applicable, practical, and make a difference. For example, a variety of United States organizations, according to Broad and Newstrom (1992), the Lakeland Research report (1995), and Cervero, Wilson, and Associates (2001), are spending billions of dollars each year on employee training and development programs. Yet, much of this training is wasted because of "continued low transfer. . . . [Rather], practitioners have emphasized and developed sophisticated delivery devices at the expense of the critical connections between the training site and the work [and other environments]" (Brinkerhoff and Montesino, 1995, p. 264). Broad and Newstrom (1992) go on to assert that for organizations to remain competitive in the global marketplace and prepare highly skilled workers, improving the transfer of learning must be a high priority.

Second, there are many issues and concerns related to the lives of adults that can be at least partially addressed through educational programs—health care reform, violence in our communities, restructuring of public education, world peace, and environmental concerns, to name a few. What is critical about so many of these issues and concerns is that solutions were needed yesterday. Therefore, what has so often been left to chance by educators—whether people, as a result of attending a variety of education and training programs, can apply what they have learned to solving these complex problems—is no longer either a viable or an ethical option.

Third, many people need assistance in reflecting changes they must make in themselves, other people, organizations, and/or society before what they have learned can be translated into concrete results. For example, some people are predisposed to change, while others need support from a variety of sources (for example, work supervisors, family members, friends) to apply what they have learned. These and other factors that enhance or block the transfer-of-learning process are discussed more in-depth in the next section.

## Factors Influencing the Transfer of Learning

Numerous reasons are identified to explain why participants either do or do not apply what they have learned as a result of attending education and training programs. Examples include program participants' perceptions about the value and practicality of program content, the presence or absence of useful transfer strategies and techniques as part of the program design, and supervisory and organizational attitudes toward changes required to apply what has been learned.

In thinking through the many ideas that are discussed about why people do or do not apply what they have learned, it is useful to categorize these ideas into a clear and manageable number of key influencing factors, as displayed below (Broad and Newstrom, 1992; Brinkerhoff and Montesino, 1995; Dodek and Ottoson, 1996; Ottoson, 1995b, 1997a; Holton III, 2000; Taylor, 2000; Hall and Hord, 2001; Yamnill and McLean, 2001).

▶ *Program participants.* Participants bring to education and training programs a set of personal experiences, diverse backgrounds, varying motivational levels to use what they have learned, and differing attitudes and values. These characteristics influence both what they learn and whether they can and even want to apply what they have learned to their personal, work, and/or public lives.

▶ *Program design and execution.* Program planners can include as part of designing and conducting education and training programs strategies and techniques for the transfer of learning. These strategies and techniques are implemented before, during, and/or after the program has been completed.

▶ *Program content.* The knowledge, skills, and/or attitudes and beliefs that are addressed through the program activities make up the program content. Program participants may or may not learn this material, either because they choose not to or because the program instructors did not teach what they said they would teach (or both).

▶ *Changes required to apply learning.* The nature of the changes required in people, professional practices, organizations, communities, and/or society to apply the learning describes the scope, depth, and enduring consequences of those changes. It also takes into account the complexity of the change process and who is responsible for making the changes.

▶ *Organizational context.* The organizational context consists of structural factors, political climate, and cultural milieu of an organization, and it either supports or inhibits the transfer of learning. This context includes the value the organization places on continuous learning and development and the concrete support that is given to education and training programs.

▶ *Community and societal forces.* The social, economic, political, and cultural conditions that exist in a specific community or society in general also play a role. This factor includes support of specific education and training programs by key leaders and groups in the community, region, and/or international arena.

These six key factors, depending on how they play out in the transfer-of-learning process, can be barriers or enhancers to that process (Kemerer, 1991; Taylor, 2000). Examples of specific barriers and enhancers linked to each factor are highlighted in Figure 10.1.

Rarely does any one of these factors affect a program in isolation. Rather, it is the interaction among a number of the factors that makes a difference in whether learners can apply what they have learned outside of the formal learning situation (Ottoson, 1995b; Dodek and Ottoson, 1996; Holton, 2000). In addition, not all of the major factors that influence learning transfer come into play for every education and training program. As illustrated in the following two examples, only a few of the factors may apply to some programs, whereas for others all may be applicable.

### Reach for Recovery Program

An initial one-day training session is required for all new Reach for Recovery volunteers. All volunteers must have had breast cancer and be willing to make home or hospital visits to newly diagnosed breast cancer patients. The objectives of the training session are fourfold: (1) to help potential volunteers explore their motivations for being volunteers, (2) to share current information about breast cancer and the Reach for Recovery program, (3) to review what is expected of volunteers on patient visits, and (4) to provide opportunities to do "simulated" patient visits. In addition, volunteers are paired with experienced volunteers to assist them with their first few visits and are given material about where to seek additional support or information. *Applicable factors:* program participants, program design and execution, and program content.

### Workplace Diversity

An organization-wide training program has been initiated on diversity in the work force. The major goals of the program are (1) to have all employees of the organization examine their own attitudes and values related to diversity issues in the workplace, (2) to provide opportunities for managers and supervisors to acquire additional knowledge and skills for working with employees who have diverse backgrounds, (3) to encourage the formulation of ad hoc teams to work on diversity issues within each

**FIGURE 10.1**

# Examples of Barriers and Enhancers to Transfer of Learning

| Barriers | Factors | Enhancers |
|---|---|---|
| • Required prior knowledge and experience are lacking<br>• Attend as "lone" individual<br>• Not motivated or do not have the confidence to make any changes<br>• Possess little power or authority to implement change<br>• Cultural differences of learners are ignored | Program Participants ⟷ | • Prior knowledge and experience are linked to what is being learned<br>• Work in collaborative teams<br>• Predisposed to learning and applying what is learned<br>• Are opinion leaders and have authority to make changes<br>• Cultural differences of learners are acknowledged |
| • Instructional methods invoke passive learning<br>• Little match between the training environment and the applications context<br>• Unrealistic transfer-of-learning strategies or no strategies are included | Program Design and Execution ⟷ | • Active learning, including application exercises, is used extensively<br>• Close match between the training environment and the applications context<br>• Transfer-of-learning strategies are useful and negotiable |
| • Not linked to the strategic goals of the organization and/or life roles of individual participants<br>• Too little content<br>• Knowledge is the focus when skill and attitude changes are required<br>• Not relevant or usable | Program Content ⟷ | • Strategic goals of the organization and/or life roles of learners are key planning variables<br>• Too much content<br>• Focus of content is on application<br>• Relevant, useful, and practical |
| • Unrealistic and too disruptive to present practice, actions, and/or beliefs<br>• Time requirements for change are not considered or unrealistic<br>• Perception is that no real opportunity exists to apply what is learned | Changes Required to Apply Learning ⟷ | • Doable and realistic<br>• Time needed to make changes is recognized<br>• Opportunities exist to integrate what is learned into current life roles |
| • Climate of resistance to innovation and change is evident<br>• Support from peers, supervisors, and managers is weak or nonexistent<br>• Financial and other resources are inadequate<br>• Reward systems work against applying what has been learned | Organizational Context ⟷ | • Innovation and change are viewed as positive<br>• Peers, key leaders, and supervisors offer concrete and useful support<br>• Adequate financial and other resources exist and are accessible<br>• Tangible rewards for learning transfer are apparent |
| • Little recognition that cultural differences affect the transfer process<br>• Key leader are hostile to this change<br>• Political climate is not right<br>• Economic conditions are adversely affected<br>• Community and/or societal norms are not supportive | Community or Societal Forces ⟷ | • Strategies for transfer take into account cultural differences<br>• Key leaders are highly supportive<br>• Receptive political climate is apparent<br>• Positively affects the economic climate<br>• Community and/or societal norms support changes |

division of the organization, and (4) to increase the number and percentage of employees in supervisory and managerial positions who are women, people of color, disabled, and/or culturally diverse. The program is envisioned as a two-year intensive effort and is supported by both the top executive officer and the board. *Applicable factors:* program participants, program design and execution, program content, changes required to apply learning, organizational context, and community and societal forces.

As is readily apparent in the above examples, the more complex the program's scope and goals, the larger the number of people affected, and the greater the magnitude of the changes; the less control over organizational and societal forces, the more difficult the transfer of learning process is.

Program planners have varying levels of control over the decisions they can make related to the factors that influence the transfer of learning. For example, an in-house program planning team consisting of team members who have the authority to make organizational changes (such as purchasing new equipment, changing the reward system) has greater control over learning transfer than do program planners who design programs for audiences from diverse settings (for example, national and international seminars and conferences, and programs for multinational corporations). This span of decision-making control over the transfer function may remain constant for some program planners but continually change for others (depending on the specific programs they are planning).

Generally, program planners have more control over some factors than they do others:

*Level 1.* (*most control*) Program design and execution

*Level 2.* Program participants, program content

*Level 3.* Organizational context

*Level 4.* Changes required to apply learning

*Level 5.* (*least control*) Community and societal forces

Because the one factor that almost all program planners have the greatest decision-making power over is the design and execution of the program, it is important that planners consider planning for the transfer of learning an integral part of the planning process.

## A Framework for Planning Learning Transfer

In planning for the transfer of learning, as shown in Exhibit 10.1, three key elements are addressed: when the transfer strategies are employed, the variety of strategies used to help in applying what has been learned, and the

**EXHIBIT 10.1**

# Framework for Transfer of Learning: People, Timing, and Strategies

| Program Planners | Instructors and Facilitators | Learners |
|---|---|---|
| **BEFORE** | | |
| • Identify clearly what is to be transferred: knowledge, skills, attitudes, and beliefs. | • Obtain a clear picture of what learning is to be transferred as a result of the activities for which they are responsible. | • Clarify what the expectations are for what learning they should transfer into their life situation (for example, work role, volunteer work, personal changes). |
| • Ascertain the contextual aspects of where the learning is to be applied (for example, political, climate for change, cultural variation, learner and sponsor expectations). | • Ask specific questions of program planners and/or learners about the contextual aspects of where the learning is to be applied. | • Select specific "things" they believe they can change related to the expectations for learning transfer. |
| • Set the guidelines for what constitutes successful transfer of learning, and make provisions for a negotiation process for changes in what determines success. | • Ask learners to select projects or other activities to complete that encompass what learning is expected to be transferred. As part of this process, request that learners think about who or what in their environments would help them successfully complete these projects or activities. | • Discuss with key people who could assist them with applying their learning (for example, work supervisors, friends, family members), the expectations for what learning is to be transferred, and how this learning should or might affect their current situations. |
| **DURING** | | |
| • Involve people who are key to the learning transfer in implementing the program (for examples, as instructors, as site coordinators). | • Use active learning techniques (for example, critical reflection, applications exercises) that enhance learning transfer. | • Actively prepare for and participate in each of the learning activities. During the activities link what they are learning to their own situations. |
| • Monitor the program to ensure instructors are incorporating instructional techniques that address transfer issues. | • Incorporate the learning context as part of the learning environment (for example, learners try out new skills in their own or similar settings). | • Try out, where possible (for example, in multiday activities), what they are learning in the settings in which this learning will be used to explore the potential for transfer. |
| • Use formative evaluation techniques to assist instructors who are not adequately addressing the transfer aspects of the program to change what and/or how they are teaching while the program is still in progress. | • Provide job aids and suggest other transfer resources (for example, people, print, and Internet sources). | • Use the job aids provided and give feedback to the instructors on whether they are useful. Ask the instructors about additional resources that might be useful. |
| | • Provide learners opportunities to develop specific application plans and assist them in | |

| Program Planners | Instructors and Facilitators | Learners |
|---|---|---|
| **DURING** *(Continued)* | | |
| • Provide alternative techniques to assist learners with transfer of learning so they can incorporate them into their own application plans (for example, support groups, peer coaching, technology-based methods).<br><br>• Provide a plan for instructors and/or teach learners about different transfer strategies and techniques so they can better select or assist in selecting which of these strategies and techniques might work better for them in applying what they have learned within their own settings. | assessing barriers and enhancers to learning transfer in their own environments.<br><br>• Teach learners about different transfer strategies and techniques so they can better select or assist in selecting which of these strategies and techniques might work better for them in applying what they have learned within their own settings. | • Develop specific application plans that include strategies that can assist them with the learning transfer and anticipate barriers and enhancers they might find in the transfer process.<br><br>• Select, with the assistance of instructors and/or planners, learning strategies and techniques that will help them most in applying what they have learned in their own settings. |
| **AFTER** | | |
| • Initiate and support the planned follow-up learning techniques to enhance the transfer process.<br><br>• Develop different transfer techniques that emerge from the needs of the learners, the instructors, or the sponsors of the program.<br><br>• Negotiate and change, as needed, what the learning transfer can realistically encompass, in cooperation with all interested parties. | • Provide follow-up assistance through a variety of techniques (for example, coaching, refresher courses, mentoring).<br><br>• Facilitate the process of initiating these different application techniques and provide support for these efforts.<br><br>• Provide feedback to program planners, learners, and other stakeholders on what learning can realistically be transferred. | • Implement their applications plans and be willing to change those plans. Use the transfer resources and seek additional support that they need.<br><br>• Initiate different transfer techniques that facilitate learning transfer within your particular context.<br><br>• Adapt what learning can and/or should be transferred based on their own experiences in the transfer process and their specific situations. |

key people involved (Baldwin and Ford, 1988; Broad and Newstrom, 1992; Ottoson, 1994, 1995b; Milheim, 1994; Broad, 2000; Cannon-Bowers, Salas, and Hilham, 2000; Yamnill and McLean, 2001).

As for the timing, transfer strategies are used before the program begins, while the program is in progress, and/or after the program is completed. Transfer strategies employed after the program is completed are usually the most difficult for program planners to influence, because of the cost and staff time that these activities normally require (Bennett, Lehman, and Forst, 1999).

The second element that is considered in planning for learning transfer is determining what strategies and techniques are the most useful in assisting learners to apply what they have learned to their personal, work, and/or public lives. These strategies and techniques range from including key people in the planning process to being aware of how contextual and cultural differences influence applying what has been learned to preferences learners have for specific techniques. To allow learners and others to be a part of this selection process, planning staff, including instructors, teach learners, supervisors, and other stakeholders about learning strategies and techniques. Providing learners and others this information permits them to make informed choices about which of these strategies and techniques are more appropriate in helping learners apply what has been learned in their own settings.

Key people—the final element to be addressed—are those who need to be involved so transfer of learning actually happens. Program planners themselves have a number of roles and functions. They first take into consideration the learners and the program instructors and facilitators in preparing transfer plans. In addition, there may be other key players who, although not necessarily involved in the program, have to be included in transfer planning. These people are most often a part of sponsoring organizations and include supervisors, managers, and community leaders. For example, in work situations, senior managers may be critical players; in community action programs, city council members, other community leaders, and "grassroots" constituents may need to be included. Examples of specific activities these players take to enhance the transfer process are displayed in Exhibit 10.1.

To ascertain which specific people should actively be involved in planning and implementing the transfer process, program planners consider whether the changes related to the learning applications are being newly initiated, are in progress, or simply need to be maintained (Rogers, 1995; Holton III, 2000; Hall and Hord, 2001). Where people and/or organizations are in the change process affects both who is involved in the transfer process and the strategies and techniques to be employed.

## Transfer-of-Learning Techniques

Program planners have a repertoire of specific techniques that are used to facilitate learning transfer. These techniques are grouped in three categories: techniques for individual learners, group techniques, and techniques that can be used either by individuals or in groups. Although a few of these

**EXHIBIT 10.2**

# Sample Techniques to Facilitate Learning Transfer

## INDIVIDUAL TECHNIQUES

- *Individual Learning Plans.* An outline of what learning objectives participants wish to pursue, how they will go about their learning, how and who will evaluate what they have learned, and a timeline for completing the plan.
- *Coaching.* Peers or supervisors who assist learners in making specific changes in their life roles through asking questions, observing what they do, listening, providing feedback, and sharing experience and knowledge in a nonjudgmental manner.
- *Job Rotation or Guided Internships.* Learners take on all or part of another person's job responsibilities that are different from their present position, with planned supervisory sessions with a person competent in this new role or function.
- *Mentoring.* A caring relationship in which a person with more experience works over an extended time period with a less experienced person to promote professional and/or personal development, through guidance, feedback, support, sharing of resources, and access to networks of other helpful people.

- *One-legged conferences.* Brief conversations, often held in hallways or at someone's door, to get some quick answers to "here and now" applications questions.
- *Job Aids.* Mechanisms for providing information, such as written checklists and charts, work samples, websites, and audio or videotapes, that give short and clear directions on how to do specific tasks or functions.
- *Portfolios.* A structured set of accomplishments that demonstrate through selected artifacts, such as technology-based, audio, or written materials, and evaluations by others, the attainment of specific competencies, standards, or outcomes.
- *Applications Notebook.* Individuals keep notebooks of ideas that have worked or not worked in the process of applying their new learning or skills. They may also add other supporting material that could assist them in the applications process.

## GROUP TECHNIQUES

- *Transfer Teams.* Teams of people are formed prior to the education and training program who are committed to working together before, during, and after the event to assist each other in the transfer-of-learning process.
- *Tuning Protocols.* Groups of learners, who usually differ each time, get together to examine specific practices they are trying out related to transfer. Through formal presentation and reflective activities, participants are honored for the good work they have done and can also "fine tune" their work.

- *Support Groups.* Groups of participants who "meet" regularly, whether in person and/or online, to share problems or practices related to learning transfer. Usually participation is voluntary, and sharing and equal status among group members is the norm.
- *Follow-Up Sessions.* Education and training programs, conducted face to face, via video or audio conferencing, or online, that all participants are expected to take part in that reinforce and extend the learning from the original activity.

## TECHNIQUES THAT COULD BE USED INDIVIDUALLY OR IN GROUPS

- *Networking.* Loosely configured groups of participants and others who have similar experiences, interests, problems, or ideas who communicate online and/or in person for the purposes of giving and receiving information and providing mutual support and assistance.
- *Action Research.* The application of research approaches (for example, ethnographic, descriptive, quasi-experimental, case study) to identify and find solutions to problems experienced with the learning transfer.

- *Reflective Practice.* Thoughtfully reflecting on one's actions, including the assumptions and feeling associated with those actions, either during an event or after an event has occurred.
- *Chat Rooms.* Web-based synchronous or asynchronous discussions that are structured in a way participants can carry on a dialogue about the transfer activities by adding comments into a running discussion.

techniques involve direct instructional activities (for example, refresher sessions, synchronous chat rooms), the majority are designed to be used within the context in which the learning transfer is taking place. Examples of some of the most popular techniques are briefly described in Exhibit 10.2. More in-depth descriptions of these and other techniques that are used in learning transfer can be found in Jackson and Caffarella (1994); Driscoll (1998); Silberman (1999); the *Journal of Staff Development* (1999); Baldwin, Ford, and Naquin (2000); and Cannon-Bowers, Salas, and Hilham (2000).

In employing these techniques, careful thought is given to matching transfer techniques to the preferences and capabilities of the learners, resource availability (for example, facilitator skills, time, technology, and money), the nature of what is to be transferred, and the context in which the transfer is to happen. For example, peer coaching and support groups may be very effective for people who are self-motivated and like to work with others, but may not work for people who need a supervisor to intervene before they will change the way they behave or practice. Likewise, learners who are highly technologically literate, especially those in organizations where technology is the major form of communication, would probably benefit more from technology-based techniques than those who have limited access to technological resources and do not use technology as a routine part of their daily activities.

## Challenges Program Planners Face in the Process

"There is no question that transfer of learning is a formidable challenge to organizations" (Holton, Baldwin, and Naquin, 2000, p. 1), and to planning staff who are responsible for ensuring transfer happens. In planning for the transfer of learning as part of the design and execution of education and training programs, program planners take into account the previously described six factors that influence the transfer of learning (program participants, program content, changes required to apply learning, organizational context, and community and societal forces). One useful tool for improving the learning-transfer process is the Learning Transfer Systems Inventory (LTSI) (Holton, 2000; Holton, Bates, and Ruona, 2000). Using this sound diagnostic instrument, program planners "can access potential factor problems . . . , investigate known transfer problems, target interventions designed to enhance transfer and incorporate evaluation of transfer as part of regular employee assessments" (Holton, 2000, p. 8).

A second helpful mechanism for responding to the challenges of the learning-transfer process is the Stages of Concerns (SOC) model proposed by Hall and Hord (2001). As people go through a change process, which, as noted earlier in this chapter, is the heart of learning transfer, "there is a developmental pattern to how [people's] feelings and perceptions evolve as the change process unfolds" (p. 57). Hall and Hord have identified and confirmed seven specific categories of concerns in the SOC model that people move through as they confront change. These seven categories are further compiled into three levels: self, task, and impact concerns. Most people go from self concerns (for example, How will using this new idea affect me?) to task concerns (for example, "I seem to be spending all of my time getting materials ready") to impact concerns (for example, "I am concerned about relating what I am doing with what my co-workers are doing") (p. 61).

There are three major techniques for assessing the levels of concern for people involved in the change process: one-legged interviews, open-ended concerns statements, and SOC questionnaires. Each of these techniques are fully described in Chapter Four of Hall and Hord's book, *Implementing Change: Patterns, Principles and Potholes.* What is useful, as learners journey through the transfer process, is knowing which stage or stages these learners are in so that planners and learners can use this information to choose appropriate transfer techniques. Learners in the self-concerns category may benefit more from techniques that that allow them to further explore the impact of implementing a new practice or making a life change (for example mentoring relationships, support groups, and reflective practice). Those in the task-concerns stage look more to techniques that give them hands-on assistance, like job aids and follow-up training sessions. And finally, learners who are in the impact-concerns arena usually want to use techniques that permit them to work with others (for example, coaching, transfer teams, Web-based chat rooms).

What is readily apparent to many program planners as they plan for the transfer of learning is that they have little influence or control over some (or even most) of the key factors that enhance or inhibit the transfer-of-learning process. As noted earlier, this lack of control is especially true when the change is extensive and the organizational, community, and/or societal forces are complex and far-reaching. Does this mean program planners should ignore this part of the program-planning process or spend little time planning for it? Obviously, the answer is no; but it does mean that program planners must understand their span of decision-making control, recognize their own limits for action, and know when and how to call on people who can and will be helpful in the transfer-of-learning process. As Ottoson (1995a) observed: "Application means getting one's hands dirty, it means having the heart to persevere in the face of obstacles, it means having the touch to apply with sensitivity, it means having the guts to make tough choices, and it means having one's feet firmly grounded in practical reality" (p. 25).

## Chapter Highlights

Devising transfer-of-learning plans—helping learners, instructors, and program sponsors to systematically think through how program participants can apply what they have learned back at work, in their personal lives, and so forth—continues to be a neglected part of the program planning process. It is assumed that this application of what was learned at an education or training program somehow just happens and that the proposed changes as a result of this learning are the worry of someone other than those responsible for planning the program. Transfer plans are based in and linked primarily to five components of the planning process—the context, program ideas and needs, program objectives, instructional plans, and program evaluation—although these plans may also be grounded in only one of those areas, such as instructional plans.

Program planners may or may not have control over the many factors that enhance or inhibit learning transfer (for example, the background and experience of the participants, the program content, the organizational and community and societal contexts). The one factor over which most planners can exert a major influence is the design and execution of the program itself. Therefore, it is important that program planners consider planning for the transfer of learning an integral part of their responsibilities. In preparing transfer-of-learning plans, planners concentrate on the following tasks:

◆ Be knowledgeable about the major factors that influence transfer of learning (for example, program participants, program design and execution, program content, changes required to apply the learning, organizational context, and community and societal forces).

◆ Decide when the transfer-of-learning strategies should be employed (before, during, and/or after the formal program).

◆ Determine the key players who should be a part of the transfer-of-learning process (for example, participants, program planning staff, instructors, work supervisors, community leaders).

◆ Teach learners, supervisors, and other interested parties about transfer-of-learning strategies and techniques so they know what strategies and techniques are available and can choose or assist in selecting appropriate ones to use in the transfer process.

◆ With the assistance of learners, instructors, and others, choose transfer strategies that are the most useful in assisting participants to apply what they have learned (for example, involving learners, supervisors, community leaders, and other stakeholders in planning the transfer process; taking into account contextual and cultural differences; ascertaining the contextual aspects of where the learning is to be applied; providing participants with opportunities to develop applications plans; and negotiating and changing what the learning transfer can realistically encompass in cooperation with all stakeholders).

◆ Select and/or assist learners and others to opt for transfer-of-learning techniques that are the most useful to them in applying what they have learned (mentoring, peer coaching, support groups, online discussions, reflective practice, transfer teams).

◆ Negotiate and change the content, skills, and/or beliefs that are to be transferred, based on barriers and enhancers to learning transfer in the application site.

As noted in the last chapter, developing transfer-of-learning plans is tied directly to the program evaluation component of the planning process, which is described in the next two chapters. Without clear and doable transfer plans, it is often difficult to trace how program activities are related to program outcomes and to provide justification for the judgments made on the worth and value of a program.

## Application Exercises

The two Application Exercises presented here are designed to help you facilitate the transfer of learning. The first assists you in identifying those factors that enhance or inhibit the learning transfer, and the second helps you incorporate transfer of learning into the design and execution of your chosen program.

## EXERCISE 10.1

## Identifying Elements That Enhance or Inhibit
## Transfer of Learning

1.  Describe briefly a program for which you planned or need to plan for the transfer of learning.

2.  Using the following chart, first list specific things (related to one or more of the six factors from Figure 10.1, page 214) that did or can enhance or inhibit the learning transfer. Next, indicate what span of decision-making control you had or have for each enhancer or inhibitor you listed. Finally, for those items for which you have indicated only some or little or no influence, list who did or could assist you in the transfer process.

| Factor | Things That Enhanced or Inhibited | Span of Decision-Making Control | People Who Did or Can Assist in Transfer |
|---|---|---|---|
| Program participants | | | |
| Program design and execution | | | |
| Program content | | | |
| Changes required to apply learning | | | |
| Organizational context | | | |
| Community and societal forces | | | |

## EXERCISE 10.2

### Planning for the Transfer of Learning in the Design and Execution of Educational Programs

1. Using a program you are currently planning or have planned or conducted, develop a transfer-of-learning plan using the chart below. List each strategy (refer to Exhibit 10.1) according to when it had or should have been used or will be used, and who did or should have used them or who will use them.

| People Involved | Strategy for Before Program | Strategy for During Program | Strategy for After Program |
|---|---|---|---|
| Program planners | | | |
| Instructors or facilitators | | | |
| Learners | | | |
| Other key players (specify) | | | |
| Other key players (specify) | | | |

2. Outline what transfer techniques were and/or should have been incorporated in a previous program or will be incorporated into a current program you are planning. Provide a justification for why each technique was or would have been useful or could be helpful in enhancing the applications process of a current program you are planning.

| Technique | Reason for Using |
|---|---|
| A. _____ | _____ |
| B. _____ | _____ |
| C. _____ | _____ |
| D. _____ | _____ |
| E. _____ | _____ |
| F. _____ | _____ |

3. Review this plan with key individuals and/or your planning group and revise your plan based on the feedback you receive.

# Chapter 11

# Formulating Evaluation Plans

Juanita wants to demonstrate that she is doing a good job as the new training coordinator for the safety training program, but she is not sure how to proceed. Her predecessor was on the job for years and ran a rather informal shop; other than a big chart displaying the number of accident-free days for the company, he kept no systematic records on the safety training. Juanita has access to some figures on the number and types of programs offered, with the number of participants in each program, but the data are incomplete; the figures were not kept for all programs, and there is a great deal of inconsistency in how the figures were gathered and recorded. Juanita asked her predecessor if there were any evaluation reports on the program, and her predecessor's response was, "You'll know if they're bad, because the trainees and/or supervisors will tell you." Juanita wonders how she can demonstrate that the safety program is doing what it is supposed to be doing— lowering the rate and severity of accidents in the plant.

Juanita is not alone in inheriting an education or training program that has had, at best, haphazard evaluation. Although systematic evaluation has "in theory" been touted as an essential part of the planning process for decades (for example, Kirkpatrick, 1976; Nadler, 1982), until fairly recently many planners have not felt the need to go beyond asking for participants' reactions or perhaps trying to gauge what knowledge has been acquired. However, with the call for greater accountability from many sectors, more planners are experimenting with practical ways of ensuring that evaluation becomes an integral part of their planning and delivery processes.

How program evaluation is defined is addressed first in the chapter, followed by a description of the heart of the evaluation process—that of judging the worth or value of an educational program. Explored next is how evaluation connects with other components of the Interactive Model of program planning. An 11-element process for conducting a systematic program evaluation, which acknowledges these connections, is then outlined, followed by a discussion of how unplanned or informal evaluation opportunities can be used. Sample approaches or models for program evaluation are then reviewed, and descriptions are given of methods and techniques to collect and analyze evaluation data. The chapter concludes with a discussion of ways judgments are made about programs on the basis of the data presented.

## Program Evaluation Defined

Program evaluation is most often defined as a process used to determine whether the design and delivery of a program were effective and whether the proposed outcomes were met. Although systematic or strategically planned evaluations are important, so are the more informal and unplanned evaluation activities. For example, systematic evaluations related to rehabilitation programs for heart attack survivors can track program outcomes over time to see if positive changes participants made in their lifestyles, eating habits, and exercise routines actually made a difference in their survival and quality of life. At the same time, informal exchanges among program staff on new research data about quality of life indicators, and alternative ways (for example, via computer bulletin boards) of getting current information to program participants can be extremely helpful in revising both the content and the delivery of the program while it is in progress.

In acknowledging the importance of both systematic and informal evaluations, evaluation becomes a continuous process that begins in the initial planning phase and continues throughout the life of the program (Tracey, 1992; Vella, Berardinelli, and Burrow, 1998; Birkenholz, 1999; Guskey, 2000; Sork, 2000). Evaluation done to improve or change a program while it is in progress is termed *formative evaluation*. When evaluation focuses on the results or outcomes of a program, it is called *summative evaluation*. In essence, good program evaluation provides useful feedback throughout the life of the program to planners, participants, instructors, organizational sponsors, community groups, and other stakeholders.

The central purposes that drive evaluation processes are gathering and analyzing data for decision-making and accountability. Planners and other stakeholders use evaluation data to make decisions about:

▶ Improving the design, delivery, management, and evaluation of program activities while in progress

▶ Negotiating outcomes as participants apply their learning in their work or personal lives

▸ Assessing how the program context (for example, political, economic, organizational) impacts program processes and outcomes

▸ Cancelling programs either before they start or while in progress

▸ Revising future programs of a similar nature

▸ Responding to needs and ideas identified for future programs (for example, feasibility, cost-effectiveness, timeliness) (Kirkpatrick, 1998; Birkenholz, 1999; Boulmetis and Dutwin, 2000; Guskey, 2000; Lee and Owens, 2000; Ottoson, 2000).

Accountability, on the other hand, often involves more than just those engaged with the program in some direct way. Although program planners have traditionally wanted to demonstrate that their programs are producing the desired results or outcomes to their immediate constituents, the external pressure for program accountability is on the rise, from such sources as the corporate sector, government, regulatory agencies, and professional associations (Phillips, 1996; Guskey, 2000; Linn, 2000). This external pressure for accountability can be a positive force for enhancing and expanding programs for adults, but also can have negative and even disastrous consequences for program participants and groups and organizations that sponsor these programs.

An example of pushing for accountability is apparent in the rhetoric around schooling for children. More specifically, this rhetoric has evidenced itself in legislative and professional associations' policies and actions related to staff development for teachers. The expectation is that when teachers attend staff-development activities, the primary result of their participation will be an increase in student achievement (Backus and others, 2000; "Revisioning Professional Development," 2000). Although this is a laudable goal, it is often very difficult to make a direct connection between the change in test scores and other student measures of increased achievement to actual participation in these programs. Therefore, funding for staff development programs for teachers has and will continue to be pulled from some programs based on student achievement data, where no real cause-and-effect relationship can be shown. It is possible there may be a connection, but it is also plausible that other variables, such as the socioeconomic level of students, school funding, and poor facilities, have more influence on student learning than the most well-designed professional development program for teachers (Linn, 2000; McNeil, 2000). These funding cuts may be demoralizing to teachers in schools that continually show little gain in student achievement, especially when these teachers believe these staff-development programs have been useful to their classroom practice. In the worst-case scenario, some of the best teachers are transferring from these low-achieving schools to schools that already had a high rating going into this accountability process so they do not get behind professionally.

## The Heart of Program Evaluation

The heart of program evaluation is judging the value or worth of education and training programs (Cervero, 1988; Rothwell and Cookson, 1997; Guskey, 2000; Sork, 2000). This judgment process is not an easy task for three major reasons. First, as noted in the example on staff development for teachers, it may be difficult to demonstrate that program outcomes are really tied to what happened in the program. Factors other than what participants did as part of a planned program may account for the occurrence or absence of changes (for example, budget increases or cuts, lack of support by key leaders, squabbling among organizational sponsors).

Second, developing clear criteria upon which judgments can be made is difficult to do, especially for program outcomes that are not quantifiable, are unclear at the onset of the program, or need to be changed as the program evolves. Even for those outcomes that are quantifiable, the time and effort it takes to formulate the types of measures needed and to collect and analyze the data may not be reasonable in terms of current program resources. (This does not mean, as is explored later in the chapter, that criteria for program success should not be developed; but program staff members may have to think differently about the evaluation processes they use and about who is involved.)

Third, some people who plan programs may not want to make judgments about their programs or have others make those judgments (Bernhardt, 2000). This stance is especially true in environments where no matter what the data show, evaluations of any kind are seen as punitive or are used primarily to advance political or personal agendas. For example, in an election year, statements are often made by politicians about the effectiveness of government-sponsored welfare-to-work programs. Whether these claims are positive or negative usually depends more on voter sentiment than whether or not the programs are actually working.

## Connecting Evaluation to Other Components of the Interactive Model

Evaluation, probably more than any other component of the Interactive Model of Program Planning, is where many of the other model components intersect and even overlap (Ottoson, 1997b, 2000; Smith and Regan, 1999; Boulmetis and Dutwin, 2000; Piskurich, 2000; Sork, 2000). This junction of components stems primarily from the data being generated and analyzed throughout the program planning and delivery process. More specifically, data gathered about the program context (see Chapter Four), the ideas for programs (see Chapter Six), the information used in developing program objectives (see Chapter Eight), and the results of transfer strategies and instructional assessments (see Chapters Nine and Ten) are often used as baseline, formative, and/or outcomes information for program assessments.

For example, in evaluating a certificate program for computer technicians, sponsored through a partnership of two community colleges and three local businesses, it is first important to understand the people and organizational contexts in which these programs are planned and delivered (Dodek and Ottoson, 1996; Sork, 2000). For example, was the planning process collaborative or more contentious in that one of the partners dominated the others for the purpose of advancing his or her own organizational agenda? Were all voices that should have been heard included in the planning process, or were some intentionally excluded and others overly represented? How was the program structured in terms of decision-making authority, and was it planned so that the cultures of each of the organizations were somehow acknowledged in the final product? These and other contextual factors often affect program outcomes regardless of whether the program was well-designed and the participants appropriately chosen. In addition, as the importance of context is recognized more and more as one of the critical variables in learning (Caffarella and Merriam, 2000), contextual data affect both the design and execution of program evaluations. Using contextual data, as stressed in planning for transfer, may mean that program processes and even outcomes may need to be negotiated throughout the program, which in turn makes the evaluation process both more complex, and yet also more realistic.

Data for program needs and ideas assessment, collected both from program participants and organizations that would most likely employ graduates of the program, are used as baseline data in a number of different ways (Gupta, 1999; Ottoson, 2000). Participants' knowledge and skill levels when they entered the program could be used in a formative way to see if there were changes occurring as they went through the program. If not, how might the program be modified to better enable participant learning? Also contextual data about these participants—for example, current job situations, language differences, and cultural ways of learning—are also helpful in both the initial design and in making needed program modifications. Are the students able to hold down full-time jobs and complete the program in the time frame and mode that is provided? Does the program need to be offered in languages other than English? And what cultural norms might inhibit or enhance the chances of these students completing the program? These same data could then be used in a summative way at the end of the program. Were there actual gains in skills and knowledge a result of completing the program? Did the program design features, related to contextual factors, make a difference in whether students actually completed the program?

The organizational data is also used in a formative way by reflecting throughout the program whether the needs and ideas as expressed by these employers were actually being addressed in the program. This type of evaluation is done by instructors and organizational representatives through review of course material and observations. In addition, program planners also use these data to see if what these employers initially expressed was actually what these graduates needed to know and do once they entered the workforce.

Program objectives, as seen later in this chapter, often form the foundation for program evaluation (for example, in the levels of evaluation, objectives-based, and accountability planner approaches). In essence, in these approaches, the evaluation is done to determine whether the stated program objectives have been adequately addressed. For example, if the program objectives state that there will be a change in the knowledge and skills needed to perform well as computer technicians, were the participants able to demonstrate those outcomes through performance and other types of tests? If the program objectives affirm that participants will be able to apply their new knowledge and skills in a work situation, were these participants able to do this? If the program objectives establish that as a result of this certificate program that 70 percent of the participants will be gainfully employed, within a month of program completion, in jobs that require the knowledge and skills learned in the program, were in fact 70 percent of the participants employed?

Information gathered as a result of transfer-of-learning strategies and instructional assessments, like the needs assessment data, is also used in formative and summative ways (Ottoson, 1997b; Vella, Berardinelli, and Burrow, 1998; Smith and Regan, 1999). Are students adequately learning the content? If so, are they able to transfer what they are learning, perhaps through formal internships or other types of experiential learning, into work situations? If not, how could courses and the overall program be changed so that content knowledge is adequate and applications of what has been learned enhanced?

In summary, when formulating evaluation plans, it is critical to think about how evaluation strategies can be interwoven into the planning process in general, and more specifically into at least five key components of that process: discerning the context, identifying program ideas and needs, developing program objectives, designing instructional assessments, and devising learning-transfer plans. One way to envision this integration is to see it as a layered process where one set of data links to another and is used for one or multiple purposes. Thinking about evaluation as a layered activity is important for both systematic and informal or unplanned evaluation formats.

## Planning for Systematic Program Evaluation

There is no one acceptable systematic process for conducting a program evaluation. Rather, a number of descriptions of the process have been developed (for example, Nadler, 1982; Kirkpatrick, 1998; Knox, 1998; Vella, Berardinelli, and Burrow, 1998; Birkenholz, 1999; Lawler and King, 2000; Ottoson, 2000; Sork, 2000). A composite description of how to design a systematic evaluation consisting of 11 elements is outlined. For each element, operational guidelines and an example from practice are given in Exhibit 11.1.

It is important to remember that planning for evaluation should not happen as an afterthought once the whole program has been planned. Rather, as illustrated earlier, evaluation is a process that occurs throughout the planning cycle and is often linked to a number of other components of the model, like contextual scans, developing program objectives, and learning transfer. As Vella, Berardinelli, and Burrow (1998) have noted: "Evaluation may be ignored if planned separately. Given the real time and resource pressures of delivering many educational programs, they must be implemented quickly (or even before) the planning is finished. Despite good intentions, the result is often that evaluation procedures are never developed or that evaluation is done on the spur of the moment, usually as the program is ending" (p. 19).

In addition, although the evaluation process may occur in logical order, in a step-by-step fashion, often, as with the Interactive Model, the various elements overlap, need to be revisited, or have already been addressed through other planning activities. For example, planners may be analyzing one set of data while collecting another. During this same time period they may also need to revise the original purpose, questions, and criteria as the program unfolds and participants attempt to incorporate into their work or personal roles what they have learned.

In doing systematic evaluations it is essential that these evaluations reflect sound evaluation practice. Guskey (2000) outlines the 30 Professional Evaluation Standards developed by the Joint Committee on Standards for Educational Evaluation (Joint Committee, 1994). "These standards are categorized into four groups corresponding to the four attributes of fair program evaluation: utility, feasibility, propriety, and accuracy" (Guskey, 2000, p. 61). Utility standards reflect the idea that an evaluation

## EXHIBIT 11.1

# Elements of a Systematic Evaluation

| | | | |
|---|---|---|---|
| **Element** | Secure support for the evaluation from those who have a stake in the results of the evaluation (for example, funding agencies, senior management, program staff, community groups). | | |
| **Operational Guidelines** | Receiving written and/or verbal support from those who are most affected by the evaluation is key. This support may take the form of memos, formal agreements, public announcements, and the like. | **Examples** | The director of the Division of Education and Training (DET) has received two memos, one from the vice president and a second from the major funding agency that endorses the overall scope and time-line for the planned evaluation. |
| **Element** | Identify the individuals who plan and oversee the evaluation. | | |
| **Operational Guidelines** | An individual or team is designated to plan and oversee the program evaluation process. Some larger organizations have personnel designated for this function. Others choose to hire outside consultants. | **Examples** | Two staff members from the DET are responsible for the overall design and execution of the evaluation. They consult with other groups (for example, instructors, managers, participants, funding agencies, community groups) as needed. |
| **Element** | Define precisely the purpose of the evaluation and how the results are to be used. | | |
| **Operational Guidelines** | The purpose of the evaluation is stated clearly and understood by all parties involved. It is especially important to meet the expectations of the major stake holders in the program (for example, participants, supervisors of participants, funding agencies). | **Examples** | The major purpose of the evaluation is to determine whether a specific educational program has produced a major change in the knowledge, skills, and problem-solving capabilities of the participants. A secondary purpose includes the improvement of the educational unit itself. |
| **Element** | Specify what is judged and formulate the evaluation questions. | | |
| **Operational Guidelines** | Major areas that are judged, depending on the purpose of the evaluation, are:<br>• Participant learning<br>• The educational program itself (for example, format, content, staff, instructional design, transfer strategies)<br>• Outcomes of the program (such as participants being able to apply what they have learned in work and/or personal life, organizational change)<br>• The policies, procedures, and practices of the educational unit/function (for example, the | **Examples** | The major area to be judged is the participants' changes in knowledge, skills, and problem-solving skills (with the educational unit itself secondary). The evaluation questions are these:<br>• Was there a change in the knowledge, skills, and problem-solving capabilities of the participants as a result of the program?<br>• Were the participants able to apply what they learned in their work settings? |

*(Continued)*

**EXHIBIT 11.1** (*Continued*)

| | | | |
|---|---|---|---|
| **Operational Guidelines** | program planning process, timely and helpful responses of staff)<br>• The impact of a program on sub-units or whole organizations<br>• The impact of a program on communities or society | **Examples** | • Were these changes in practice maintained over a 12-month period?<br>• How could the DET be changed to better meet the requirements of the major funding agency and the organization as a whole? |
| **Element** | Determine who supplies the needed evidence and/or if some of that data are already available. | | |
| **Operational Guidelines** | Evidence is gathered from a number of people, such as participants, their supervisors, program staff members, instructors, managers, customers, community members, and outside consultants. In addition, staff determine if there are existing data that are appropriate to use. | **Examples** | Evidence is gathered primarily from participants, their supervisors, and the funding agency. Education and training staff, including instructors, are also asked to supply some of the data. It is determined that no existing data were appropriate for this evaluation process. |
| **Element** | Delineate the evaluation approach. | | |
| **Operational Guidelines** | The chosen approach matches the purpose of the evaluation, the nature of the program, and the evaluation questions. The optimal choice of approach may not always be the most feasible or practical. | **Examples** | An objectives-based approach, one of the most often-used approaches, is selected. The program objectives regarding participants' learning, changes in their practice in their work settings as a result of this learning, and the operation of the educational unit provide the focus for the evaluation. |
| **Element** | Choose which data collection techniques to use, when the data are to be collected, and/or how the existing data can be put into useable forms. | | |
| **Operational Guidelines** | The techniques and timing of data collection are primarily determined by the purpose of the evaluation, the approach chosen, and the type of data collected. Characteristics of the respondents, the expertise of the evaluators, and the time and cost requirements are also considered. In addition, staff members put existing data into useable forms so they can be integrated with the new data being collected. | **Examples** | Four primary techniques are used to conduct the evaluation: interviews, written questionnaires, observations, and a review of performance records. Data are collected prior to the program (as part of the needs assessment process), during and after the formal instructional activities, as part of the formal transfer of learning processes, and 12 months after the program has been completed. In addition, data gathered through informal means are integrated into the overall database. |

**EXHIBIT 11.1 (*Continued*)**

| Element | | Indicate the analysis procedure(s). |
|---|---|---|
| **Operational Guidelines** | The analysis procedures are related directly to the evaluation questions, the approach, and the type of data collected. For quantitative data, these procedures range from simple numerical counting or computing of percentages to very sophisticated statistical analysis. Qualitative data are also analyzed in numerous ways (for example, the constant comparative method, case, and cross-case analysis). | **Examples** — As the quantitative data are at the nominal level, the analysis consists of frequency counts and a chi-square statistical procedure. The qualitative data from the interviews are analyzed for patterns and general themes, through the constant-comparative method |

| Element | | Stipulate the criteria to use in making judgments about the program or what process to apply in determining the criteria. |
|---|---|---|
| **Operational Guidelines** | The criteria chosen indicate the level of learning or change that is considered acceptable. Criteria are set for each major evaluation question. For programs where the criteria cannot be predetermined, a process for how criteria will eventually emerge is outlined. This same process could also be used when there is a need to revise the evaluation purpose, questions, approach, and the like. | **Examples** — • Participants are able to demonstrate at the end of the program that they have acquired at least 90 percent of the knowledge, skills, and problem-solving capabilities presented and are able to successfully apply these in their own work settings. Eighty percent of the participants demonstrate they are applying what they have learned 12 months after completion of the program. In addition, participants and their supervisors show the changes in practice have resulted in enhanced service and a 10-percent higher level of productivity.<br>• The DET demonstrates, as a result of this program evaluation, at least five major changes they have made in policies, procedures, and/or productivity that better meet the requirements of the funding agency and the organization. |

| Element | | Determine the specific timeline, the budget, and other necessary resources. |
|---|---|---|
| | | **Examples** — The timeline for the quantitative evaluation is this:<br>• *Cycle One:* Baseline knowledge, skill, and problem-solving |

*(Continued)*

**EXHIBIT 11.1 (*Continued*)**

| | | | |
|---|---|---|---|
| **Operational Guidelines** | The timeline is set and specific (such as before, during the transfer phase, and after a specified program) or continuous (as in the recording of change in the learning of participants for all programs). Program evaluations cost money, so a realistic budget is negotiated prior to initiating the process. | **Examples** | capabilities of the participants are ascertained through the needs assessment process. <br><br> • *Cycle Two:* Levels of knowledge, skill, and problem-solving capabilities acquired are assessed after each major educational activity. <br> • *Cycle Three:* Levels of knowledge, skill, and problem-solving capabilities that have been applied are assessed after the formal program, including the transfer of learning activities. <br> • *Cycle Four:* Levels of knowledge, skill, and problem-solving capabilities continue to be applied in the work setting 12 months after the formal training program has been completed. <br> Qualitative data are collected throughout the project, including a contextual analysis of the worksites where the learning is to be applied. The budget for the evaluation has been set at $3,000 (excluding staff time). |
| **Element** | Monitor and complete the evaluation, make judgments about the value and worth of the program, and think through ways the evaluation data can effectively be used. | | |
| **Operational Guidelines** | It is clear who monitors the evaluation process and how and when that monitoring occurs. Judgments about the program reflect the purpose, questions, and criteria upon which the program is to be appraised. Staff ensures that the evaluation data can effectively be used in making decisions about the program. | **Examples** | The monitoring of the evaluation is done by the two staff members from the DET who are responsible for coordinating the evaluation process. Judgments about the value and worth of the program are made by this same evaluation team in consultation with selected stakeholders (for example, instructors, supervisors, participants). A task force, consisting of the volunteer coordinator, two supervisors, and the director of DET, ensures the data are used in making changes to the program and the DET. |

provides useful information to the various stakeholders, while feasibility standards speak to an evaluation being realistic, cost-effective, and politically viable. Propriety standards address the issues of legality, ethical practice, and call for "due regard for the welfare of those involved in the evaluation, as well as those affected by the results" (Guskey, 2000, p. 63). Ensuring that an evaluation generates technically accurate information that justifies the conclusions drawn is the focus of the accuracy standards. Using these standards as a guide for practice helps mitigate against evaluators and other stakeholders abusing their power and influence as they move through the evaluation process.

Even though systematic program evaluations are a desirable and necessary part of the programming process, Knowles (1980); Rothwell and Kazanas (1993); Vella, Berardinelli, and Burrow (1998); and Bernhardt (2000) have cautioned program planners of four major pitfalls. First, as noted earlier, the outcomes of some educational programs may be too complicated and the number of variables affecting those outcomes too numerous to allow planners to demonstrate that a given program actually produced the desired ratings. For example, it appeared that one three-week (two hours per day, twice a week) training program increased the proficiency of staff in the use of a new computer networking system. This conclusion was reached by comparing pre-test and post-test scores of all workshop participants on the use of the system once the program was completed. Yet, when the participants were asked what key element had helped them to increase their proficiency, 95 percent cited on-the-job trial and error. They said that the training program had, in fact, hindered their progress more than helped, because the instructor often gave poor and incomplete descriptions of how to use the new system and there were not enough work stations to go around.

A second pitfall is that current evaluation procedures, however scientifically rigorous, may not be able to provide hard evidence that the more subtle, and at times the most important, aspects of the education and training programs have been achieved. For example, education and training programs whose major objectives are to foster changes in personal, organizational, and/or societal values and beliefs are especially difficult to evaluate. Third, conducting systematic program evaluations costs time and money, neither of which some organizations and groups are willing to provide, especially when an evaluation appears to be an "afterthought" once the program has begun. Fourth, when staff know that no action will or can be taken on the basis of evaluation findings, it may be better not to collect the data at all, because the evaluation process raises expectations on the part of participants and/or sponsors that changes will be forthcoming.

## Informal and Unplanned Evaluation Opportunities

Although most models of program planning advocate a systematic or strategic process of evaluating programs, informal and often unplanned evaluation opportunities are also very useful. In some cases, they are a critical part of a program planner's responsibilities (Knox, 1998; Champion, 2000; Hall and Hord, 2001). As with systematic evaluation, these informal evaluation strategies are used prior to the start of the program, during the program, or after a program has been completed. Several informal and/or unplanned evaluation strategies are illustrated in the following scenarios.

### Prior to the Program—A Possible Failure in the Making

Wen-Hauer Li, the director of the English as a Second Language (ESL) program at the local community college, has been overseeing, with the help of an outside consultant, the planning of a two-day professional development program for all teaching staff. He has a feeling that what has been proposed—even though it seems to address the problems that have been identified with the delivery of services by his department—is not really what the instructors need to know to do their jobs more effectively. He decides to talk with three key staff members, people he knows will give him direct and honest feedback about both the format and content of the proposed program. If their reactions are similar to his, he has enough time and the authority to either ask for changes in the program or, if needed, cancel the consultant's contract.

### During the Program—Instructor Problems

The atmosphere of the workshop has been tense. The instructors during the morning sessions did not deliver what they had promised, and the participants have been very verbal about how poor the program has been thus far. Sally, the program coordinator, decides to ask the instructors to meet with her over lunch. Prior to the luncheon meeting, she spends a quick 15 minutes with three of the participants, getting their reactions to the morning session. Armed with that information and her own perceptions, Sally decides to "lay the major problems on the table" and hopes that the instructors will be able to respond in a positive manner.

### During the Program—A Look from the Top

Diego, the vice president for human resource development, decides to attend part of the new training program for nonexempt personnel. He is interested in finding out how receptive the employees are to the training events. Diego randomly chooses three sessions that fit into his schedule. He times his arrival and departure around the coffee break so that he can hear what the trainees are saying informally about the program.

### During the Program—Will They Ever Be Able to Apply This Stuff?

In training faculty on the use of new computer systems, Christina wonders if they will ever be able to apply what she has been teaching them. Part of the problem is that not all of the participants have the same systems, and some of the faculty do not even have the proper software on their machines. In addition, the majority of those who do have the needed hardware and software appear not to take the time to practice what they have learned, complaining that this task is one more thing on top of everything else they have to do. What is frustrating to Christina is that she knows that if they do adopt these systems that their workload in some areas could be reduced, such as grading procedures and interoffice communications. She wonders if a job aid of some type might help, plus some one-on-one tutoring. In addition, she is contemplating a meeting with the dean to impress upon her the seriousness of the problem of inadequate computer systems.

### After the Program—It's Not Taking

Dave, the principal of Shelly High School, has heard both directly and through the teacher grapevine that a recent two-day district-wide conference on how to initiate a new literacy program was perceived by his teachers as worse than even he thought it was. The content was a jumbled mess of unclear information and how-to tips that were unrealistic for a district of this size. The major outcome of this program appears to be that some teachers are even more opposed to this new initiative; and even those who supported it before are having major doubts. Dave knows that the superintendent and the board are committed to implementing this new literacy program within the next year. He decides to check with three or four other principals to see if they and their teachers reacted the same way to the program. If these principals and their staff had the same reaction, he will ask one or two of these colleagues to join him at an informal breakfast meeting with the assistant superintendent and the superintendent, who happen to be golfing buddies of his. At the breakfast, he plans to provide them with his informal feedback about the program and offer to help in planning further informational and action agendas around this new initiative.

What is common among these scenarios is that people were willing to observe what was happening, listen to feedback about programs, and then take action on what they learned.

Whether program evaluations are systematic or informal, it is useful for staff members involved with the program planning process to have a working knowledge of the following elements of the evaluation process: evaluation approaches, data collection techniques, data analysis procedures, and making judgments about the program. These elements, which are discussed in the remainder of this chapter, are the nuts and bolts of the evaluation process.

## Approaches to Program Evaluation

There are numerous approaches to or designs for evaluating education and training. These consist of a framework with relatively explicit perspectives and procedural methods for conducting evaluation. Because evaluation is often a multifaceted endeavor, more than one approach or design may be employed in combination in the evaluation process.

Salient examples of evaluation approaches, along with sample questions and data collection techniques appropriate for each approach, are given in Exhibit 11.2 (Worthen and Sanders, 1987; Wholey, Hatry, and Newcomer, 1994; Ottoson, 1997b, 2000; Athanasou, 1995; Kirkpatrick, 1998; Merriam, 1998; Vella, Berardinelli, and Burrow, 1998; Denzin and Lincoln, 2000; Guskey, 2000; Tedlock, 2000; Berg, 2001). As is evident from the description of each approach, there are overlaps and commonalities of focus and techniques between and among the approaches. The broadest overlaps are among the objectives-based, the "levels of evaluation," and the accountability planners approaches, because these three approaches focus on similar areas. In addition, some of the approaches—for example, the case study method—are sometimes used as part of the data collection and analysis process for other approaches.

The "levels of evaluation" approach—more specifically, the participant level of that approach—is still the most commonly used form of evaluation (Munson, 1992; Guskey, 2000). Participants are usually asked to complete

**EXHIBIT 11.2**

# Various Approaches to Program Evaluation

| Approach | Description | Sample Questions | Sample Data Collection Techniques |
|---|---|---|---|
| **"Levels of Evaluation" Review (Kirkpatrick, 1998; Guskey, 2000)** | Measures four different levels: (1) participant reactions; (2) participant learning; (3) behavior change or use of new knowledge and skills; and (4) results or outcomes (for example, organizational support and change, increased productivity, client or customer learning, social action). Focus is primarily on participant reactions and changes and on organizational changes. This approach is most often coupled with the objectives-based model. | • Did participants like the program?<br>• What knowledge or skills were learned?<br>• What values or attitudes were changed?<br>• What changes in participant behavior have resulted that can be linked to the program?<br>• What overall impact has program had on the organization (for example, reduced cost, improved quality, and so on) or community (cleaner air, more job opportunities, increase in "green space")?<br>• What overall impact has the program had on the client or customers of the organization (for example, student learning in staff development programs for teachers, greater customer satisfaction)? | • Written questionnaires<br>• Tests<br>• Performance reviews<br>• Product reviews<br>• Focus groups<br>• Cost-benefit analysis |
| **Accountability Planner (Vella, Berardinelli, and Burrow, 1998)** | Accounts for four types of evaluative data: (1) skills/knowledge/attitudes (SKAs) and achievement of broad objectives; (2) education process elements (learning, tasks, and materials); (3) anticipated changes (learning, transfer, and impact); | • What is the learner expected to know, do, or believe as a result of the program?<br>• What are/were the educational processes used by program instructors and facilitators and the participants themselves for each content area or achievement-based objective? | • Observations<br>• Tests<br>• Interviews<br>• Review of program materials and transfer plans |

*(Continued)*

**EXHIBIT 11.2** *(Continued)*

| Approach | Description | Sample Questions | Sample Data Collection Techniques |
|---|---|---|---|
| | and (4) evidence of change (context, process, qualitative, and quantitative). Evaluation viewed as a process that is interwoven through-out the program plan-ning cycle with docu-mentation required for each type of data. This approach is similar to the "Levels of Evaluation Review." | • What are the anticipated changes related to learn-ing, application, and pro-gram impact?<br>• What evidence, either quantitative or qualitative, do you have of change related to the content and the process aspects of the program? | • Product reviews<br>• Computer simulations<br>• Focus groups |
| **Situated Evaluation Framework (Ottoson, 2000)** | Situates the learner and what is being learned at the junction of the program, participant practice, and evaluative context. Components of the situated evaluation framework are pro-gramming (the what and how), valuing (who decides what is valuable and how), knowledge construction (what counts as evidence), and utilization of evaluation findings (for what ends and by whom). | • What internal and exter-nal factors influence the program, what has been learned, and how that learning is applied?<br>• What are the criteria for program success, who determines these criteria, and how are they devel-oped?<br>• What counts as real evidence of success, and does what counts vary by stakeholder?<br>• What kinds of evaluation are acceptable, who makes this decision, and what is the time frame for the use of the evaluation data? | • Review of program structures, methods, content and skills taught, and character-istics of educational and practice contexts<br>• Reflection on criteria (who determines and how)<br>• Product or perfor-mance review (types of products/perfor-mances allowed, who has control over deciding the types)<br>• Review of evaluation data (acceptable, by whose standards, uses for, and time frame for use) |
| **Systems Evaluation** | Provides feedback on the effectiveness of the program planning and execution process, the structure of the educa-tional unit or function, and the efficiency of | • Has the process of plan-ning and implementing the program been effective and efficient? | • Written questionnaires |

**EXHIBIT 11.2** (*Continued*)

| Approach | Description | Sample Questions | Sample Data Collection Techniques |
|---|---|---|---|
| | the use of resources in relation to the outcomes of education and training programs. One emphasis is cost-benefit analysis. | • Have resources been used wisely in relation to the benefits of the program? | • Interviews<br>• Cost-benefit analyses |
| **Case Study Method** | Gives a "thick description" of what a program looks like from the viewpoint of participants, staff, sponsors, and/or other stakeholders. It characterizes how a program has been implemented and received. | • What are the prominent events or activities respondents highlight?<br>• What is the context of the learning site and where that learning will be applied?<br>• What value do participants, staff, and stakeholders place on the program?<br>• What are the program's strengths and weaknesses from the participants' and other stakeholders' perspectives? | • Observations<br>• Interviews<br>• Organizational or community records and documents<br>• Self-assessments |
| **Quasi-Legal Evaluation** | Determines program quality through adversarial hearings. Panels hear a range of evidence (for example, opinions, data-based studies, belief statements) presented in a legalistic fashion. The judgments rest with a majority opinion of the panel members. | • Which point of view represents the best judgment about the value or worth of a program?<br>• Should the program be continued, modified, or eliminated based on a specified body of evidence? | • Interviews<br>• Organizational or community records and documents<br>• Product reviews<br>• Tests<br>• Cost-benefit analyses |
| **Professional or Expert Review** | Relies on a panel of experts making judgments, usually based on a predetermined set of categories and standards, about a program (such as | • Does the program meet a predetermined set of standards related to the processes and outcomes of the program? | • Interviews<br>• Organizational records and documents |

(*Continued*)

**EXHIBIT 11.2** (*Continued*)

| Approach | Description | Sample Questions | Sample Data Collection Techniques |
|---|---|---|---|
| | program accreditation, formal program reviews). Most often focuses on the resources, processes, and outcomes of large education and training programs. | • Is the program doing what it claims it is doing? | • Product reviews |
| Ethnography | Involves evaluators entering into a close and prolonged interaction with people in their everyday lives (for example, work, community activism, home) for the purpose of placing their actions, encounters, events, changes, and the like into a fuller and larger context. Qualitative descriptions in such forms as narratives, travelogues, stories, and memoirs result. | • What themes emerge from the stories of participants about how they have changed related to a series of education and training programs?<br>• What has been observed about the context in which these stories are set and how that context influences the characters, plot, and outcomes of the stories? | • Interviews<br>• Observations<br>• Story-telling<br>• Field notes<br>• Immersion in context (people and organizational)<br>• Travelogues<br>• Building of life histories and memoirs |

some form of questionnaire indicating their opinion on such items as content, instructors, instructional techniques, facilities, and food service. They are also sometimes asked to more generally list the strengths and weaknesses of the program, what they perceive they have learned, and recommendations for future activities. Soliciting participant reactions is most often done at the end of the formal program activities. In addition, some program planners also like to request participant feedback for individual sessions within longer programs. For example, at workshops or conferences where there are numerous instructional events, from small-group sessions to large-group presentations, evaluation data are collected at the end of each session. When evaluation data are generated for individual sessions, these data are used in two ways. The first is to provide feedback to individual instructors and presenters. The second is to contribute to a larger data set focused on evaluating the program as a whole (see Chapter Nine). Two examples of participant reaction forms—a brief form and a more comprehensive one—are given in Exhibits 11.3 and 11.4. In addition, a sample evaluation form for transfer-of-learning activities from the participants' perceptions is given in Exhibit 11.5. Two other sources of practical evaluation forms are Piskurich (2000) and Dick, Carey, and Carey (2001).

---

**EXHIBIT 11.3**

## Sample Participant Questionnaire (Short Form)

**Title of Program:**                                                    **Date:**

Please circle the ratings that best describe your reaction to this session:

*1 = No*          *2 = Somewhat*          *3 = Yes, definitely*

| | | | |
|---|---|---|---|
| 1. Were the session objectives clear? | 1 | 2 | 3 |
| 2. Were the instructional techniques and materials helpful in your learning of the material? | 1 | 2 | 3 |
| 3. Did the instructor focus the presentation on the session objectives and use the instructional techniques and methods well? | 1 | 2 | 3 |
| 4. The overall session contributed to my knowledge and/or skill base. | 1 | 2 | 3 |

5. Please identify any information and/or skills you can use from the program:

6. Please suggest improvements for this session:

---

**EXHIBIT 11.4**

## Sample Participant Questionnaire (Long Form)

**Title of Program:**                                    **Date:**

Please assist us in evaluating the quality of the program by completing this questionnaire. For each question, circle the number that best represents your view:

*1 = No*          *2 = Somewhat*          *3 = Yes, definitely*

Your specific comments and suggestions for improvement are most appreciated, especially for those items you marked "No" or "Somewhat."

Have you had prior experience and/or training in this content area? If so, what?




**Part 1:  Session Content and Process**

1. Were the program objectives clear and realistic?                                    1    2    3
   Comments/suggestions:


2. Did you learn what you expected to learn?                                    1    2    3
   Comments/suggestions:


3. Was the material presented relevant and valuable to you?                    1    2    3
   Comments/suggestions:


4. Was the material presented at an appropriate pace?                          1    2    3
   Comments/suggestions:


5. Was there an adequate amount of time allotted to each topic?                1    2    3
   Comments/suggestions:


6. Did the instructional and presentation techniques used
   assist you in adequately learning the material?                            1    2    3
   Comments/suggestions:


7. If there were opportunities for you to actively participate in
   the various sessions, was this participation beneficial to you?            1    2    3
   Comments/suggestions:


8. Could you relate the material to your particular life situation?            1    2    3
   Comments/suggestions:

9. Did the instructional materials and aids used (transparencies, manuals, videotapes, and the like) enhance the learning process?          1     2     3
   Comments/suggestions:

10. Was the program well organized and effectively conducted?          1     2     3
    Comments/suggestions:

**Part 2:  Presenter Skills\***

1. Were the presenters enthusiastic?          1     2     3
   Comments/suggestions:

2. Were the presenters well spoken?          1     2     3
   Comments/suggestions:

3. Did the presenters have expert knowledge of the content?          1     2     3
   Comments/suggestions:

4. Did the presenters make an effort to help you feel comfortable?          1     2     3
   Comments/suggestions:

5. Did the presenters provide you with adequate assistance in learning the material?          1     2     3
   Comments/suggestions:

6. Did the presenters communicate well with the participants (for example, use nonsexist language, attend to diversity of audience)?          1     2     3
   Comments/suggestions:

7. Did the presenters hold your interest?          1     2     3
   Comments/suggestions:

8. Did the presenters cover the content adequately in the allotted time?          1     2     3
   Comments/suggestions:

**Part 3:  Logistical Arrangements**

1. Were the registration procedures "participant-friendly"?          1     2     3
   Comments/suggestions:

*\*This part can be modified to enable participants to give feedback on individual presenters or instructors; alternatively, separate evaluation forms can be used for each session.*

(Continued)

**EXHIBIT 11.4** (*Continued*)

2. Was the program schedule well planned (for example, allowing enough time between sessions for lunch and networking)?         1     2     3
   Comments/suggestions:

3. Would you recommend that these facilities be used again?         1     2     3
   Comments/suggestions:

4. Would you want the same food menus again for breaks and meals?         1     2     3
   Comments/suggestions:

**Part 4:  Overall Program**

1. Will you be able to apply what you have learned in your work, at home, and/or in your personal life?         1     2     3
   Comments/suggestions:

2. Were you challenged by the content and the way the material was taught?         1     2     3
   Comments/suggestions:

3. How do you rate the program overall?         1     2     3
   Comments/suggestions:

4. Please comment on the major strengths of the program and changes you would recommend.

   Major strengths:

   Suggestions for improvement:

   Additional observations:

*Thank You For Your Help!*

**EXHIBIT 11.5**

# Sample Participant Questionnaire for Transfer Activities

**Title of Program:**                               **Date:**

Please assist us in evaluating the quality of the transfer activities by completing this questionnaire. For each question, circle the number that best represents your view:

*1 = No      2 = Somewhat      3 = Yes, definitely*

Your specific comments and suggestions for improvement are also most appreciated.

**Part 1: Clarity of What Is Expected in Applying What You Learned**

1. Was it clear what content and skills were to be applied in your own setting
   or life situation?      1    2    3

2. Was the uniqueness of your setting or life situation taken into account in thinking
   through how to apply what you have learned?      1    2    3

3. Were the guidelines clear as to what constitutes successful learning transfer?      1    2    3

4. If you needed to change what you were expected to apply to your own setting
   or life situation, were you able to easily negotiate those changes?      1    2    3
   Comments/suggestions:

**Part 2: Role of People in the Transfer-of-Learning Process**

1. Did the instructor or facilitator of the various program activities and events you
   attended use techniques that helped you apply what you had learned?      1    2    3

2. Did the instructor or facilitator of the various program activities and events you
   attended provide you with job aids or other resources that helped you
   apply what you had learned?      1    2    3

3. Please specify who assisted you and what they did in helping you to apply what you had learned to
   your setting or life situation.

| Who | What They Did | Ratings | | |
|---|---|---|---|---|
| _____ Work supervisor | | 1 | 2 | 3 |
| _____ Coworkers | | 1 | 2 | 3 |
| _____ Family | | 1 | 2 | 3 |
| _____ Friends | | 1 | 2 | 3 |
| _____ Other (please specify) | | 1 | 2 | 3 |

Observations/suggestions:

*(Continued)*

**EXHIBIT 11.5** (*Continued*)

**Part 3:  Use of Transfer Techniques**

1. Please indicate which transfer techniques you used, and whether they were helpful in applying what you had learned.

| Transfer Techniques | Helpful | | |
|---|---|---|---|
| _____ Individual learning plan | 1 | 2 | 3 |
| _____ Mentoring | 1 | 2 | 3 |
| _____ Coaching | 1 | 2 | 3 |
| _____ Job aids | 1 | 2 | 3 |
| _____ Job rotation | 1 | 2 | 3 |
| _____ Guided internships | 1 | 2 | 3 |
| _____ Portfolios | 1 | 2 | 3 |
| _____ Transfer teams | 1 | 2 | 3 |
| _____ Follow-up sessions | 1 | 2 | 3 |
| _____ Support group | 1 | 2 | 3 |
| _____ Networking | 1 | 2 | 3 |
| _____ Reflective practice | 1 | 2 | 3 |
| _____ Chat rooms | 1 | 2 | 3 |
| _____ Listservs | 1 | 2 | 3 |
| _____ Other(s); please specify_____ | 1 | 2 | 3 |

2. Which techniques were the most helpful and why?

3. Observations/suggestions:

**Part 4:  Overall Transfer Activities**

1. In general, did the planned transfer activities assist you in applying what you had learned?                                    1    2    3

   a.  If these activities were helpful, briefly explain why

   b.  If these activities did not help, briefly explain why

2. How do you rate the transfer part of the program overall?        1    2    3

3. Please comment on the major strengths of the transfer portion of the program and changes you would recommend.

   Major strengths:

   Suggestions for improvement:

4. Any additional observations/suggestions:

*Thank You For Your Assistance!*

A second approach that is also often used for program evaluation is the objectives-based approach. In this approach, the program objectives serve as the basis for program evaluation. The purpose, design, and criteria for the evaluation are all drawn from these objectives. Focusing on the program objectives does not mean that other aspects of the program (such as facilities or on-site coordination) are excluded from the evaluation; rather, the program objectives serve as the primary guidepost for the evaluation process. Within this approach, the objectives may address changes in individual participants; the procedures and practices of the education or training unit or the program itself (for example, program formats, instructor competence, program coordination); the organization; and/or in the community or society. If these objectives need to change as the program evolves, so too might the evaluation purpose, approach, data collection and analysis tools, and criteria.

## Collecting Evaluation Data

There are a number of techniques for collecting evaluation data, whether in systematic or informal ways. Selecting these data collection techniques depends on the purpose, the evaluation approach, and the type of information needed. Other important variables to consider are the types of people administering and responding to the evaluation and the cost of using a given technique. Eleven of the most widely used techniques for collecting evaluation data are described in Exhibit 11.6 along with a list of operational guidelines. Helpful resources that include more detailed descriptions of specific evaluation techniques include Tracey (1992); Wholey, Hatry, and Newcomer (1994); Phillips (1996); Tenopyr (1996); Mitchell (1998); Smith and Ragan (1999); Marienau (1999); Guskey (2000); and Berg (2001).

Many of the same data collection techniques, as noted earlier in this chapter, are used for program evaluation as well generating ideas for programs, instructional assessment, and as part of the transfer process. For example, information gathered by on-the-job observations as part of a needs analysis could be used as baseline data for an evaluation study. After an education or training program was completed, the change in job performance would be measured against the original needs analysis data. (The type and form of the data would need to be equivalent in both phases, of course.) In addition, some of these techniques (for example, tests, product reviews, and interviews) are also used for instructional evaluation and as part of the transfer process.

Evaluation data can be collected at three major points: prior to the program, during the program (including the transfer process), and after the program is completed. The types of information collected at these three

**EXHIBIT 11.6**

# Techniques for Collecting Evaluation Data

| Technique | Description | Operational Guidelines |
|---|---|---|
| **Observations** | Watching participants at actual or simulated tasks and recording the knowledge, skills, problem-finding and -solving capabilities, and/or values and attitudes participants display. | Determine whether these should be open-ended or formally structured (with specific behaviors to observe). Observers must have a clear picture of who, how, and what they are observing. |
| **Interviews** | Conversations with people (for example, learners, program planners, supervisors, customers) individually or in groups, in person, by phone, and/or via computer-based means (for example, email, chat rooms, listservs). | Determine whether these should be open-ended or formally structured (with specific questions to ask). For formally structured interviews, the interview schedule should be pilot-tested. Interviewers must listen to responses without judgment. |
| **Written Questionnaires** | Gathering of opinions, attitudes, perceptions, or facts by means of a written series of questions. | Choose from among a variety of question formats: open-ended, ranking, checklists, scales, or forced choices. These can be administered by mail or given to individuals or groups to complete. |
| **Tests** | Paper-and-pencil or computer-generated tests used to measure participants' knowledge, skills, problem-finding or -solving, and/or values and attitudes. | Know what the test measures (knowledge, skills, problem-finding or -solving, and/or attitudes and values) and use it as an evaluation tool for only those areas. In addition, make sure the test is both reliable and valid. Choose a test carefully. Check to see whether what it measures is important and relevant. |
| **Product Reviews** | Tangible items that participants produce as a result of the program (for example, written materials, portfolios, clay pots, rebuilt engines, flower arrangements, videotapes, websites, computer simulations, multimedia presentations). | Clearly and precisely define the nature of the project and the criteria on which it will be judged. Participants, whenever possible, should be able to use the products. |

| Technique | Description | Operational Guidelines |
|---|---|---|
| **Performance Reviews** | Demonstration of a specific skill or procedure (for example, team building, responding to customer complaints, answering a health information line) in either a simulated or a real situation. | Identify specifically what the elements and criteria are for the performance to be evaluated. Determine what tool will be used in the process (such as, checklists, rating scales, experts' judgment) and ensure consistency. |
| **Organizational and Community Records and Documents** | Written materials, often found in computerized data-based systems, developed by organizations and communities. Examples include performance appraisals, production schedules, financial reports, records of absenteeism or attendance, job efficiency indexes, annual reports, committee and board minutes, and records showing hours of training time and numbers of participants involved. | Systematically collect and record data so that the information is easy to retrieve and sort. |
| **Portfolios** | A purposeful collection of learners' work assembled over time that documents events, activities, products, and/or achievements. | Include items produced by the learners and attestations from others (for example, honors, awards certificates). Portfolios may take the form of notebooks or be computer-based and are used in a number of different ways (for example, for active reflection by learners while the program is in progress, as summative evaluative tools). |
| **Cost-Benefit Analysis** | A method for assessing the relationship between the outcomes of an educational program and the costs required to produce them. | Develop the cost side of the equation. Include both direct and indirect costs. Calculate the benefit side by focusing on either increasing revenues or decreasing expenses. Evaluators must have quantitatively measurable outcomes to use this technique. |
| **Focus Groups** | Informal small-group discussion, guided by an experienced facilitator, designed to obtain in-depth qualitative data on a particular topic or issue (for example, whether program participants could apply what they had learned, overall effectiveness of the program). | Facilitators pose no more than three or four questions, one at a time, with participants building on the responses of other group members. The conversation is primarily among the participants, with facilitators encouraging interaction and ensuring all participants have a voice. Group interactions are most often audio- or videotaped and then transcribed at a later date. |

*(Continued)*

| EXHIBIT 11.6 (*Continued*) | | |
|---|---|---|
| **Technique** | **Description** | **Operational Guidelines** |
| **Self-Assessment** | Individually or in groups, learners appraise what they have learned and whether they have been able to apply that learning in their own contexts. Program planners, instructors, and other stakeholders can also use this process, but these people usually focus on the program structure, processes, and organizational or community-wide impact of the program. | Identify methods for doing self-assessments (for example, personal journals and diaries, videotaping, using portfolio materials). Specify the time frame, what is to be recorded or discussed, and whether the process will be done individually, with one or two other people, or in groups. Guarantee confidentiality for sensitive areas, especially related to learners' personal lives and feelings. |

major points and examples of where, when, how, and what types of information that can be gathered are outlined in Exhibit 11.7.

Evaluation data that are collected before the program include information about the context of where the learning is to take place and/or be applied, and baseline data on individual learners or groups of learners (see Chapters Four and Six). Data gathered during and at the close of programs contain material that is tied directly to the instructional processes (see Chapter Nine). One example of this type of data is information that instructors request either prior to or right at the start of a learning activity, such as the current knowledge and skill levels of participants in relation to the course content. A second example is the data collected either during or after the instructional portion to determine what participants have learned. For programs where only instructional data are collected, these data become the main criteria for making judgments about the value of the program. For example, if the major objective of a program is to teach individual participants specific skills (such as CPR or other emergency medical procedures), then the only data needed might be those that are collected during the instructional phase. For educational and training programs that have objectives beyond individual change, the evaluation data generated as a part of the instructional portion of the program are only one part of the databank that is needed.

Likewise, evaluation data is collected during the transfer-of-learning activities (see Chapter Ten). For example, data can be collected as part of support-group activities, through group interviews, or observations. Again, as stressed in this chapter and throughout the book, the various components of the program planning and implementation process often overlap and therefore are not necessarily done as separate tasks.

# EXHIBIT 11.7
## When, Where, and How Evaluation Data Are Collected and Types of Evaluation Data

| | Prior to the start of the program | During the program | At the end of the program | During the transfer phase of the program | Well after the program is completed |
|---|---|---|---|---|---|
| **When the Data Are Collected** | | | | | |
| **Where the Data Are Collected** | Program site and/or the application site (if different) | At the program | At the program | At the applications site of the participants | At the applications site of the participants |
| **How Data Might Be Collected** | • Observations<br>• Interviews<br>• Review of group, organizational, and community records and reports<br>• Focus groups<br>• Questionnaires<br>• Tests<br>• Self-assessments | • Questionnaires<br>• Interviews<br>• Tests<br>• Self-assessments | • Questionnaires<br>• Interviews<br>• Tests | • Interviews<br>• Observations<br>• Self-assessment<br>• Focus groups | • Observations<br>• Interviews<br>• Reviews of organizational records<br>• Cost-benefit analyses<br>• Written documents<br>• Questionnaires<br>• Product and performance reviews<br>• Focus groups |
| **Type of Data Collected** | • Baseline data on participants' present knowledge, skills, problem-finding and problem-solving capabilities, and/or values and attitudes; group, organizational, or community and societal information (for example, policies, operating procedures, specific behaviors, expressed values and attitudes)<br>• Data on the people, organizational and environ-mental context where participants are expected to apply their learning | • Data on participants' learning; participant and staff reaction to the program while it is still in progress | • Data on participants' learning; participant and staff reactions to the program | • Data on whether participants can apply their learning in their own situations<br>• Observations by those in the applications settings of whether the context is amenable to this change in practice or attitudes and values | • Data on participants' knowledge level, performance, and/or beliefs, values, and attitudes<br>• Organizational information (for example, changes in policies, procedures, costs)<br>• Community and societal information (for example, knowledge, actions, values and attitudes) |

## Data Analysis

At whatever point the evaluation data are collected, it is important to have set procedures for analyzing the data, because one of the most frequent flaws in the evaluation process is the inadequate planning of data analysis procedures. The following scenario illustrates this problem.

### *Chaotic Data*

Karen, the director of judicial education for the state and municipal court system, has been asked to prepare an evaluation report covering the last two years of the program. She believes that putting together this report should be a fairly easy process, because she has required the collection of evaluation information on all programs. However, due to the time constraints of her staff, very little actual analysis of the data has been completed (especially in the last year) except on the new education and training activities. Karen decides to do a cursory review of the data prior to turning the information over to the two new members of her staff who will actually complete the analysis and draft the report. To her dismay, what she finds in the computer reports is a set of figures that do not make sense. Not only have the data been entered differently across programs, but the data recorded are not consistent from program to program. She also finds five file boxes full of written questionnaires that have never been entered into the system and a large stack of handwritten notes from evaluation interviews with key judges and administrative staff. Karen wonders how she and her staff are going to make sense out of all these different sets of data.

Two major kinds of data are generated from program evaluations: quantitative and qualitative (Creswell, 1994; Wholey, Hatry, and Newcomer, 1994; Punch, 1998; Guskey, 2000; Berg, 2001). Quantitative data give precise numerical measures, while qualitative data provide rich descriptive materials. What some program planners do not realize is that these two major types of data are very different, as pictured in Exhibit 11.8, and therefore require vastly different competencies of the staff in the analysis phase (Punch, 1998; Berg, 2001).

For some evaluations, only quantitative data or qualitative data are needed; for others, both types of data are required. In addition, some program evaluations rely on single data sources (such as questionnaires or performance demonstrations), whereas others require multiple data sources before complete responses to evaluation questions can be provided. This notion of single and multiple data sources linked to specific evaluation

**EXHIBIT 11.8**

# Types of Data Collected in Quantitative and Qualitative Analysis

| Focus of Evaluation | Types of Data Generated |
|---|---|
| **Evaluations Focusing on Participants' Learning** | *Quantitative*<br>Participants take tests that measure changes in their knowledge, skill levels, and/or beliefs, attitudes, values, and feelings. These test scores are recorded in the training records and compared to the pre-test scores. These tests are given after the on-site program and also during the transfer-of-learning phase.<br><br>*Qualitative*<br>Observations are made by the instructors, work supervisors, or community leaders, on the extent of change in participants' knowledge, skill levels, and/or beliefs, attitudes, values, and feelings. These observations result in 25 pages of acceptable data. |
| **Evaluations Focusing on Program Operations** | *Quantitative*<br>Using a five-point Likert Scale, department heads and selected participants rate specific procedures and practices of the education and training unit (for example, people skills of staff, ways program ideas are generated, program formats, how participants for programs are chosen, funding for programs). These ratings are then compiled and analyzed, and a two-page numerical summary is given to all education staff.<br><br>*Qualitative*<br>Department heads and staff are interviewed, using open-ended questions about their perceptions of the effectiveness of the education and training unit. About 100 pages of transcripts, transcribed from 10 audiotapes, are analyzed. |
| **Evaluations Focusing on Organizational Issues** | *Quantitative*<br>After a training program for new agency volunteers, the percentage of new volunteers who remain with the program is assessed. The director of volunteers does a percentage count after one month, and then again after three months, by checking the computer records kept on all volunteer activities.<br><br>*Qualitative*<br>The director of volunteers, the staff who work directly with the volunteers, and a selected group of volunteers are asked if the training program made a difference in the way they provide services to the clients of the agency. Notes are taken at each of the group interviews and transcribed so that staff and volunteers can review them. |
| **Evaluations Focusing on Societal Issues** | *Quantitative*<br>A random sample of community members is surveyed via a structured telephone interview to determine whether a recent series of newspaper articles on violent acts in the community has led to more people becoming involved in neighborhood programs for safer communities. Whenever respondents indicate that they have become more active, the type of activity and the setting are recorded.<br><br>*Qualitative*<br>Staff and members of five neighborhood groups for safer communities are asked in focus group meetings if they perceive the newspaper articles as having been useful in generating community support for their programs. Extensive notes are taken by two recorders and then transcribed and reviewed. |

questions, data collection techniques, and resulting types of data is illustrated in Exhibit 11.9. When different kinds of data and multiple data sources are used, a failure to outline the data analysis procedures clearly beforehand can be especially problematic, as was illustrated earlier in the last scenario.

In choosing data analysis procedures, the evaluation questions, approaches, data collection techniques, and kinds of data collected are considered. For evaluations that produce quantitative data, as discussed earlier, some sort of numerical values is assigned, from simple counting to complex statistical analysis. Qualitative analysis provides in-depth descriptions, usually in the form of words or visuals rather than numbers (Denzin and Lincoln, 2000; Berg, 2001). Content and thematic analysis is one of the most often used methods for reviewing qualitative data. More detailed descriptions of specific quantitative and qualitative analysis procedures can be found in McMillan and Schumacher (2000); Krathwohl (1993); Wholey, Hatry, and Newcomer (1994); Kraut (1996); Punch (1998); Denzin and Lincoln (2000); Guskey (2000); and Berg (2001).

If the program planning staff is unfamiliar with how to do data analysis, especially when complex procedures are needed, an outside consultant can be a good investment. "People with such expertise may be higher education specialists or may be engaged in evaluation or market research in a business or community agency" (Knox, 1998, p. 168).

## Making Judgments About the Program

Program planners make judgments on the worth and value of the program as they interpret the data compiled during the analysis phase. This judgment process involves bringing together various pieces of the information gathered and supplying answers to the evaluation questions (Tracey, 1992; Guskey, 2000; Sork, 2000). Was what the participants learned in the program worthwhile? Were the objectives of the program addressed in an effective and efficient manner? Were the learners able to apply what they learned back into their work and/or other life situations? Do management and administrative personnel believe the education and training programs give vital assistance in fulfilling the mission and goals of the organization? Does the program address compelling community and societal concerns? These judgments provide the basis for making final conclusions and recommendations concerning the content and the operation of education and training programs. Making program recommendations is discussed in Chapter Twelve.

Judgments about programs should be based primarily on criteria related to the program processes and/or outcomes and are reached by comparing

**EXHIBIT 11.9**

# Examples of Single and Multiple Evaluation Data Collection Sources

| *Single Data Source* | | |
|---|---|---|
| **Sample Evaluation Questions** | **Sample Data CollectionTechniques** | **Kinds of Data** |
| What new skills were learned by participants as a result of the train-the-trainer program? | Observations of participants before and after training | Qualitative Quantitative |
| Did participants perceive the instructors as effective and the content as useful in the program on communication skills? | Questionnaires administered right at the end of the on-site program | Quantitative |
| Did the parents believe that the information and skills taught to them through a series of seminars on "Coping with Your Teenager" were useful? | Telephone interviews a month after the seminar series was completed | Quantitative Qualitative |
| Was there a reduction in the rate of turnover for new employees that could be attributed to the orientation program? | Review of company turnover rates for new employees three months after the program | Quantitative |

| *Multiple Data Sources* | | |
|---|---|---|
| **Sample Evaluation Questions** | **Sample Data CollectionTechniques** | **Kinds of Data** |
| What changes in the participants' job performances were outcomes of the leadership development program? | On-the-job observations, interviews, and performance appraisals three and then six months after the program | Qualitative Quantitative |
| As a result of the training program, are the volunteers more effective instructors of adults? | Questionnaires, observations, and interviews during the transfer phase and three months after the program | Qualitative Quantitative |
| Did the education of staff on customer service result in a cost savings to the organization? | Review of company records and a cost-benefit analysis on a quarterly basis for two years | Quantitative |
| Are more and different groups of people participating in community performing arts events as a result of educational programs on the arts for children and parents in area schools? | Review of ticket sales over a six-month period and questionnaires sent to parents | Quantitative |

results of the data analysis with the criteria that were set (or emerged) for each evaluation question or objective. For those criteria that were predetermined and are measurable, the judgments are quite simple: the changes produced by the program either meet the criteria or they do not. Examples of this are given in Exhibit 11.10.

A word of caution is given for program planners, even where the criteria are predetermined and measurable. Unless the evaluation approach is sophisticated enough to control for variables that could affect the outcomes, program planners must be careful not to attribute success or lack of success to their education or training programs without qualifying what those other variables are.

It is much more difficult to make judgments about programs for which the criteria are less clear and/or cannot or should not be stated in advance. The following scenario illustrates a program for which criteria are difficult to develop. The planners for this program usually are not able to describe upfront exactly what the tangible outcomes might be.

### *Mountain Plains Community College*

The major staff development goal for administrators and instructors of Mountain Plains Community College is to have all staff use open and honest communication styles and to work on rebuilding trust between and among staff members. Those who have been working at the college for the last two years know that communication has been a problem; little trust exists between the instructors and administrators and between and among some of the instructional staff. It is a tough agenda, but one that most staff are committed to, even those who have been the most angry and disillusioned. The catalyst for this commitment has been twofold: the hiring of a new president and public statements by respected instructors that students are being negatively affected by the actions of both instructors and administrators. A two-day retreat will be held at a rustic mountain resort as the initial activity for addressing this problem.

Education and training programs that focus on the kinds of changes that are difficult, if not impossible, to quantify (such as the program described in this scenario) challenge program planners to think differently about who should define criteria, when and how those criteria are determined, and the judgment process itself. The use of qualitative approaches, such as in-depth case studies, often does not allow for developing upfront criteria. In most qualitative evaluation studies, the criteria for judging the worth and value of the program are grounded in the major themes that

**EXHIBIT 11.10**

## Examples of Judgments Made on Education and Training Programs Using Quantitative Evaluation Criteria

### FOCUSING ON PARTICIPANTS' LEARNING

**Evaluation Question**    Did the participants in the program on supervisory skills gain sufficient knowledge in this content area?

| Criterion | Findings Based on Analysis Process | Interpretation and Conclusions |
|---|---|---|
| Participants will score 85 or better on a knowledge test of supervisory skills. | Thirty-eight of the 40 participants scored 85 or better on a knowledge test of supervisory skills. | The majority of participants mastered the material; thus the program was termed highly successful. |

### FOCUSING ON PROGRAM OPERATIONS

**Evaluation Question**    Are the program staff effective instructors and facilitators for inhouse educational programs?

| Criterion | Findings Based on Analysis Process | Interpretation and Conclusions |
|---|---|---|
| Staff members will achieve a four-point rating or better on a five-point scale on their skills as instructors and facilitators. The data will be drawn from 25 randomly selected programs over a six-month period. | All but one of the staff members were given an overall four-point rating based on the data drawn from 25 program evaluations of randomly selected educational programs. | The staff as a whole are seen as very effective instructors and facilitators for in-house educational programs. |

### FOCUSING ON ORGANIZATIONAL ISSUES

**Evaluation Question**    Was there a reduction in the turnover rate for new employees that could be attributed to the orientation program?

| Criterion | Findings Based on Analysis Process | Interpretation and Conclusions |
|---|---|---|
| There will be a reduction of 20 percent in the turnover rate of new employees over a six-month period. | The turnover rate was reduced by 10 percent during a specified six-month period. | The orientation program did not produce the desired effect. Therefore, the problem of high turnover needs to be examined for alternative interventions (for example, changes in supervisory behavior or working conditions). |

*(Continued)*

**EXHIBIT 11.10 (Continued)**

**FOCUSING ON SOCIETAL ISSUES**

| Evaluation Question | Was there an increase in the number of people who became volunteers for their local neighborhood action programs for safer communities as a result of a series of newspaper articles, neighborhood informational meetings, and flyers sent to all community households? |
| --- | --- |

| Criterion | Findings Based on Analysis Process | Interpretation and Conclusions |
| --- | --- | --- |
| There will be a 5-percent increase in the number of people who volunteer to work with their neighborhood action programs for safer communities. | The percentage of volunteers increased an average of 8 percent. | Since the increase in the percentage of new volunteers exceeded program goals, the educational efforts via newspaper articles, neighborhood meetings, and flyers were judged to be highly successful. |

emerge during the evaluation process and are highly contextual to that particular setting. Unfortunately, qualitative evaluations are usually costly and call for evaluators with high levels of expertise. So how else could this be done?

A second strategy in the case of hard-to-quantify outcomes is to ask program participants to serve as the primary judges of whether the program has worked. Therefore, the criteria for program success start with individual perceptions of worth and value rather than preset standards. For most programs, these criteria continue to change as the program unfolds. For some programs, such as the retreat for staff members of Mountain Plains College, it is important to make the emerging individual criteria public, with the explicit goal of working toward criteria that are mutually agreed upon. For other programs, such as support or self-help groups, the criteria often remain highly personalized for each program participant. Allowing participants the freedom to form their own criteria for judging program quality and success, whether these criteria remain personalized or become a collective statement, means acceptance by program planners of multiple ways of saying programs are worthwhile. For example, returning to the scenario, criteria could range from explicit statements such as, "Trust means that when I ask people to do something they will do it, and do it well," to very open-ended observations such as, "I feel better, and therefore the program was great," or "The new communication system just feels right, even though

I can't put my finger on exactly why it's working." Ways in which these kinds of judgments are made include self-reflection, reflective group procedures, and reviews of participants' journals. In some cases, an outside consultant is required to assist in making this kind of judgment process work.

## Chapter Highlights

Program evaluation is a process used to determine whether the design and delivery of a program were effective and whether program outcomes were achieved, including those outcomes that emerged as the program progressed as well as those that were anticipated. The heart of program evaluation lies in judging the value and worth of a program, which is not an easy assignment. The program design and delivery are usually easier to evaluate than program outcomes; outcome measures are often elusive, and using them in judging whether a specific program is worthwhile or not is problematic. Evaluation, more than other elements of the Interactive Model of Program Planning, is where many of the other components of the model overlap. This junction comes primarily from evaluative data being generated and analyzed throughout the program planning process.

Program planners take advantage of informal and unplanned evaluation opportunities that take place throughout the program as well as systematic program evaluation procedures. In formulating evaluation plans, program planners therefore consider both formal and informal evaluation processes as valid sources of evaluation data. In preparing evaluation plans, planners concentrate on six major tasks:

- Develop, as warranted, systematic program evaluation procedures.

- Use informal and unplanned evaluation opportunities to collect formative and summative evaluation data (for example, observing participant behavior during a program, listening to learners' comments during break times, and checking to see if participants can apply what they have learned in their specific situations).

- Specify the evaluation approach or approaches to be used (for example, objectives-based, accountability planner, levels of evaluation, quasi-legal).

- Determine how evaluation data are to be collected (for example, observations, questionnaires, product reviews) and/or if some evaluation data already exists.

- Think through how the data are to be analyzed, including how to integrate the data that were collected through any informal evaluation processes.

◆ Describe how judgments are made about the program, using predetermined and/or emergent evaluation criteria for program success.

In using the evaluation process as a tool for making program recommendations and for revising or eliminating current programs and planning future programs, it is important to examine programs that are judged to be failures as well as those that are perceived as successful. In addition, communicating these recommendations and results is also critical. Both of these important tasks, making program recommendations and communicating program results, are discussed in the next chapter.

## Application Exercises

These Application Exercises assist you in planning a systematic program evaluation, reflecting on informal or unplanned evaluation opportunities, and making program judgments.

## EXERCISE 11.1

# Planning a Systematic Program Evaluation

1. Briefly describe an education or training program for which you have or have to develop a systematic program evaluation.



2. Using the program situation you described above, analyze the evaluation process you conducted or are developing using the 11-element model in the chart below. Use exhibits and tables provided in Chapter Eleven (specifically, Exhibit 11.1) as guides for completing your evaluation plan.

| Elements | Your Evaluation Plan |
|---|---|
| Secure support for the evaluation effort from those who have a stake in the results of the evaluation. | |
| Identify the individuals to be involved in planning and overseeing the evaluation process. | |
| Define precisely the purpose of the evaluation and how the results are to be used. | |
| Specify what is judged and formulate the evaluation questions. | |
| Determine who supplies the needed evidence and/or if some of that evidence is already available. | |
| Delineate the evaluation approach. | |
| Choose the data collection techniques to use, when the data will be collected, and /or how the already available data can be put into useable forms. | |

*(Continued)*

## EXERCISE 11.1 (Continued)

| | |
|---|---|
| Indicate the analysis procedure(s). | |
| Stipulate what criteria to use in making judgments about the program or what process to apply in determining the criteria. | |
| Determine the specific time line, budget, and other necessary resources. | |
| Monitor and complete the evaluation, make judgments about the value and worth of the program, and think through ways the evaluation data can be effectively used. | |

3.  **Ask a colleague and/or your planning group to review the evaluation plan you have analyzed or proposed. Revise your plan based on the feedback you receive.**

## EXERCISE 11.2

## Informal and Unplanned Evaluation Opportunities

List at least three ways you have used in evaluating education and training programs. Indicate next to each whether what you did was helpful, and describe briefly why or why not.

| Informal or Unplanned Ways to Evaluate Education and Training Programs | Helpful? (Why or Why Not) |
|---|---|
| 1. | |
| 2. | |
| 3. | |

## EXERCISE 11.3

## Making Judgments About Programs

1.  Using information from a program evaluation in which you were involved, fill in the following chart. Use Exhibit 11.10 (page 259) as a resource in completing this activity.

| | | | |
|---|---|---|---|
| **Evaluation Question or Area Judged** | | | |
| **Way Data Were Collected and Analyzed** | | | |
| **Criteria Used** | | | |
| **Interpretations and Conclusions** | | | |

2.  Were any of the processes or procedures used unclear? Are there blank spaces on your chart? If the answer to either question is yes, how might you have made this evaluation a more complete process? More specifically, what might you have done differently?

# Chapter 12

# Making Recommendations and Communicating Results

Barbara, the director for continuing professional education for a consortium of hospitals, has just completed a very successful continuing education program for emergency room personnel on revised patient care procedures. The majority of staff members who attended displayed a high level of knowledge about the new procedures and also were able to demonstrate they had applied this knowledge into their emergency room practices. Barbara had garnered, prior to the start of the program, the backing of key physicians, nurses, and support personnel from all shifts at each of the participating hospitals for the proposed changes in practice. In addition, she had included in her program plan suggested strategies and techniques that both the medical and support personnel could use in translating what they had learned into their work roles. As part of this transfer plan, she had taken into account the differences in the practice context among the hospitals and the three work shifts and made sure these differences were apparent in both the instructional and transfer phases of the program. As part of the evaluation procedures, Barbara collected data about the program strengths and areas for improvement and used these data in formative ways as the program progressed. She also planned to use these data, and the ideas she collected for future programs as part of the final evaluation report on this program. As Barbara contemplated putting together the final evaluation report, she wondered how she could accomplish three objectives:

1. Let program participants and other stakeholders know that she listened to what they had to say and how she had and would

use their feedback and the other evaluation data collected to make recommendations for current and future programs

2.  Give a strong statement to "the powers that be" that this program resulted in positive changes in emergency room procedures for all participating hospitals

3.  Present the material in such a way that grabs people's attention and keeps them engaged in what is she is trying to communicate

In addition, Barbara also wanted to reframe her annual report on the activities of the Office of Continuing Professional Education, which was due in the next two months. She had not been happy with the format, nor with the overall response to the success of the program and the recommended changes.

In general little attention is given to communicating in useable and effective ways the recommendations and the results of education and training programs. Communications of this nature could assist in the planning of current and future programs, either in terms of planning individual programs or in demonstrating the value and worth of the overall education and training program initiatives and operations. Program participants, more than any other stakeholders, are often left out of this feedback loop. In addition, although program planners usually generate a number of different types of program reports for varying audiences (for example, evaluation reports, quarterly reports, annual reports), these reports tend to be perfunctory at best, and boring at worst. Even when these reports are lively and interesting, often no real thought is given to getting key decision-makers and stakeholders to review and then use the information.

Examined first in this chapter are what constitutes program successes as well as failures. Suggestions for formulating recommendations about current and future programs are then given. Outlined next are five important factors program planners consider when communicating program recommendations and results, through preparing different kinds of reports on education and training programs. This discussion is followed by a brief exploration of the audiences and timing of program reports. The chapter concludes by stressing the importance of follow-up activities with key individuals and/or groups to clarify questions about the program recommendations and results, and ensuring the right people have heard this information.

## Examining Program Successes and Failures

In examining education and training programs, both the program successes and failures are explored in terms of identifying the realities of programming situations (Sork, 1991a). Discussed first is an example of how a planner used an in-depth evaluation process to highlight a program success.

## Highlighting Program Successes

Going back to Barbara's situation in the opening scenario, it is important for her to help various stakeholders, from participants to funding sources, understand how the program had a positive impact on both individual practice and the ways emergency rooms operate. Barbara examined and used data from a variety of sources in this process. First, she compared the original ideas and needs, which were collected through a systematic needs assessment, with data collected both after the program was completed and six months later. Barbara was checking to see if the program had addressed these identified ideas and needs, and if changes were made in practice, grounded in these ideas and needs, as a result of the training program. These data were collected through preconference meetings with program attendees and managers from each hospital, during and after the formal classroom instruction, and at the transfer-of-learning phase.

These data were used to help program participants and sponsors see how the program was revised through ongoing feedback, and how the outcomes were negotiated for each hospital site, depending on the context in which the learning was applied. In addition, this information clearly showed the relationship between the program and how practices and operations within the emergency rooms changed, which Barbara chose to report in a briefing for selected senior managers from each hospital as part of their regular bi-monthly meetings. Part of Barbara's overall objective in being so thorough with reporting this program's success was that she was well aware of the public criticism these emergency rooms had been receiving, both in the local newspapers and on the nightly news. In addition, Barbara made sure the marketing departments of each of the hospitals also received a short evaluation report, with key data, that would be useful in their work. In addition, as Barbara was also interested in gaining more resources in general for her department, she ensured that all major stakeholders had a clear picture of what was recommended for future programs and what level of resources was needed to provide quality programs in these areas.

## Understanding Program Failures

Although it is important that Barbara and other program planners focus on their program successes, too often only the successes are examined thoroughly, while analyzing the failures is neglected. Sork (1991b) argues that examining program failures can be as important as program successes, as much can be learned from mistakes planners make. Sork (1991a), based on his earlier work (1987), and that of Sork, Kalef, and Worsfold (1987), developed the following typology of four program failures.

In Type 1 problems, planning for the program is partially completed but is terminated before implementation. Likely causes of failure include:

- ▶ Unclear organizational goals or mandates
- ▶ Ill-defined client and/or customer systems
- ▶ Incomplete knowledge of resource constraints
- ▶ Excessively costly or complex tentative design
- ▶ Lack of follow-through

In Type 2 problems, planning for the program is completed, but because the program does not attract sufficient enrollment, it is canceled. These problems are often due to:

- ▶ Inappropriate pricing, scheduling, and/or location
- ▶ Lack of interest by potential participants, organizations, and/or the community
- ▶ Poorly focused or timed marketing
- ▶ More attractive competition
- ▶ Market saturation
- ▶ Inadequate support services

In Type 3 problems, planning for the program is completed and the program is offered, but the program does not provide the participants what they expected. The participants then either fail to complete the program or react negatively to it. The fault may lie with:

- ▶ Poor instruction
- ▶ Poor coordination
- ▶ Unclear objectives
- ▶ Mismatch between content and the participants' needs
- ▶ Poor quality of noninstructional resources

In Type 4 problems, the program is offered and the participants express satisfaction, but there is clear evidence that the program failed to achieve the goals and objectives for which it was designed. Among the likely causes of failure are these:

- ▶ Ineffective instruction
- ▶ Unclear objectives
- ▶ Miscommunication of objectives

- ▶ Unrealistic expectations
- ▶ Mismatch between objectives and program format and instructional techniques
- ▶ Inadequate provision for learning transfer (Sork, 1991b, pp. 90–92)

Sork (1991b) goes on to discuss how to use these program failures to develop sound principles and practices of program development. For example, a Type 3 failure—a program that does not provide participants what they expected—might be avoided by planners who pay careful attention to ensuring that the program objectives match the participants' needs; select instructors who are competent, knowledgeable, and have a reputation for delivering what they say they will deliver; and choose instructors who are willing to make changes in the program while it is being conducted if it is not meeting the participants' expectations and/or is not being delivered as promised.

In addition, Sork (1981, 1991a, 1991b) has outlined ideas for specific procedures for analyzing and responding to program mistakes and failures. One systematic process for doing this is a postmortem program audit (Sork, 1981; Sork, Kalef, and Worsfold, 1987). Examples of important questions used for such an audit are these:

- ▶ What was the dollar value of personnel time devoted to this activity?
- ▶ How much money (other than for personnel) was expended on this activity?
- ▶ What event or evidence led to this activity being judged a failure?
- ▶ What are the consequences associated with this failure?
- ▶ What could have been done to avoid this failure?

More specific procedures and worksheets for doing this kind of audit are contained in a manual by Sork, Kalef, and Worsfold (1987). These authors stress that postmortem program audits should be timely and include as many staff members who were involved with the program activity as possible. In addition, they caution that these procedures are very difficult to do, because not all the facts are always known and what *is* known may be the product of people's imagination.

## Formulating Recommendations

One of the final steps in examining program successes and failures is formulating recommendations concerning education and training programs (Tracey, 1992; Birkenholz, 1999). These recommendations focus on both reviewing current and planning future programs. Recommendations are made utilizing the framework of revising or eliminating current programs and/or planning new programs. The focal points of these recommendations are on program planning and delivery, program content, instructional and transfer strategies and techniques, program evaluation, program outcomes and impact, and how the education or training function could more effectively and efficiently serve the organization or community. For example, it is recommended that administrators and managers become more active in planning programs for their staff.

The program recommendations are clear about what areas are being considered, grouped by major issues or topic, and include any new observations that emerged. Each recommendation also includes strategies for tackling the recommendations and a list of the resources that are needed to respond. One useful format for recommendations is outlined below:

I.  Area Being Addressed

II.  Recommended Actions

III.  Alternative Strategies for Addressing the Recommended Actions

IV.  Resources Needed to Respond

For example, recommendations regarding future evaluation address such issues as the usefulness of the evaluation questions, the appropriateness of the evaluation approach and data collection techniques, and the clarity of the analysis and reporting procedures. Additionally, detailed recommendations are made concerning the format and questions on an instrument used to gather evaluation data. More specifically, a questionnaire was perceived as too long, too technically worded, and thus too cumbersome for many of the respondents to complete.

## Preparing Reports on Results of Education and Training Programs

The only reason to do reports on education and training programs is "to make a splash, to have that impact, to change situations in a desired direction" (Hendricks, 1991, cited in Hendricks, 1994, p. 549). "Some call this 'speaking truth to power,' but what good is speaking truth if power isn't listening? Unless we find more effective ways to help our audiences listen, all of our good works are likely to go for naught" (Hendricks, 1994, p. 594).

In moving reports from "ripples to splashes," program planners have to report program results regularly and frequently, and make these reports simple, but direct. The focus of these reports is on what has happened, including recommendations that help people make decisions on what to do next—in other words, the spotlight is on action, not merely what has gone before. In developing reports that make a difference in practice there are seven important factors to consider: function, scope, audience, content, structure, style, and format. Each of these factors is discussed in the following sections.

## Function

Reports on education and training programs fill one or more major functions. First, reports are used to discuss how evaluation data from participants and other stakeholders was and will be used to improve, eliminate, or plan new programs. Second, reports are employed to educate and gain support from key people and groups, and to facilitate and inform decision-making about current and future programs. Third, documentation for permanent records is provided in reports and often this material is drawn upon to demonstrate program accountability. Fourth, reports are also used to market current and future programs and serve as catalysts for future involvement and action (Rothwell and Kazanas, 1998; Tracey, 1992; Hinrichs, 1996; Knox, 1998; Vella, Berardinelli, and Burrow, 1998). The people responsible for preparing the report have a clear understanding of how the report of program results will be used before they put it together.

## Scope and Audience

Decisions also are made about the scope and audience for the report (Hendricks, 1994; Milano with Ullius, 1998). How comprehensive should the report be? Will it describe only a specific education or training event, selected parts of a program, or the education and training program as a whole? What kinds of data are needed? Who should receive the report? There are one or multiple audiences, depending on the function and scope of the communication. In addition, the audience is a key determiner in how the reports on program results are structured and the style and format these reports take. Common audiences for reports on education and training programs are listed in Exhibit 12.1.

## Content

The content of a report on program results is tailored to the issues and concerns of the recipients as well as the reporting function (Hendricks, 1994; Guskey, 2000; Kemp, 2000). A typical content outline is shown in Exhibit 12.2. In developing the content Kemp (2000) cautions that programmers "not become too detailed or use technical language" (p. 88), but support data with graphics and pictorial displays.

---

**EXHIBIT 12.1**

# Common Audiences for Reports on Education and Training Programs

- ❖ Past, current, and future participants
- ❖ Instructors
- ❖ Program planning staff
- ❖ Supervisors of participants
- ❖ Senior and middle management and administrators
- ❖ Members of advisory boards and committees or other ad hoc planning committees or teams

- ❖ Clientele of the organization
- ❖ Regulatory or licensing groups
- ❖ Funding agencies
- ❖ Professional groups and organizations
- ❖ Community leaders
- ❖ Community groups and organizations
- ❖ Public libraries
- ❖ General public

---

**EXHIBIT 12.2**

# Typical Content Outline

**1. Opening section**
   a. "Catchy" title, including pictorial or other symbolic representation of the program
   b. Executive summary highlighting key results and recommendations
   c. Persons who wrote report and will supply additional information as requested

**2. Major body of the report**
   a. Introduction (purpose, and what is addressed in the report (an "advanced organizer"))
   b. Program description(s)
   c. Program participants
   d. Review of the organizational and/or community context in which the program(s) were held
   e. Characterization, if different, of the organization or community context in which the learning was applied
   f. Ways data were collected and analyzed
   g. Key results of the program(s) including realistic recommendations for future actions

**3. Appendices**

---

## Structure and Style

Reports are structured as a series of short reports or one all-inclusive text or folio. Action-oriented reports often consist of short, focused documents or other mediums and usually address only one or two program functions. Thinking back to Barbara's situation from the opening scenario, she opted, for example, to have a series of short reports for program participants and other stakeholders on how their feedback influenced the program while it was in operation and how the context where the learning is applied influenced the final outcomes in each emergency room setting. She gave this information orally throughout the formal instructional program and also sent participants and other stakeholders via listservs several short accountings of how practice had changed in each setting. For the senior management team, as noted earlier, she gave a briefing at one of their bimonthly meetings, primarily focused on the impact the program had on emergency room treatment protocols, and she supplied each manager with a colorful pictorial display of these changes. In addition, she gave this pictorial display to the marketing department and asked them to provide each emergency room with information about the changes and relay the changes in practice and services to the general public. Barbara also included in a prominent place in the annual report the results of this particular program, including recommendations made for future programs and the resources needed to continue with her record of successful programs for medical and support personnel. In all of her program reports, both the brief and longer ones, Barbara emphasized a style that is active; contains anecdotes, short stories, and photos; and incorporates clear numerical data.

### Format

The format—the means by which the information is to be communicated to the appropriate audience(s)—is handled in a number of ways, as outlined in Exhibit 12.3 (Rothwell and Kazanas, 1998; Hendricks, 1994; Hinrichs, 1996; Guskey, 2000).

Although reports on program results may use a single format, a combination of formats may be more effective. For example, although a formal written report with an executive summary is developed, in presenting the report program planners may use PowerPoint presentations and display boards to illustrate important content. Whatever format is chosen, the challenge is to find the best way to present the information so that the audience will be receptive and willing to "listen" to and/or act on the materials presented.

Those who construct program reports find it helpful to map out each of the seven factors prior to developing a report. One method for doing this mapping, with specific examples given for each factor, is illustrated in Exhibit 12.4. Completing this sort of preliminary exercise makes it easier to develop a report that is well organized, clear, and concise.

## Communicating the Report to Key Individuals and Groups

Program reports, as noted earlier, "should be made frequently to individuals and groups intimately involved in the program" (Knowles, 1980, p. 190) and at least annually, where applicable, to senior managers and

**EXHIBIT 12.3**

# Examples and Descriptions of Formats for Reports

| Type of Report | Description |
|---|---|
| *Formal written report* | A formal, detailed, written description of program objectives, results, and recommendations. The depth and scope of the report depends on the purpose and audience for the document. |
| *Executive summary of formal written report* | A one- or two-page summary of a formal written report highlighting the major components of that report. A summary is found at the beginning of the complete report and/or distributed separately. |
| *Series of short written, oral, and/or pictorial reports* | Brief reports that focus on only one or two aspects of a program, which are often used for a single function (for example, decision making, marketing). |
| *Briefings sessions* | Bringing together key actors to discuss specific issues and lay the initial draft plans for future action. Briefings consist of preparing the selected materials, including charts and handouts; setting the stage for the event; delivering the content well; and encouraging interaction. |
| *Draft report* | Sharing of a report in its draft form for comments and action. A draft is used to bring out sensitive issues that staff members do not want in the final report and/or areas that demand more attention. |
| *Journalistic-style report* | A report written in newspaper style describing the program and highlighting a specific aspect of the program (for example, participants, activities, results). |
| *Media presentation* | A formal presentation using some kind of media, such as PowerPoint presentations, videotapes, videodiscs, or transparencies. Often formal reports are enhanced by the use of media. |
| *Case study report* | A report that describes a specific educational event or situation. The case is used to illustrate a major facet of the program. |
| *Product display* | An exhibit of products produced as a result of education and training programs. This exhibit is usually used in combination with a second format, such as a written report or an informational brochure. |
| *Poster or display board* | A sign illustrating the results of education and training programs. This display board is used as part of an oral presentation or placed in a strategic place in the organization where key personnel and participants are able to see it. |
| *Oral report* | A formal or informal oral presentation highlighting specific aspects of education and training program. Although this type of report can be planned, it is often given on a spontaneous basis at staff or committee meetings. |
| *Informational brochure* | A written document describing the program or series of programs and highlighting the results. Brochures are mailed to people, placed in display racks, or handed out in organizational meetings or at future programs. |
| *Electronic communication systems* | Text and/or graphics about a program entered into an email system or on websites. This communication format is especially useful when key audiences are primary users of electronic communication. Also other types of reports (for example, brief reports, case studies, full written reports) can be relayed via electronic communication systems. |

**EXHIBIT 12.4**

## Sample Applications of Factors to Consider When Reporting

| Primary Function | Scope | Audience | Content | Structure and Style | Format |
|---|---|---|---|---|---|
| To educate and gain support from key people and groups | Selected parts of the program (for example, volunteer training and community action and information components) | • Current and future participants<br>• Senior management<br>• Advisory board members<br>• Community leaders<br>• Community groups and organizations<br>• Public at large | • Description of participants and program activities<br>• Results of the program<br>• Suggested recommendations for program changes and new programs | • Short, focused reports | • Journalistic-style report<br>• Media presentation<br>• Oral report |
| To influence and inform decision-makers about current and future programs | Selected parts of the program (for example, new program initiatives) | • Instructors<br>• Program planning staff<br>• Ad hoc advisory teams<br>• Key supervisors<br>• Senior managers | • Short overview of previous programs<br>• Suggestions for new program initiatives | • All-inclusive, action-oriented text | • Briefing sessions<br>• Draft reports<br>• Executive summary<br>• Written report<br>• Media presentation<br>• Email |
| To provide documentation for permanent records | Education and training program as a whole | • Instructors<br>• Program planning staff | • Numbers of participants who attended each event or program<br>• Types of activities<br>• Topic areas addressed<br>• Numbers of hours or days for each event or program<br>• Program results | • Focused documents and products | • Short reports<br>• Graphic representations<br>• Sample products |

| To demonstrate program accountability | Education and training program as a whole | • Senior managers and administrators<br>• Funding agencies<br>• Regulatory bodies | • Brief description of program participants and activities<br>• Detailed description of program results in terms of on-the-job performance<br>• Recommended actions for organizational changes<br>• Cost-effectiveness of the program | • All-inclusive text | • Formal written report with executive summary<br>• Media presentations<br>• Display board |
|---|---|---|---|---|---|
| To market the program | A specific education or training event | • Potential participants<br>• Supervisors<br>• Professional organizations and groups | • Description of participants, topic areas, and program outcomes for similar audiences | • Series of short documents | • Posters displayed in high-visibility areas<br>• Informational brochures |

administrators, other stakeholders, and to the public. As stressed earlier in this chapter, the audience for the report is chosen carefully prior to the report preparation. The information has a much better chance of being "heard" and acted upon if it is in the language and the "mindset" of the primary recipients. For example, in program reports addressing the general public as part of a marketing effort, it is in most cases better to use a colorful poster or informational brochure highlighting the results of the program rather than a formally written report. If the primary language of that general audience is other than the official language of the area (for example, if a large percentage of the target group is Spanish speakers in an English-speaking area), whatever text is used in the poster should reflect both languages. This issue of using more than one language is handled either through a dual printing (in each language) or by incorporating both languages on a single poster. In contrast, a program report prepared for organizational sponsors to demonstrate program accountability, which highlights the cost-effectiveness of a program, includes a more formal traditional text, and elaborate graphs and tables. Again, the key is making the content and style of the report understandable to the primary audience.

The timing of the program report is critical in determining whether the information is actually used. For example, a report sent to work supervisors during their busiest production season is probably put aside or given only a cursory review. On the other hand, a report sent to those same supervisors during budget preparation time demonstrating that production costs were reduced by 5 percent as a result of an educational program in all probability is given a very thorough review. Therefore, based on the situational realities, it is important to plan not only to whom and in what format the report is released, but also when. The examples shown in Exhibit 12.5 offer guidelines for completing this task.

In summary, when communicating the value of education and training programs, program planners make sure the reports are clear and understandable. Careful thought is given to the appropriate audience(s) and timing of the reports.

## Following Up

In many situations it is important to initiate additional conversations with key individuals and groups after a report or series of reports have been released. Additional conversations may clarify any questions or concerns about the program, make sure the information has been heard, and provide opportunities for comments on proposed program changes. This

**EXHIBIT 12.5**

# Examples of the What, Who, and When of Distributing Program Reports

| | |
|---|---|
| **Report Title (Content):** | Technical Training: A Six-Month Review |
| **Who Should Receive Report** | Instructors |
| | Technical supervisors |
| | Training staff |
| | Technical training advisory committee |
| | Senior management |
| **Format of Report** | Journalistic-style report |
| | Briefing sessions |
| **When Report Should Be Released** | Immediately after a successful changeover to new equipment requiring all technical staff to learn a series of new skills |
| **Report Title (Content):** | The Leadership Development Program: Making Diversity Work |
| **Who Should Receive Report** | Program participants |
| | Participants' supervisors |
| | Senior managers and administrators |
| | Program planning staff |
| | Members of advisory committee |
| **Format of Report** | Formal report with an executive summary |
| | Oral media presentation |
| | Poster display |
| **When Report Should Be Released** | Mid-January, to coincide with Martin Luther King, Jr. Day |
| **Report Title (Content):** | The Wellness Program: A Year of Success |
| **Who Should Receive Report** | Program participants |
| | Program staff |
| | Community groups and organizations |
| | General public |
| **Format of Report** | Poster display |
| | Informational brochure |
| | Journalistic-style report |
| **When Report Should Be Released** | January 2 (right after the holiday season) |
| **Report Title (Content):** | The Neighbor-to-Neighbor Program: Actions Speak Louder Than Words |
| **Who Should Receive Report** | Program participants |
| | Community groups and organizations |
| | General public |
| **Format of Report** | Journalistic-style report |
| | Posters |
| | Community presentations |
| | Product display |
| **When Report Should Be Released** | After each successful project and/or when more community volunteers are needed |

communication may be informal, such as during hallway conversations or coffee breaks. These follow-ups also may be more formal like Web-based communication systems, planned conversations, lunches, or planned sessions.

Returning to Barbara's situation, here is her follow-up process. Although Barbara knows she has prepared and given useful reports to her various constituents, she is also aware that in the fast-changing world of health care, she must continue to make a case for continuing professional education programs and the credibility of her own unit. She first hires a consultant to develop and maintain a website that is easy to navigate and well-designed for both novice and expert users. The purpose of the website is fourfold: to give hospital staff members, managers, and other interested parties up-to-date information on current and upcoming programs; to provide a direct information channel to her and her staff on issues related to the consortium's activities and plans; to offer a feedback loop on evaluative data being collected and decisions made based on those data; and to supply general information about the consortium and her office operations.

Second, Barbara makes sure that she and her staff members are visible "in the right places," both at key meetings and activities of the consortium. She has a carefully laid-out plan to ensure this happens because of the complexity of the program and the hospital systems in which she works. Barbara herself is also viewed as a valuable process consultant for meetings involving complex problem-finding and -solving sessions by all of the hospitals in the consortium. This role gives her access to information about critical issues for which professional development is at least a part of the solution. And finally, Barbara stresses to her staff that hallway conversations, coffee breaks, the health club, and other social activities are useful places to listen and learn about hospital problems and to form alliances with key people. One way Barbara fosters these forms of interaction is to have a space in each hospital for her and her staff to work. She also provides health club and cafeteria benefit packages, and allots funds in her budget for luncheon meetings, celebrations, and other informal social gatherings.

In a situation similar to Barbara's, Walter, who is the director of human resources at a software company, believes it is important that all department heads of the organization thoroughly understand the implications and recommendations of his recent report on the quality-of-service program planned and delivered by his unit. Therefore, he and his associate director, Jean, meet personally with each of the department heads to discuss the report and respond to any questions they have. Walter sends department heads, prior to their meeting, a second copy of the executive summary of the report with an addendum outlining what actions have been taken thus far. In addition, Jean buttonholes many of the supervisors over coffee or lunch to gather their opinions on whether the program has made a difference in the day-to-day operations.

## Chapter Highlights

Program planners often overlook communicating program recommendations, results, and the value of education and training programs. Educators have to tell their stories in such a way that the various publics hear their message and receive a clear picture of what education and training programs for adults are all about—learning and change. In completing this component, program planners carry out the following tasks:

◆ Examine program successes and failures and formulate recommendations to revise or eliminate current programs and/or plan new programs.

◆ Tell the story well through program reports that are framed by the following elements: the program function, scope, audience, content, structure and style, and format.

◆ Select the format for the report carefully (for example, journalistic-style reports, briefing sessions, posters, product displays, electronic communication) so the audiences are receptive and willing to "listen" and/or act on the information presented.

◆ Time the release of the report when the audience is most likely to review it.

◆ Follow up as needed with appropriate individuals and groups to clarify any questions or concerns about the program, to make sure the information has been heard, and to provide opportunities for comments on proposed program changes.

The benefits of making program recommendations, developing quality program reports, and communicating these materials to appropriate parties are well worth the extra time and effort.

Often the success or failure of a program is tied to "behind the scenes" concepts of the planning process—those critical components participants are not usually aware of until they receive information about the program or when they actually arrive on the scene (and perhaps not even then). Selecting formats, schedules, and staff; preparing budgets and marketing plans; and coordinating facilities and on-site events comprise these components of the planning process. These important components are discussed in the next three chapters.

## Application Exercises

These Application Exercises are designed to help you examine program failures, formulate program recommendations, prepare reports on education and training programs, and communicate program results to key individuals and groups.

---

### EXERCISE 12.1

### Examining Program Failures

1.  **Briefly describe an education or training program you helped plan that, in your opinion, was a failure.**

2.  **Using the Sork four-part typology (see page 268) for understanding program failures, determine the type of program failure that happened in the program you described above. Then list the probable causes of the failure, and outline what you could do differently next time to develop a better program.**

    Type of failure:

    Probable causes of failure:

    What you could do to develop a better program:

---

## EXERCISE 12.2

# Formulating Program Recommendations

1.  Using information from a program evaluation you currently are completing or have completed, fill in the following chart.

| Recommended Actions | Alternative Strategies for Addressing Recommended Actions | Resources Needed to Respond |
|---|---|---|
| | | |
| | | |
| | | |

2.  Review your plan with a colleague. Is or was your plan realistic? Are or were there any additional actions or strategies that you can add or delete? Were the resources you required readily available?

## EXERCISE 12.3

## Preparing Reports on Education and Training Programs

1.  Describe briefly a situation for which you have prepared or need to prepare a report on a specific education or training event or program.

2.  Using the following chart, outline the primary function(s), scope, audiences, content, structure(s) and style(s), and format(s) for that report. See Exhibit 12.5 for examples.

| |
| --- |
| **Primary Function(s)** |
| **Scope** |
| **Possible Audience(s)** |
| **Content** |
| **Structure and Style** |
| **Format(s)** |

3.  Review your past report or your plan for a current report with a colleague. Reflect on the past report and revise the current report plan as appropriate.

## EXERCISE 12.4

## Communicating Program Results to Key Individuals and Groups

1. **Using the following chart, develop a one-year plan for communicating the results of an education or training program to key individuals and groups, both internal and external to the organization.**

   *Report Title (Content):*

   *Who Should Receive Report:*

   *Format of Report:*

   *When Report Should be Released:*

2. **Review your plan with two or three colleagues and/or your planning team, and then revise as needed.**

# Chapter 13

# Selecting Formats, Schedules, and Staff Needs

As part of her work with the planning team responsible for putting together a three-year training grant for teachers working in literacy programs in both the public and private sectors, Cassie has been asked to provide the group some alternative ideas for how the program could be structured. In the past, the training program has consisted primarily of a week-long summer workshop, access to a statewide resource center, and individual consultation services. This move to restructure the training program and provide some different formats for learning has come from two sources. The first is the funding guidelines, which specifically state that grants that incorporate a technological component as part of the training program will have a higher priority for funding. The second is that the background and needs of many of the teachers have changed. The teachers now comprise a wide mixture of generations, have more experience with adult learners, and express more frustration with fitting the week-long training session in with their other professional and personal obligations. Cassie wonders which of the many training formats might work best for what has become a very diverse group of learners. She is intrigued by how she might use a Web-based program, but she is unsure that present staff members have the expertise to take part in this form of learning without a lot of upfront training. With these two parameters in mind, she decides the best strategy in suggesting how to restructure the training program is to ask the current teachers about their preferences for learning formats and what their expertise is in the more technologically-based formats.

With the alternatives widening for how education and training programs are structured and delivered, dilemmas around the "right" choice or choices for learning formats are not uncommon for program planners. In selecting which formats are appropriate, planners are knowledgeable about the current options and also keep up to date on newly developed formats. Programmers also understand how their choices of formats affect the manner in which programs are scheduled and staffed.

This chapter first describes five major formats for learning, with specific examples given for each. Attention is then given to which formats have the best promise for building learning communities among participants and staff members. Outlined next are samples of program schedules, which demonstrate both single and combined uses of program formats. The chapter concludes with a discussion of staffing issues, including the different roles staff members play, the use of external consultants, and the importance of obtaining effective instructors and facilitators.

## Determining Program Formats

A program format refers to how education and training activities are structured and organized. Five kinds of formats are used in these programs: individual learning, small-group (face to face) learning, large-group (face-to-face) learning, distance learning, and community learning (Knowles, 1980; Houle, 1996; Driscoll, 1998; *Journal of Staff Development*, 1999). These are not discrete categories; indeed, some formats easily fit into more than one category. For example, although a workshop is usually viewed as a small-group activity, it also is used for a large group of people (with the large group divided into smaller workgroups so that the "flavor" of the intensive interaction and product orientation is not lost). In addition, program formats are often used in combination. A video conference, for example, might be integrated into a locally sponsored program at which participants also become involved in face-to-face small- or large-group interactions and/or individualized learning formats.

In the past, education and training programs for adults have been equated primarily with face-to-face learning in groups. With the advent of expanding technological options and the recognition that learning via individual modes is a key way adults learn, program planners are incorporating more of these formats into their programs. The methods and techniques within the individual and small-group face-to-face formats often are similar or the same as instructional and transfer techniques (see Chapters Nine and Ten). Brief descriptions of a variety of options within each of the five categories of learning formats are given in Exhibit 13.1.

**EXHIBIT 13.1**

# Descriptions of Program Formats

## Individual Formats

- *Apprenticeship.* Formal relationship between an employer and an employee by which the employee is trained for a craft or skill through practical experience under the supervision of experienced workers.

- *Coaching.* One-on-one learning by demonstration and practice, with immediate feedback, conducted by peers, supervisors, and/or experts in the field.

- *Computer-Based Technologies.* Computer-based (for example, CD-ROM) and Web-based training, which is highly structured. Individuals work at their own pace and address "structured problems that are designed to teach knowledge, comprehension, and application skills that can be assessed by observation of measurable outcomes" (Driscoll, 1998, p. 53).

- *Interactive Tutorials.* Face-to-face or computer-based instruction in which an individual works with an assigned tutor who is a content expert in the area the learner is exploring.

- *World Wide Web Searches.* Individuals, using a search engine such as Yahoo! (www.yahoo.com) or AltaVista (www.altavista.com), locate information about specific topics of interest to them. Through the Web, learners can access numerous kinds of sources including catalogues of major public and university libraries, information centers (such as the Educational Resources Information Center [ERIC] databases), and other websites (Owston, 1998).

- *Self-Directed Learning.* A form of study in which learners have the primary responsibility for planning, carrying out, and evaluating their own learning experiences. Adults use people, such as friends, family, and content experts, and other types of resources (for example, websites, travel, books) in this process. A personalized learning plan or contract is often used to document this type of format.

- *Mentoring.* An intense, caring relationship in which someone with experience works with a less experienced person to promote both professional and personal growth. Mentors model expected behavior and values and provide support and a sounding board for the mentoree.

- *Clinical Supervision.* A collegial practice designed to support and provide feedback to experienced staff who generally are good at what they do. The process, consisting of five steps (pre-observation conference, observation and data collection, analysis and strategy session, follow-up conference, and post-conference analysis), is used to refine practice.

- *On-the-Job Training (OJT)/Job-Embedded Training).* Instruction provided by experienced individual or groups of workers, either peers or supervisors, to new employees or volunteers while both are on the job and engaged in productive work. "The experienced employer [or volunteer] demonstrates and discusses new areas of knowledge and skill and then provides opportunities for practice and feedback" (Jacobs, 1992, p. 499).

- *Email.* Via the Internet, learners communicate with instructors or other participants. Information is shared, questions are asked, and concerns or issues are raised. In addition, learners may also choose to communicate with experts who are not formally a part of the program.

- *Writing.* Writing of all kinds is included (for example, reflective journals, articles, poetry, books). Although writing provides a powerful individual format for learning, it is also is used as a small-group format (if, for example, writers work together to share and critique their work).

## Small-Group (Primarily Face-to-Face) Formats

- *Courses on Classes.* Groups with a definite enrollment that meet at predetermined times for the purpose of learning a specified content area under the direction of an instructor. These classes

- *Clinics.* Sessions that focus on a single problem or skill as participants present case illustrations of practice problems to an expert or panel of experts. The experts serve in consultant roles.

## Small-Group (Primarily Face-to-Face) Formats

are held at educational institutions, workplaces, or in community settings. They also are a part of a distance-learning program or held at only one site. In addition, learners use, as part of these classes, a variety of technologically based sources (for example, email, Internet chat groups).

- *Seminars.* A focus on learning from discussions of knowledge, experiences, and projects of group members. Participants in these groups have knowledge and skills in the content of the seminar. Instructors act primarily as resource persons and facilitators.

- *Workshops.* Intensive group activities that emphasize the development of individual skills and competencies in a defined content area. The emphasis in this format is on group participation and the transfer and application of new learning (Fleming, 1997).

- *Action Learning.* Process aimed at helping organizations solve real problems, while at the same time developing individuals and groups within the organization. Most often occurring in team situations, groups of learners "pinpoint the cause of problems, solve the problems, formulate goals, work toward achieving goals, establish a shared vision of the future, and work toward realizing [that shared vision]" (Rothwell, 1999, p. 5).

- *Collaborative Research Projects.* Groups of people working together to respond to research questions related to practice. The final product includes both research findings and conclusions, and an action plan related to these materials.

- *Field Visits.* A group visits a work or other situation that is similar to theirs for on-site observation and learning, usually of a short duration (one or two days). Field visits provide the opportunity for further experiences with people, places, and situations that cannot be found in a formal classroom setting.

- *Support Groups.* Groups in which people work together on shared problems or practices. Usually participation is voluntary, and sharing and equal status among group members is the norm. In some cases, a trained facilitator works with this type of learning group.

- *Decision Support Labs.* Groups of learners, using an interactive computer network, make group decisions and learn a variety of decision-making and problem-solving techniques.

- *Cohort Groups.* Groups of learners take a series of courses, workshops, or other learning experiences together over an extended time period. In addition to the content or skills being learned, instructors stress team building and participant support of one another.

- *Networks.* Loosely configured groups of people with similar experiences, interests, problems, or ideas who come together to give and receive information and to provide mutual support and assistance.

## Large-Group (Face-to-Face) Formats

- *Conferences and Conventions.* One or more days of meetings, one of the primary purposes of which is education—to present information, exchange experiences, improve skills, learn new skills, engage in problem-solving activities, and/or establish learning networks. Sessions include large- and small-group meetings, networking, and a variety of formal and informal instructional strategies are used.

- *Clubs and Other Types of Organized Groups.* Groups that frequently engage in activities that foster learning as part of their agenda (for example, hobby clubs, physical fitness groups, computer users groups), although sponsoring education and training programs are not their

- *Theater.* Use of formal and informal acting situations for a variety of learning purposes. For example, theater serves "as a medium for the dissemination of information with the objective of encouraging learners to adopt certain attitudes or practices" (Bates, 1996, p. 226).

- *Educational Tours.* An event in which participants travel for a longer period of time (for example, one week to a month) for the express purpose of learning about educational systems and programs, often in cultural settings different than their own situations. Activities include visits to different types of programs, sessions with educational leaders and teachers, conversations with learners, and touring of cultural sites.

**EXHIBIT 13.1  (Continued )**

### Large-Group (Face-to-Face) Formats

primary purpose. These groups can also be a small-group format, depending on the size of the club or group.

- **Institutes.** Intensive sessions, usually over several days, emphasizing the acquisition of knowledge and skill in a specialized area of practice.

- **Exhibits.** A stationary display of ideas, products, and/or processes. Resource people may be available to respond to questions about the content of the exhibit.

- **Residential Learning.** Participants live and learn together, 24 hours a day, as they complete a common program. The residential experience could be part of a larger program, which also includes other formats, or a stand-alone event. Residential programs are hosted in a variety of venues, such as retreat centers, university conference centers, and outdoor settings (Fleming, 1998).

- **Lecture Series.** A series of presentations by one or more speakers who offer material on a given topic over a specified period of time.

### Distance Learning Formats

- **Correspondence Study.** Prepared printed instructional materials (for example, course syllabi, manuals, texts, worksheets) that are delivered to the home or office. Participants engage in reading and/or other learning activities and send assignments to instructors to evaluate.

- **Audioconferencing.** The linking of one or more sites by telephone to provide for live, interactive verbal exchanges of information between and among program participants and instructors. Conference phones and networks are used to enhance group interaction.

- **Videoconferencing.** Delivery of education and training programs via one-way video or two-way video to one or more locations. With two-way video, distinct sites send and receive both motion video and audio.

- **Interactive Computer-Based Instruction.** Delivered while participants and instructors are online at the same time (synchronous interactions) or done on learners' and instructors' own time (asynchronous interactions). Interactive computer-based "classrooms" enable "learners to control the path, rate, and depth of content" (Driscoll, 1998, p.100), and provide instructors a means for directing attention to critical material. Examples of techniques employed include Hypertext/media, chat rooms, listservs, and forums.

- **Broadcast and Cable Television.** Education and training programs transmitted by private and public broadcasting stations and cable television companies. The television production may stand alone or be part of a larger program effort (for example, college courses that are offered via television).

- **Satellite Communication.** Delivery of video and audio educational programs that are picked up by satellite reception dishes in homes, hotels, businesses, and other sites. This format does not generally provide for interaction among learners and instructors, however (as does videoconferencing).

- **Web-Based Conferences.** Use of the World Wide Web to share information and promote interactive communication among participants in a structured format. These conferences last days or weeks, and are open to anyone interested in the topic, but most often are targeted to specified audiences. As with computer-based classrooms, these conferences are done in real-time (synchronous interactions) or designed as asynchronous interactions (for example, presenters post papers and participants respond through threaded discussions which they can enter at any time during a specified period).

---

### Community-Learning Formats

- **Community Resource Centers.** Centers that offer learning opportunities to individuals and groups within the community. Examples of these types of centers include museums, libraries, community schools, and learning exchanges.
- **Community Development.** Centered on educators who serve as resource people or consultants to action-oriented groups focusing on community change. The community serves as the laboratory for learning.
- **Popular Theater.** Involves participants identifying, interpreting, and acting out their "own social, economic, cultural, and political conditions" (Bates, 1996, p. 225) with the purpose of spawning collective action aimed at changing these conditions in their own communities. This form of theater allows learners to develop and reflect on their own aims and objectives and gives facilitators an opportunity to build on the social and cultural backgrounds of the participants.

- **Community Action Groups.** Groups formed for the primary purpose of social action (for example, church groups, human rights groups, civic organizations). Although their primary purpose may not be learning, many of these groups organize activities that foster learning and development.
- **Virtual Communities.** "A group of people who regularly interact online and share common goals, ideas, or values" (Owston, 1998, p. 60). These communities can provide a rich source for personal, professional, and community growth and development across geographic boundaries.
- **Learning Cities.** A geographic entity, like a town, city, region, or even a village, that harnesses and integrates its "economic, political, educational, social, cultural, and environmental structures toward developing the talents and human potential of all its citizens" (Longworth, 1999, p. 110). The glue that holds these cities together is a focus on learning for the common good of all, and the ability to reach out to other cities and establish linkages among these communities.

---

More detailed information about these formats can be found in Galbraith (1990, 1998); Jackson and Caffarella (1994); Imel (1996); Gibson (1998); Owston (1998); *Journal of Staff Development* (1999); Longworth (1999); Rothwell (1999); and Collison, Elbaum, Haavind, and Tinker (2000). Again, as stressed earlier and noted in some of the format descriptions, this categorization of format examples is only *one* of the illustrative categories that are used. What is key is that program planners think in terms of alternative formats for learning, recognizing that there is no one right (and sometimes no one best) way to structure a specific program.

In choosing a format or formats for learning, seven factors, which are similar to choosing instructional techniques (see Chapter Nine), are considered: the background and experience of the participants, availability and expertise of staff, cost, types of facilities and equipment, program content, program outcomes, and the context in which the learning is to take place. Especially for more comprehensive programs, planners are advised to include more than one format so that a wide range of styles and conditions for learning can be accommodated. "Besides, a variety of formats adds to the aesthetic quality of a program by giving it a sense of liveliness and rhythm, and a richer texture" (Knowles, 1980, p. 130). More recently, educational planners have also been interested in using different formats to build communities of learners.

## Building Learning Communities

### *A Graduate Class Becomes a Learning Community*

Participants in a graduate class in adult learning were both excited by what had happened in their class and also saddened that the class had come to an end. These feeling came from a sense that they had built a learning community, one that evolved over time. As one student commented: "I truly believed it was an open, honest, and safe environment in which to ask questions and offer my ideas."

Both students and the instructor believed that the different formats used for learning—small- and large-group interactions (both in terms of time and intensity), lively listserv "chats," a retreat weekend, and learning in partnerships—helped create this learning community. The norms that the class set for themselves also contributed to the sense of community (for example, actively listening to each other, respecting one another, being truly interested in learning about each other, providing positive and useful feedback, being willing to challenge each other, and addressing any problems or concerns of the class, or among class members and the instructors). There was also a sense that participants had fun learning and that "no one person had to 'carry' the total load of leadership for the community. Obviously, you [meaning the instructor] had ultimate responsibility for the class, but everyone seemed willing to help."

A number of different forces are driving the movement towards building learning communities as part of developing education and training programs for adults. Among these forces, four stand out as especially critical: learning as a collaborative process, the globalization of learning, learning in cyberspace, and the purposeful goal of establishing learning organizations (Watkins and Marsick, 1993; Rhinesmith, 1996; DiBella and Nevis, 1998; Owston, 1998; Saltiel, Sgroi, and Brockett, 1998; Garmston and Wellman, 1999; Palloff and Pratt, 1999). What each of these forces have in common is that as our learning environments expand from individual formats and self-contained classrooms to organizational learning and virtual communities, diversity among learners, political and ethical questions about which learners should be served and why, and complexity of plan-

---

**EXHIBIT 13.2**

## Sample Formats for Building Learning Communities

| Small-Group Formats | Large-Group Formats | Distance-Learning Formats | Community-Learning Formats |
|---|---|---|---|
| Action learning projects | Clubs and other organized groups | Interactive computer-based instruction | Community action groups |
| Collaborative research projects | Residential learning (for example, retreats) | Web-based formal and informal conferencing | Virtual communities |
| Cohort groups | Educational tours | Interactive video-conferencing combined with Web-based learning | Learning cities |

---

ning programs are the norm. Sample formats that lend themselves to building learning communities are listed in Exhibit 13.2.

Just using these sample formats will not create learning communities. Program planners, instructors, facilitators, and learners work together to create a climate that engenders respect, collaborative interaction, trust, caring, and openness to diversity of both people and ideas. Being willing and able to challenge conventional ways of thinking and knowing also is critical to this process. More specific techniques for allowing a learning community to develop and grow are included in Chapters Four and Ten, as well as in the final section of this chapter.

## Scheduling the Program

Once the format is chosen, program planners identify the appropriate length and breakdown of the program and set specific dates and program schedules. Three examples of program schedules are given in Exhibit 13.3. Whatever schedule is chosen, thought is given to such things as travel time and means of travel for the participants. For example, when participants are driving in for a local event, how does rush-hour traffic affect the opening and closing time of the program? Other coordinating functions like ensuring materials and other resources are readily available, registration, locating facilities, and setting up breaks and meals also are carefully planned (see Chapter Fifteen).

In finalizing the dates for the program, planners must take care that the times chosen fit into the participants' personal and/or job schedules. Few,

**EXHIBIT 13.3**

# Sample Program Schedules

**Sample 1   Individual-, Large-, and Small-Group Formats: Three-Day Conference**

*Day 1*

| | |
|---|---|
| 10:00 A.M.–Noon | Registration |
| Noon–1:45 P.M. | Opening luncheon with speaker |
| 2:00–3:30 P.M. | Individual and team time to develop learning plans for the conference and transfer-of-learning strategies with conference staff support |
| 3:30–4:00 P.M. | Break and time to network |
| 4:00–5:30 P.M. | **Session 1**   *Participant choice of small-group sessions* |
| 6:00–7:00 P.M. | Reception |
| 7:00–9:00 P.M. | Dinner with entertainment |

*Day 2*

| | |
|---|---|
| 8:30–10:00 A.M. | General session |
| 10:00–10:30 A.M. | Break and time for networking |
| 10:30–Noon | **Session 2**   *Participant choice of small-group session* |
| 12:45–1:45 P.M. | Conference luncheon |
| 2:00–5:00 P.M. | **Session 3**   *Participant choice of workshops* |
| 5:00–7:00 P.M. | Networking and free time |
| 7:00–9:00 P.M. | Awards Banquet |

*Day 3*

| | |
|---|---|
| 9:00–10:30 A.M. | **Session 4**   *Participant choice of small-group session* |
| 10:30–11:00 A.M. | Break and time for networking |
| 11:00–Noon | Time for group and team planning for learning transfer with conference staff support |
| 12:15–2:00 P.M. | Lunch with closing session and evaluation |

**Sample 2   Field Site Visit, Combined with Large- and Small-Group Interactions**

| | |
|---|---|
| 8:00 A.M. | Departure from home organizations |
| 9:30 A.M. | Arrival at destination for site visit |
| 9:30–10:00 A.M. | Refreshment and stretch break to prepare for day |
| 10:00–11:00 A.M. | Introductory session with whole group to organization and programs |
| 11:00 A.M.–12:30 P.M. | Tour of facilities with whole group |
| 12:30–1:45 P.M. | Lunch in organization's cafeteria and break time |
| 1:45–3:45 P.M. | Choice of one of three seminar groups related to different operating divisions of the organization |
| 3:45–4:15 P.M. | Refreshment break and time for networking |
| 4:15–5:15 P.M. | Choice of small-group sessions to form mail and/or face-to-face interest groups as a transfer-of-learning strategy |
| 5:15–6:00 P.M. | Wrap-up session and evaluation with whole group |
| 6:00 P.M. | Departure (trip includes dinner at restaurant in the area) |
| 10:00 P.M. | Arrival at home organizations |

**Sample 3    Distance-Learning Formats Combined with Small-Group On-Site Discussion and Support Groups: Four-Week Training Program with Transfer-of-Learning Support**

***Week One***

| | | |
|---|---|---|
| Monday | 9:00–Noon | Small on-site groups meet with facilitator and technical support staff to introduce training program and ensure participants know how to use the Web-based system. |
| Tuesday–Friday | | Individuals, using an interactive computer-based system, are required to review materials online and participate in at least two chat room discussions. They log on and do this work at their convenience. |

***Week Two***

| | | |
|---|---|---|
| Tuesday | 9:00–Noon | Small on-site groups meet with facilitator to review and discuss what they have learned thus far and to plan for learning transfer both during and after the training program. |
| Wednesday–Friday | | Same format as previous week, except that participants are required to also take part in two real-time (synchronous) interactions (Wednesday, 1:00–3:00, and Friday, 9:00–11:00). |

***Week Three***

| | | |
|---|---|---|
| Tuesday | 9:00–11:00 | On-site small groups meet for purpose of peer support. |
| Tuesday–Thursday | | Same online format as Week One. |
| Friday | 9:00–Noon | On-site small groups meet with facilitator to review and discuss applications of what they have learned from the training experience. |

***Week Four***

| | | |
|---|---|---|
| Monday–Thursday | | Same online format as Week Two. |
| Friday | 9:00–2:00 | On-site small groups meet with facilitator to review and discuss applications of what they have learned, ensure transfer plans are in place, complete program evaluation, and host a group celebration. |

***Transfer-of-Learning Component After the Training: Six-Month Period***

✓ On-site small groups meet biweekly either by themselves or with a facilitator.

✓ Online support chat groups continue.

✓ Two formal full-day sessions are held on-site, which include online real-time interaction with whole-group and small-group interactions.

✓ Other transfer techniques used by individual program participants (for example, supervisor support for transfer, job rotation, coaching).

if any, education and training programs should be scheduled around times when the target audiences have other commitments, such as a seasonally heavy workload, family responsibilities, and religious celebrations. For example, to hold education and training programs for managers or their administrative assistants during budget preparation time is not advisable. Likewise, programs should not be planned on or near major holidays or vacation times, unless a vacation package option is a part of the marketing strategy (including, for example, sightseeing tours and special hotel rates).

Contingency plans are thought through if the scheduled program has to be scaled back or cancelled. For example, if the registration for a particular program is lower than expected, the program format and design may have to be changed to accommodate the lower numbers. In addition, payment for instructors and other program resources may have to be renegotiated. In the case of internal staff, some of those working with the program may need to be reassigned to other activities. If a program is cancelled, it is critical that those who have registered are notified as soon as possible and that a process for making refunds for registration fees is in place. Depending on the geographic scope of the conference, a "go or no go" decision has to be made far enough in advance so that participants do not incur travel costs that cannot be either refunded or used for other travel (for example, airline reservations). Staff members and facilities costs, among other concerns, also have to be taken care of, either through negating those costs if possible, and if not, negotiating with the various people and organizations involved what must be paid, depending on the contracts that have been signed. For example, outside program consultants normally expect payment for design work completed thus far, but may be willing to forgo compensation for work not yet completed, such as actually giving presentations or conducting evaluation studies.

## Identifying Program Staff

Staff members design, coordinate, conduct, and evaluate education and training programs. One person may take on all of these tasks or the tasks may be divided among a number of people, depending on the size and complexity of the program being planned. However the tasks are divided, program planners assume these four major roles (Rothwell and Kazanas, 1998; Killion and Harrison, 1997; Rothwell and Cookson, 1997; Milano with Ullius, 1998; Collison, Elbaum, Haavind, and Tinker, 2000):

- *The program designer and manager* role includes designing and managing the program. This role entails such tasks as gathering ideas for programs, setting program priorities, developing program objectives, planning transfer-of-learning activities, and preparing budgets and marketing plans.

- *The event coordinator* role involves coordinating specific program events and ensuring that all logistical tasks related to planning, conducting, and evaluating a particular program are completed in a timely manner (see Chapter Fifteen). Such tasks include arranging facilities, registering participants, and monitoring on-site programs. In carrying out this role, individuals act as information givers, brokers, counselors, resource specialists, and/or administrators.

- *The instructor/learning facilitator* role entails designing and/or delivering the instruction and directly assisting participants to achieve their learning objectives using a variety of learning techniques and devices. The development of more complex instructional packages (for example, computer-based instruction) requires staff with specialized expertise, from instructional designers to computer support specialists.

- *The program evaluator* role consists of making judgments about the value and results of the program (after specifying who judges what, how, and on what criteria).

Some of the program designer's specific tasks (such as compiling lists of ideas for programs, determining program objectives, and planning transfer-of-learning activities) are discussed in Chapters Six, Seven, Eight, and Ten, as well as earlier in this chapter. A more detailed description of the evaluator role is given in Chapter Twelve, while the roles of instructor and coordinator are discussed in Chapters Nine and Fifteen, respectively. The various tasks of the four roles are not necessarily independent of each other. For example, although the program coordinator usually arranges the facilities and equipment, the program designer may choose to do this task because of specific design requirements that a coordinator may not understand. For smaller programs, the roles of program designer, coordinator, instructor, and evaluator may all be handled by one person or shared by a team of people.

## Deciding to Use External Staff

Program staff, whether they are paid or volunteer, may be internal to the organization or hired from the outside. Sometimes a mix of organizational personnel and external consultants are used. For example, while internal staff members coordinate and evaluate an education or training program, outside consultants are responsible for the design and delivery of that program. Parry (1996) and Mitchell (1998) cite five major reasons for hiring outside consultants: expertise, short-term expansion of staff, political leverage, cost-effectiveness, and opportunities for internal staff to learn new skills and competencies. In selecting external consultants, guidelines and questions to judge their quality and performance are recommended in Exhibit 13.4 (Munson, 1992; Parry, 1996; Mitchell, 1998).

---

**EXHIBIT 13.4**

## Guidelines and Questions for Selecting External Consultants

❖ *Caliber and Beliefs of the People.* Are the individuals both competent and capable? Are they credible to your organization and the participants? What are their approaches to and beliefs about education and training?

❖ *Quality of Their Resources.* Are the resources the outside consultants use or develop (for example, training manuals, videos, simulations) of good educational quality? Are these resources useful to the participants?

❖ *Problem-Solving Capabilities.* Do the outside consultants have a solid understanding of the problem(s) being tackled? Does what they are proposing lead to positive changes?

❖ *Adaptability.* Are the outside consultants willing to tailor their work (for example, presentations, resources) to meet the requirements of the buying organization?

❖ *Scope and Depth of Available Resources.* Do the outside consultants add to the scope and depth of the present educational resources of the organization?

❖ *Context Knowledge.* Do the outside consultants know something about the organization and the business of that organization (for example, banking, communications, agriculture)?

❖ *Cost.* Do the outside consultants cost more than internal staff for the same activity? If so, is this additional cost justifiable?

---

There are two primary sources for locating outside staff: other organizations and private consulting firms. It is critical that program planners check out consultants carefully prior to signing a formal contract. This process should involve face-to-face discussions, a review of materials, and, when possible, sitting in on a session the person or consulting group is conducting. In addition, information about prospective consultants can be gathered by talking with knowledgeable colleagues and the consultants' current clients. In considering using university faculty as consultants, planners also find it helpful to ask the opinion of current or former students and faculty colleagues of these faculty.

Outside staff members are usually paid in one of three different ways: time plus expenses, a fixed fee, or by a percentage of the income generated by a specific program. No matter how they are paid, however, it is important that the hiring organization negotiate a written contract for services. The following checklist, based on the work of Munson (1992), Tracey (1992), and Parry (1996), indicates what the negotiation process and the contract or letter of agreement include:

- A brief description of the program, project, or service
- What the consultant's responsibilities are (for example, developing instructional modules, serving as the instructor, developing and conducting the program evaluation)

- Time requirements and schedule for which the consultant provides services (for example, two days of off-site preparation and two days of program delivery time)

- Costs for the consultant's professional fees and per diem expenses

- Costs for program resources and aids (for example, technological sources, participant manuals, shipping charges, books, handouts, participant evaluations, and certificates)

- Expectations for on-site support services (such as administrative assistance, copying, office space)

- Project or service start and completion dates

- Contract extension or termination conditions

- Internal staff contact (for example, project manager, principal, director of training, manager of human resource division, executive director, division director)

- How fees for services and expenses are billed and what forms are completed

- Rights to use any copyrighted material to be distributed and/or use such material after the contract is completed

- Protection of the employing organization's intellectual property and overall confidentiality (for example, a statement promising nondisclosure of proprietary information)

Although negotiating a written contract or letter of agreement does not guarantee a good working relationship between outside consultants and internal staff members, this contract helps set the stage for making the process work and ensuring the desired results.

## Obtaining Effective Instructors and Facilitators

Instructors and facilitators play a key role in making education and training events a success, because they are responsible for assisting participants to achieve what they want to learn (see Chapter Nine). Therefore, it is very important to obtain effective personnel for this role. But how does one determine who will be good? Nine selection criteria, proven to be helpful, are outlined in Exhibit 13.5 (Apps, 1996; Palmer, 1998; Phillips, 1997; Pratt and Associates, 1998; English and Gillen, 2000). With the increase of online learning, it is critical that instructors possess the skills to effectively facilitate this form of instruction. Helpful resources in ascertaining these skills include Gibson (1998); Collison, Elbaum, Haavind, and Tinker (2000); and Salmon (2000).

Instructors come from a variety of sources, again both internal and external to the sponsoring organization. Although adult educators, trainers,

---

**EXHIBIT 13.5**

## Nine Criteria to Consider When Obtaining Instructors

1.  ***Content Knowledge.*** Instructors are knowledgeable about their content areas and, where applicable, are successful practitioners of their knowledge and/or skills.

2.  ***Competence in the Processes of Instruction.*** Instructors are competent in a number of instructional techniques and processes, match those techniques to their subject matter and the learners, and are able to use a variety of methods. They also know how to provide helpful feedback and evaluate what the participants have learned.

3.  ***Ability to Respond Effectively to the Background and Experience of the Participants.*** Instructors work well with specific groups of participants (for example, culturally diverse groups, low-income participants, people of color, women and men, differing educational levels) and demonstrate capability to tap into their participants' varied and diverse experiences and backgrounds.

4.  ***Belief That Caring for Learners Matters.*** Instructors care about learners and provide an environment where respect, trust, and cultural richness are key norms. Giving "space" to participants to negotiate when and how they will learn when "adult life" gets in the way of their learning is important in demonstrating a caring attitude.

5.  ***Credibility.*** Instructors demonstrate credibility based on their position, background, experiences, and/or personal impact. High credibility predisposes participants to accept more readily the material presented.

6.  ***Enthusiasm and Commitment.*** Instructors are enthusiastic, even passionate about their subject and committed to teaching it to others.

7.  ***Personal Effectiveness.*** Instructors are organized and prepared. They use humor effectively and have a genuine interest in whether or not the participants learn. They also adjust their presentation to the needs of the audience and model the behaviors and/or attitudes they are teaching.

8.  ***Enterprise Knowledge.*** Instructors have basic information about the organizations or groups from which the participants come (for example, products, services, culture).

9.  ***Ability to Teach from the Heart and Spirit, as well as the Mind.*** Instructors know and share who they are—that is, they are authentic in what they do and say. They also acknowledge the "personhood" of each learner and that participants search for personal and communal meanings for their lives through learning experiences.

---

and staff developers are the main sources, there are many people without this specialized background who, through experience and/or training, are competent instructors. For example, technical employees often provide instruction for other technical staff, and volunteers serve as peer coaches and instructors for other volunteers.

Geigold and Grindle (1983) have cautioned program planners to be on the lookout for "Dr. Fox" in choosing instructors. Dr. Fox is an instructor "who has a wealth of personal charm, podium presence, and funny stories, but who conveys little else to the group" (p. 63). Although Dr. Foxes may demonstrate competence in the processes of instruction and personal effectiveness, they fall short in content knowledge, credibility, and commitment to teaching their content expertise to others. Although audiences react positively to these Dr. Fox instructors, they learn little, if anything.

## Chapter Highlights

Making decisions about how programs are organized, scheduled, and staffed is an important part of the program planning process. This component of the planning process is complex as format choices and staff members' expertise in designing and implementing these formats have expanded (primarily through the wider use of technology-based formats). More specifically, the following tasks are completed during this phase of the planning process:

♦ Choose the most appropriate format or combination of formats for the learning activity (for example, individual, small-group [primarily face-to-face], large-group [face-to-face], distance learning, or community-learning formats).

♦ Take into account the desire to build a community of learners as part of the goals and objectives of the program.

♦ Devise a program schedule that fits the formats chosen, the specific activities planned, and the participants' personal and/or job commitments.

♦ Identify staff needs (that is, program designers and managers, program coordinators, instructors and facilitators, and program evaluators).

♦ Determine whether internal staff (paid or volunteer) will plan and conduct the program and/or whether external consultants are required.

♦ Make careful choices about instructors and/or learning facilitators for the various activities to ensure that content expertise, competence in teaching adults, and the ability to respond effectively to the background and experiences of the learners are evident.

Formats, schedules, and staff needs are often connected to the financial resources that are available. How to link these financial resources to the planning process is discussed in the next chapter, along with how to prepare marketing plans for education and training programs.

## Application Exercises

This chapter's Application Exercises are intended to assist you in determining program format and staffing and help you put together a schedule for a specific program activity.

## EXERCISE 13.1

## Determining the Program Format and Staff

1.  Identify an education or training program that you are in the process of developing or will be planning, and give a short description of that program.

2.  Identify at least two alternative formats (or combinations of formats) that are appropriate for this program, and outline the reasons why you chose them.

    Alternative One

    Alternative Two

    Which of these formats would you use, and why?

    If one of the objectives of this program is to build a learning community, does the format(s) you have chosen enable the participants and instructors to accomplish this goal? If yes, how does that format(s) address building learning communities? If no, what format(s) might be more applicable?

3.  Using the following chart, identify the specific staff members that are or will plan and carry out the program.

| Staff Role | Specific Person or Persons Who Carry Out Each Role | Internal or External to the Organization | Paid or Volunteer Staff Members |
|---|---|---|---|
| **Program Designer and Manager** | | | |
| **Event Coordinator** | | | |
| **Instructor and Facilitator** | | | |
| **Program Evaluator** | | | |

## EXERCISE 13.2

## Scheduling the Program

Using the same example you gave in Exercise 13.1, lay out a program schedule that takes into account the participants' personal and/or job situations, and when, where, and how the program is being or will be held. Use Exhibit 13.3 (page 294) to guide you.

# Chapter 14

# Preparing Budgets and Marketing Plans

SCENARIO

Terri, the director of continuing education at a small private college, has proposed her division increase its revenues by 10 percent for each calendar year for the next three years. She would use this additional money for two primary purposes: to provide faculty incentive funds for developing new programs for adults and to develop additional distance-learning programs.

Prior to making this proposal, Terri first discussed with her staff members whether this operational program objective is doable and, if so, what strategies could be used to accomplish it. Her staff is very positive—they view the idea as a proactive way to respond to the needs of adult students and the faculty simultaneously. They were able to come up with at least three strategies for making this objective a reality. These strategies include marketing their student portfolio development guide nationally to other small colleges, increasing the offerings for five current high-demand, high-revenue-generating programs, and charging fees for certain services that were formerly offered without charge.

Terri also conferred with a number of faculty leaders over lunch to see whether they believe their colleagues would be responsive to such an incentive plan for program development. In addition, she had two preliminary planning sessions with chairs and faculty who expressed interest in offering part or all of their programs via distance learning. Again, Terri received positive feedback on her proposal. The faculty members were especially responsive to the idea of their being able to apply for incentive funds for planning. This procedure breaks with the current campus norms, whereby faculty are paid only for what they actually deliver, not for the time and effort of developing an innovative program.

As illustrated by the scenario, planning programs requires a whole range of activities that go beyond thinking through the educational components of the plan. People who are responsible for program planning need to recognize that budget management and other behind-the-scenes tasks are integral components of the planning process and serve as the driving forces behind program development efforts. Two of these key tasks are discussed in this chapter: preparing program budgets and developing marketing plans.

Discussed first are critical details of the budgeting process. Worksheets for program planners to use in estimating the cost and income for specific programs are provided as part of this discussion. Managing program budgets and developing cost contingency plans are described next. Marketing education and training programs is then explored starting with an overview of four key tenets essential to the marketing process, the importance of knowing the potential audiences and the contexts within which these audiences function, and how to do both a target and contextual analysis. Addressed next are four critical aspects of marketing: product, price, place, and promotion. Specific materials and strategies used in promoting education and training programs are highlighted as part of this discussion. The chapter concludes with a description of what is included in a marketing campaign and how an organization's or group's promotional assets are assessed.

## Preparing Program Budgets

Preparing a program budget is essentially translating intended program activities into monetary terms. Some education and training units are funded as budget centers and therefore have organizational funds in addition to whatever income they generate. Other units operate on a cost basis and have to break even, while the remainder are required to be profit centers and make money (Tracey, 1992; Birkenholz, 1999).

### Understanding the Terminology

In working with budgets, some key words and phrases are used (Matkin, 1985; Ericksen, 1994; Watkins and Sechrest, 1998). A brief review of these terms provides a foundation for the subsequent discussion.

• *Income and expense budget:* The income or revenue side of a budget includes whatever monies are generated to support education and training activities, while the expense or cost side consists of the actual cost of developing, delivering, and evaluating those activities.

• *Direct and indirect costs:* Direct program costs are funds actually spent (also referred to as "out-of-pocket" expenses) that support specific program activities, such as instructors' salaries, travel costs, and money for instructional materials. Indirect program costs are those expenses that usually are not attributable to individual programs and do not cost actual dollars, but are necessary to maintain the program as a whole. Indirect costs include overhead such as space, utilities, management and administrative support, payroll and accounting services, and fringe benefits like health and life insurance. What are considered indirect costs may become direct costs (and vice versa), depending on the program and the organization. For example, if a training program is held at the host organization's facilities, the space and equipment items are usually considered indirect costs; if the program is housed at a motel or conference center, these same expenses are considered direct costs.

• *Fixed and variable expenses:* Fixed expenses are those items that usually remain stable no matter the number of participants or even whether the program is held or cancelled (for example, publicity and initial development costs). In contrast, variable expenses are costs that typically change depending on specific program requirements and how many participants sign up for a program (for example, meals, and breaks, travel, and materials). Again, as with direct and indirect costs, what is a fixed expense for one program may be a variable expense for another. For example, instructor fees, which are most often thought of as fixed expenses, are sometimes negotiated based on the number of participants who actually complete a program: the more participants who complete the program, the more the instructors are paid. In other situations, instructor costs may be lowered through a negotiated process, if fewer people register than anticipated so that expenses are met. In these cases, instructor fees are part of the variable costs.

• *Profit:* Profit refers to making money, whether it is the education and training unit that makes money or the organization as a whole. As stated earlier, some organizations expect the educational function to turn a profit. Other organizations simply expect the outcomes of education and training programs to have a positive effect on the overall profitability of that organization.

• *Return on investments:* The term return on investment (ROI) describes the benefits (or savings) program activities provide in relationship to the total program costs. A ratio is calculated of the costs to the benefits, which is expressed as a percentage of return. "Basically, positive ROIs are good, and the more positive the better. A negative ROI means that, as far as can be calculated, the company is not getting enough of a benefit to justify the expenditure required for a program" (Piskurich, 2000, p. 40).

• *Cost-benefit analysis:* The costs of education and training programs are related to the benefits they produce. These benefits are spelled out in monetary terms to determine the economic viability and efficiency of a program or set of activities. The cost side of the equation is often easier to spell out, while the benefits side is more difficult. The need to demonstrate a positive economic benefit has become more pressing in recent years. As organizations infuse an increasing amount of money into education and training programs, they question whether this investment is worth it, especially if financial resources are scarce or the bottom line is shrinking. Yet despite this demand for more explicit financial accounting, few cost-benefit studies on education and training programs are actually done (Swanson, 1998). Major reasons given by organizations for not doing cost-benefit analyses are time, cost, difficulty in producing the necessary quantifiable data, and lack of know-how by educators and trainers. Two ways program staff can address these concerns are to become knowledgeable about how to do cost-benefit studies and to ask for assistance from others in the organization that are experts in financial analysis. Examples of helpful resources on how to do cost-benefit analysis for education and training programs include Blomberg (1989); Tracey (1992); Swanson and Gradous (1988); Kruse and Keil (2000); and Piskurich (2000).

## Estimating the Cost of Educational Programs

There are three basic kinds of costs or expenses associated with each program offered: development costs, delivery costs, and evaluation costs (Laird, 1985; Tracey, 1992; Watkins and Sechrest, 1998). Expense items in these categories usually include staff costs, instructional materials, facilities, food, travel, equipment, special services, promotional materials, and general costs (for example, overhead and benefits). In developing budgets for specific programs, program planners must know ahead of time whether they need to account for both direct and indirect costs (rather than just direct costs) and which items are considered fixed versus variable expenses. A sample worksheet for estimating program expenses is outlined in Exhibit 14.1.

In preparing budgets for some programs, all of the budget items are estimated, while for others only selected items are. For example, when programs are in-house, costing out the facilities, travel, and equipment may be unnecessary. In another example, when delivering already-developed programs, costs for developing instructional and promotional materials are not calculated. Another consideration in the budget preparation process is whether to be high or more on target in determining the costs. Birkenholz (1999)

**EXHIBIT 14.1**

# Worksheet for Estimating Program Expenses

| Budget Items | Development Costs | Delivery Costs | Evaluation Costs | Subtotal |
|---|---|---|---|---|
| **Internal Staff** | | | | |
| Program planners | _____ | _____ | _____ | _____ |
| Instructors/facilitators | _____ | _____ | _____ | _____ |
| Technology specialists | _____ | _____ | _____ | _____ |
| Clerical and other support staff | _____ | _____ | _____ | _____ |
| **External Staff** | | | | |
| Program consultants | _____ | _____ | _____ | _____ |
| Instructors/facilitators | _____ | _____ | _____ | _____ |
| Technology specialists | _____ | _____ | _____ | _____ |
| Support staff | _____ | _____ | _____ | _____ |
| **Instructional Materials** | | | | |
| PowerPoint presentations | _____ | _____ | _____ | _____ |
| Books and articles | _____ | _____ | _____ | _____ |
| Manuals | _____ | _____ | _____ | _____ |
| Videotapes | _____ | _____ | _____ | _____ |
| Videodiscs | _____ | _____ | _____ | _____ |
| Audiotapes/CDs | _____ | _____ | _____ | _____ |
| Overhead transparencies | _____ | _____ | _____ | _____ |
| Slides | _____ | _____ | _____ | _____ |
| Computer charges | _____ | _____ | _____ | _____ |
| Satellite uplink/downlink | _____ | _____ | _____ | _____ |
| Videoconferencing | _____ | _____ | _____ | _____ |
| Telephone charges | _____ | _____ | _____ | _____ |
| Other (specify) | _____ | _____ | _____ | _____ |
| **Facilities** | | | | |
| Large meeting rooms | _____ | _____ | _____ | _____ |
| Break-out rooms | _____ | _____ | _____ | _____ |
| Staff work rooms | _____ | _____ | _____ | _____ |
| Social/entertainment areas | _____ | _____ | _____ | _____ |
| Sleeping accommodations | | | | |
|   Staff | _____ | _____ | _____ | _____ |
|   Participants | _____ | _____ | _____ | _____ |
| Computer access | | | | |
|   Staff | _____ | _____ | _____ | _____ |
|   Participants | _____ | _____ | _____ | _____ |
| Telephone/fax | _____ | _____ | _____ | _____ |
| Parking | _____ | _____ | _____ | _____ |
| Signage | _____ | _____ | _____ | _____ |
| **Food** | | | | |
| Catered meals | | | | |
|   Staff | _____ | _____ | _____ | _____ |
|   Participants | _____ | _____ | _____ | _____ |

| Budget Items | Development Costs | Delivery Costs | Evaluation Costs | Subtotal |
|---|---|---|---|---|
| **Food (*Continued*)** | | | | |
| Special needs | | | | |
|   Staff | _____ | _____ | _____ | _____ |
|   Participants | _____ | _____ | _____ | _____ |
| Refreshment breaks | _____ | _____ | _____ | _____ |
| Special functions (such as social hours, receptions, hospitality suites) | _____ | _____ | _____ | _____ |
| **Travel** | | | | |
| Planning/follow-up meetings | _____ | _____ | _____ | _____ |
| To and from program | | | | |
|   Staff | | | | |
|     In-house | _____ | _____ | _____ | _____ |
|     External consultants | _____ | _____ | _____ | _____ |
| Participants | _____ | _____ | _____ | _____ |
| Educationally related outings | _____ | _____ | _____ | _____ |
| Entertainment outings | _____ | _____ | _____ | _____ |
| **Equipment** (rent or purchase) | | | | |
| Media playback | _____ | _____ | _____ | _____ |
| Media record | _____ | _____ | _____ | _____ |
| Computers | _____ | _____ | _____ | _____ |
| Video projectors | _____ | _____ | _____ | _____ |
| Overhead projectors | _____ | _____ | _____ | _____ |
| LCD projectors | _____ | _____ | _____ | _____ |
| Screens | _____ | _____ | _____ | _____ |
| Other (specify) | _____ | _____ | _____ | _____ |
| **Special Services for Participants** (For example, sign language experts, note takers, interpreters) | _____ | _____ | _____ | _____ |
| **Marketing Plans** | | | | |
| Target and contextual analysis | _____ | _____ | _____ | _____ |
| Promotional materials | _____ | _____ | _____ | _____ |
|   Design | _____ | _____ | _____ | _____ |
|   Purchase | _____ | _____ | _____ | _____ |
|   Printing | _____ | _____ | _____ | _____ |
|   Distribution/mailing | _____ | _____ | _____ | _____ |
|   Return processing | _____ | _____ | _____ | _____ |
| **General Costs** | | | | |
| Overhead | _____ | _____ | _____ | _____ |
| Benefits | _____ | _____ | _____ | _____ |
| **Other Costs** | _____ | _____ | _____ | _____ |
| ***Subtotal for each type of cost*** | $_____ | $_____ | $_____ | $_____ |

**Grand Total Costs =** $_____

suggests, "It is best to estimate expenses on the high side" (p. 129), especially when the sources of funding are fixed and/or depend primarily on participant fees.

Tracey (1992) offers further guidance for estimating program development expenses. For example, he provides worksheets for computing costs for specific types of educational materials. As an example, the costs for audiovisual materials include some combination of the following: purchase costs, rental costs, development costs (including materials, labor, and processing), and distribution costs. In addition, Tracey outlines ways to figure other development costs, explaining how to calculate different types of indirect costs and unit costs (such as costs per square foot, costs per hour, and equipment costs per hour). Piskurich (2000) also offers a helpful list of costs for both development and delivery of primarily media-based programs (for example, cost of materials, Web programmers, and Web-based instruction).

Some organizations, especially for-profit companies, require that participant costs also be computed, either as a separate expense budget or as part of the total program budget. Although some of those items, such as costs for participant travel and accommodations, are included in Exhibit 14.1, others are not.

Laird (1985) and Watkins and Sechrest (1998) offer these useful ideas for computing participant costs:

- ▶ *Salary.* Number of participants (by pay group) × median salary × hours/days of educational programming
- ▶ *Benefits.* Number of participants × hourly fringe benefit charges × hours/days
- ▶ *Travel.* Total from expense reports (or median costs × number of participants)
- ▶ *Per diem.* Total from expense reports (or median allowance × number of participants × number of days)
- ▶ *Materials.* Material costs × number of participants
- ▶ *Participant replacement costs.* Number of hours × median salary
- ▶ *Lost productivity of participants.* Value per unit × number of lost units (or value per unit × the reduced production)

In calculating participant costs, planners may use only some of the line items or all of them, depending on the financial policies and procedures of organizational sponsors.

## Determining How the Program Is Financed

The income or revenue sources for education and training programs vary depending on the type of institution (that is, for-profit versus non-profit); the purpose, content, and format of the program; and whether or not fees are charged for the program. The primary income sources for educational programs are parent organizational subsidy, sponsorship funds, participant fees and tuition, auxiliary enterprises and sales, grants and contracts, government funds, profits from the education or training unit itself, and miscellaneous income (Knowles, 1980; Watkins and Sechrest, 1998; Birkenholz, 1999; Bates, 2000). Brief descriptions of these income sources are listed in Exhibit 14.2, with examples of each.

As funding for programs are often pieced together, it is important that program planners have a good understanding of their funding sources and the policies and regulations that govern each revenue stream. For example, a series of programs on retirement for low-income people might be funded through a number of sources including a local community center, government funds, and/or in-kind contributions (such as volunteer instructors, donated refreshments, and printing of materials).

Just as it is necessary to estimate the expense side of the budget, it is also necessary to account for the income side. A worksheet for estimating program income is displayed in Exhibit 14.3. In estimating the income side, it is best to estimate "revenues on the conservative side" (Birkenholz, 1999, p. 129). Estimating on the conservative side is especially wise if the program is expected to break even or make a profit.

## Keeping Accurate Budget Records

It is important to keep accurate financial records that are clear, simple, and practical. The type of formal record keeping that is readily available depends on the accounting system of the organization in which the program is housed. Large organizations have computerized systems, while some smaller organizations and groups still require manual entries. The specific system within an organization may not allow for program-by-program record keeping; yet if records of income and expenses for individual programs are necessary, program planning staff members develop their own set of record-keeping procedures.

## Managing Program Budgets

Managing program budgets is as important as preparing them and demands both financial analysis skills and the ability to read program situations well. As Mitchell (1998) observes, careful construction and

**EXHIBIT 14.2**

## Sample Income Sources

| Income Source | Description | Example |
|---|---|---|
| **Organizational subsidy** | The educational function receives operating funds from the parent or partnership organizations as part of the internal budgeting mechanism. | The Division of Correctional Educators (DCE) receives an expense budget of $200,000 annually for salaries, materials and equipment, travel, general office supplies, and printing. In addition, a collaborative partnership of which the DCE is a part of also provides $100,000 in additional revenues for new technology-based programs. |
| **Sponsorship funds** | Other organizations (for example, business, philanthropic, professional, and trade groups) and individuals give financial support to a specific program or series of programs. | Two local businesses, one philanthropic organization, and three individual donors have agreed to underwrite some of the costs for a series of outdoor adventure programs for a group of adults who are disabled. These organizations and individuals will sponsor the program in conjunction with a community-based program and the local university that provides services for adults with disabilities. |
| **Participant fees and tuition** | Participants are charged a fee or tuition for attending a program. | Eighty percent of all adult literacy and GED programs sponsored by the local school district must break even. Thus the participants' fees must cover all expenses of those programs. |
| **Auxiliary enterprises and sales** | Revenue is earned from the sale of materials, publications, technology-based programs, and services provided by the educational unit to other organizations and individuals. | A nationally prominent accounting firm has developed an excellent computer-based training program and is now selling it to other organizations for profit. |
| **Grants and contracts from foundations and other organizations** | Foundations, businesses, trade and professional organizations, labor unions, special interest groups, and other organizations award funds to an educational unit to develop a specific program. Usually these awards go to nonprofit organizations. | Funding is given to a community action agency that serves low-income people of color to increase their participation in local, state, and national elections. |

| Income Source | Description | Example |
|---|---|---|
| **Government funding (federal, state, and local)** | Government funds are awarded or given to an education or training unit to develop a specific program. These funds may be given to for-profit or nonprofit agencies (depending on the regulations governing the funds). | A local community college, in partnership with a workplace learning program, is awarded a grant to initiate a job-training program for unemployed workers. |
| **Profit from the educational unit** | The educational unit produces an overall profit from the operation, which in turn can be used for future programs. | A national continuing education program for judicial personnel on average nets a 10-percent profit from the Conferences and Institutes Division. These funds are used to sponsor new program ventures. |
| **Miscellaneous income** | This category covers all other sources of funding that are not listed above. A sampling of these sources includes endowments, royalty income, fundraising events, and in-kind contributions. | The miscellaneous income for the mentoring program for new faculty is used to host luncheons for the mentors and their protégés. |

---

**EXHIBIT 14.3**

## Worksheet for Estimating Income Sources

| Income Source | Amount of Income/Subsidy |
|---|---|
| **Parent organizational subsidy** | $_____ |
| **Sponsorship funds** | $_____ |
| **Participant fees** | |
| (fee × # of estimated participants) | $_____ |
| **Auxiliary enterprises and sales** | |
| (item or service to be sold × # of | |
| estimated customers) | $_____ |
| **Grants and contracts** | |
| (List each source of funding with amount) | |
| 1. | $_____ |
| 2. | $_____ |
| 3. | $_____ |
| **Government funds** | |
| (List each source of funding with amount) | |
| 1. | $_____ |
| 2. | $_____ |
| 3. | $_____ |
| Profit from any educational units | $_____ |
| **Miscellaneous income** | $_____ |
| **Total Income** | $_____ |

"allocation of financial resources . . . [is] a good way to develop political friends" (p. 343). In addition, when budgeting is done well it demonstrates the planners' ability to connect planning with monetary resources, execute programming priorities, and demonstrate their understanding of overall organization goals and objectives.

Programmers often do juggling acts in working with budgets. They decide what a program costs and manage situations when costs are too high. Conversely, they know how to handle the revenue side, which is discussed later in this chapter, to cover those costs.

## Cost Contingency Plans

The process of determining costs has a number of wrinkles and may require developing contingency plans. Three situations often become problematic: when costs exceed the projected budget, when revenue is lower than expected, and when programs are cancelled. As programs take shape, sometimes the costs are higher than what was estimated. In that case, program costs have to come down. Exhibit 14.4 contains a list of strategies

---

**EXHIBIT 14.4**

## Strategies for Use During the Planning Stage to Reduce Program Costs

- ❖ Substitute less expensive instructional materials or eliminate certain materials altogether.
- ❖ Reduce the number of staff members who plan, deliver, and/or evaluate the program. Be especially cognizant of the cost of outside consultants.
- ❖ Reduce the number of participants.
- ❖ Employ less expensive learning format(s) and/or techniques so that the same number of participants (or more) can be involved.
- ❖ Use either a less expensive facility or one that does not cost direct dollars.
- ❖ Hold the program at a facility close to where participants live and/or work so they do not have to pay for overnight accommodations.
- ❖ Have participants pay for their own meals rather than including meals as part of the program package.
- ❖ Require that participants find the cheapest mode of travel to and from the program (for example, car pool, train, and plane).
- ❖ Change the program to a date when the prices for the facilities, meals, and so forth are lower (for example, a weekend or an off-season time at a resort area).
- ❖ Make promotional material for the program less elaborate.
- ❖ Shorten the program and tighten the design.
- ❖ Use a lending library of materials rather than producing all the materials for the participants.
- ❖ Take the program to the participants rather than gathering the participants at a different site if it costs less to deliver the program.
- ❖ Consider subcontracting some of the programs if the costs are lower.

for reducing program costs while the program is in its initial development stage, based on Davis and McCallon (1974), Nilson (1989), and Bellman (1993).

The other two situations—when revenue is low or when a program is canceled—occur after programs have been developed, but before they are delivered. Often, revenues do not materialize due to participant numbers being down, but also if funds from other sources are less than expected. In response, program planners take a hard look at the program and cut out activities, services, and the like that can be scaled back or do not need to be provided. If participant numbers are low they also can save by reducing the funds being spent on instructors and facilitators, instructional materials, food, travel, and equipment. Some of these items are difficult to alter if these services are already contracted and no clause is negotiated in the contract to allow for changes. If changes are made in the program that affect what has been advertised, contact participants and other funding sources and give them the choice to opt out as they no longer will be getting the program that was promised. Although this notification creates short-term problems, being honest about these changes most likely will pay off in future program endeavors. If cost projections allow, programmers may also lower the participants' price when major program changes are made.

If the program is canceled for the lack of adequate projected revenue, again often due to low participant numbers, planners must somehow absorb the already expended or encumbered costs within other revenue streams. For programs that are funded primarily from parent or partner organizations or other "hard" monies, this absorption is less problematic than when participant fees or other "soft" monies are the primary funding sources. The most often used strategy for covering these costs are to set aside a certain percentage of the total operating budget for this purpose, reallocate funds, and build into other programs the costs expended for cancelled programs. Another way that costs are recovered is to use the instructional materials that were developed for other programs. If contracts for food, travel, facilities, external staff, and the like are written so they can be negated with little or no penalty, this is helpful if program cancellations are made.

## Paying for Programs

Managing the income side of the equation is also vital. For some sources of income, the amounts are fixed for a given time period, like organizational subsidies, grants and contracts, and government funds. Although these sources are usually fixed, planners still pay attention to which sources fund each program and ensure monies are appropriately used. In addition, as noted in the previous section, programmers build in "safety systems" within these fixed sources of funds to cover unexpected costs, program changes, and program cancellations.

For revenue that is customarily variable, like sponsorship funds and participant fees, knowing how much to ask sponsors to donate and what to charge participants can be tricky. For example, establishing participant fees depends on a number of factors like what the market will bear, what other sources of income are available, the perceived need for the program, and knowing the target audience. Establishing minimum enrollment figures, especially for non-profit organizations, is often "one of the most arbitrary and subjective decisions [that] educators make in the planning process. However, the decision to establish a minimum enrollment may significantly affect participant fees and, ultimately, whether programs have to be canceled due to insufficient enrollments" (Birkenholz, 1999, p. 128). Even organizations that use extensive historical data, marketing surveys, and established policies and procedures rely heavily on "hunches" and "intuitive guesses" to project enrollment numbers. For programs that rely primarily on participant fees, establishing the final registration fee is critical to the overall success of the program. If potential participants perceive the cost as too high, they may not come. At the same time, if the fee if too low, they may wonder about the program quality and therefore choose not to enroll.

## Marketing the Program

With increased competition for education and training programs for adults in many sectors, marketing is an essential element of the program planning process. This demand for marketing is especially true of educational programs where participation is voluntary and potential participants are not affiliated with the sponsoring organization. Successful marketing is defined by Simerly as "a process for ensuring that an organization reaches its goals and objectives by exchanging its products, services and knowledge for program registrations" (1989a, p. 445).

Marketing is done primarily for three reasons: to ensure adequate participation for programs, to communicate with various organizations what the programs are about, and to convince other publics that specific topics are important even if the majority of the public believes otherwise (Birkenholz, 1999). Ensuring adequate participation, as discussed in the previous section, can make or break a program even prior to it being held. Communicating a message that this program is useful and meaningful to potential participants is critical in ensuring participation. In addition, though, it is crucial to communicate well to other publics, such as sponsoring organizations, funding agencies, and the general community the value and importance of the planned program (Blomberg, 1989; Tracey, 1992). Finally, not all programs are "wanted" by or even perceived as needed by the wider community, but other groups see their necessity. For example, initially, AIDS prevention programs were not welcomed by most community members, and even today, educational programs on diversity, workplace harassment, and sexual preferences are perceived as unnecessary by a large segment of the population.

In developing successful marketing campaigns, there are four key tenets that are essential to these processes (Mitchell, 1998; Craven and DuHamel, 2000).

▶ *Develop and maintain credibility.* Develop a track record of well-run, high-quality programs that build respect and trust with your regular participants and convey to potential audiences that they will get their money's worth.

▶ *Build on successes.* Listen to the participants, both in terms of suggestions on how to change current programs and practices and what future programs they might attend and why.

▶ *Know the competition.* Knowledge about the competitions' programs, what they are charging, who their participants are, how they attract these participants, and so on can assist in designing and marketing current and future programs. In addition, it may pay off to form alliances or partnerships around selected program areas that could increase the viability and quality of these offerings and benefit all involved parties.

▶ *Find a market niche.* Although the probably of overlap in services by organizations in similar market areas is not unusual, groups and organizations should find unique content areas and ways of offering programs that are theirs alone.

The first two tenets, program credibility and success, appear to be givens and not worth much attention. Planners often choose to overlook these tenets when their minds are on short- versus long-term gains. However, ensuring adequate participation and finding market niches are directly connected to being knowledgeable about potential audiences and contents.

## Potential Audiences

Knowing the diverse background and experiences of potential audiences or customers is one of the first steps in developing a marketing plan. There are two major ways programmers go about doing this task: being "customer-oriented," and conducting target audience analyses (Havercamp, 1998; Russell, 1999; Smith and Ragan, 1999; and Sternthal and Tybout, 2001).

### Being Customer- or Participant-Oriented

Current and even potential participants often look to see if program sponsors and staff are participant- or customer-oriented, or if they are there just to improve the bottom line. Although improving the bottom line is often a necessity, current and potential audiences like to feel they are important, that their opinions and ideas count, both in terms of expressing their ideas and needs (see Chapter Six) and for some, through involvement in framing the marketing process. Havercamp (1998) urges that programmers "use traditional and nontraditional strategies to understand customers, clients, and users of programs and services" (p. 381). He and Russell (1999) suggest a number of ways to gain a more general understanding of these groups and what their program preferences are. Sample methods are:

▶ *Track all topics requested, even when they are out of the usual scope of programs offered.* What kinds of insights do these requests give about what sorts of programs should be on the drawing board, and what topics might constitute new horizons in programming for the organization or group? What are the characteristics of people making these requests?

▶ *Monitor websites and listservs whose audience is similar to those served by your organization.* What kinds of promotional materials do they use for education and training programs? What are people discussing? What are they interested in knowing more about?

▶ *Make contacts in person, via the phone, or on the Web to ask about how these contacts might promote a particular program.* Does the program idea sound feasible? Who might the target audiences be? What promotional strategies would they suggest be used to reach the audiences they suggested?

▶ *Conduct focus groups composed of a diversity of former and potential participants to ask them what kinds of marketing campaigns they find useful and which turn them off.* Which kinds of promotional materials do they like and which ones do they "delete" immediately or throw into their "circular files"? How much notice do they prefer on upcoming programs? Where do they like programs to be held?

▶ *Use task forces and advisory groups to assist in designing and conducting marketing endeavors* (see Chapter Five). Is the proposed program worthwhile, and who might be the best target audience or customer? How should the program be priced? Where should the program be held? Are members willing to develop and/or review promotional materials?

▶ *Organize community forums when launching new programs that affect all or large segments of the community.* Does the program make sense? Why or why not? Who are the potential participants? How could these potential participants best be reached to let them know about the program?

Although these strategies are useful in helping current or potential participants feel they are important to the organization and in gaining their perspective about possible marketing strategies, programmers go further once an idea has been solidified for a specific program. They gain more detailed information about the potential audiences or customers.

## Doing a Target Audience Analysis

Completing a target audience analysis is one way to gather information on characteristics of potential participants. This process assumes that staff know which individuals or groups of people are or might be interested in attending the program to be offered. A target audience analysis is useful for both open enrollment programs and programs that have eligibility requirements (for example, about specific types of jobs or educational background). These data can assist in determining whether audiences for these types of programs exist in the designated market area and as a screening device for potential participants (Tracey, 1992; Sternthal and Tybout, 2001).

The target audience analysis entails answering some or all of the questions displayed in Exhibit 14.5, depending on the potential participants (Richey, 1992; Rothwell and Kazanas, 1998; Smith and Ragan, 1999; Lee and Owens, 2000; Sternthal and Tybout, 2001).

"A common error resulting from failure to analyze the characteristics of an audience is assuming that all learners are alike. An even more common error is assuming that the learners are like the [program planners]" (Smith and Ragan, 1999, p. 46). When program planners make this second error, they design program and marketing plans that appeal to them versus their participants or customers. The target audience analysis is done in a number of ways. One primary, although often incomplete, source for this information are data collection efforts done for other components of the program planning process, like identifying program ideas (see Chapter Six) or preparing instructional and transfer-of-learning plans (see Chapters Nine and Ten respectively). When additional or all new information is required, program planners also use other existing databases, conduct interviews, do observations, have participants fill out assessment instruments, examine job descriptions, conduct surveys, and/or review texts and materials that pertain to the potential participants (see Chapter Six) (Smith and Ragan, 1999).

---

**EXHIBIT 14.5**

## Questions for Target Audience Analysis

---

- ❖ How many people might be involved?
- ❖ At what times are the potential participants able to attend sessions?
- ❖ Where are the potential participants located (for example, different geographic locations or all from one organization)?
- ❖ What are the ages of the potential participants?
- ❖ What are the educational levels of the potential participants?
- ❖ What race, gender, ethnicity, and social class are the potential participants?
- ❖ What are the language abilities or preferences of the potential participants?
- ❖ Do the potential participants have any special requirements (such as learning disabilities or loss of hearing) that call for specific program formats, instructional strategies, and/or special services?
- ❖ What can be assumed about the knowledge, skills, and experiences that potential participants bring to the program in relation to the content being offered (for example, on-the-job training, as parents, students, community volunteers)?
- ❖ How do participants believe they process information best?
- ❖ What are the potential participants' attitudes about education and training programs? About the organizations or groups that are sponsoring these programs?
- ❖ Are the potential participants in any identifiable career stages (such as the entry level or retirement) or life roles (for example, parent, spouse, partner, volunteer) that influence the content or process of the program to be offered?
- ❖ Why do the potential participants want to enroll or be involved in the program?
- ❖ Are the potential participants motivated to learn this material, and if so, what are the primary motivators?
- ❖ What are the costs (for example, for fees, loss of job time, travel, and childcare) to the potential participants for attending the program?

---

One note of caution in using a target audience analysis to assess the characteristics and needs of the potential audience for education and training programs is that the potential program participants and the program audience may or may not be one and the same. For example, in planning an educational program for entry-level managers, program planners might assume that those entry-level managers are their prime audience. This assumption may be true, but other scenarios could also be built depending on the situation. The impetus for that particular program may have come from upper-level management, and thus a dual audience may exist: the entry-level managers and upper-level managers. In this latter instance, upper-level management may in fact be the primary audience. Therefore, program planners may need to go beyond a target audience analysis (perhaps by conducting interviews with selected upper-level managers) in order to get a complete picture of their audience.

### Context Analysis

Having a clear picture of the potential audience is not enough for program planners to develop solid marketing plans. They also call for a sense of the people, organizational, and environmental contexts from which their potential participants or customers are drawn. Although a more complete description of each of these contextual elements and how to obtain information about them is given in Chapter Four, the following questions are specifically useful in preparing marketing plans.

- In addition to the potential participants, who else in the participants' public or private sphere might need "to be sold" on the value and worth of the program (for example, work supervisors, senior management, family members and friends)?

- For the people who have been identified, what types of promotional materials would most likely capture their attention? Would different copy or pictures make a difference in reaching this wider audience?

- What organizational factors should be highlighted to attract potential participants into the program? For example, for organizations that are team-based, describing how the program is designed for teams of participants is a good marketing strategy.

- Are there wider environmental factors related to the program content that might influence potential participants to attend? If so, how could attention be drawn to these factors in the promotional materials?

- Where learning transfer is important (see Chapter Ten), how might programmers get across the idea that a well-designed transfer plan is incorporated into the program? Does that transfer plan fit the contexts in which the participants will apply their new knowledge and skills?

Much of this information may have already been gathered through earlier efforts to discern the context. If programs have been previously planned for the same or similar organizations or groups of people, and/or the environments in which programs are held or will be held remain relatively stable, there is even a greater chance that these data are available.

## The Product, Price, Place, and Promotion

In addition to a good picture of the potential audience and the contexts of that audience, program planners should address four key aspects of marketing: product, price, place, and promotion (Simerly and Associates, 1989; Galbraith, 1997; Krishnamurthi, 2001).

## Product

Obviously, program planners have to know their "product"; that is, they are able to provide a comprehensive and understandable description of the programs for which they are responsible. They also are able to choose the right product (that is, the right program) to fit the needs and desires of their audience.

## Price

If there is to be a cost charged to participants for a program, the right price is determined. How much are the potential customers—whether they are individuals, groups, or organizations—willing to pay? In thinking through costs, program planners consider both the cost to participants for the program itself and the participants' travel expenses. In addition, some organizations compute costs in terms of participants' time away from the job. In setting prices, the actual cost of planning and implementing the program, the demand for the program, what customers are willing to pay, the competition, and the life cycle of the program are taken into account (Simerly, 1989a; Watkins and Sechrest, 1998; Krishnamurthi, 2001). For example, lowering the price to increase the demand for a program can be a good decision, especially if the market is a highly competitive one. On the other hand, when the competition is marginal and the demand high, increasing the price is appropriate. In addition, pricing by program costs may deny access to segments of the population who really need the program. In these cases, as discussed earlier, education and training units set aside special funds for the overall budget, so these programs can be subsidized.

## Place

Choosing where to offer education and training programs is also important. The location must be consistent with the program design, audience, and budget (Carson, 1989). For example, hosting a three-day national conference in a place relatively inaccessible by air (which usually means higher airfares) is generally not a good decision, especially if the participants have to obtain low airfares to attend the conference. Other common mistakes in marketing the location of the program include overemphasizing the place rather than the program, and being too "glowing" about the features and attractions of the location.

## Promotion

Not all education and training activities are promoted. Some are required—the participants are told they must go. Others are in such high demand that the job of the program planners is to select participants from a large applicant pool. For the most part, though, program planners promote or sell programs to their potential audiences. Many programs fail because of poor promotion. "People just never heard about them [the programs] or did not realize how good they were" (Knowles, 1980, p. 176).

Promotion involves developing strategies and materials aimed at generating or increasing enrollments for education and training programs. Examples of promotional materials and strategies used to foster interest in education and training programs are in Exhibit 14.6 (Nilson, 1989; Simerly and Associates, 1989; Galbraith, 1997; Havercamp, 1998; and Russell, 1999). More complete descriptions of how to develop these types of materials and strategies are given in Nilson (1989), Simerly and Associates (1989), and Galbraith (1997).

---

**EXHIBIT 14.6**

# Examples of Promotional Materials and Strategies

| Promotional Materials | Strategies | |
|---|---|---|
| **Brochures** | A written document describing a specific program or series of programs. A three-fold piece measuring 4 x 9 inches (which can fit into a business-size envelope) is used most often. | → Direct mail<br>→ Placement in appropriate offices and public places (such as coffee rooms, cafeterias)<br>→ Participant packets (for brochures promoting future programs)<br>→ By hand at appropriate meetings |
| **Flyers or announcements** | A single sheet, preferably color, $8\frac{1}{2} \times 11$ inches, promoting an activity or a group of related activities to people with specialized interests. | → Direct mail<br>→ Bulletin boards<br>→ Participant packets (for brochures promoting future programs) |
| **Email (personal and listservs)** | A brief message that has a catchy title in the subject line is sent to selected individuals and listservs. Use attachments or direct access to a website for more detailed information. Employ this medium sparingly, as people are becoming very discriminate in what they open. Know which potential participants do not have regular or any access to email. | → Internal organizational electronic mail<br>→ More widely used communication networks external to the organization |
| **Website information** | Eye-catching promotional materials on the websites of sponsoring organizations and groups. Make sure this information is easy to navigate and all materials are functional. If possible, allow people to access further information and register directly | → Internal organizational websites<br>→ Websites found on the Internet that link well to your program interests |

*(Continued)*

**EXHIBIT 14.6**

## Examples of Promotional Materials and Strategies (*Continued*)

| Promotional Materials | Strategies | |
|---|---|---|
| **Website information** (*Continued*) | from the website. Link your website to other sites to broaden the access to other potential audiences. Remember that there are some potential participants that do not or choose not to have access to the Internet. | |
| **Form letters and memos** | These letters and memos can be used in two ways. First, use as a cover letter mailed with a brochure or sent electronically with other promotional material (with the letter focusing the reader's attention on certain activities described in the promotional piece). Second, send as a separate mailing (written or electronic) to make an appeal to a specific group of people. Planners can choose to personalize each letter or memo by addressing it to a specific individual. | ➜ Direct paper or email |
| **Newspaper or newsletter publicity** | An information piece describing a specific program or series of activities. Fostering good relationships with a local reporter or editor of a newsletter often helps in ensuring programs from your organization stay in the public eye. | ➜ Distribution by the organization that owns or is responsible for the publication |
| **Postcards** | Postcards can be used in a variety of ways—from initial program announcements to reminders of how to register. Keep the message and the graphics clear as well as fun and creative. Also make sure a contact address (for example, email, telephone, fax) is always in the same place on the card. | ➜ Direct mail<br>➜ Participant packets (for brochures promoting future programs) |
| **Catalogues** | A description of the programs and services of an organization's educational activities, with course and activity descriptions usually included. | ➜ Direct mail<br>➜ Placement in offices and public display areas<br>➜ In-person distribution through various departments or units of an organization |
| **Posters** | A sign used to attract attention about a specific program or event. It should be attractive and eye-catching. | ➜ Bulletin boards and other appropriate places (such as office doors, cafeteria, coffee room, restaurants, local businesses) |
| **Personal contacts** | Program planning staff, other organizational personnel, and/or past participants who tell others about the program. This dissemination can be planned or done on an informal basis. | ➜ Individual in-person conversations, telephone conversations, email messages, and announcements in group meetings |

| Promotional Materials | Strategies | |
|---|---|---|
| **Newsletter, newspaper, and magazine ads** | An ad placed in appropriate publications announcing the program. There is usually a cost associated, except for in-house newsletters. | ➜ Distribution by the organization that owns or is responsible for the publication |
| **Radio, television, and audio and videotapes** | Production of these promotional materials is often costly, but free "air time" may be given to non-profit organizations | ➜ Local radio and television stations<br>➜ Direct mail (for example, videotapes) |
| **Exhibits or booths** | Displays that clearly portray what the program is all about. The space, allocations, cost, expected attendance, storage, and available staff determine the size and materials allowed. | ➜ Set up at conferences, trade shows, conventions, libraries, museums, shopping malls, and other public places (with information given by staff or, if exhibit is not staffed, picked up by interested parties) |
| **Coupons** | The giving of coupons for a certain percentage off the regular program fee (may be conditions like signing up by a certain date, registering a new person for the program). | ➜ Direct mail<br>➜ Participant packets of current programs<br>➜ In-person distribution<br>➜ Placement in offices and public display areas |

## The Marketing Campaign

Having a clear picture of the audience to be reached and the contexts in which they live and work, as noted earlier, is the essential first step to any marketing campaign. For example, a promotional piece targeted at older adults will be poorly received if many of the people who receive the material do not consider themselves to be old. This audience and context targeting does not have to be done in an overt way but can come through in a more subtle manner—for example, in the illustrations, pictures, or language used in a brochure.

The second step, that the marketing campaign is well planned, is also essential. The planning phase includes building a promotional budget and determining how that budget will be spent. Two examples illustrating this planning process are outlined in Exhibit 14.7.

The third marketing step is preparing and distributing the promotional material. The most popular promotional materials are brochures, online announcements and materials, and newsletter pieces. The preparation of copy and images (for example, graphics and pictures) that are readable and attractive is key to this third step. Shipp (1981), Simerly (1989b), and Mitchell (1998) outline four classic elements of a good promotional piece.

**EXHIBIT 14.7**

# Sample Marketing Campaign Plans

|  | Example 1 | Example 2 |
|---|---|---|
| **Name of program and proposed date** | Preparing Transfer-of-Learning Plans (one-day invitation only in-house conference for selected members of state-level nursing professional organizations) | Conducting Cost-Benefit Analysis (workshop sponsored by a local chapter of the American Society for Training and Development [ASTD]) |
| **Target audience** | Staff who plan education and training programs as part of their work roles<br><br>Full-time managers of staff and/or patient education | Human resource managers and staff, performance improvement staff, consultants |
| **Types of promotional material to use** | Personalized invitational letters to individuals<br><br>Personalized invitational letters to executive vice presidents and managers for nursing services at in-patient facilities, and other directors of nursing services for outpatient and home care programs.<br><br>Brochures to go with invitational letters<br><br>Follow-up postcards<br><br>Personal contacts with nurse opinion leaders | ASTD website and newsletter<br><br>Email to all chapter members with direct link to the local chapter's web page for more detailed information, which includes online registration<br><br>Brochures mailed to each member, plus other potential customers' lists (for example, members of other professional associations, graduate students in human resource development program); also available at local chapter meetings<br><br>Personal contacts |
| **Target time for distribution** | November 1<br>November 1<br>November 1<br>November 15–December 1<br>Mid-November–mid-December | January 15<br>January 15<br>January 30<br>Push three to four weeks before program |
| **Proposed cost** | November 1           $ 40<br>November 1           $ 10<br>November 1           $ 100<br>November 15–<br>December 1          $ 20<br>Mid-November–     No direct cost<br>mid-December | January 15–No direct cost (considered in-kind contributions)<br><br>January 15–No direct cost (considered in-kind contribution)<br><br>January 30–$700<br><br>Push three to four weeks before program; no direct cost |

The piece catches the reader's attention, creates interest, engages the reader, and inspires action. More specifically, Simerly (1989b) and Mitchell (1998) give the following pointers for preparing good promotional materials:

- ▶ Keep the intended audience's interests, experiences, backgrounds, and contexts in which they live and work at the forefront.

- ▶ Keep it simple. Use short sentences, familiar words, and clear images.

- ▶ Use as few words as possible. Say what you want to say and no more.

- ▶ Ensure images match and illuminate the text.

- ▶ Use the present tense and action words and images to give the message a sense of urgency.

- ▶ Use personal pronouns and images to which the audience responds. "Speak" to the audience just as you would to a colleague or friend.

- ▶ Do not use jargon, and do not overuse or crowd images. These flaws disrupt the flow of the message.

- ▶ Emphasize benefits. Participants should be able to easily see what they will learn and do.

- ▶ Convey enthusiasm. Convince the consumer to share your excitement.

Developing a fact sheet before preparing the actual copy is helpful. The questions on the fact sheet are the same ones that program planners answer when preparing the actual program: who, what, when, where, why, and how.

It is helpful to both track and evaluate marketing campaigns. Tracking marketing campaigns entails keeping on file selected information such as copies of all promotional materials, distribution lists, cost of promotion, and a description of problems and strategies used to solve these problems over a set period of time. "Keep [the tracking] . . . simple so the task is not daunting" is the advice given by Craven and DuHamel (2000, p. 61). Then, at specified times, review and evaluate this marketing information and look for trends and ways to improve marketing efforts. Birkenholz (1999, p. 119) states: "The primary questions to be addressed in this evaluation are 'How did the participants [and organizations and groups from which they came] learn about the program?' and 'What factors were most influential in their decision to participate?'"

## Your Promotional Assets

Ascertaining and strengthening your promotional assets and capabilities is an important part of any marketing effort. Program planners can use a checklist (Farlow, 1979; Simerly and Associates, 1989) for doing this task, rating each asset and capability as present, readily obtainable, or hard to obtain. For a sample checklist, see Exhibit 14.8.

**EXHIBIT 14.8**

**Sample Checklist to Help Determine Available Promotional Assets and Capabilities**

| Asset | Present | Readily Available | Hard to Obtain |
|---|---|---|---|
| **Personnel (paid staff and/or volunteers)** | | | |
| *Copywriters* | | | |
| *Photographers* | | | |
| *Graphic artists* | | | |
| *Design specialists* | | | |
| *Web masters* | | | |
| *Computer communications experts* | | | |
| *Desktop computer publishers* | | | |
| *Clerical assistants* | | | |
| *Other staff* | | | |
| Access to printers, duplicating equipment, computers, and/or print shops | | | |
| Access to copy machines for small jobs | | | |
| Up-to-date mailing lists | | | |
| Coding and tracking system for mailing lists | | | |
| Established relationships with media people (for example, those working with newsletters, newspapers, radio, TV) | | | |
| Access to email, bulletin boards, and websites | | | |
| Access to a good reference library | | | |
| Access to good demographic studies of potential audiences | | | |

## Chapter Highlights

Preparing and managing program budgets and marketing plans is one of the key components of the planning process, depending on the organizational setting in which the programs are planned. If the programs are expected to break even or be profit-making ventures, these aspects of the overall plan are critical to the very survival of the planning enterprise. In carrying through this important component, program planners center on 11 major tasks:

◆ Estimate the expenses for the program, including costs for the development, delivery, and evaluation of the program (for example, costs for staff salaries, participant expenses, facilities, instructional materials, and transfer-of-learning strategies).

◆ Determine how the program is financed (for example, by participant fees, organizational subsidy, government funding), and estimate the program income.

◆ Manage the program budget and keep accurate budget records.

◆ Develop contingency budget plans for programs that are scaled back or cancelled.

◆ Pay the bills for the program by managing the income side of the budget.

◆ Build and maintain program credibility, success, and market niches when marketing education and training programs. Demonstrate being participant- or customer-orientated.

◆ Conduct a target audience analysis to help determine the background and experiences of the potential audience as one of the starting places for the marketing plan.

◆ Use already existing contextual information and/or generate it to help frame the marketing plan.

◆ Select and prepare promotional materials for the program (such as brochures, website materials, emails, newsletter copy, flyers) that "tell the story well" of the what (the product), the cost (the price), and the where (the place) of the program.

◆ Prepare a targeted and lively promotional campaign, paying careful attention to the target audience, the different contexts of the potential participants, the type of promotional materials to use, the time frame, and the cost.

◆ Ascertain and strengthen your promotional assets and capabilities. These behind-the-scenes tasks of preparing and managing program budgets and marketing plans can have disastrous effects on the learning portion of the program if they are not done well.

Discussed next is a more visible component of the planning process, at least to the participants—dealing with the logistical aspects of the program. More specifically, these logical aspects entail determining the importance of obtaining suitable facilities, the role of the site coordinator, the setting of positive climates for learning, and the tasks completed once the program is over.

## Application Exercises

This chapter's Application Exercises address the issues of budgeting for and marketing education and training programs. The first is designed to help you create a budget for your program, the second is a tool for conducting audience and contextual analyses, and the third deals with marketing a program.

---

## EXERCISE 14.1

## Preparing Program Budgets

1. **Choose an educational program that you are presently or will be planning and prepare an estimated expense budget for that program using the following chart. Put an *X* in the space provided if no costs are incurred for that item.**

### Worksheet for Estimating Program Expenses

| Budget Items | Development Costs | Delivery Costs | Evaluation Costs | Subtotal |
|---|---|---|---|---|
| **Internal Staff** | | | | |
| Program planners | | | | |
| Instructors/facilitators | | | | |
| Technology specialists | | | | |
| Clerical/other support staff | | | | |
| **External Staff** | | | | |
| Program consultants | | | | |
| Instructors and facilitators | | | | |
| Technology specialists | | | | |
| Support staff | | | | |
| **Instructional Materials** | | | | |
| PowerPoint presentations | | | | |
| Books and articles | | | | |
| Manuals | | | | |
| Videotapes | | | | |
| Videodiscs | | | | |
| Audiotapes/CDs | | | | |
| Overhead transparencies | | | | |
| Slides | | | | |
| Computer charges | | | | |
| Satellite uplink/downlink | | | | |
| Videoconferencing | | | | |
| Telephone charges | | | | |
| Other | | | | |
| **Facilities** | | | | |
| Large meeting rooms | | | | |
| Break-out rooms | | | | |
| Staff work rooms | | | | |
| Social/entertainment areas | | | | |
| Sleeping accommodations | | | | |
|     Staff | | | | |
|     Participants | | | | |
| Computer access | | | | |
|     Staff | | | | |
|     Participants | | | | |
| Telephone and fax | | | | |
| Parking | | | | |
| Signage | | | | |

*(Continued)*

| Budget Items | Development Costs | Delivery Costs | Evaluation Costs | Subtotal |
|---|---|---|---|---|
| **Food** | | | | |
| Catered meals | | | | |
| Staff | _____ | _____ | _____ | _____ |
| Participants | _____ | _____ | _____ | _____ |
| Special needs | | | | |
| Staff | _____ | _____ | _____ | _____ |
| Participants | _____ | _____ | _____ | _____ |
| Refreshment breaks | _____ | _____ | _____ | _____ |
| Special functions (such as social hours, receptions, hospitality suites) | _____ | _____ | _____ | _____ |
| **Travel** | | | | |
| Planning and follow-up meetings | _____ | _____ | _____ | _____ |
| To and from program | | | | |
| Staff | | | | |
| In-house | _____ | _____ | _____ | _____ |
| External consultants | _____ | _____ | _____ | _____ |
| Participants | _____ | _____ | _____ | _____ |
| Educationally related outings | _____ | _____ | _____ | _____ |
| Entertainment outings | _____ | _____ | _____ | _____ |
| **Equipment** (rent or purchase) | _____ | _____ | _____ | _____ |
| Media playback | _____ | _____ | _____ | _____ |
| Media record | _____ | _____ | _____ | _____ |
| Computers | _____ | _____ | _____ | _____ |
| Video projectors | _____ | _____ | _____ | _____ |
| Overhead projector | _____ | _____ | _____ | _____ |
| LCD projectors | _____ | _____ | _____ | _____ |
| Screens | _____ | _____ | _____ | _____ |
| Other | _____ | _____ | _____ | _____ |
| **Special Services for Participants** (sign language experts, note takers, interpreters) | _____ | _____ | _____ | _____ |
| **Marketing Plans** | | | | |
| Target and contextual analysis | _____ | _____ | _____ | _____ |
| Promotional materials | | | | |
| Design | _____ | _____ | _____ | _____ |
| Purchase | _____ | _____ | _____ | _____ |
| Printing | _____ | _____ | _____ | _____ |
| Distribution and mailing | _____ | _____ | _____ | _____ |
| Return processing | _____ | _____ | _____ | _____ |
| **General Costs** | | | | |
| Overhead | _____ | _____ | _____ | _____ |
| Benefits | _____ | _____ | _____ | _____ |
| **Other Costs** | _____ | _____ | _____ | _____ |
| *Subtotal for each type of cost* | $_____ | $_____ | $_____ | $_____ |
| | | | **Grand Total Costs** = | $_____ |

**2.** **If you need to cover all or part of these program costs, identify what sources of income you will use and estimate how much funding will come from each source.**

### Worksheet for Estimating Income Sources

| Income Source | Amount of Income/Subsidy |
|---|---|
| **Parent organizational subsidy** | $_____ |
| **Sponsorship funds** | $_____ |
| **Participant fees** (fee × # of estimated participants) | $_____ |
| **Auxiliary enterprises and sales** (item or service to be sold × # of estimated customers) | $_____ |
| **Grants and contracts** (list each source of funding with amount) | |
| 1. | $_____ |
| 2. | $_____ |
| 3. | $_____ |
| **Government Funds** (list each source of funding with amount) | |
| 1. | $_____ |
| 2. | $_____ |
| 3. | $_____ |
| **Profit from any educational units** | $_____ |
| **Miscellaneous income** | $_____ |
| Total Income | $_____ |

**3.** **If your expense and income sources are not in line, describe how you would adjust either one or both in order to achieve your budget objective (for example, breaking even on expenses, earning 10 percent over cost).**

**4.** **Review your budget plans with other members of your planning team and/or with people from your organization or sponsoring group. Revise your expense and income estimates and your ideas on how to meet your budget objective as needed.**

## EXERCISE 14.2

### Conducting Target and Contextual Analyses

1.  **Identify an educational or training program that you are or will be in the process of developing and give a short description of that program.**

2.  **Complete a target audience analysis for that program by responding to any of the following questions that are appropriate for your situation.**

    How many people might be involved?

    At what times are the potential participants able to attend sessions?

    Where are the potential participants located (for example, where geographically, or all from one organization)?

    What are the ages of the potential participants?

    What are the educational levels of the potential participants?

    What race, gender, ethnicity, and social class are the potential participants?

    What are the language abilities or preferences of the potential participants?

    Do the potential participants have any special requirements (such as learning or physical disabilities) that call for specific program formats, instructional strategies, and/or special services?

What can be assumed about the knowledge, skills, and experiences that potential participants bring to the program in relation to the content being offered (for example, on-the-job training, as parents, students, community volunteers)?

How do participants believe they process information best?

What are the potential participants' attitudes about education and training programs? About the organizations or groups that are sponsoring these programs?

Are the potential participants in any identifiable career stages (such as entry level or retirement) or life roles (for example, parent, spouse, partner, volunteer) that influence the content or process of the program to be offered?

Why do the potential participants want to enroll or be involved in the program?

Are the potential participants motivated to learn this material, and if so, what are the primary motivators?

What are the costs (for example, for fees, loss of job time, travel, and childcare) to the potential participants for attending the program?

*(Continued)*

3.  **Complete a contextual analysis for the program you identified in Exercise 14.1 by responding to any of the following questions that are appropriate to your situation.**

    In addition to the potential participants, who else in the participants' public or private sphere might need "to be sold" on the value and worth of the program (for example, work supervisors, senior management, family members and friends)?

    For the people who have been identified, what types of promotional materials would most likely capture their attention? Would different copy or pictures make a difference in reaching this wider audience?

    What organizational factors are important to highlight in order to draw potential participants into the program? (For example, for organizations that are team-based, describing how the program is designed for teams of participants is a good marketing strategy.)

    Are there wider environmental factors related to the program content that might influence potential participants to attend? If so, how could attention be drawn to these in the promotional materials?

    Where learning transfer is important (see Chapter Ten), how might programmers get across the idea that a well designed transfer plan is incorporated into the program that fits the contexts in which the participants will apply the material?

4.  **How can you use the information you have generated from the target audience and contextual analyses in the planning process?**

## EXERCISE 14.3

## Marketing the Program

1. **Choose a program for which you have completed a marketing plan or one for which you need to do a marketing plan. Using the following chart, outline either how you did or would go about preparing the plan.**

| | |
|---|---|
| **Name of Program and Proposed Date** | |
| **Target Audience** | |
| **Types of Promotional Material to Use** | |
| **Target Time for Distribution** | |
| **Proposed Cost** | |

2. **Choose either 2a or 2b, depending on your situation.**

   a. If you have already delivered the program, are there ways you could have improved your marketing efforts? If so, how?

   b. If you are still preparing the marketing plan, ask at least two people who are either involved in the planning process with you or are knowledgeable about your organization and/or the program to review your plan. Based on the feedback, complete a revision of the marketing plan as needed.

# Chapter 15

# Coordinating Facilities and On-Site Events

**THERE IS NOTHING** more frustrating to program participants and presenters than discovering that the logistical end of the program has received little or no attention. This problem is illustrated in the following scenarios.

### Poor Choice of Conference Facilities

Sue is really not enjoying the conference, primarily because the facilities range from poor to mediocre. She has thought to herself a number of times that the meeting rooms must have been designed by people who never attend education and training events. The chairs are extremely uncomfortable, the lighting is terrible, and the temperature fluctuates between hot and cold. The food service and quality have been poor both for the breaks and the meals, and the hotel rooms are noisy and small. In addition, because the hotel is located in a questionable part of the city, Sue does not really feel safe. She tells herself that this is the last time she will attend a conference sponsored by this group, even though the program itself has been good, because her complaints to the conference staff about facilities have been virtually ignored.

### Meeting Room Problems

Brandon, a workshop presenter, arrives at the room in which he is to present and finds it in total disarray. The room has dirty glasses, napkins, and crumbs scattered all over the tables. Although he requested a specific seating arrangement, the chairs and tables are all over the place. In addition, the video projector and screen he ordered are not in place. He looks through his presenter packet to see if it has any instructions on how to get assistance. Finding none, Brandon decides to remedy the situation as best he can by moving the chairs and tables and figuring out how to do his presentation without the video projector. This endeavor is awkward, because the program participants have started to arrive. Then, when everything is as set as can be and Brandon is about to start, who should arrive but the person who was supposed to make sure all the room arrangements were in order.

### Ignoring the Schedule of Events

The program participants are beginning to get restless. According to the schedule, this session should have been over 15 minutes ago. A number of people have already walked out of the session, while new arrivals looking for their next session keep opening and closing the door. Still, Julie, who is the presenter, goes on and on, seemingly oblivious to the time. Finally someone who has just entered the room—Jim, who is the next presenter—tries in a very diplomatic way to let Julie know that his session is scheduled in this room next. Julie's response to this interruption is to tell him to wait his turn because she still has some important material to cover.

Thinking through the many logistical details of education and training programs is not always fun, but it is a task program planners must tackle (*before* the last minute). One of the hallmarks of top-notch planners who have the responsibility for logistics is they are detail-oriented and keep track of numerous tasks in a timely manner. The larger the program, the more important it is to spend the time and effort before, during, and after the program to make sure it runs as smoothly as possible.

This chapter first addresses the importance of obtaining suitable program facilities. Included in that discussion is both facility and meeting room checklists for helping planners with this task. Explored next are the logistical tasks on-site coordinators do prior to the opening of the program. This section is followed by how coordinators create positive climates for learning once the participants have arrived and ways coordinators monitor the program once it is in progress. The chapter concludes with suggestions for tasks that program coordinators complete in concluding programs and in tying up loose ends once the participants have left.

## Obtaining Suitable Facilities

The physical environment in which education and training activities take place affects participants' learning (Hiemstra, 1991; Finkel, 1996; Russell, 1999; Hartwig, 2000). A learning environment is defined by Finkel (1996) as "the quality of every detail in the environment within which your programs are held and how they contribute to attendee learning" (p. 982). For example, Brooks-Harris and Stock-Ward (1999) observe that the "physical arrangements communicate information about levels of both power and authority" (1999, p. 105), even when presenters may not want to portray this message. Standing behind a podium or up on a stage removes presenters from the audience and, unless they purposely do something to connect with participants, gets in the way of learning for some. To minimize this nonverbal disconnection and message of power, presenters can step out from behind the podium and move off the stage for part of their presentations, walk among the audience, invite audience participation, and connect with them through story-telling and humor.

The most important space for education and training programs is the meeting rooms, whether they are designed for large groups, break-out groups, or individual learning. In addition, program planners consider other space, such as places for meals and breaks, overnight accommodations, and opportunities for recreation and socializing.

## Investigating Facilities

There are five types of facilities commonly used for education and training activities: in-house organizational facilities, hotel and motel facilities, conference and retreat centers, college and university facilities, and resort areas. Each type of facility has its advantages and disadvantages, depending on the objectives of the activity, the instructional techniques to be used, the participants, the program presenters and facilitators, the cost, the accessibility, and the type of services the facility provides (Nadler and Nadler, 1987; Munson, 1992). For example, for an organization's three-hour workshop for in-house personnel, the organization's seminar room is probably the best choice of facilities. If that same workshop is offered to people from a wide geographic area, however, a central meeting place in a local hotel or community college probably works better.

If outside facilities are used, program planners check them out thoroughly. The checklist, given in Exhibit 15.1, helps with this task (Nadler and Nadler, 1987; Munson, 1992; Conner and Waldrop, 1994; Hartwig, 2000).

In investigating facilities, two other areas are key: estimating costs and negotiating contracts. Outlined in Chapter Fourteen is a sample worksheet for costing out expenses for facilities as well as other items. This cost estimation is completed prior to negotiating any contract with the rental facilities. Negotiating contracts is not always an easy task, but it is a necessary process. As Simerly (1990) stresses: "There are many legal issues to be aware of and traps to avoid" (p. 103) when planners attempt to negotiate favorable contracts for rental space. Conner and Waldrop (1994, p. 73) offer a

**EXHIBIT 15.1**

# Checklist for Selecting Facilities

| Items | Notes |
|---|---|

***Availability of program dates***

_____ First choice _____

_____ Second choice _____

_____ Other _____

***Location***

_____ Good transportation access

(for example, plane, car, ground transportation) _____

_____ Participant appeal _____

_____ Safe and secure (for example, lighting, security staff) _____

_____ Ease of parking _____

***Meeting rooms: General sessions, break-out rooms, social and entertainment areas***

(See Exhibit 15.2 for a description of each of these features.)

_____ Size _____

_____ Appearance _____

_____ Lighting _____

_____ Décor _____

_____ Furnishings _____

_____ Ventilation, heating, and cooling _____

_____ Sound projection _____

_____ Electrical outlets _____

_____ Computer hookups _____

***Support services (at same or different facility where program will be held)***

_____ On-site meals (catered by same

or different group) _____

_____ Accommodations _____

_____ Restaurants _____

_____ Recreation, fitness facilities _____

_____ Phones, fax, and Internet access _____

_____ Business center _____

_____ Equipment services _____

***On-Site transportation (frequency, convenience, cost)***

_____ Public _____

_____ Private _____

***Accessibility requirements under Americans with Disabilities Act (ADA)***

_____ Accessible parking spaces _____

_____ Ramps, lifts _____

_____ Elevators _____

_____ Accessible sleeping rooms _____

_____ Accessible public restrooms _____

_____ Doorway and corridor width for wheelchairs _____

*(Continued)*

---

**EXHIBIT 15.1 (*Continued*)**

| Items | Notes |
|---|---|
| _____ Floor surfaces smooth and firm | _____ |
| _____ Lowered public telephones | _____ |
| _____ Telecommunications device for deaf (TDD) | _____ |
| _____ Readable signs with large lettering, Braille, or raised symbols | _____ |
| _____ Sufficient lighting in rooms and corridors | _____ |
| _____ Emergency warnings in multiple delivery methods | _____ |

***General factors***

| | |
|---|---|
| _____ Attractions and entertainment in area | _____ |
| _____ Experience in hosting educational programs | _____ |
| _____ Site personnel | _____ |
| _____ Safety issues | _____ |
| _____ Medical and emergency services | _____ |

---

number of useful tips prior to signing a contract. A sampling includes:

- Meeting dates are accurate.
- Agreed-upon meeting rooms and group meal rooms are reserved.
- Correct number of lodging rooms are secured for the accurate dates.
- Deposit requirements are outlined.
- Cancellation clauses are present.
- Liabilities are clearly articulated.
- All costs, gratuities, and taxes are identified and fixed.
- Conditions that might trigger price increases are clear.
- Master accounts and direct billing are arranged.
- Agreements on late fees and charges are complete.

Having a contract protects the program sponsors and also guides planners in budget planning and management (see Chapter Fourteen).

## Choosing Meeting Rooms

Different learning activities require different types of meeting rooms (from large auditoriums to small seminar rooms) and seating arrangements. For example, instructors who foster group interaction and team-building do not want a huge room with chairs arranged in rows (preventing participants from seeing each other). Rather, they prefer chairs placed around tables or in circles in rooms that are appropriate for the number of participants. These room arrangements provide much better learning environments for these kinds of activities. In addition, some types of learning activities require special facilities, such as space for prototype machinery or equipment.

In choosing meeting rooms, the accent is on details. "These details will influence the degree to which participants will be able to spend their time valuably" (Finkel, 1996, p. 984). In addition, instructors, facilitators, and coordinators must present, communicate, and handle the program logistics to ensure the most productivity. Important details that are checked when arranging for meeting room space are outlined in Exhibit 15.2, which includes recommendations for each factor (Nadler and Nadler, 1987; Munson, 1992; Finkel, 1996; Mitchell, 1998).

Reality often sets in with a bang for those selecting meeting rooms. Some program planners have no real choice. For example, they may have to use the space available in their organization even though it is not the best environment for learning. In situations like these, it is important to think how the available space can be used to its best advantage. If the lighting is poor, can extra lights be obtained for the session? If the placement of outlets is inconvenient, are extension cords available and can they be placed so that people are not tripping over them? If the room is too warm, could quiet fans be used to cool it down? Could more comfortable chairs be borrowed from another room just for this session?

## Arranging Meeting Rooms

This question is often asked of program staff: "How do you want the meeting rooms arranged?" Often the response is a quickly scribbled picture on a napkin or other scrap of paper. It is more helpful to have a set of diagrams available to give to the persons responsible for arranging the rooms (such as custodial staff, convention center managers). Figure 15.1 shows arrangement options for large rooms, while Figure 15.2 presents diagrams of the most frequently used set-ups for meeting rooms.

## Arranging for Instructional Equipment

In arranging facilities, program planners know whether the necessary instructional equipment (for example, screens, overhead projectors, video players) is available at the site. For education and training programs held at the host organization, this checking usually only involves scheduling the equipment, but equipment may also have to be borrowed or leased if the host organization does not own what is required.

When facilities are rented, arranging for instructional equipment may be more complicated. The host organization, presenters, the rental facility, or an outside rental agency may supply equipment. All of these arrangements have both advantages and disadvantages, as highlighted in Exhibit 15.3.

Whether planners are arranging for in-house or rental equipment, three considerations are taken into account: Will the equipment be in good

---

**EXHIBIT 15.2**

# Paying Attention to Meeting Room Details

---

◆ **Access.** Choose rooms that are barrier-free and accommodate persons with special needs (for example, places with wheelchair access to all floors, audio equipment, signs in other languages and/or Braille). Ensure that all ADA requirements are met for access.

◆ **Room size.** Avoid overcrowding and cavernous, oversized rooms. Participants want elbow room and some personal space.

◆ **Room structure.** Watch out for narrow rooms and posts in wrong places. The ideal room structure is square.

◆ **Windows.** Selecting rooms that have or do not have windows is still a personal and controversial issue. Some prefer the natural light and even the ambiance of the out-of-doors in selected settings. Others insist that meeting rooms should not have windows because they detract from the learning. When windows are present, ensure that they can be covered if low-light is needed or direct sunlight may hinder the presentation of the program.

◆ **Furnishings.** Make sure tables are designed for flexible use and are movable, and chairs are comfortable and provide good back support. If participants desire writing and workspace, ensure these are available. In addition, provide instructors and presenters with tables and chairs.

◆ **Color.** Look for warm pastel shades and soft beiges. Stay away from white and dark colors.

◆ **Pictures and clocks.** Check to see whether pictures, clocks, or other types of wall decorations can be taken down.

◆ **Floor coverings.** Choose rooms carpeted in solid shades, not patterns, and that are ADA acceptable.

◆ **Lighting.** Look for indirect, warm fluorescent lighting with dimming controls. Make sure the lighting is sufficient for note-taking and that ADA requirements for lighting are met.

◆ **Glare.** Eliminate all sources of glare.

◆ **Temperature.** Make sure heat and air conditioning controls are accessible, and ensure you are able to regulate the temperature. Keep the temperature between 68 and 72 degrees. If you must err, err on the cool side.

◆ **Ventilation.** Keep the air circulating in the room. Smoking is never permitted.

◆ **Noise.** Check for noise from heating, ventilating, and air-conditioning systems in adjacent rooms, corridors, and outside the building.

◆ **Acoustics.** Check on the bounce and absorption of sound. Use different types of voices for this testing process. Make sure to meet ADA requirements for acoustics.

◆ **Electrical outlets.** Identify the location and type of outlets (for example, grounded outlets). Ideally there should be electrical outlets every six feet along the wall and also floor outlets for media equipment.

◆ **Computer hookups.** Check for telephone or ethernet jacks that allow for computer hookups.

◆ **Technological "smart rooms."** Check to see if there are any meetings rooms that are especially designed for high-technology access (for example, distance-learning equipment, LCD panels, videotaping, and play-back capability).

◆ **Access to other areas.** Check for easy access to restrooms, vending machines, eating facilities, and so on. Make sure to comply with all ADA requirements for access to these areas.

**FIGURE 15.1**

## Large Meeting Room Arrangements

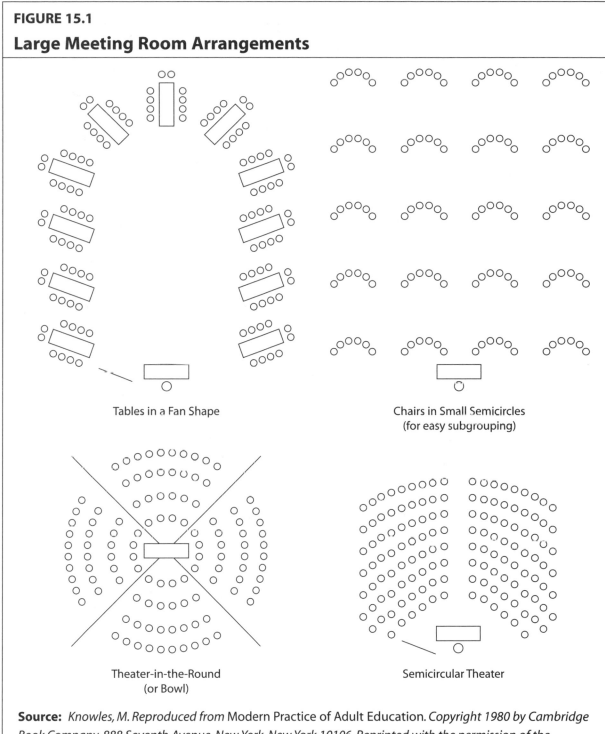

Tables in a Fan Shape

Chairs in Small Semicircles
(for easy subgrouping)

Theater-in-the-Round
(or Bowl)

Semicircular Theater

**FIGURE 15.2**

# Layouts for Setting Up Meeting Rooms

The physical environment in a meeting space can make or break how active and participatory the meeting will be. No setup is ideal, but there are many options from which to choose. The "interior decorating" of meetings is fun and challenging, especially when the furniture is less than ideal. In some cases, furniture can be easily rearranged to create different setups. If you choose to do so, ask participants to help move tables and chairs. That makes them "active" too.

**Conference Tables.** It is best if the table is round or square. This arrangement minimizes the importance of the meeting leader and maximizes the importance of the participants. Each person is equally distant from others and can see the others easily.

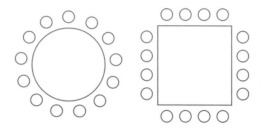

A long rectangular table often creates a sense of formality, especially if the facilitator is at the head of the table. If you only have access to a long, rectangular table, sit in the middle of the wider side.

You can form a conference table arrangement by joining together several smaller tables.

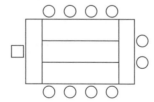

**U-Shaped Arrangements.** A U-shape is an all-purpose setup for a meeting in which there are presentations. With this setup, participants have a reading and writing surface, they can see the facilitator and a visual medium easily, and they are in face-to-face contact with one another. It is also easy to pair up participants, especially when there are two seats per table. The arrangement is ideal for distributing handouts quickly too because you can enter the U and walk to different points with sets of materials. You can set up oblong tables in a squared-off U.

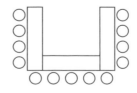

Be sure there is enough perimeter space in the room so that subgroups of three or more participants can pull back from the tables and face one another.

When there are more than sixteen participants, a U can start to resemble a bowling alley or a bridge. It is much better, in this case, to bring all participants in closer contact by seating some participants inside the U, as shown.

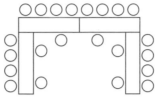

**Circles.**  Simply seating participants in a circle without tables promotes the most direct face-to-face interaction. A circle is ideal for full-group discussion. Assuming there is enough perimeter space, you can ask participants to arrange their chairs quickly into many subgroup arrangements.

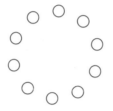

If you want a table surface available for participants, use a peripheral arrangement.

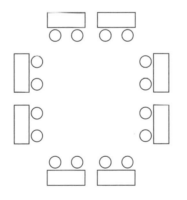

**Team Style.**  In large meetings, grouping circular or oblong tables around the room enables you to promote team interaction. You can place seats fully around the tables for the most intimate setting. If you do, some participants will have to turn their chairs around to face the front of the room to see you, a flip chart, a blackboard, or a screen.

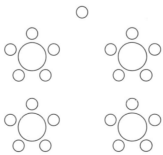

*(Continued)*

**FIGURE 15.2  (*Continued*)**

Or you can place seats around the tables so that no participant has his or her back to the front of the room.

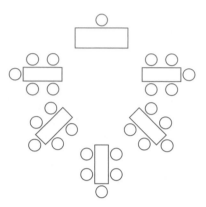

**Group on Group.**  This arrangement allows you to conduct fishbowl discussions. The most typical design is two concentric circles of chairs.

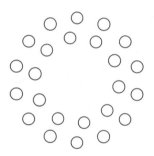

A conference table is ideal for a fishbowl discussion. Designate the participants seated at one side of the table as the discussants. Other participants observe and listen. If you wish, rotate the discussion to a different side of the table.

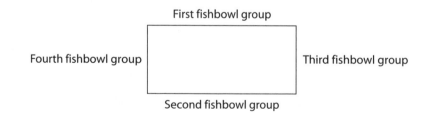

**Breakout Groupings.**  If the room is large enough or if nearby space is available, arrange (in advance when feasible) tables and/or chairs that subgroups can go to for team-based discussion and problem-solving. Keep the break-out settings as far from one another as they can be so that no team is disturbed by the others. However, avoid using breakout spaces that are so far from the main room that the connection to it is difficult to maintain.

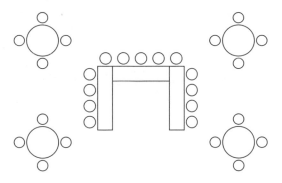

**Paired Seating.**  This arrangement requires seating (with or without tables or desks) in twos. Everyone is together in one group, but discussion partners are already in place.

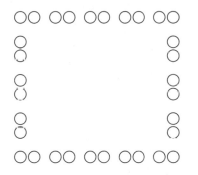

**Chevron.**  A traditional "classroom" setup (rows of tables) is not desirable for active meetings. However, when there are many participants (thirty or more) and only oblong tables are available, it is sometimes necessary to arrange participants classroom style. A repeated V or chevron arrangement, when possible, creates less distance between people and better frontal visibility. It also provides participants with a greater opportunity to see one another than the traditional classroom setup does. In this arrangement, it is best to place aisles off-center.

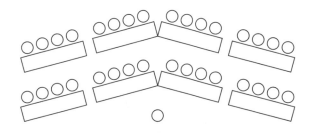

**Traditional Classroom.**  If you have no choice but to use a series of straight rows of desks or tables and chairs, all is not lost. Group chairs in pairs to allow for the use of discussion partners. Try to create an even

*(Continued)*

**FIGURE 15.2  (*Continued*)**

number of rows and enough space between them so that pairs of participants in the odd-number rows can turn their chairs around and create a quartet with the pair seated directly behind them.

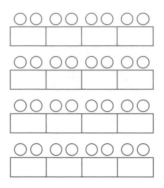

**Auditorium.**  Although an auditorium is a very limiting environment for active meetings, there is still hope. If the seats are movable, place them in an arc to create greater closeness and to allow participants to see one another better.

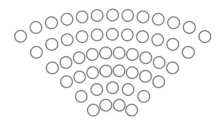

If the seats are fixed, ask participants to seat themselves as close to the center as possible. Be assertive about this request; consider cordoning off sections of the auditorium.

*Remember:*  No matter how large the auditorium and the size of the audience, you can still pair up participants for discussion purposes.

*Silberman, M. (Assisted by Kathy Clark.)* 101 Ways to Make Your Meetings Active: Surefire Ideas to Engage Your Group. *San Francisco: Jossey-Bass/Pfeiffer, 1999.*

working order on the day of the program? Will the equipment be available at the times requested? Who will be responsible for setting up and checking the equipment prior to presentation times? If the organization responsible for the equipment has a good track record for supplying working equipment in a timely manner, then program staff members feel confident that they, too, will have equipment that works and is where it is supposed to be at the requested time. If, on the other hand, staff members have heard that this organization's equipment has not worked properly in the past and/or there have been scheduling difficulties, they may well decide that another company should be brought in to manage the equipment for the

**EXHIBIT 15.3**

**Advantages and Disadvantages of Equipment Arrangements**

| Type of Arrangement | Advantages | Disadvantages |
|---|---|---|
| Supplied by host organization | • The equipment usually is in good working order.<br>• The program coordinator usually has control over scheduling and setting up the equipment. | • On-site staff members may not be available to move and set up equipment if the program is hosted in an off-site facility.<br>• The program coordinator often is responsible for making sure the equipment is set up properly and that it works. |
| Supplied by presenters | • Presenters feel more comfortable using their own equipment.<br>• Presenters are able to supply highly specialized equipment that is not usually available (for example, CRT screens). | • Many presenters do not have easy access to the equipment.<br>• Some presenters do not want or are not physically able to cart their own equipment. |
| Supplied by on-site rental facility | • The equipment is available on-site, and therefore no arrangements need to be made to get the equipment to and from the host organization.<br>• Staff from the on-site facility handle all setting up and taking down of equipment. | • The equipment may not be well maintained and thus may work poorly at best.<br>• The program coordinator loses some control in ensuring the equipment is set up. |
| Supplied by outside rental agency | • The equipment is transported to and from the facility by the rental agency staff, who also usually handle all setting up and taking down of equipment. | • The equipment may not be well maintained and thus may work poorly at best.<br>• The program coordinator loses some control in ensuring the equipment is set up.<br>• The program coordinator or presenter may not be familiar with how the rental equipment operates. |

program. The third task—setting up and checking the equipment—is also assigned beforehand. Will staff from the host organization be responsible for this task, or will it be done by staff from the rental facility or outside agency?

# On-Site Coordination

*SCENARIO*

### Preparing for a Conference

Dominique is busily checking all the last-minute program arrangements for a two-day conference that starts tomorrow. The conference is being held in one of the local hotels. This is the first time he has used these facilities, so he has double-checked all the arrangements, such as accommodations, food, and equipment. Dominique plans to go to the hotel later in the day to meet with the hotel sales director to make sure all is in order. Dominique's major worry at this point is the weather. Rain with heavy fog is forecasted, and this weather could wreak havoc with the arrival of both conference participants and instructional staff. He has been thinking all day about possible contingency plans if one or more of the major presenters is not able to arrive on time and/or the participant numbers are much lower, especially during the first morning of the conference. Dominique has called an emergency meeting of the conference planning committee to help him work out the details of a possible reorganization for at least the first day of the conference. This committee will meet later over dinner.

Most personnel who coordinate education and training programs agree that carrying out a program is very hectic. All of the program arrangements are confirmed, and thought is given to how the program is opened, monitored, and concluded. One person may be responsible for all these tasks (as well as the instructional portion, perhaps) or a number of people may be involved, depending on the complexity of the event. In addition, as illustrated in the above scenario, those doing the program coordination may also need to address unexpected last-minute changes, such as major schedule changes and a reorganization of part or all of the planned program event.

The on-site coordination function is highly visible and can make or break a program. Although most program participants are unaware of or indifferent to what went into *planning* a program, they are usually immediately cognizant of the details related to a program's on-site coordination, and they form opinions about the program based on those details. For example, were the on-site registration procedures easy or difficult? Was all of the signage for meeting rooms and other spaces clear? Did the different sessions start and end on time? Was there adequate parking? Did the coordinator handle the "unexpected changes" well? Because of this visibility, it is important that education and training programs are well coordinated from start to finish, with special attention paid to those details that directly affect the participants.

## Overseeing the Program Arrangements

One of the first tasks of program coordinators is to assure that all program arrangements are completed. This task is done the day before, for the most part, although some things, such as checking on meeting room arrangements and equipment, may have to be done on the day of the program. A

**EXHIBIT 15.4**

# Program Arrangements Checklist

*Meeting rooms* (general sessions, breakouts, social and entertainment areas)

_____ Lighting is adequate.

_____ Ventilation is good.

_____ Temperature is comfortable.

_____ Layout of room (for example, arrangement of table and chairs, placement of equipment) is what was requested.

*Meals, refreshment breaks, social functions*

_____ Menus reflect what was requested.

_____ Special meals have been ordered.

_____ Final count of people for each meal, break, and social function is done.

_____ Exact times for meals and breaks are established.

*Sleeping accommodations*

_____ Reservations are in order for both participants and staff.

_____ Special room accommodations are in place.

_____ Rooms are clean and comfortable.

*ADA requirements*

_____ Parking is accessible.

_____ Ramps are clear; lifts and elevators are working.

_____ Accommodations have been made for special needs.

*Instructors and program staff*

_____ All staff has a clear understanding of their roles.

_____ All presenters, leaders, and instructors are present.

_____ Staff has been assigned to host keynote speakers and other instructors.

_____ Presenters' and other instructional staff's materials are ready.

*Equipment*

_____ An equipment schedule is complete.

_____ The type and quantity of equipment requested is available.

_____ The right equipment is placed in the right rooms.

_____ All equipment is working properly.

_____ Extension cords, backup parts, and equipment are easily accessible.

*Materials*

_____ All handouts and other participant materials are complete.

_____ The number of copies of participant materials is correct.

_____ The materials are arranged in order of use.

_____ Requested instructor materials are all in place (for example, flip charts, marker pens, overheads, masking tape, Post-It notes)

*Transportation*

_____ Transportation needs are provided for (for example, travel to and from the site, parking, vans, or buses among sites).

_____ Responsibility for assisting participants and/or program presenters and instructors with transportation is assigned.

*(Continued)*

---

**EXHIBIT 15.4**

## Program Arrangements Checklist (*Continued*)

---

*Transportation (continued)*

_____ When and for whom transportation is needed is determined.

*Program schedule*

_____ People have been assigned to introduce sessions and activities and have them start on time.

_____ People have been assigned responsibilities for ending the sessions and activities on time.

_____ Methods for keeping on schedule have been agreed upon (for example, open and close doors at start and completion of session).

*On-site registration*

_____ Procedures are clear and customer-friendly.

_____ The physical setup is correct.

_____ The times when registration will be open are posted.

_____ Registration packets are complete.

_____ Name tags are made.

*Message and information center*

_____ The form of the center has been decided (for example, table, bulletin board).

_____ Who will staff the center has been determined.

_____ Ways to up-date program information have been established.

_____ Information on public transportation, restaurants, entertainment, and other attractions in the area are available.

_____ Ways to handle emergency messages and information are clear.

---

program arrangement checklist is given in Exhibit 15.4, showing the items that are finalized prior to the start of the program (Nadler and Nadler, 1987; Munson, 1992; Conner and Waldrop, 1994; Lawson, 1998; Hartwig, 2000).

Not all items on this list are checked for every program, of course. What is important is that on-site coordinators know about and pay attention to those items essential for their specific programs. The key to finalizing the program arrangements is ensuring that everything that *can* be in place *is* in place *prior to the arrival of the participants* (Munson, 1992). There is nothing more frustrating to participants than a learning event that is disorganized before it even begins.

## Opening the Program

It is crucial to create a positive climate for learning at the opening of the education and training event. Knowles spoke often to this point: "I am convinced that what happens in the first hour or so of any learning activity (course, seminar, workshop, institute, tutorial, etc.) largely determines how productive the remaining hours will be" (1980, p. 224). Climate setting starts as soon as the participants, instructors, and presenters arrive. Are they greeted warmly and given a hot or cold drink, or do they wander around trying to figure out where they should be? Is someone available to introduce the participants and instructional staff to one another and provide name tags? Are the people responsible for on-site registration friendly and helpful, or do they seem to be just doing a job? Do staff growl at participants and other staff members who have problems such as incomplete registration materials and inadequate room set-ups, or do they try to be of assistance? Do the coordinating staff seem harried, or do they appear calm and in control?

The way participants are oriented to the actual learning activities at the opening of the program is also very important (Sisco, 1991; Brooks-Harris and Stock-Ward, 1999; and Silberman, 1999). Items included in this orientation process are staff and participant introductions, an explanation of the goals and objectives for the program, clarification of program requirements (such as attendance, outside assignments, instructor and participant expectations), and basic administrative information (for example, start and finish times, contact people for assistance and problems, discussing or generating ground rules or norms for interactions). The orientation can be done formally (perhaps in a session where the sole purpose is orienting participants) or informally (at the opening of the program and/or in individual program sessions). Making the orientation activities active is always a challenge, one that Silberman (1999) provides some very useful ways to tackle (for example, ways to learn names, exercises to wake up or relax a group). The size of the group and the format for learning are two of the major factors that determine how the orientation process is conducted.

For *small and midsize groups* (under 100), the orientation process is usually done with the whole group, whether as a separate session or as a part of opening the program. The staff is introduced to the group first. If there are many staff members, only key personnel, such as the program coordinator and the primary instructional staff members, are introduced at this time. All these introductions are brief and to the point.

If the group is small (20 or fewer), program participants are also introduced or introduce themselves to the whole group. If the number of people is between 21 and 100, the coordinator or instructor usually chooses to divide the group into smaller groups or into triads or dyads for the initial introductions. Although these groupings do not allow the learners to get a snapshot of all the other participants, it does give them the opportunity to become acquainted with at least one or more of their fellow participants. This type of activity is especially important when learners do not know each other or have just a passing acquaintance.

How the actual participant introductions are done in small and midsize groups varies, depending on the goals and objectives of the program and the time allotted for this part of the program. Participants may simply introduce themselves; they may, after an initial conversation with a second participant, introduce each other; and/or they may take part in more elaborate warm-up or icebreaker activities (Bianchi, Butler, and Richey, 1990; Corbett, 1992; Silberman, 1999). What people say or do may be straightforward (such as the sharing of names, occupations, and reasons for attending the program), or include other information about themselves (such as interests, hobbies, expertise they bring to the event). Introductions may also take on different forms when icebreakers or warm-up activities are used. All but the straightforward introductions may also be used to address the program content in some way. For example, participants are asked to share special problems, issues, or questions they hope to have addressed and/or to describe any prior knowledge and experience they have related to the program content. If this sharing is done, instructional staff has to acknowledge which of their ideas will be discussed and which cannot, and recognize their prior knowledge and experience throughout the program. It is a real turn-off to participants if what they have put on the table is ignored.

For *very large groups*, orientation to the program is handled in a number of different ways: whole-group sessions set aside just for orientation, small-group sessions, written and/or computerized information, and individual assistance programs. For example, a major national conference hosts small-group sessions for people attending for the first time, assigns mentors or helpers to first-time attendees, and provides written and/or computerized information systems for all participants. In addition, individual volunteer or paid staff members are placed at key locations to offer help in answering questions and concerns. Two useful information sources for developing orientation activities and creating positive learning climates for large programs are Nadler and Nadler (1987) and Simerly (1990).

The learning format also plays a part in determining what the orientation process is like (and even what content is addressed). For example, if the learning format calls for active involvement of the participants, then this involvement is modeled in the participant introductions. On the other hand, for learning situations that do not call for participant interaction, such as public lectures, participant introductions may not be needed or even appropriate.

## Monitoring the Program

Experienced program planners know that things *do* go wrong while the program is in process (Munson, 1992; Hartwig, 2000). Some of these things, such as a major speaker's illness, are out of the coordinator's control. Other problems are in the coordinator's purview (and can be avoided), such as having insufficient copies of handouts or equipment that does not function. No matter what the source of the problems, the key is to find solutions quickly that allow the program to keep functioning at an optimal level. This need for quick response to problems means that coordinators must continually monitor the program, remain flexible, and at times be highly creative. For example, if a major presenter becomes ill right before the start of a program, either another speaker has to be found or the order and timing of the program have to be rearranged. Either solution calls for fast action on the part of the coordinator and the ability to make sound, but swift, decisions.

Even if the program appears to be running smoothly, it is important that program coordinators continue to monitor the proceedings (Munson, 1992; Conner and Waldrop, 1994). This task includes checking to see that:

▶ All presenters and other staff are present and prepared.

▶ Rooms continue to be arranged, as requested, as sessions change.

▶ Participant concerns and problems are addressed in a timely and courteous manner.

▶ Equipment is available and working.

▶ Food and refreshments are well prepared and delivered on time.

▶ Correct handouts and other resources are available.

▶ Evaluation data are being collected as planned.

▶ Time schedules are being followed by presenters and instructors.

▶ Special services are being delivered.

An additional way to monitor the program is by having participants give evaluative feedback to program staff at designated times during the event. This type of feedback is especially useful for programs longer than one day, when changes in the program's format or content can realistically be made. There are a number of ways this kind of feedback is obtained, including administering short written questionnaires and having the respondents critique the program in small groups.

In an intriguing variation on the small-group approach, program coordinators conduct focus-group interviews with selected participants using semi-structured questions to find out what participants think of the program. The participants' perceptions are then given to program staff so that changes can be made in the program for the next day (Long and Marts, 1981; Berg, 2001). This evaluation process is integrated into the program, rather than just being tacked on at the end of the day. Participants are selected at random to participate and are given an advance invitation requesting their involvement. Because the job of focus-group leaders is critical, they are well versed in the process and willing to record and share all comments, no matter how negative.

The most critical component of the monitoring process, no matter how it is done, is using feedback to make program adjustments in anything from the time schedule to the content of the program. It is the responsibility of program coordinators to ensure that necessary changes are made.

## Concluding the Program

In concluding the program, program coordinators accomplish three tasks. The first task is to ensure that all data required for the evaluation are collected. Depending on the evaluation design, the data collection may be done throughout the program, at the end of the program, or at both times. When participants are asked to give written evaluative comments, it is helpful to offer some kind of incentive for completion. Door prizes, for example, are awarded to participants who complete session evaluations during individual program sessions. A piece of candy or fruit to eat on the way home is given to participants who complete participant reaction forms at the end of the program.

A second task is to give participants recognition for taking part in the program. For some programs, such as recertification classes for continuing medical and other health professionals, this recognition is usually formal, whereas for other types of programs it is informal. One common practice for giving formal recognition is to award certificates (or other written documentation) to all participants who successfully meet certain pre-established minimum requirements. These requirements range from simple attendance to participant demonstration that learning has occurred. A second practice is to give formal academic credit, often in the form of continuing education units, to participants who meet agreed-upon standards. This assignment of credit is set up formally in advance with either an accredited post-secondary institution or a professional association. Other less formal but very effective ways to recognize successful program completion include: giving mementos (such as mugs or t-shirts) to program participants, taking group photos, highlighting participants' involvement via in-house communications or the local press, and hosting informal celebrations.

The third task at the end of a program is to thank both participants and staff for being a part of the program. This thanks is done either at a group session and/or individually, depending on the learning format and what is most appropriate. These thank-yous are personalized (for example, recognizing something unique a staff person has done) and expressed with sincerity.

### Tying Up Loose Ends

The coordinator also ties up all the loose ends, such as picking up extra handouts, returning equipment, and scrutinizing the bills, after the program is completed. When coordinators compile closing checklists prior to the start of programs, they are less likely to miss the details of this step due to tiredness. A sample checklist of tasks to complete after the program follows (Conner and Waldrop, 1994):

_____ Go through facilities and, where necessary, put meeting rooms and other spaces back in order.

_____ Pick up and store extra handout materials.

_____ Make sure all equipment is accounted for and stored away.

_____ Complete all administrative forms.

_____ Reconcile and pay bills.

_____ Conduct a staff debriefing.

_____ Write letters of appreciation to instructional staff and other resource people, including facilities' personnel.

_____ Jot down suggestions for program improvements

In programs where there are a large number of participants, these tasks are shared among a number of people and planned ahead of time. Whether the groups are large or small, no one person should feel like she or he is always stuck with the "clean-up work."

## Chapter Highlights

Handling the logistical end of the program often feels like a thankless task; yet if these chores are not done well, they can negatively affect all aspects of education and training programs. One of the hallmarks of program planners who handle these types of arrangements in an effective and efficient manner is that they understand the importance of keeping track and staying on top of all of the detail work. Eight specific tasks are completed in this component:

◆ Obtain suitable facilities that provide the optimum environment for learning, and arrange for instructional materials and equipment that works.

◆ Make sure facilities meet all Americans with Disabilities Act (ADA) requirements.

◆ Oversee all of the on-site program arrangements (supervise those dealing, for example, with facilities, instructors and other staff members, equipment, program schedules).

- ◆ Create a positive climate for learning from the moment the participants arrive through offering user-friendly registration systems, participant orientations, and introductions.

- ◆ Provide systems for monitoring programs and making sound, quick decisions when program changes are required.

- ◆ Gather data for program evaluations and provide incentives for completing the on-site evaluation processes.

- ◆ Give recognition to program participants (for example, certificates, mugs, celebrations) and thank both staff members and participants for being a part of the program.

- ◆ Tie up all loose ends after the program is completed (such as storing equipment, completing administrative forms, reconciling and paying bills, conducting staff debriefings).

This chapter on coordinating facilities and handling on-site events completes the discussion of each of the 12 components of the Interactive Model of Program Planning. In the final chapter, a review is provided of the Interactive Model, its key components and tasks, and how program planners find the model to be useful.

## Application Exercises

This chapter's Application Exercises focus on coordinating facilities and on-site events. The first assists you in selecting program facilities, while the second helps you in choosing meeting rooms. The third allows you to reflect on program arrangements that were made at a recent event that you either planned or attended, and the fourth addresses creating a positive climate for learning.

## EXERCISE 15.1

## Selecting Program Facilities

1. **Either choose a program you are currently planning or work with someone who is. Using the following checklist, visit at least one possible program facility and evaluate it for its suitability for the program being planned.**

**Checklist for Selecting Facilities**

*Availability of program dates*

_____ Ist choice _____

_____ 2nd choice _____

_____ Other _____

*Location*

_____ Good transportation access
(plane, car, ground transportation)  _____

_____ Participant appeal  _____

_____ Safe and secure (lighting, security staff)  _____

_____ Ease of parking  _____

*Meeting rooms: General sessions, break-out rooms, social and entertainment areas*
(See Exhibit 15.2 for a description of each of these features)

_____ Size  _____

_____ Appearance  _____

_____ Lighting  _____

_____ Décor  _____

_____ Furnishings  _____

_____ Ventilation, heating,
and cooling  _____

_____ Sound projection  _____

_____ Electrical outlets  _____

_____ Computer hookups  _____

*Support services (at same or different facility than where the program will be held)*

_____ On-site meals (catered by same
or different group)  _____

_____ Accommodations  _____

_____ Restaurants  _____

_____ Recreation, fitness facilities  _____

_____ Phones, fax, and internet access  _____

_____ Business center  _____

_____ Equipment services  _____

*(Continued)*

*On-Site transportation (frequency, convenience, cost)*

_____ Public          _____

_____ Private         _____

*Accessibility requirements under Americans with Disabilities Act (ADA)*

_____ Accessible parking spaces        _____

_____ Ramps, lifts          _____

_____ Elevators             _____

_____ Accessible sleeping rooms        _____

_____ Accessible public restrooms      _____

_____ Doorway and corridor width for wheelchairs   _____

_____ Floor surfaces smooth and firm        _____

_____ Lowered public telephones            _____

_____ Telecommunications device for deaf (TDD),
            readable signs with large lettering, Braille,
            or raised symbols                     _____

_____ Sufficient lighting in rooms and corridors   _____

_____ Emergency warnings in multiple delivery methods  _____

*General factors*

_____ Attractions and entertainment in area    _____

_____ Experience in hosting educational programs   _____

_____ Site personnel                        _____

_____ Safety issues                         _____

_____ Medical and emergency services        _____

2.   **Discuss your evaluation with others involved in this program planning process.**

## EXERCISE 15.2

## Choosing Meeting Rooms

1. **No meeting room is perfect. Knowing that, choose from the list below your top seven requirements for a room that is adequate for the education or training program you described in Exercise 15.1.**

   _____ The room has barrier-free access.

   _____ The room is square.

   _____ Window placements and view are not distracting to participants, or there are no windows.

   _____ The chairs are comfortable with good back support, and there is adequate work space available for every participant and instructor.

   _____ The color of the room is cheerful.

   _____ The room is clean and well-maintained.

   _____ The floors are tastefully carpeted.

   _____ The lighting is good.

   _____ There are no sources of glare in the room.

   _____ The temperature of the room can be controlled.

   _____ There is good air circulation.

   _____ There is no background noise that might distract participants.

   _____ The acoustics of the room are good.

   _____ There are plenty of electrical outlets spaced adequately around the room.

   _____ There are convenient computer hookups.

   _____ The room is a good size for the number of participants.

   _____ The room is close to restrooms, vending machines, and other needed conveniences.

   _____ Technologically smart rooms are available.

2. **Compare with two or three others what you checked. Discuss first your areas of differences and then those that were similar. Examine what factors you think entered into the decisions that you each made.**

## EXERCISE 15.3

## Overseeing the Program Arrangements

1. Describe an education or training program you recently attended or coordinated.

2. Reflect on this program you described above using the following chart, and critique the program arrangements that were made. Write "NA" (not applicable) next to those items for which program arrangements were not needed.

| Categories of Items | What Was Good About the Arrangements | What Problems Were There with the Arrangements? | How Could the Arrangements Have Been Improved? |
|---|---|---|---|
| Meeting Rooms | | | |
| Meals, Breaks, and Social Functions | | | |
| Sleep Accommodations | | | |
| ADA Requirements Met | | | |
| Roles of Instructors and Program Staff | | | |
| Equipment | | | |
| Materials | | | |
| Transportation | | | |
| Program Schedule | | | |
| On-Site Registration | | | |
| Message and Information Center | | | |
| Other (Please Specify) | | | |

## EXERCISE 15.4

## Creating a Positive Climate for Learning

1. **Describe a program which you are currently planning or will be planning.**

2. **Using the following chart, indicate how you can create a positive climate for learning for the program you described above.**

| Part of Programs | How would you handle each item to help create a positive climate for learning? |
| --- | --- |
| Registration | |
| Introduction of staff | |
| Introduction of participants | |
| Introduction of the program | |
| Explanations of program requirements | |
| Clarification of staff and participant expectations | |
| Discussion or generation of ground rules or norms for interaction | |
| Other (please specify) | |

3. **Discuss your ideas with two or three other people. Do they view your ideas as helpful? What other suggestions do they have?**

# Chapter 16

# Revisiting the Interactive Model of Program Planning

Swimming in the ocean—yes, it's a lot like planning programs for adults. Sometimes planners are swimming with the sharks, at other times with the dolphins. Swimming with either sharks or dolphins has challenges and surprises, some which fit each of their images while others do not. Sharks, for example, although they may appear scary, are quite harmless and may even offer protection. In other cases they are "deadly" and literally out to get whoever crosses their path. So, too, it is with the dolphins. Dolphins often frolic with swimmers near the beach, while at other times beckon swimmers to swim with them to deeper and sometimes dangerous waters.

Although swimming or just playing in the ocean is fun, there also are times when even the most ardent water lovers just want to lie on the beach, and relax or perhaps read. They are soothed by the lapping waves and warmed by the sun. Beach lovers also like to walk along the surf and find interesting items that wash up on shore. They are excited when they come across colorful shells, crabs darting here and there, or see schools of fish that just happen by. So, too, it is with program planners. They also need to get out in the water, no matter how calm or rough, take time to listen to and feel what is around them, and discover new things, no matter how small, about their practice as planners and the environments in which they work.

This book presents an opportunity for educators and trainers to be on the beach and allows them to reflect on their practice as planners, reinforce or gain new knowledge and skills, and refine or try out these ideas and skills. This chapter provides practitioners a summary and a checklist of what they have read and/or experienced as a result of using and reflecting on the materials in this book. First, a brief overview of the Interactive Model of Program Planning is given. Highlighted in this overview are three key factors that make this model a viable resource: the practicality and usefulness as a technical description of the planning process, the emphasis on people being the heart of this process, and the importance of context as a centering point for action. A detailed checklist of the major tasks program planners do to tackle each component of the Interactive Model, which can be shared with others, is then offered as a guide for practice. The chapter concludes with a short personal reflection from the author on the writing of this second edition of *Planning Programs for Adult Learners*.

## Reviewing the Model

The Interactive Model of Program Planning provides practical descriptions of and ways that planners engage in the complex and often befuddling process of organizing education and training programs for adults. Composed of twelve components, as pictured in Figure 16.1, this model takes into account the major tasks that program planners undertake, which are often seen as technical in nature. In other words, these tasks comprise the knowledge and skills that planners use in their everyday planning activities.

Although the Interactive Model is technical, being able to use it effectively calls for planners to have finely tuned people skills, as it is people who

**FIGURE 16.1**

**Interactive Model of Program Planning**

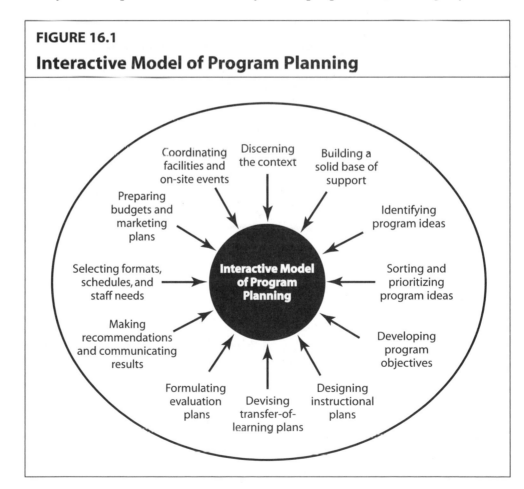

plan programs. Some of the interactions among planners and/or other stakeholders are collaborative; others are cordial, but distant; and still others are downright hostile. Interactions that are especially tricky include times when those responsible for planning program do not follow through on their tasks, use the planning process for their own ends, or covertly try to sabotage parts of the planning and/or delivery of education and training programs.

In addition to the importance of the people aspects of planning, using the Interactive Model requires program planners to acknowledge the contextual nature of the planning process, that is, the organizational and wider environmental factors that influence the planning process, in both positive and negative ways. For example, organizational leaders may either strongly endorse professional development as a critical component of a healthy organization and put funds into these programs, or just give "lip service" to the idea. Likewise the wider social, economic, and political climate within which planners work may overtly encourage social change through education, or covertly and even openly block any education or training programs that have a chance of bringing about change in social norms and actions. Again, planners have a better chance of fostering social change when the wider community is with them in both spirit and resource support than if they are not.

Taking into account the people and contextual factors in the planning process demands that program planners be flexible in their practice. Being flexible means that planners can choose to use the various components and tasks of the model differently depending on their planning situations. In many programs for adults, for example, learning transfer is critical to whether the program outcomes are achieved, like changes in job practices, learning to deal with a major life change, or alleviating the AIDS crisis in affected African countries. In other programs, like listening to public radio or attending a concert, no specific transfer activities are necessary. A short description of the major tasks for each component of the model is presented in the next section through a detailed checklist for planning.

## Tasks Within Each Component of the Interactive Model

The major tasks within each component of the Interactive Model of Program Planning offer a framework for making decisions about the what, who, when, where, and why of the program planning process. As emphasized throughout the book, not all of the components and therefore not all of the tasks, given in Exhibit 16.1, are addressed in developing every program. Rather, planners choose those components and tasks that are critical to people with whom they work and their specific planning situations.

**EXHIBIT 16.1**

# A Checklist for Planning Programs

### Discerning the Context

— Be knowledgeable about the people, the organization, and the wider environmental contextual factors that affect decisions made throughout the planning process.

— Be well-informed about the issue of power that is present in most planning situations and the influences that power relationships have in the planning process.

— Cultivate and/or enhance negotiation skills required to navigate situations in which power is a central issue. Negotiation requires that planners have finely tuned people skills, are able to listen to multiple voices, are good analytical thinkers, are willing to communicate effectively through a variety of means, have excellent group facilitation skills, understand what taking risks means, and have the ability to operate effectively within relationships of power.

— Ensure that beliefs and actions being displayed in one's practice are ethical. Being reflective in practice and stating personal, unit, and organizational beliefs related to planning programs for adults are essential in being consistently ethical in practice.

— Know and be able to access sources of information about the context of the planning situation (for example, written documents, technology-based sources, professional and trade associations, group meetings and gatherings, and interactions with individuals).

### Building a Solid Base of Support

— Ensure support from key constituent groups including: current and potential learners, all levels of organizational personnel, and other stakeholders through such mechanisms as active participation in planning and conducting education and training activities, transfer-of-learning strategies, and formal and ad hoc group and board work.

— Cultivate continuous organizational support through establishing structural processes that work (for example, mission and goals statements, standard operating procedures and policies, authority unit has over programs). The choice of these processes depends primarily on the centrality of the education or training function.

— Promote an organizational culture in which formal, job-embedded, self-directed learning activities and continuous learning are valued.

— Obtain and maintain support from the wider community through formal and ad hoc groups and boards, where the following key underlying assumptions are in place: ideas and observations from members are heard and used, democratic planning is fostered, and collaborative interaction is the operative norm.

— Build and sustain collaborative partnerships with other organizations and groups that provide different vehicles for program planning and delivery that are in the best interests of all involved parties.

### Identifying Program Ideas

— Decide what sources to use in identifying ideas for education and training programs (for example, current or potential program participants, employers, organizational and community leaders, life events and personal issues, government regulations and legislative mandates, community and societal problems).

— Generate ideas through a variety of techniques. Example of the most-often used techniques include questionnaires, interviews, observations, group sessions, job analysis, review of print and

*(Continued)*

**EXHIBIT 16.1** (*Continued*)

computer-based materials, social indicators, and conversations with colleagues. Remain open to gathering program ideas using a wide variety of techniques that may not have been predetermined or even thought about.

— Be aware that highly structured needs assessments are not the only way to identify ideas for education and training programs. In reality generating program ideas in this manner is not often used. Rather, less formal and informal ways are employed more than highly structured processes.

— Ensure you can defend why a highly structured needs assessment is warranted and choose and or/develop a model for conducting this assessment that is appropriate to the situation.

— Consider contextual issues that affect or might affect how ideas for programs are generated.

— Understand that in most planning situations program planners cannot use all of the program ideas that have been identified, and therefore planners usually have to sort and prioritize these ideas.

### Sorting and Prioritizing Program Ideas

— Be knowledgeable about how priority ideas are defined, and what the typical issues and problems are that call for interventions, other than education and training programs.

— Analyze and sort the program ideas into two piles—those appropriate for educational activities and those that require alternative interventions.

— Select people who will do the actual prioritizing process. These may or may not be the same individuals who analyzed and sorted the original program ideas.

— Be well-informed about two approaches for prioritizing ideas for education and training programs: quantitative and qualitative.

— Use systematic methods for prioritizing program ideas. The critical ingredient in this process is the establishment of clear criteria for making decisions about each of the ideas.

— Be familiar with alternative interventions and how they are selected and implemented. Work on creating and nurturing networks of people who will listen and act when these alternative interventions are required.

### Developing Program Objectives

— Write program objectives that reflect what participants will learn, the resulting changes from that learning, and the operational aspects of the program. The program objectives related to participant learning are often then translated into learning objectives (see Chapter Nine).

— Ensure that both measurable and nonmeasurable program outcomes, as appropriate, are included.

— Check to see whether the program objectives are written clearly enough so they can be understood by all parties involved (for example, participants, sponsoring organizations).

— Use the program objectives as an internal consistency and "do-ability" checkpoint (to determine, for example, whether the instructional, transfer-of-learning, and evaluation plans match the objectives).

— Negotiate changes in program objectives, as needed, among the parties involved with the planning process.

### Designing Instructional Plans

— Develop clear and understandable learning objectives for each instructional session and ensure they match the proposed learning outcomes (acquiring new knowledge, enhancing cognitive and psychomotor skills, problem-finding and -solving capacities, and changing attitudes, beliefs, values, and/or feelings).

— Select and organize the content based on what participants "must learn." This "must learn" content is grounded in the learning objectives. Content that supplements the essential material should be included only if time allows. Be cognizant there is no best way to select and sequence the content.

— Choose instructional techniques that match the focus of the proposed learning outcomes, the instructor is capable of using, and that take into account the backgrounds and experiences of the learners and the learning context (for example, lectures, case studies, Web-based instruction, story-telling, games, or metaphor analysis).

— Select and/or develop instructional resources that enhance the learning effort (for example, "real things," printed materials, visual aids, audio- and video-based materials, computer-based resources, or interactive technologies).

— Choose an assessment component for each instructional segment that improves participants' learning and ascertains whether the instructional event actually produced the desired result.

— Use instructional assessment data in formative and summative ways for both the instructional aspects of the program as well as the program as a whole.

— Prepare clear and concise instructional plans as roadmaps that can assist instructors to stay focused as they move through the instructional process.

— Make the instructional process work by ensuring instructors know their content, are competent learning facilitators, care about learners, use instructional and assessment techniques appropriately and skillfully, and are well-prepared for each instructional event.

### Devising Transfer-of-Learning Plans

— Be knowledgeable about the major factors that influence transfer of learning (for example, program participants, program design and execution, program content, changes required to apply the learning, organizational context, and community and societal forces).

— Decide when the transfer-of-learning strategies should be employed (before, during, and/or after the formal program).

— Determine the key players who should be a part of the transfer-of-learning process (for example, participants, program planning staff, instructors, work supervisors, community leaders).

— Teach learners, supervisors, and other interested parties about transfer-of-learning strategies and techniques so they know what strategies and techniques are available and can assist in selecting appropriate ones to use in the transfer process.

— Choose, with the assistance of learners, instructors, and others, transfer strategies that are the most useful in assisting participants to apply what they have learned (for example, involving learners, supervisors, community leaders, and other stakeholders in planning the transfer process; taking into account contextual and cultural differences; ascertaining the contextual aspects of where the learning is to be applied; providing participants with opportunities to develop applications plans; and negotiating and changing what the learning transfer can realistically encompass in cooperation with all stakeholders).

— Select and/or assist learners and others to opt for transfer-of-learning techniques that are the most useful to them in applying what they have learned (mentoring, peer coaching, support groups, online discussions, reflective practice, transfer teams).

— Negotiate and change the content, skills, and/or beliefs that are to be transferred, based on barriers and enhancers to learning transfer in the application site.

### Formulating Evaluation Plans

— Develop, as warranted, systematic program evaluation procedures.

— Use informal and unplanned evaluation opportunities to collect formative and summative evaluation data (for example, observing participant behavior during a program, listening to learners' comments during break times, and checking to see if participants can apply what they have learned in their specific situations).

*(Continued)*

**EXHIBIT 16.1** *(Continued)*

— Specify the evaluation approach or approaches to be used (for example, objectives-based, accountability planner, levels of evaluation, quasi-legal).

— Determine how evaluation data are to be collected (for example, observations, questionnaires, product reviews) and/or if some evaluation data already exist.

— Think through how the data are to be analyzed, including how to integrate the data that were collected through any informal evaluation processes.

— Describe how judgments are made about the program, using predetermined and/or emergent evaluation criteria for program success.

*Making Recommendations and Communicating Results*

— Examine program successes and failures and formulate recommendations to revise or eliminate current programs and/or plan new programs.

— Tell the story well through program reports that are framed by the following elements: the program function, scope, audience, content, structure and style, and format.

— Select the format for the report carefully (for example, journalistic-style reports, briefing sessions, posters, product displays, electronic communication) so the audiences are receptive and willing to "listen" and/or act on the information presented.

— Time the release of the report when the audience is most likely to review it.

— Follow up as needed with appropriate individuals and groups to clarify any questions or concerns about the program, to make sure the information has been heard, and to provide opportunities for comments on proposed program changes.

*Selecting Formats, Schedules, and Staff*

— Choose the most appropriate format or combination of formats for the learning activity (for example, individual, small-group [primarily face-to-face], large-group [face-to-face], distance-learning, or community-learning formats).

— Take into account the desire to build a community of learners as part of the goals and objectives of the program.

— Devise a program schedule that fits the format(s) chosen, the specific activities being planned, and the participants' personal and/or job commitments.

— Identify staff requirements (that is, program designers and managers, program coordinators, instructors and facilitators, and program evaluators).

— Determine whether internal staff (paid or volunteer) will plan and conduct the program and/or whether external consultants are required.

— Make careful choices about instructors and/or learning facilitators for the various activities to ensure that such areas as content expertise, competence in teaching adults, and ability to respond effectively to the background and experiences of the learners are evident.

*Preparing Budgets and Marketing Plans*

— Estimate the expenses for the program, including costs for the development, delivery, and evaluation of the program (for example, costs for staff salaries, participant expenses, facilities, instructional materials, and transfer-of-learning strategies).

— Determine how the program is financed (for example, by participant fees, organizational subsidy, government funding), and estimate the program income.

— Manage the program budget, and have accurate budget records.

— Develop contingency budget plans for programs that are scaled back or cancelled.

— Pay the bills for the program by managing the income side of the budget.

— Build and maintain program credibility, success, and market niches when marketing education and training programs. Also demonstrate being participant- or customer-oriented.
— Conduct a target audience analysis to help determine the background and experiences of the potential audience as one of the starting places for the marketing plan.
— Use already existing contextual information or generate it to help frame the marketing plan.
— Select and prepare promotional materials for the program (such as brochures, website materials, emails, newsletter copy, flyers) that "tell the story well" of the what (the product), the cost, and the where of the program.
— Prepare a targeted and lively promotional campaign, paying careful attention to the target audience, the different contexts of the potential participants, the type of promotional materials to use, the time frame, and the cost.
— Ascertain and strengthen your promotional assets and capabilities.

***Coordinating Facilities and On-Site Events***
— Obtain suitable facilities that provide an optimum environment for learning and arrange for instructional materials and equipment that works.
— Make sure facilities meet all Americans with Disabilities Act (ADA) requirements.
— Oversee all of the on-site program arrangements (those dealing, for example, with facilities, instructors and other staff members, equipment, program schedules).
— Create a positive climate for learning from the moment the participants arrive, through offering user-friendly registration systems, participant orientations, and introductions.
— Provide systems for monitoring programs and making sound, quick decisions when program changes are required.
— Gather data for program evaluations and provide incentives for completing the on-site evaluation processes.
— Give recognition to program participants (for example, certificates, mugs, celebrations), and thank both staff members and participants for being a part of the program.
— Tie up all loose ends after the program is completed (such as storing equipment, completing administrative forms, reconciling and paying bills, conducting staff debriefings).

Program planners use this checklist differently, depending primarily on their level of experience with planning education and training programs for adults and the planning context. Novice planners are often overwhelmed by all of the details in the checklist and wonder where they should start and how many of these tasks they can realistically take on with their limited experience and knowledge base. One strategy novice planners find helpful in using the checklist is to work collaboratively, either in actually planning programs with and/or in a mentoring or coaching relationship with more experienced planners. These experienced planners help novice planners select which components and tasks to direct their attention to and why, and how the program context plays a part in this section. A second strategy that novice planners find useful is to address at first each component, and the tasks within those components, in an almost linear fashion.

They start with the first component and work their way through the Interactive Model from start to finish, and actually do only the tasks they can handle and that appear to be essential to their specific planning situation. Finally, novice planners use the application exercises to help them frame and reflect on their practice.

More experienced planners use different strategies in employing the checklist as a planning tool. Some planners use the checklist as a job aid for themselves and/or their planning teams to keep track of which tasks are important for a particular planning process. In utilizing the checklist with planning groups, group members collectively decide on which tasks are essential, who will do each task, and when that task has to be completed to keep the planning process running as smoothly as possible.

Another strategy experienced planners employ while using the checklist is to make sure they capture, while in the throes of the planning process, the components and tasks that are new to them, and therefore not currently a routine part of their practice. Using the many figures and exhibits given throughout the book that describe these tasks in a concise format and that provide examples of what these tasks look like in practice is another way planners gain knowledge and skills in utilizing these new tasks. In addition, the Application Exercises at the end of each chapter provide a structured format for practicing and reflecting on each of the major tasks.

Finally, experienced planners use the checklist to educate others who are new or unfamiliar with planning education and training programs about the complexities of this process. For example, they may refer to and/or give copies of the checklist to stakeholders who have a commitment to educating adults about specific topics, but have no idea how much time and effort this process actually entails, especially for endeavors that require major changes in individuals, organizations, and/or the wider community.

## Closing Reflections

In writing this second edition of *Planning Programs for Adult Learners*, I found myself both updating components and tasks of the initial version of the Interactive Model of Program Planning, and either adding new or describing differently critical components of the planning process, such as discerning the context, identifying program ideas, and devising transfer-of-learning plans.

I was challenged tremendously by taking into account the new knowledge we have about adult learners, the importance of context in planning, the influence technology has on both the planning and delivery of programs, and the global and diverse nature of our world. These four themes changed my views about the overall planning process, what the critical components and tasks are within that process, and the assumptions upon which the Interactive Model is grounded. For example, knowing where learning takes place, such as in classrooms, via Web-based instruction, or embedded in adults' everyday life roles, is as crucial to adult learning as the content being taught. This knowledge totally changed my thinking about the importance of discerning the context for planning. Without this contextual knowledge and how to use that knowledge, program planners are less able and often cannot realistically plan education and training programs that provide opportunities for adults to apply what they have learned in their own spheres of life. That is, these learners are unable to transfer what they have learned to make desired or needed changes in themselves, in the groups and organizations within which they function, and/or the wider communities in which they live.

In closing, my hope is that this second edition of *Planning Programs for Adult Learners* is as helpful to those who read and use it in planning education and training programs as it has been to me in re-conceptualizing the planning process. In addition, I will consider this rethinking of the Interactive Model of Program Planning successful only if practitioners, myself included, are actually able to use, critique, and mold the model in a way that is useful to them.

# References

Alessi, S. M., and Trollip, S. R. (2001). *Multimedia for Learning: Methods and Development.* (3rd ed.) Boston, Mass.: Allyn & Bacon.

American Cancer Society (no date). "You Are Not Alone. We Can Help . . ." Greeley, Colo.: Weld County Unit, Northeastern Colorado.

Angelo, T. A., and Cross, K. P. (1993). *Classroom Assessment Techniques: A Handbook for College Teachers.* (2nd ed.) San Francisco: Jossey-Bass.

Apps, J. W. (1988). *Higher Education in a Learning Society: Meeting New Demands for Education and Training.* San Francisco: Jossey-Bass.

Apps, J. W. (1991). *Mastering the Teaching of Adults.* Malabar, Fla.: Krieger.

Apps, J. W. (1996). *Teaching from the Heart.* Malabar, Fla.: Krieger.

Aragon, S. R., and Hatcher, T. (Eds.) (2001). "Ethics and Integrity in HRD: Case Studies in Research and Practice." *Advances in Human Resource Development, 3*(1).

Archie-Booker, D. E., Cervero, R. M., and Langone, C. A. (1999). "The Politics of Planning Culturally Relevant AIDS Prevention Education for African-American Women." *Adult Educator Quarterly, 49*(4), pp. 163–175.

Athanasou, J. (1995). "Issues in the Evaluation of Adult Education." In G. Foley (Ed.), *Understanding Adult Education and Training.* St. Leonards, New South Wales, Australia: Allen and Unwin.

Backus, D., and others (2000). "What Can I Do? Voices of Advocacy." *Journal of Staff Development, 21*(3), pp. 24–36.

Baldwin, T. T., and Ford, J. K. (1988). "Transfer of Training: A Review and Directions for Future Research." *Personnel Psychology, 41,* pp. 63–105.

Baldwin, T. T., Ford, J. K., and Naquin, S. S. (2000). "Managing Transfer Before Learning Begins: Enhancing the Motivation to Improve Work Through Learning." In L. F. Holton III, T. T. Baldwin, and S. S. Naquin (Eds.), *Managing and Changing Learning Transfer Systems.* Advances in Developing Human

Resources, no. 8. Baton Rouge, La.: Academy of Human Resource Development and San Francisco: Berrett-Koehler Communications.

Bates, A. W. (Tony) (2000). *Managing Technological Change: Strategies for University and College Leaders.* San Francisco: Jossey-Bass.

Bates, R. A. (1996). "Popular Theatre: A Useful Process for Adult Educators." *Adult Education Quarterly, 46*(4), pp. 224–236.

Bellman, G. M. (1993). "Trimming Your Waste Line." *Training and Development Journal, 47*(3), pp. 28–31.

Bennett, J. B., Lehman, W.E.K., and Forst, J. K. (1999). "Change, Transfer Climate, and Customer Orientation: A Contextual Model and Analysis of Change-Driven Training." *Group and Organizational Management, 24*(2), pp. 188–216.

Berg, B. L. (2001). *Qualitative Research Methods for the Social Sciences.* (4th ed.) Boston: Allyn & Bacon.

Bernhardt, V. L. (2000). "Intersections: New Routes Open When One Type of Data Crosses Another." *Journal of Staff Development, 21*(1), pp. 33–36.

Bianchi, S., Butler, J., and Richey, D. (1990). *Warmups for Meeting Leaders.* San Diego: University Associates.

Birkenholz, R. J. (1999). *Effective Adult Learning.* Danville, Ill.: Interstate Publishers.

Blankespoor, H. D. (1997). "Classroom Atmosphere. A Personal Inventory." In J. K. Roth (Ed.), *Inspiring Teaching: Carnegie Professors of the Year Speak.* Bolton, Mass.: Anker.

Blomberg, R. (1989). "Cost-Benefit Analysis of Employee Training: A Literature Review." *Adult Education Quarterly, 39*(2), pp. 89–98.

Bloom, B. (1956). *Taxonomy of Educational Objectives: The Classification of Educational Goals.* New York: McKay.

Bolman, L. G., and Deal, T. E. (1997). *Reframing Organizations: Artistry, Choice, and Leadership.* (2nd ed.) San Francisco: Jossey-Bass.

Boulmetis, J., and Dutwin, P. (2000). *The ABCs of Evaluation: Timeless Techniques for Program and Project Managers.* San Francisco: Jossey-Bass.

Boyle, P. G. (1981). *Planning Better Programs.* New York: McGraw-Hill.

Bradley, M. K., Kallick, B. O., and Regan, H. B. (1991). *The Staff Development Manager.* Needham Heights, Mass.: Allyn & Bacon.

Bridges, W. (1991). *Managing Transitions: Making the Most of Change.* Cambridge, Mass.: Perseus Books.

Brinkerhoff, R. O., and Montesino, M. U. (1995). "Partnerships for Training Transfer: Lessons from a Corporate Study." *Human Resource Development Quarterly, 6*(3), pp. 263–274.

Broad, M. L. (2000). "Managing the Organizational Learning Transfer System." In L. F. Holton III, T. T. Baldwin, and S. S. Naquin (Eds.), *Managing and Changing*

*Learning Transfer Systems.* Advances in Developing Human Resources, no. 8. Baton Rouge, La.: Academy of Human Resource Development and San Francisco: Berrett-Koehler Communications.

Broad, M. L., and Newstrom, J. M. (1992). *Transfer of Training.* Reading, Mass.: Addison-Wesley.

Brockett, R. G. (Ed.) (1988). *Ethical Issues in Adult Education.* New York: Teachers College Press.

Brookfield, S. D. (1986). *Understanding and Facilitating Adult Learning: A Comprehensive Analysis of Principles and Effective Practices.* San Francisco: Jossey-Bass.

Brookfield, S. D. (1990). *The Skillful Teacher: On Technique, Trust, and Responsiveness in the Classroom.* San Francisco: Jossey-Bass.

Brookfield, S. D. (1992). "Giving Helpful Evaluations to Learners." *Adult Learning,* 3(8), pp. 22–24.

Brookfield, S. D., and Preskill, S. (1999). *Discussion as a Way of Teaching: Tools and Techniques for Democratic Classrooms.* San Francisco: Jossey-Bass.

Brooks-Harris, J. E., and Stock-Ward, S. R. (1999). *Workshops: Designing and Facilitating Experiential Learning.* Thousand Oaks, Calif.: Sage.

Buckley, F. J. (2000). *Team Teaching: What, Why, and How?* Thousand Oaks, Calif.: Corwin.

Burge, E. J. (2000). *The Strategic Use of Learning Technologies.* New Directions for Adult and Continuing Education, no. 88. San Francisco: Jossey-Bass.

Caffarella, R. S. (1985). "A Checklist for Planning Successful Training Programs." *Training and Development Journal,* 39(3), pp. 81–83.

Caffarella, R. S. (1988). *Program Development and Evaluation Resource Book for Trainers.* New York: Wiley.

Caffarella, R. S. (1992). *Psychosocial Development of Women: Linkages to Teaching and Leadership in Adult Education.* Columbus, Ohio: ERIC Clearinghouse on Adult, Career, and Vocational Education.

Caffarella, R. S. (1993). "Facilitating Self-Directed Learning as a Staff Development Option." *Journal of Staff Development,* 14(2), pp. 30–34.

Caffarella, R. S. (1994). "Characteristics of Adult Learners and Foundations of Experiential Learning." In L. Jackson and R. S. Caffarella (Eds.), *Experiential Learning: A New Approach.* New Directions for Adult and Continuing Education, no. 62. San Francisco: Jossey-Bass.

Caffarella, R. S. (1998–1999). "Planning Programs for Adult Learners: An Interactive Approach." *Adult Learning,* Winter, pp. 27–29.

Caffarella, R. S., and Merriam, S. B. (2000). "Linking the Individual Learner to the Context of Adult Learning." In A. L. Wilson and E. R. Hayes (Eds.), *Handbook of Adult and Continuing Education.* San Francisco: Jossey-Bass.

Cahoon, B. (Ed.) (1998). *Adult Learning and the Internet.* New Directions for Adult and Continuing Education, no. 78. San Francisco: Jossey-Bass.

Cannon-Bowers, J., Salas, E., and Hilham, L. M. (2000). "The Transfer of Team Training: Propositions and Preliminary Guidance." In L. F. Holton III, T. T. Baldwin, and S. S. Naquin (Eds.), *Managing and Changing Learning Transfer Systems.* Advances in Developing Human Resources, no. 8. Baton Rouge, La.: Academy of Human Resource Development and San Francisco: Berrett Koehler Communications.

Carson, C. R. (1989). "Choosing the Best Locations for Continuing Education Programs." In R. G. Simerly and Associates, *Handbook of Marketing for Continuing Education.* San Francisco: Jossey-Bass.

Cervero, R. M. (1988). *Effective Continuing Education for Professionals.* San Francisco: Jossey-Bass.

Cervero, R. M., and Wilson, A. L. (1991). "Perspectives on Program Planning in Adult Education." Proceedings of the 32nd Annual Adult Education Research Conference, University of Oklahoma, Stillwater, Okla .

Cervero, R. M., and Wilson, A. L. (1994). *Planning Responsibility for Adult Education: A Guide to Negotiating Power and Interests.* San Francisco: Jossey-Bass.

Cervero, R. M., and Wilson, A. L. (Eds.) (1996). *What Really Matters in Program Planning.* New Directions for Adult and Continuing Education, no. 69. San Francisco: Jossey-Bass.

Cervero, R. M., and Wilson, A. L. (1998). "Working the Planning Table: The Political Practice of Adult Education." *Studies in Continuing Education*, 20(1), pp. 5–21.

Cervero, R. M., and Wilson, A. L. (1999). "Beyond Learner-Centered Practice: Adult Education, Power, and Society." *CJSAE/RCEEA*, 13(1), pp. 27–38.

Cervero, R. M., Wilson, A. L., and Associates. (2001). *Power in Practice: Adult Education and the Struggle for Knowledge and Power in Society.* San Francisco: Jossey-Bass.

Champion, R. (2000). "Got a Minute? A Stairwell Talk Can Turn Evaluation into Everyday Business." *Journal of Staff Development*, 21(3), pp. 57–60.

Clark, M. C., and Caffarella, R. S. (Eds.) (1999). *An Update on Adult Development Theory: New Ways of Thinking About the Life Course.* New Directions for Adult and Continuing Education, no. 84. San Francisco: Jossey-Bass.

Collison, G., Elbaum, B., Haavind, S., and Tinker, R. (2000). *Facilitating Online Learning: Effective Strategies for Moderators.* Madison, Wis.: Atwood.

Conner, M. E., and Waldrop, K. (1994). *Program Management: Managing Deadlines, Details, Activities, and People. JERITT Monograph Five.* Michigan State University, East Lansing, Mich.: The Judicial Education Reference, Information and Technical Service.

Corbett, A. H. (1992). "Give Participants Responsibility for Learning: Techniques for Opening a Workshop." *Journal of Staff Development*, 13(1), pp. 40–42.

Craig, R. L. (Ed.) (1996). *The ASTD Training and Development Handbook. A Guide to Human Resource Development.* (4th ed.) New York: McGraw-Hill.

Craven, R. F., and DuHamel, R. F. (2000). "Marketing Realities in Continuing Professional Education." In V. W. Mott and B. J. Daley (Eds.), *Charting a Course for Continuing Professional Education: Reframing Our Practice.* New Directions for Adult and Continuing Education, no. 86. San Francisco: Jossey-Bass.

Creswell, J. W. (1994). *Research Design: Qualitative and Quantitative Approaches.* Thousand Oaks, Calif.: Sage Publications.

Daley, B. J., and Mott, V. W. (2000). "Continuing Professional Education: From Vision to Reality." In V. W. Mott and B. J. Daley (Eds.), *Charting a Course for Continuing Professional Education: Reframing our Practice.* New Directions for Adult and Continuing Education, no 86. San Francisco: Jossey-Bass.

Daloz, L. A. (1999). *Mentor: Guiding the Journey of Adult Learners.* San Francisco: Jossey-Bass.

Daloz, L. A., Keen, C. H., Keen, J. P., and Parks, S. D. (1996). *Common Fire: Lives of Commitment in a Complex World.* Boston: Beacon Press.

Darkenwald, G. G., and Merriam, S. B. (1982). *Adult Education: Foundations of Practice.* New York: HarperCollins.

Davis, L. N., and McCallon, E. (1974). *Planning, Conducting, Evaluating Workshops.* Austin, Tex.: Learning Concepts.

Denzin, N. K., and Lincoln, Y. S. (Eds.) (2000). *Handbook of Qualitative Research.* (2nd ed.) Thousand Oaks, Calif.: Sage.

Deshler, D. (1998). "Measurement and Appraisal of Program Success." In P. Cookson (Ed.), *Program Planning for the Training and Continuing Education of Adults.* Malabar, Fla.: Krieger.

Diamond, R. M. (1998). *Designing and Assessing Courses and Curricula.* San Francisco: Jossey-Bass.

DiBella, A. J., and Nevis, E. C. (1998). *How Organizations Learn: An Integrated Strategy for Building Learning Capacity.* San Francisco: Jossey-Bass.

Dick, W., Carey, L., and Carey, J. O. (2001). *The Systematic Design of Instruction.* (5th ed.) New York: Longman.

Dietz, M. E. (1999). " Portfolios." *Journal of Staff Development*, 20(3), pp. 45–46.

Dirkx, J. M., and Prenger, S. M. (1997). *A Guide for Planning and Implementing Instruction for Adults.* San Francisco: Jossey-Bass.

Dixon, N. M. (1997). "The Hallways of Learning." *Organizational Dynamics*, 25(4), pp. 23–34.

Dodek, P. M., and Ottoson, J. M. (1996). "Implementation Link Between Clinical Practice Guidelines and Continuing Medical Education." *The Journal of Continuing Education in the Health Professions*, 16, pp. 82–93.

Donaldson, J. F., and Kozoll, C. E. (1999). *Collaborative Program Planning: Principles, Practices, and Strategies.* Malabar, Fla.: Krieger.

Driscoll, M. (1998). *Web-Based Training: Using Technology to Design Adult Learning Experiences.* San Francisco: Jossey-Bass/Pfeiffer.

DuFour, R. P. (1991). *The Principal as Staff Developer.* Bloomington, Ind.: National Educational Service.

English, L. M., and Gillen, M. A. (Eds.) (2000). *Addressing the Spiritual Dimensions of Adult Learning: What Educators Can Do.* New Directions for Adult and Continuing Education, no. 85. San Francisco: Jossey-Bass.

Ericksen, C. G. (1994). "Developing and Managing Adult Education Budgets." In P. Mulcrone (Ed.), *Current Perspectives on Administration of Adult Education Programs.* New Directions for Adult and Continuing Education, no. 60. San Francisco: Jossey-Bass.

Ewert, D. M., and Grace, K. A. (2000). "Adult Education for Community Action." In A. L. Wilson and E. R. Hayes (Eds.), *Handbook of Adult and Continuing Education.* San Francisco: Jossey-Bass.

Farlow, H. (1979). *Publicizing and Promoting Programs.* New York: McGraw-Hill.

Farquharson, A. (1995). *Teaching in Practice: How Professionals Can Work Effectively with Clients, Patients, and Colleagues.* San Francisco: Jossey-Bass.

Finkel, C. L. (1996). "Meeting Facilities." In R. L. Craig (Ed.), *The ASTD Training and Development Handbook: A Guide to Human Resource Development.* New York: McGraw-Hill.

Fleming, J. A. (Ed.) (1997). *New Perspectives on Designing and Implementing Effective Workshops.* New Directions for Adult and Continuing Education, no. 76. San Francisco: Jossey-Bass.

Fleming, J. A. (1998). "Understanding Residential Learning: The Power of Detachment and Continuity." *Adult Education Quarterly,* 48(1), pp. 245–259.

Forest, L., and Mulcahy, S. (1976). *First Things First: A Handbook of Priority Setting in Education.* Madison: Division of Program and Staff Development, University of Wisconsin Extension.

Forester, J. (1989). *Planning in the Face of Power.* Berkeley: University of California.

Fox, R. D. (1984). "Fostering Transfer of Learning to Work Environments." In T. J. Sork (Ed.), *Designing and Implementing Effective Workshops.* New Directions for Adult and Continuing Education, no. 22. San Francisco: Jossey-Bass.

Fuller, J., and Farrington, J. (1999). *From Training to Performance: Navigating the Transition.* San Francisco: Jossey-Bass/Pfeiffer.

Funk, S. L., and McBride, D. (2000). "Training in the Twenty-First Century." In S. Tobias and Fletcher, J. D. (Eds.), *Training and Retraining: A Handbook for Business, Industry, Government, and the Military.* New York: Macmillan References USA.

Galbraith, M. W. (Ed.) (1990). *Adult Learning Methods.* (1st ed.) Malabar, Fla.: Krieger.

Galbraith, M. W. (1997). *Administering Successful Programs for Adults: Promoting Excellence In Adult, Community, and Continuing Education.* Malabar, Fla.: Krieger.

Galbraith, M. W. (Ed.) (1998). *Adult Learning Methods.* (2nd ed.) Malabar, Fla.: Krieger.

Garmston, R. J., and Wellman, B. M. (1999). *The Adaptive School: A Sourcebook for Developing Collaborative Groups.* Norwood, Mass.: Christopher-Gordon.

Geigold, W. C., and Grindle, C. R. (1983). *In Training: A Practical Guide to Management Development.* Belmont, Calif.: Lifetime Learning.

Gibson, C. C. (Ed.) (1998). *Distance Learners in Higher Education: Institutional Responses for Quality Outcomes.* Madison, Wis.: Atwood.

Gordon, W., and Sork, T. J. (2001). "Ethical Issues and Codes of Ethics: Views of Adult Education Practitioners in Canada and the United States." *Adult Education Quarterly, 51*(3), pp. 202–218.

Gupta, K. (1999). *A Practical Guide to Needs Assessment.* San Francisco: Jossey-Bass/Pfeiffer.

Guskey, T. R. (2000). *Evaluating Professional Development.* Thousand Oaks, Calif.: Corwin.

Guy, T. C. (1999a). "Culturally Relevant Adult Education: Key Themes and Common Purposes." In T. C. Guy (Ed.), *Providing Culturally Relevant Adult Education: A Challenge for the Twenty-First Century.* New Directions for Adult and Continuing Education, no. 82. San Francisco: Jossey-Bass.

Guy, T. C. (Ed.) (1999b). *Providing Culturally Relevant Adult Education: A Challenge for the Twenty-First Century.* New Directions for Adult and Continuing Education, no. 82. San Francisco: Jossey-Bass.

Hall, G. E., and Hord, S. M. (2001). *Implementing Change: Patterns, Principles, and Potholes.* Boston: Allyn & Bacon.

Hartwig, M. C. (2000). "Programming: Nuts and Bolts." In D. L. Liddell and J. P. Lund (Eds.), *Powerful Programming for Student Learning: Approaches That Make a Difference.* New Directions for Student Services, no. 20. San Francisco: Jossey-Bass.

Havercamp, M. J. (1998). "Program Promotion and Marketing." In P. S. Cookson (Ed.), *Program Planning for the Training and Continuing Education of Adults: North American Perspectives.* Malabar, Fla.: Krieger.

Hayes, E. (1994). "Developing a Personal and Professional Agenda for Change." In E. Hayes and S.A.J. Colin III (Eds.), *Confronting Racism and Sexism.* New Directions for Adult and Continuing Education, no. 61. San Francisco: Jossey-Bass.

Hayes, E., and Colin III, S.A.J. (Eds.) (1994). *Confronting Racism and Sexism.* New Directions for Adult and Continuing Education, no. 61. San Francisco: Jossey-Bass.

Hayes, E., Flannery, D. D., and Associates. (2000). *Women as Learners: The Significance of Gender in Adult Learning.* San Francisco: Jossey-Bass.

Hendricks, M. (1994). "Making a Splash: Reporting Evaluation Results Effectively." In J. S. Wholey, H. P. Hatry, and K. E. Newcomer (Eds.), *Handbook of Practical Program Evaluation.* San Francisco: Jossey-Bass.

Hendricks, S. M. (2001). "Contextual and Individual Factors and the Use of Influencing Tactics in Adult Education Program Planning." *Adult Education Quarterly, 51*(3), pp. 219–235.

Hiemstra, R. (Ed.) (1991). *Creating Environments for Effective Adult Learning.* New Directions for Adult and Continuing Education, no. 50. San Francisco: Jossey-Bass.

Highum, A. C., and Lund, J. P. (2000). "Partnership in Programming: Relationships That Make a Difference." In D. L. Liddell and J. P. Lund (Eds.), *Powerful Programming for Student Learning: Approaches That Make a Difference.* New Directions for Student Services, no. 20. San Francisco: Jossey-Bass.

Hinrichs, J. R. (1996). "Feedback, Action Planning, and Follow-Through." In A. I. Kraut (Ed.), *Organizational Surveys: Tools for Assessment and Change.* San Francisco: Jossey-Bass.

Holt, M. E. (1998). "Ethical Considerations in Internet-Based Adult Education." In Cahoon, B. (Ed.), *Adult Learning and the Internet.* New Directions for Adult and Continuing Education, no. 78. San Francisco: Jossey-Bass.

Holton, III, E. F. (2000). "What's *Really* Wrong: Diagnosis for Learning Transfer." In L. F. Holton III, T. T. Baldwin, and S. S. Naquin (Eds.), *Managing and Changing Learning Transfer Systems.* Advances in Developing Human Resources, no. 8. Baton Rouge, La.: Academy of Human Resource Development and San Francisco: Berrett-Koehler Communications.

Holton, III, E. F., Baldwin T. T., and Naquin, S. S. (2000). *Managing and Changing Learning Transfer Systems.* Advances in Developing Human Resources, no. 8. Baton Rouge, La.: Academy of Human Resource Development and San Francisco: Berrett-Koehler Communications.

Holton, III, E. F., Bates, R. A., and Ruona, W.E.A. (2000). "Development of a Generalized Learning Transfer System." *Human Resource Development Quarterly, 11*(4), pp. 333–360.

Holton, III, E. F., Bates, R. A., Seyler, D. L., and Carvalho, M. B. (1997). "Toward Construct Validation of a Transfer of Climate Instrument." *Human Resource Development Quarterly, 8*(2), pp. 95–113.

Houle, C. O. (1972). *The Design of Education.* (2nd ed.) San Francisco: Jossey-Bass.

Houle, C. O. (1989). *Governing Boards: Their Nature and Nurture.* San Francisco: Jossey-Bass.

Houle, C. O. (1996). *The Design of Education.* (2nd ed.) San Francisco: Jossey-Bass.

Imel, S. (Ed.) (1996). *Learning in Groups: Exploring Fundamental Principals, New Uses, and Emerging Opportunities.* New Directions for Adult and Continuing Education, no. 71. San Francisco: Jossey-Bass.

Jackson, L., and Caffarella, R. S. (Eds.) (1994). *Experiential Learning: A New Approach.* New Directions for Adult and Continuing Education, no. 62. San Francisco: Jossey-Bass.

Jacobs, R. L. (1992). "Structured On-the-Job Training." In H. D. Stolovitch and E. K. Keeps (Eds.), *Handbook of Human Performance Technology.* San Francisco: Jossey-Bass.

Johnson, K. E. (1999). "Toward Green Challenge Courses." *The Journal of Experiential Education, 22*(3), pp. 149–153.

Joint Committee on Standards for Educational Evaluation. (1994). *The Program Evaluation Standards.* (2nd ed.) Newbury Park, Calif.: Sage.

*Journal of Staff Development.* (1999). *20*(3), pp. 9–60.

Kaufman, R., Rojas, A. M., and Mayer, H. (1993). *Needs Assessment: A User's Guide.* Englewood Cliffs, N.J.: Educational Technology.

Kaufman, R., and Stone, B. (1983). *Planning for Organizational Success.* New York: Wiley.

Kemerer, R. W. (1991). "Understanding the Application of Learning." In T. J. Sork (Ed.), *Mistakes Made and Lessons Learned: Overcoming Obstacles to Successful Program Planning.* New Directions for Adult and Continuing Education, no. 49. San Francisco: Jossey-Bass.

Kemp, J. E. (2000). *An Interactive Guidebook for Designing Education for the 21st Century.* Bloomington, Ind.: TECHNOS.

Kemp, J. E., Morrison, G. R., and Ross, S. M. (1996). *Designing Effective Instruction.* Upper Saddle River, N.J.: Merrill.

Killion, J. P., and Kaylor, B. (1991). "Follow-Up: The Key to Training for Transfer." *Journal of Staff Development, 12*(1), pp. 64–67.

Killion, J., and Harrison, C. (1997). "The Multiple Roles of Staff Developers." *Journal of Staff Development, 18*(3), pp. 34–44.

Kirkpatrick, D. L. (1976). "Evaluation of Training." In R. L. Craig (Ed.), *Training and Development Handbook.* New York: McGraw-Hill.

Kirkpatrick, D. L. (1998). *Evaluating Training Programs: The Four Levels.* (2nd ed.) San Francisco: Berrett-Koehler.

Knowles, M. S. (1980). *The Modern Practice of Adult Education.* New York: Cambridge University Press.

Knox, A. B. (1998). *Evaluating Adult and Continuing Education.* Information Series, no. 375. The Ohio State University, Columbus, Ohio: ERIC Clearinghouse on Adult, Career, and Vocational Education.

Krathwohl, D. R. (1993). *Methods of Educational and Social Science Research.* White Plains, N.Y.: Longman.

Kraut, A. I. (Ed.) (1996). *Organizational Surveys: Tools for Assessment and Change.* San Francisco: Jossey-Bass.

Krishnamurthi, L. (2001). "Pricing Strategies and Tactics." In D. Iacobucci (Ed.), *Kellogg on Marketing.* San Francisco: Jossey-Bass.

Kruse, K., and Keil, J. (2000). *Technology-Based Training: The Art and Design, Development and Delivery.* San Francisco: Jossey-Bass/Pfeiffer.

Laird, D. (1985). *Approaches to Training and Development.* (2nd ed.) Reading, Mass.: Addison-Wesley.

Lakeland Research. (1995). "1995 Industry Report." *Training, 32*(10), pp. 38–74.

Langdon, D. G. (1999). "Selecting Interventions." In D. G. Langdon, K. S. Whiteside, and M. M. McKenna (Eds.), *Intervention Resource Guide: 50 Performance Resource Tools.* San Francisco: Jossey-Bass/Pfeiffer.

Langdon, D. G., Whiteside, K.S., and McKenna, M. M. (Eds.) (1999). *Intervention Resource Guide: 50 Performance Resource Tools.* San Francisco: Jossey-Bass/Pfeiffer.

Latimer, J. (1999). "Cross-Border Knowledge Transfer." *Technical Training, 10*(5), pp. 49–53.

Lawler, P. A. (2000). "Ethical Issues in Continuing and Professional Education." In V. W. Mott and B. J. Daley (Eds.), *Charting a Course for Continuing Profesional Education: Reframing Practice.* New Directions for Adult and Continuing Education, no. 86. San Francisco: Jossey-Bass.

Lawler, P. A., and King, K. P. (2000). *Planning for Effective Faculty Development Using Adult Learning Strategies.* Malabar, Fla.: Krieger.

Lawson, K. (1998). *Train-the-Trainer Facilitator's Guide.* San Francisco: Jossey-Bass/Pfeiffer.

Lee, W. W., and Owens, D. L. (2000). *Multimedia-Based Instructional Design: Computer-Based Training, Web-Based Training Distance, Broadcast Training.* San Francisco: Jossey-Bass/Pfeiffer.

Leigh, D., Watkins, R., Platt, A., and Kaufman, R. (2000). "Alternative Models of Needs Assessment: Selecting the Right One for Your Organization." *Human Resource Development Quarterly, 11*(2), pp. 87–93.

Linn, R. L. (2000). "Assessments and Accountability." *Educational Researcher, 26*(2), pp. 4–15.

Long, J. S., and Marts, J. A. (1981). "The Focused Group Interview—An Alternative Way to Collect Information to Evaluate Conferences." Pullman: Cooperative Extension Service, Washington State University.

Longworth, N. (1999). *Making Lifelong Learning Work: Learning Cities for a Learning Century.* London: Kogan Page.

Loucks-Horsley, S. (1989). "Managing Change: An Integral Part of Staff Development." In S. D. Caldwell (Ed.), *Staff Development: A Handbook of Effective Practice.* Oxford, Ohio: National Staff Development Council.

Mager, R. F. (1984). *Preparing Instructional Objectives.* (2nd ed.) Belmont, Calif.: David S. Lake.

Marienau, C. (1999). "Self-Assessment at Work: Outcomes of Adult Learners' Reflection on Practice." *Adult Education Quarterly, 49*(3), pp. 135–146.

Matkin, G. W. (1985). *Effective Budgeting in Continuing Education: A Comprehensive Guide to Improving Program Planning and Organizational Performance.* San Francisco: Jossey-Bass.

McCullum, P. C. (2000). "6 Points of a Partnership." *Journal of Staff Development, 21*(2), p. 39.

McMillan, J. H. (2001). *Classroom Assessment: Principles and Practice for Effective Instruction.* (2nd ed.) Boston: Allyn & Bacon.

McMillan, J. H., and Schumacher, S. (2000). *Research in Education: A Conceptual Introduction.* Reading Mass.: Addison Wesley.

McNeil, L. M. (2000). "Creating New Inequalities: Contradictions of Reform." *Phi Delta Kappan, 81*(10), pp. 728–734.

Mehrens, W. A., and Lehmann, I. J. (1991). *Measurement and Evaluation.* (4th ed.) Troy, Mo.: Holt, Rinehart & Winston.

Merriam, S. B. (Ed.) (1993). *An Update on Adult Learning Theory.* New Directions for Adult and Continuing Education, no. 57. San Francisco: Jossey-Bass.

Merriam, S. B. (1998). *Qualitative Research and Case Study Applications in Education.* (2nd ed.) San Francisco: Jossey-Bass.

Merriam, S. B., and Caffarella, R. S. (1999). *Learning in Adulthood: A Comprehensive Guide.* (2nd ed.) San Francisco: Jossey-Bass.

Merriam, S. B., and Mohamad, M. (2001). "How Cultural Values Shape Learning in Older Adulthood: The Case of Malaysia." *Adult Education Quarterly, 51*(1), pp. 45–63.

Mezirow, J., and Associates. (1990). *Fostering Critical Reflection in Adulthood: A Guide to Transformative and Emancipatory Learning.* San Francisco: Jossey-Bass.

Milano, M., with Ullius, D. (1998). *Designing Powerful Training: The Sequential-Iterative Model.* San Francisco: Jossey-Bass/Pfeiffer.

Milheim, W. D. (1994). "A Comprehensive Model for the Transfer of Training." *Performance Improvement Quarterly, 7*(2), pp. 95–104.

Mills, D. P., Cervero, R. M, Langone, C. A., and Wilson, A. L. (1995). "The Impact of Interests, Power, Relationships, and Organizational Structure on Program Planning Practice: A Case Study." *Adult Education Quarterly*, 46(1), pp. 1–16.

Mitchell, G. (1998). *The Trainer's Handbook: The AMA Guide to Effective Training.* (3rd ed.) New York: AMACOM.

Moller, G. (1999). "You Have to Want to Do This Job." *Journal of Staff Development*, 20(4), pp. 10–5.

Munson, L. S. (1992). *How to Conduct Training Seminars.* (2nd ed.) New York: McGraw-Hill.

Nadler, L. L. (1982). *Designing Training Programs: The Critical Events Model.* Reading, Mass.: Addison-Wesley.

Nadler, L., and Nadler, Z. (1987). *The Comprehensive Guide to Successful Conferences and Institutes.* San Francisco: Jossey-Bass.

Newman, M. (1995). "Program Development in Adult Education and Training." In G. Foley (Ed.), *Understanding Adult Education and Training.* New South Wales, Australia: Allen & Unwin.

Newstrom, J. W., and Lilyquist, J. M. (1979). "Selecting Needs Analysis Methods." *Training and Development Journal, 33*(10), pp. 52–56.

Nilson, C. (1989). *Training Program Workbook and Kit.* Englewood Cliffs, N.J.: Prentice Hall.

O'Donnell, J. M., and Caffarella, R. S. (1998). "Learning Contracts." In M. W. Galbraith (Ed.), *Adult Learning Methods: A Guide for Effective Instruction.* (2nd ed.) Malabar, Fla.: Krieger.

Ottoson, J. M. (1994). "Transfer of Learning: Not Just an Afterthought." *Adult Learning, 5*(4), p. 21.

Ottoson, J. M. (1995a). "Reclaiming the Concept of Application: From Social to Technological Process and Back Again." *Adult Education Quarterly*, 46(1), pp. 17–30.

Ottoson, J. M. (1995b). "Use of a Conceptual Framework to Explore Multiple Influences on the Application of Learning Following a Continuing Education Program." *CJSAE/RCEEA, 9*(2), pp. 1–18.

Ottoson, J. M. (1997a). "After the Applause: Exploring Multiple Influences on Applications Following An Adult Education Program." *Adult Education Quarterly*, 47(2), pp. 92–107.

Ottoson, J. M. (1997b). "Beyond Transfer of Training: Using Multiple Lenses to Assess Community Education Programs." In A. D. Rose and M. A. Leahy (Eds.), *Assessing Adult Learning in Diverse Settings: Current Issues and Approaches.* New Directions for Adult and Continuing Education, no. 75. San Francisco: Jossey-Bass.

Ottoson, J. M. (2000). "Evaluation of Continuing Professional Education: Toward a Theory of Our Own." In V. W. Mott and B. J. Daley (Eds.), *Charting a Course for Continuing Professional Education.* New Directions for Adult and Continuing Education, no. 86. San Francisco: Jossey-Bass.

Owston, R. (1998). *Making the Link: Teacher Professional Development on the Internet.* Portsmouth, N.H.: Heinemann.

Palloff, R. M., and Pratt, K. (1999). *Building Learning Communities in Cyberspace: Effective Strategies for the Online Classroom.* San Francisco: Jossey-Bass.

Palmer, P. J. (1998). *The Courage to Teach: Exploring the Inner Landscape of a Teacher's Life.* San Francisco: Jossey-Bass.

Parry, S. B. (1996). "Consultants." In R. L. Craig (Ed.), *The ASTD Training and Development Handbook: A Guide to Human Resource Development.* (4th ed.) New York: McGraw-Hill.

Pearce, S. (1998). "Determining Program Needs." In P. S. Cookson (Ed.), *Program Planning for the Training and Continuing Education of Adults: North American Perspectives.* Malabar, Fla.: Krieger.

Pennington, F., and Green, J. (1976). "Comparative Analysis of Program Development Processes in Six Professions." *Adult Education,* 27(1), pp. 13–23.

Pershing, J., and Pershing, J. (2001). "Ineffective Reaction Evaluation." *Human Resource Development Quarterly,* 12(1), pp. 73–90.

Phillips, J. J. (1996). "Measuring the Results of Training." In R. L. Craig (Ed.), *The ASTD Training and Development Handbook.* (4th ed.) New York: McGraw-Hill.

Phillips, S. (1997). "Opportunities and Responsibilities: Competence, Creativity, Collaboration, and Caring." In J. K. Roth (Ed.), *Inspiring Teaching: Carnegie Professors of the Year Speak.* Bolton, Mass.: Anker.

Piskurich, G. M. (2000). *Rapid Instructional Design: Learning ID Fast and Right.* San Francisco: Jossey-Bass.

Pratt, D. D., and Associates. (1998). *Five Perspectives on Teaching in Adult and Higher Education.* Malabar, Fla.: Krieger.

Pratt, D. D., Kelly, M., and Wong, W.S.S. (1999). "Chinese Conceptions of 'Effective Teaching' in Hong Kong: Towards Culturally Sensitive Evaluation of Teaching." *International Journal of Lifelong Education,* 18(4), pp. 241–258.

Punch, K. (1998). *Introduction to Social Research: Quantitative and Qualitative Approaches.* San Francisco, Calif.: Sage.

Rees, E. F., Cervero, R. M., Moshi, L., and Wilson, A. L. (1997). "Language, Power, and the Construction of Adult Education Programs." *Adult Education Quarterly,* 47(2), pp. 63–77.

"Revisioning Professional Development." (2000). *Journal of Staff Development,* 21(3), pp. 1–19 (insert).

Rhinesmith, S. H. (1996). "Training for Global Operations." In R. L. Craig (Ed.), *The ASTD Training and Development Handbook: A Guide to Human Resource Development.* (4th ed.) New York: McGraw-Hill.

Richey, R. (1992). *Designing Instruction for the Adult Learner.* London: Kogan Page.

Rogers, E. M. (1995). *Diffusion of Innovations.* (4th ed.) New York: Free Press.

Rohnke, C. E. (1990). "Ropes Courses: A Constructed Adventure Environment." In J. C. Miles and S. Priest (Eds.), *Adventure Education.* State College, Pa.: Venture Publishing.

Rossett, A. (1987). *Training Needs Assessment.* Englewood Cliffs, N.J.: Educational Technology Publications.

Rossett, A. (1996). "Job Aids and Electronic Performance Support Systems." In R. L. Craig (Ed.), *The ASTD Training and Development Handbook: A Guide to Human Resource Development.* New York: McGraw-Hill.

Rossett, A. (1998). *First Things First: A Handbook for Performance Analysis.* San Francisco: Jossey-Bass.

Rossett, A., and Gautier-Downes, J. (1991). *A Handbook of Job Aids.* San Diego: Pfeiffer.

Roth, J. K. (Ed.) (1997). *Inspiring Teaching: Carnegie Professors of the Year Speak.* Bolton, Mass.: Anker.

Rothwell, W. (1999). *The Action Learning Guidebook: A Real-Time Strategy for Problem Solving, Training Design, and Employee Development.* San Francisco: Jossey-Bass.

Rothwell, W. J., and Cookson, P. S. (1997). *Beyond Instruction: Comprehensive Program Planning for Business and Education.* San Francisco: Jossey-Bass.

Rothwell, W. J., and Kazanas, H. C. (1993). *The Complete AMA Guide to Management Development.* New York: American Management Association.

Rothwell, W. J., and Kazanas, H. (1998). *Mastering the Instructional Design Process: A Systematic Approach.* (2nd ed.) San Francisco: Jossey-Bass.

Russell, L. (1999). *The Accelerated Learning Fieldbook: Making the Instructional Process Fast, Flexible, and Fun.* San Francisco: Jossey-Bass.

Salmon, G. (2000). *E-Moderating: The Key to Teaching Online.* London: Kogan Page.

Saltiel, I. M. (1998). "Defining Collaborative Partnerships." In I. M. Saltiel and A. Sgroi (Eds.), *The Power and Potential of Collaborative Practice.* New Directions for Adult and Continuing Education, no. 79. San Francisco: Jossey-Bass.

Saltiel, I. M., Sgroi, A., and Brockett, R. G. (1998). "The Power and Potential of Collaborative Learning Projects." In I. M. Saltiel and A. Sgroi (Eds.), *The Power and Potential of Collaborative Practice.* New Directions for Adult and Continuing Education, no. 79. San Francisco: Jossey-Bass.

Schein, E. H. (1999). *The Corporate Culture Survival Guide.* San Francisco: Jossey-Bass.

Scott, J. (2000). *Social Network Analysis.* (2nd ed.) London: Sage.

Sgroi, A., and Saltiel, I. M. (1998). "Human Connections." In I. M. Saltiel and A. Sgroi (Eds.), *The Power and Potential of Collaborative Practice.* New Directions for Adult and Continuing Education, no. 79. San Francisco: Jossey-Bass.

Shipp, T. (1981). "Building a Better Mousetrap in Adult Education." *Lifelong Learning: The Adult Years, 5*(1), pp. 4–6.

Shipp, T. (1998). "The Role of Programmer." In Cookson, P. (Ed.), *Program Planning for the Training and Continuing Education of Adults.* Malabar, Fla.: Krieger Publishing.

Silberman, M. (1996). *Active Learning: 101 Strategies to Teach Any Subject.* Boston: Allyn & Bacon.

Silberman, M. (1999). *101 Ways to Make Your Meetings Active: Surefire Ideas to Engage Your Group.* San Francisco: Jossey-Bass.

Silverman, S. L., and Casazza, M. E. (2000). *Learning and Development: Making Connections to Enhance Teaching.* San Francisco: Jossey-Bass.

Simerly, R. G. (1989a). "A Ten-Step Process to Ensure Success in Marketing." In R. G. Simerly and Associates, *Handbook of Marketing for Continuing Education.* San Francisco: Jossey-Bass.

Simerly, R. G. (1989b). "Writing Effective Advertising Copy: Eight Principles for Success." In R. G. Simerly and Associates, *Handbook of Marketing for Continuing Education.* San Francisco: Jossey-Bass.

Simerly, R. G. (1990). *Planning and Marketing Conferences and Workshops: Tips, Tools, and Techniques.* San Francisco: Jossey-Bass.

Simerly, R. G., and Associates. (1989). *Handbook of Marketing for Continuing Education.* San Francisco: Jossey-Bass.

Sisco, B. R. (1991). "Setting the Climate for Effective Teaching and Learning." In R. Hiemstra (Ed.), *Creating Environments for Effective Adult Learning.* New Directions for Adult and Continuing Education, no. 50. San Francisco: Jossey-Bass.

Smith, B. J., and Delahaye, B. L. (1987). *How to Be an Effective Trainer.* (2nd ed.) New York: Wiley.

Smith, P. L., and Ragan, T. J. (1999). *Instructional Design.* (2nd ed.) Columbus, Ohio: Merrill.

Sork, T. J. (1981). "The Postmortem Audit: Improving Programs by Examining 'Failures.'" *Lifelong Learning: The Adult Years, 5*(3), pp. 6–7, 31.

Sork, T. J. (1982). *Determining Priorities.* Vancouver: British Columbia Ministry of Education.

Sork, T. J. (1987). "Toward a Causal Model of Program Failure in Adult Education." *Proceedings of the 28th Annual Adult Education Research Conference.* Laramie: University of Wyoming.

Sork, T. J. (1988). "Ethical Issues in Program Planning." In R. G. Brockett (Ed.), *Ethical Issues in Adult Education.* New York: Teachers College Press.

Sork, T. J. (1990). "Theoretical Foundations of Educational Program Planning." *The Journal of Continuing Education in the Health Professions, 10,* pp. 73–83.

Sork, T. J. (Ed.) (1991a). *Mistakes Made and Lessons Learned: Overcoming Obstacles to Successful Program Planning.* New Directions for Adult and Continuing Education, no. 49. San Francisco: Jossey-Bass.

Sork, T. J. (1991b). "Tools for Planning Better Programs." In T. J. Sork (Ed.), *Mistakes Made and Lessons Learned: Overcoming Obstacles to Successful Program Planning.* New Directions for Adult and Continuing Education, no. 49. San Francisco: Jossey-Bass.

Sork, T. J. (1996). "Negotiating Power and Interests in Planning: A Critical Perspective." In R. M. Cervero and A. L. Wilson (Eds.), *What Really Matters in Program Planning: Negotiating Power and Interests.* New Directions for Adult and Continuing Education, no. 69. San Francisco: Jossey-Bass.

Sork, T. J. (1997). "Workshop Planning." In J. A. Fleming (Ed.), *Newer Perspectives on Designing and Implementing Effective Workshops.* New Directions for Adult and Continuing Education, no. 76. San Francisco: Jossey-Bass.

Sork, T. J. (1998). "Program Priorities, Purposes, and Objectives." In P. S. Cookson (Ed.), *Program Planning for the Training and Continuing Education of Adults: North American Perspectives.* Malabar, Fla.: Krieger.

Sork, T. J. (2000). "Planning Educational Programs." In A. L. Wilson and E. R. Hayes (Eds.), *Handbook of Adult and Continuing Education.* San Francisco: Jossey-Bass.

Sork, T. J., and Caffarella, R. S. (1989). "Planning Programs for Adults." In S. B. Merriam and P. M. Cunningham (Eds.), *Handbook of Adult and Continuing Education.* San Francisco: Jossey-Bass.

Sork, T. J., and Fielding, D. W. (1987). "Identifying Learning Needs." In J. R. Arndt and S. Coons (Eds.), *Continuing Education in Pharmacy.* Alexandria, Va.: American Association of Colleges of Pharmacy.

Sork, T. J., Kalef, R., and Worsfold, N. E. (1987). *The Postmortem Audit: A Strategy for Improving Programs.* Vancouver, Canada: Intentional Learning Systems.

Sparks, D. (1998). "The Politics of Culture and the Struggle to Get an Education." *Adult Education Quarterly, 48*(4), pp. 245–259.

Sparks, D. (2000). "Partnerships Need Purposes." *Journal of Staff Development, 21*(2), p. 3.

Sparks, D. and Hirsh, S. (1997). *A New Vision for Staff Development.* Alexandria, Va.: Association for Supervision and Curriculum Development.

Starratt, R. J. (1991). "Building an Ethical School: A Theory in Educational Leadership." *Educational Administration Quarterly, 27,* pp. 185–202.

Starratt, R. J. (1994). *Building an Ethical School: A Practical Response to the Moral Crisis in Schools*. Washington, D.C.: Falmer Press.

Sternthal, B., and Tybout, A. M. (2001). "Segmentation and Targeting." In D. Iacobucci (Ed.), *Kellogg on Marketing*. San Francisco: Jossey-Bass.

Sugrue, B., and Clark, R. E. (2000). "Media Selection for Training." In S. Tobias and J. D. Fletcher (Eds.), *Training and Retraining: A Handbook for Business, Industry, Government, and the Military*. New York: Macmillan References USA.

Swanson, R. A. (1998). "Demonstrating the Financial Benefit of Human Resource Development: Status and Update on the Theory and Practice." *Human Resource Development Quarterly, 9*(3), pp. 285–287.

Swanson, R. A., and Gradous, D. B. (1988). *Forecasting Financial Benefits of Human Resource Development*. San Francisco: Jossey-Bass.

Taylor, D., Marienau, C., and Fiddler, M. (2000). *Developing Adult Learners: Strategies for Teachers and Trainers*. San Francisco: Jossey-Bass.

Taylor, M. C. (2000). "Transfer of Learning in Workplace Literacy Programs." *Adult Basic Education, 10*(1), pp. 3–20.

Tedlock, B. (2000). "Ethnography and Ethnographic Representative." In N. K. Denzin and Y. S. Lincoln (Eds.), *Handbook of Qualitative Research*. (2nd ed.) Thousand Oaks, Calif.: Sage Publications.

Tennant, M. (2000). "Adult Learning for Self-Development and Change." In A. L. Wilson and E. R. Hayes (Eds.), *Handbook of Adult and Continuing Education*. San Francisco: Jossey-Bass.

Tennant, M. C., and Pogson, P. (1995). *Learning and Change in the Adult Years: A Developmental Perspective*. San Francisco: Jossey-Bass.

Tenopyr, M. L. (1996). "Testing." In R. L. Craig (Ed.), *The ASTD Training and Development Handbook*. (4th ed.) New York: McGraw-Hill.

Tisdell, E. J. (1995). *Creating Inclusive Adult Learning Environments: Insights from Multicultural Education and Feminist Pedagogy*. Information Series no. 361. Columbus, Ohio: ERIC Clearinghouse on Adult, Career, and Vocational Education, Center on Education and Training for Employment, College of Education, The Ohio State University.

Tracey, W. R. (1992). *Designing Training and Development Systems*. (3rd ed.) New York: AMACOM.

Tyler, R. W. (1949). *Basic Principles of Curriculum and Instruction*. Chicago: University of Chicago Press.

Umble, K. E., Cervero, R. M., and Langone, C. A. (2001). "Negotiating About Power, Frames, and Continuing Education: A Case Study." *Adult Education Quarterly, 51*(2), pp. 128–145.

Van Kavelaar, E. K. (1998). *Conducting Training Workshops: A Crash Course for Beginners*. San Francisco: Jossey-Bass/Pfeiffer.

Vella, J. (1994). *Learning to Listen, Learning to Teach: The Power of Dialogue in Educating Adults.* San Francisco: Jossey-Bass.

Vella, J. (2000). *Taking Learning to Task: Creative Strategies for Teaching Adults.* San Francisco: Jossey-Bass.

Vella, J., Berardinelli, P., and Burrow, J. (1998). *How Do They Know They Know? Evaluating Adult Learning.* San Francisco: Jossey-Bass.

Walker, D. F. (1971). "A Naturalistic Model for Curriculum Development." *School Review, 80*(1), pp. 51–65.

Walker, D. (1990). *Fundamentals of Curriculum.* Fort Worth, Tex.: Harcourt Brace College Publishers.

Watkins, K. E., and Marsick, V. J. (1993). *Sculpting the Learning Organization: Lessons in the Art and Science of Systematic Change.* San Francisco: Jossey-Bass.

Watkins, K. E., and Sechrest, T. L. (1998). "Adding Value: Program Financing for Program Planners." In P. S. Cookson (Ed.), *Program Planning for the Training and Continuing Education of Adults: North American Perspectives.* Malabar, Fla.: Krieger.

Welton, M. R. (1993). "The Contributions of Critical Theory to Our Understanding of Adult Learning." In S. B. Merriam (Ed.), *An Update on Adult Learning Theory.* New Directions for Adult and Continuing Education, no. 57. San Francisco: Jossey-Bass.

Whiteside, K. S. (1999). "Implementing Interventions." In D. G. Landgon, K. S. Whiteside, and M. M. McKenna (Eds.), *Intervention Resource Guide: 50 Performance Resource Tools.* San Francisco: Jossey-Bass/Pfeiffer.

Wholey, J. S., Hatry, H. P., and Newcomer, K. E. (Eds.) (1994). *Handbook of Practical Program Evaluation.* San Francisco: Jossey-Bass.

Wiggenhorn, A. W. (1996). "Organization and Management of Training." In R. L. Craig (Ed.), *The ASTD Training and Development Handbook: A Guide to Human Resource Development.* (4th ed.) New York: McGraw-Hill.

Wiggins, G. (1998). *Educative Assessment: Designing Assessments to Inform and Improve Student Performance.* San Francisco: Jossey-Bass.

Wilson, A. L., and Cervero, R. M. (1996a). "Learning from Practice: Learning to See What Matters in Program Planning." In R. M. Cervero and A. L. Wilson (Eds.), *What Really Matters in Adult Education Program Planning: Lessons in Negotiating Power and Interests.* New Directions for Adult and Continuing Education, no. 69. San Francisco: Jossey-Bass.

Wilson, A. L., and Cervero, R. M. (1996b). "Paying Attention to the People Work When Planning Educational Programs." In R. M. Cervero and A. L. Wilson (Eds.), *What Really Matters in Adult Education Program Planning: Lessons in Negotiating Power and Interests.* New Directions for Adult and Continuing Education, no. 69. San Francisco: Jossey-Bass.

Wilson, A. L., and Cervero, R. M. (1996c). "Who Sits at the Planning Table: Ethics and Planning Practice." *Adult Learning, 8*(2), pp. 20–22.

Wilson, A. L., and Hayes, E. R. (Eds.) (2000). *Handbook of Adult and Continuing Education.* San Francisco: Jossey-Bass.

Winston, R. B., and Creamer, D. G. (1998). "Staff Supervision and Professional Development: An Integrated Approach." In W. Bryan and R. A. Schwartz (Eds.), *Strategies for Staff Development: Personnel and Professional Education in the Twenty-First Century.* New Directions for Student Affairs, no. 84. San Francisco: Jossey-Bass.

Witkin, B. R., and Altschuld, J. W. (1995). *Planning and Conducting Needs Assessments: A Practical Guide.* Thousand Oaks, Calif.: Sage.

Wlodkowski, R. J. (1998). *Enhancing Adult Motivation to Learn: A Comprehensive Guide for Teaching All Adults.* (rev. ed.) San Francisco: Jossey-Bass.

Wlodkowski, R. J., and Ginsberg, M. B. (1995). *Diversity and Motivation: Culturally Responsive Teaching.* San Francisco: Jossey-Bass.

Worthen, B. R., and Sanders, J. R. (1987). *Educational Evaluation.* White Plains, N.Y.: Longman.

Xiao, J. (1996). "The Relationship Between Organizational Factors and the Transfer of Training in the Electronics Industry in Shenzhen, China." *Human Resource Development Quarterly, 7*(1), pp. 55–73.

Yamnill, S., and McLean, G. N. (2001). "Theories Supporting Transfer of Training." *Human Resource Development Quarterly, 12*(2), pp. 195–208.

Yang, B. (1999). "How Effectively Do You Use Power and Influence?" In M. Silberman (Ed.), *The 1999 Training and Performance Sourcebook.* New York: McGraw-Hill.

Yang, B., Cervero, R. M., Valentine, T., and Benson, J. (1998). "Development and Validation of an Instrument to Measure Adult Educators' Power and Influence Tactics in Program Planning Practice." *Adult Education Quarterly, 48*(4), pp. 227–244.

Yelon, S. (1992). "M.A.S.S.: A Model for Producing Transfer." *Performance Improvement Quarterly, 5*(2), pp. 13–23.

Yelon, S. L., and Ford, J. K. (1999). "Pursuing a Multidimensional View of Transfer." *Performance Improvement Quarterly, 12*(3), pp. 58–77.

Yelon, S. L., and Sheppard, L. M. (1999) "The Cost-Benefit Transfer Model: An Adaptation From Medicine." *Performance Improvement Quarterly, 12*(3), pp. 78–93.

Zemke, R., and Kramlinger, T. (1982). *Figuring Things Out.* Reading, Mass.: Addison-Wesley.

Zinn, L. M. (1998). "Identifying Your Philosophical Orientation." In M. W. Galbraith (Ed.), *Adult Learning Methods.* (2nd ed.) Malabar, Fla.: Krieger.

# Index